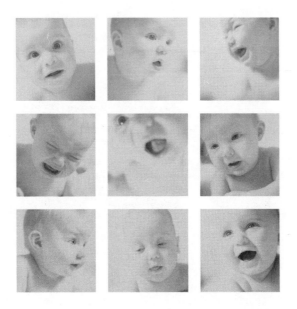

There are two ways to live your life.

One is as though nothing is a miracle.

The other is as though everything is a miracle.

Albert Einstein (1879-1955)

finding our way
life with triplets, quadruplets and quintuplets

A Collection of Experiences
Edited by Suzanne Lyons
Foreword by Cécile Dionne

Publication Team
Patricia Harber, Diane Myers,
Donna Patterson, Maureen Tierney

Triplets, Quads & Quints Association
Canada
2001

Edited by Suzanne Lyons

Published by
Triplets, Quads & Quints Association
2968 Nipiwin Drive
Mississauga, Ontario Canada
L5N 1X9
www.tqq.com

National Library of Canada Cataloging in Publication Data
Main entry under title:

Finding our way: life with triplets, quadruplets and quintuplets

Includes bibliographical references.
ISBN 0-9687160-0-8
1. Triplets. 2. Quadruplets. 3. Quintuplets. 4. Child rearing. 5. Multiple pregnancy – Popular works. I. Lyons, Suzanne, 1965-   . II. Triplets, Quads & Quints Association.

HQ777.35.F56 2001   649'.144
C2001-930557-5

Grateful acknowledgement for permission to reprint is made as follows:
Infertility Awareness Association of Canada for "Could You Make the Choice?" by Donna Zidar; Triplet Connection for "Music and Motherhood" by Karen Rotenberg and "It Seems Like Only Yesterday" by Ken Johnson; Multiple Births Canada (formerly POMBA Canada) for "What Will They Think of Next" and "Our Toilet –Training Marathon" by Barbara Morrison and "Toilet-Training Quadruplets" by Valerie Koning Keelan; Mississauga News for the Harrison's picture photographed by Rob Beintema; National Post for the Vlahiotis's picture photographed by Kevin Van Paassen.

This project was financially assisted by Health Canada and various other generous supporters. The views expressed herein do not necessarily represent the official policy of Health Canada.

Cover Design by Thumbnail Art Direction & Design
Typesetting and Design by Thumbnail Art Direction & Design

Printed in Canada by Webcom Ltd.

The Triplets, Quads & Quints Association is a non-profit, Canadian peer and professional network which enhances the quality of life of higher order multiple birth individuals and their families.

For more information about TQQ and to purchase a copy of *Finding Our Way*, please contact us through our website www.tqq.com

introduction

Seven years ago, a small group of parents met every Tuesday evening in a young mother's home to swap stories and concerns about their kids. Some of the women had only recently found out they were pregnant. A few already had newborn babies or toddlers, while the others were bracing for the bittersweet day their children would start school. Like each of their lives, their stories and concerns were unique. What drew them together was the shared experience of a higher order multiple birth. They were parents of triplets, quadruplets or quintuplets, searching for the kind of advice and support that their families, friends and parenting books were not able to provide.

That's where this book began, long before my husband and I found out that we were expecting three babies. Three babies. At once! Somehow, inexplicably, I was pregnant with triplets. We laughed hysterically at the news, at once thunderstruck and delighted with our remarkable, unlikely achievement. The tears came just a few moments later, as the implications of having triplets became more obvious with every minute. Our lives were about to change in ways we couldn't begin to imagine. What we needed was informed advice about the risks and how to prepare for the babies once they were home. Aside from this small group of parents, there were no other sources of support and information especially suited for our experience.

Later we discovered there were many other families in our same situation. Every year in Canada, growing numbers of parents are told they are expecting three, four or five babies. What follows is an uncertain, and sometimes frightening leap into the world of high risk hospitals, financial worries and monumental changes, not just for the expectant parents but for families and friends as well.

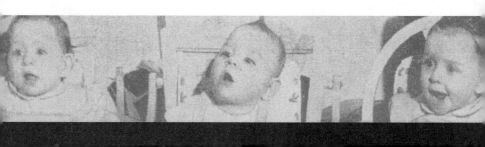

As a group, parents of higher order multiple birth children face issues that are quite distinct from those who have one baby at a time, and even twins. Pregnancy care for triplets or more babies shifts into high gear, emphasizing preterm labour prevention, bedrest, and in some cases, fetal reduction. Caring and bonding with premature babies who remain in hospital is a constant, underlying concern. Plans to breastfeed may be questioned. Parents worry about extreme, ongoing fatigue, the financial demands of hiring help at home, the unforeseen demands and isolation of stay-at-home parents, and the effects on their marriage and relationships with other children.

These were some of the topics of conversation among the parents who began meeting seven years ago. Several of the mothers saw the wisdom of asking individuals in the group and others across Canada to share their experiences in print. In effect, they wanted to expand the conservation and fill the void encountered by other families that would follow. The result is this collection of real-life narratives by parents, siblings, healthcare professionals, volunteers, grandparents and individuals who are multiple birth children themselves. As a collection, it is the voice of experience from which readers can draw support, reassurance and information.

Developing and refining this volume of material through the past five years has been a challenging and enlightening experience for each member of the publication team. The team evolved to include Diane Myers, Donna Patterson, Maureen Tierney, Patricia Harber and then, finally, me. As parents of multiple birth children, we were taken aback and captivated by the honesty of the authors.

By asking for contributions, it seems we had released a fountain of observations and support that always existed but had never been expressed. For every story that was finally selected for our book, there were a great many more that could not be included.

Many, many nights were spent debating subject matter. Our decisions were influenced by our own perceptions as parents and with the guidance of an international review team who read and offered suggestions after the first draft. But we had our doubts. At times, we questioned if submissions from professionals belonged in a book written primarily by and for parents and their families. Ultimately, the dearth of solid information specializing in higher order multiple births compelled us to include articles written by doctors and other specialists when appropriate. More troublesome were our doubts when the content grew dark in chapters covering prematurity, family stresses, depression and even, death. We questioned if expectant or new parents could benefit from this knowledge. In the end, we concluded that acknowledging extreme emotional strains was a necessary counterbalance to the always sunny reflections of our lives in the media. Accepting that our experiences may be difficult can help us to cope and to recognize that unexpected responses may not be as unusual as we believe.

Your interpretation of the stories will be shaped by your own experience. This book cannot offer absolutes or explanations, only insight from others who have been there. With such insight, we hope that parents feel better prepared to make decisions and choose the course that is best for them and their children.

Suzanne Lyons

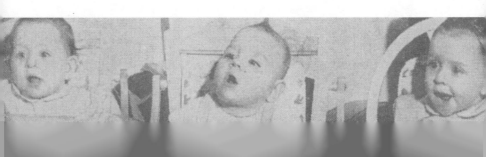

foreword
for the children

When I was first asked to contribute to this book, I was honoured and rather excited. I imagined myself sitting down and dispensing bits of wisdom to the parents of these special children — words that would perhaps alter the course of the lives of these families. Without a doubt, I feel a natural connection to you and yours, a very tender regard for you.

But when I sat down to put pen to paper, I couldn't quite understand why I stared blankly at the paper for so long. I began to think that perhaps I shouldn't have agreed to do this. After all, what do I know about raising multiples? I've never done it. And though the circumstances of my birth were said to be miraculous, I was no more than an ordinary person born in extraordinary circumstances. As much as I wanted to address the parents who were undergoing such life-altering changes, the words wouldn't come. And then it hit me. I realized that my role as advisor to these parents was futile. All the wisdom in the world would never give me the right to dispense parental advice, for I am not the parent of an unbelievable birth, but the child. I am the child, one of the Dionne quintuplets, and a thread, as tenuous and mysterious as it may seem to you, exists between your children and me. That is my role, to be the voice of your children, for they may not be able to tell you. Please listen to the children.

I can only imagine the shock, whether it be negative or positive, of finding out that you are about to become parents of not one, but several children. While I'm sure some people receive this news with glee, for the majority of people, it must be a rather confusing and frightening time. But don't blame the children coming along, for what has happened is simply a biological equation that has resulted in more than a single birth. All parents require patience. But you will require more.

Mom and Dad, please allow us to go through every stage of childhood just as other kids do. While there are many of us going through this together, we cannot suppress our behaviour or hurry up the stages or be wise or well behaved beyond our years. We are

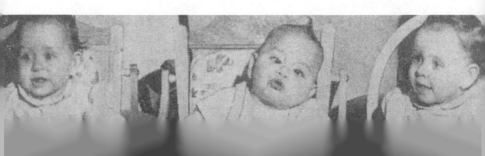

not small adults, with your control and understanding. We are little children who depend on you for love, guidance and acceptance. Please find a way to give it to us. When it seems too much, pause. There are many loving people around you who would love to help — aunts, uncles, grandparents, friends, neighbours. Accept or ask for their helping hands. We need them too. We need their attention, their time, their smiles. You are only human and can only give so much. We just don't realize that yet. So don't blame us for our incessant demands and needs. We are not to blame.

Treat us as individuals. It is part of everyone's basic needs to feel that there is no one else on this earth who is exactly like them. We are no different. Though on the surface it might seem to everyone that my siblings and I are exactly alike — we are not. Look for those differences and nurture them. Don't encourage similarities by dressing us alike or giving us similar names. Look for differences among us, even when, as in the case of monozygotic children, they are subtle. We need to develop our own uniqueness and self-esteem, and it is you who can help us to do that. The bond between my siblings and me is already so strong. At times, it is stronger than the bond between parent and child. So help me become my own person and not an extension of a multiple birth. Spend time with me and me alone, for sharing is what I have done all my life. I've never had you to myself, right from the very beginning, so indulge me.

Most of all, just love me. Make me feel loved and cherished and wanted. Make me feel part of a strong family unit. You are my protector, my lifeline, my shield against the world, which is so often eager to exploit me in any number of ways. Listen to me, dry my tears and rejoice in my laughter. Though it may all seem overwhelming, remember that one day, when I am grown, you will long for those silly moments and look back with tears in your eyes. Please make them tears of joy.

Cécile Dionne

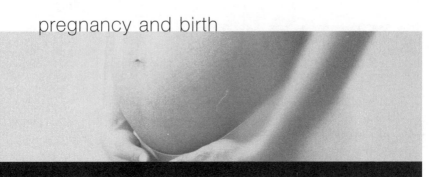

pregnancy and birth

the first year

CHAPTER 6 - Fragile Lives - Prematurity

CHAPTER 7 - Many Mouths to Feed

CHAPTER 8 - Early Days at Home & Hospital

Delayed Bonding

Home at Last

CHAPTER 9 - Coping with Stress & Change

Working and Parenthood

CHAPTER 10 - Our Supporters

CHAPTER 11 - Overnight Celebrities

CHAPTER 12 - Remember When

lifetime experiences

CHAPTER 13 - Toddler Years

Safety

CHAPTER 14 - Preschool Years

Toilet-Training

CHAPTER 15 - Growing Up

CHAPTER 16 - Pregnant Again

CHAPTER 17 - Special Needs

CHAPTER 18 - Losing a Child

CHAPTER 19 - Individuality

CHAPTER 20 -A Word From the Experts

pregnancy and birth

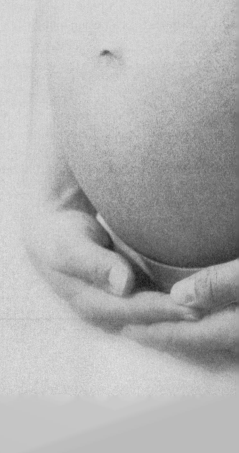

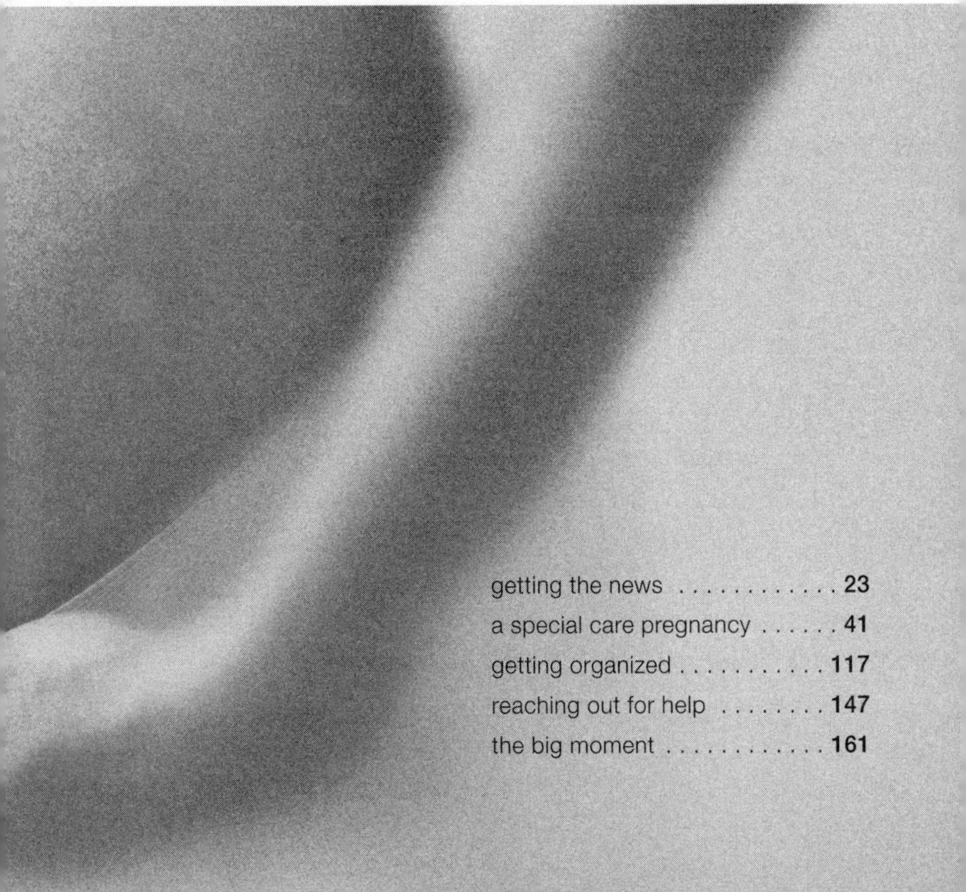

1

getting the news

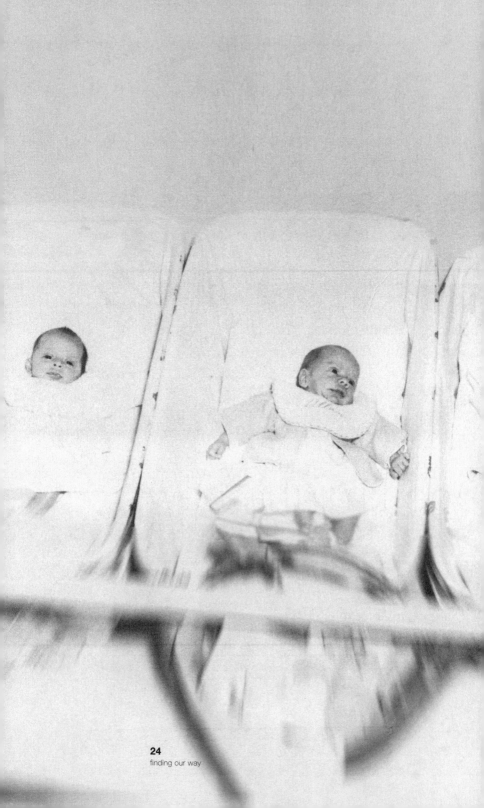

believe it or not
Diane Myers

The news was unreal

It was January 1990 when I was on my way to an ultrasound of our second pregnancy. Craig, our first baby, was about 13 months old. I told my husband, John, that I had an ultrasound scheduled at 12 weeks because my doctor thought we had miscalculated the dates. I was getting quite large. John was on his way to Hong Kong that day, so he was not sure if he could make the appointment. Since we had been through a pregnancy before, I didn't feel there was a compelling reason for him to be there. My parents were able to watch Craig, so I headed to the ultrasound on my own.

Shortly after the technician started the procedure, she stopped and asked me if I had taken any infertility medication. After answering no, I was left alone in the room for a moment to consider this as she went for assistance. "Cool — maybe twins," I thought.

The technician returned with another technician and showed her the screen. They looked at each other, asked me if I was alone and told me that this was going to take a while. I said that my husband was probably not coming and asked what was the matter. What was the matter with my baby? They told me that I would have to speak to my doctor about the results of this visit. I was not about to let them proceed until they told me what was wrong. They claimed that nothing was wrong.

"Then tell me!"

After some conversation, they told me that everything seemed fine, but that I was carrying four babies.

"Yeah right! Please tell me what's going on."

They showed me the ultrasound picture and pointed out four tiny babies.

Apparently, the rumour spread quickly through the office and reached the receptionist just as John arrived. John announced that he was there to see me and was asked to wait until they were finished the ultrasound. He recalls a bit of commotion buzzing through the office but had no idea that we were the cause. Finally, John was escorted into the ultrasound room just as the technicians and I were discussing who was going to tell him the news.

"Well, John, we didn't miscalculate the dates. But (how to word this) how many children do you want?"

A quizzical look from John, and then he said, "Oh, I get it. Twins! That's neat."

I shook my head.

"Three!" he said.

"Nooooo … "

"What's going on?"

"John, we are going to have four babies."

"Yeah right! Let me see. I know every millionth ultrasound you freak out the parents by putting on a tape of a quadruplet pregnancy. Let me see you do the ultrasound again." So the technician did the ultrasound again. "Oh, my!"

At this point John quickly ran up to our doctor's office, which happened to be on the third floor of the same building. Unfortunately she was not in, but her nurse quickly got her on the phone. John needed to confirm the reality of all this. Not an easy task — it still seems unreal. I slowly followed John upstairs. After some conversation with our doctor over the phone, John headed to the airport and I headed to the grocery store. Many of our family and friends were stunned that we just carried on with our routine after getting the news. But life goes on. We needed milk. And very likely, I needed a sense of normalcy as I tried to comprehend the unbelievable.

Looking back, it's amazing how we even managed to function. Well, sort of. I must have looked like quite a nut pushing a big cart around the store with one bag of milk in it and periodically breaking out into giggling fits.

John did get on the plane and headed to Hong Kong. On the plane he called his family and best friend to tell them the news. At some point the steward must have overheard his conversation because after they confirmed the story with John, they started pouring him champagne. Luckily, some of John's colleagues were meeting him at the airport because he apparently required some assistance departing the plane.

telling family and friends
Believe it or not

Spreading the word was great fun! From the doctor's office, we called my parents to tell them we were going to be late. In John's haste he hadn't considered that this kind of news may come as a shock or that it may cause great concern. John called my mother and said, "Joan, we'll be late, we're having quadruplets," and then he hung up.

I am not sure of my parents' initial reaction, but when I returned home about two hours later, my mom was in a bit of a panic. "You're having what? What's a quadruplet? Oh my ... four babies at once ... can you do that?" After we all calmed down, the next call was to my sister and brothers. What fun that was! "Hi, it's Diane. Just called to tell you that all went well with the ultrasound and we are having more than one." The responses had slight variations but typically went like this. "More than one? Twins, wow! We don't have any twins in the family. Not twins? Three? Not three? What are you talking about? Diane, tell me what's going on! Four! Get out! Get out! How can you have four? Oh my! When can I tell people?"

After a little practice, we became very good at prolonging the agony for our friends.

did you say three?
Brenda Stewart-Brown

I was expecting bad news — not triplets

My husband and I were not expecting another pregnancy. In fact, we had very nearly given up on the idea of having any more children.

We had lost our first son at 19 weeks due to premature rupture of membranes. Ten months later, our second son, John, was born at just 31 weeks gestation for the same reason. Both deliveries had been complicated by a strep infection. John spent four weeks in the Neonatal Intensive Care Unit before coming home. At four months of age, he was diagnosed with severely advanced hydrocephalus and was rushed to hospital for emergency surgery to insert a shunt in his brain to drain cerebrospinal fluid. Over the next year and a half, there was a blur of developmental checkups, physiotherapy appointments, neurosurgical checkups, two shunt revisions and a scrotal hernia repair. At that time, having another child was the furthest thing from our minds.

But time passed, John remained healthy and was developing normally, and we began to muse the pros and cons of him being an only child. Then we tried conceiving another baby for about a year. I took temperatures, plotted ovulation dates, and went for exams and ultrasounds to make sure there was nothing abnormal, and still no pregnancy. We were not prepared to pursue the matter any further with medication or invitro fertilization, and decided to let it drop for the time being and just relax. Two months later I was pregnant. We decided not to tell anyone about the pregnancy at that point because I was at such a high risk of having another premature baby or miscarriage. I visited my family doctor at six weeks and asked for an immediate referral to an obstetrician/gynecologist. My first appointment was two weeks later.

After seven weeks and three days, I noticed some blood spotting and called the obstetrician. I was sure this was leading up to a miscarriage. (I'd had some spotting early on in the first pregnancy.) Also, I just didn't feel pregnant. I had absolutely no morning sickness, not even a queasy stomach. I was just a little more tired than usual.

I was convinced something was wrong

My obstetrician said that a cervical polyp was most likely causing the bleeding, but she sent me for an ultrasound just to be sure noth-ing else was wrong. I was agitated and worried as I waited for the ultrasound technician to take me in to be scanned because I was still convinced something was wrong. I laid down on the table and the technician started to do the ultrasound after asking a few general questions about my history — how many weeks gestation, and so on. She had done only a few cursory sweeps of the abdomen with the wand when she frowned and asked, "Have you been taking any drugs?" For a moment I was taken aback. What did she mean? Narcotics? Antibiotics? "Have you been on any medications?" she asked again when I didn't reply.

"No, no, nothing," I stammered. "What's wrong?"

"I'm sorry, but I'll have to call the radiologist to come down and examine you," she said. My heart sank. My worst fears had been realized. There was either something seriously wrong with the fetus or it was dead.

I waited and waited for what seemed like an eternity. Thoughts of the previous miscarriage, of our hopes for a brother or sister for John, of my reluctance to even believe in this pregnancy in case something should go wrong, were all going through my head. The technician came in again and tried to smile reassuringly at me. "The radiologist should be down shortly; he must have gotten tied up somewhere. I'll try calling him again."

"Excuse me," I said, "but I have a medical background. I prom-ise I won't fall apart if it's bad news. Can't you just tell me what you've found?"

"I'm sorry," she replied. "But you must understand that we can't tell you anything until it's verified by a radiologist. Don't worry."

"Yeah, right," I thought. "Easy for you to say."

About 10 minutes after the initial call the radiologist finally arrived. He sat down on the edge of the narrow bed, scanned my abdomen for about 30 seconds and said, "Yep, there's definitely three in there. Congratulations!"

I was completely stunned into silence! My jaw dropped, and I'm sure I looked like a complete fool. I just could not comprehend what he had said. It was absolutely the last thing on my mind. I had prepared myself for the worst and was handed the complete oppo-site. A multiple pregnancy was incomprehensible.

"Congratulations — in a few months you are going to be as big as a house"

"Wha... wha... what did you say?" I managed to blurt out. "Did you say three?"

"Yes," he repeated. "You are having triplets. Congratulations — in a few months you are going to be as big as a house!"

And while I lay in stunned disbelief trying to comprehend this piece of wonderful but totally unexpected news, a progression of all the nurses on the floor, it seemed, came in to see the ultrasound. Apparently some had never seen triplets on ultrasound. I felt like a display from a medical textbook. Everyone had lots of questions. "Did you take fertility drugs?" "Are there multiples in your family?" "Do you have any other children?" "How are you going to manage?" I realize now that the questions will never end, they just change with the stage of the pregnancy, and afterwards, with the babies. But all I wanted then was to get the ultrasound over with so that I could find a quiet spot alone and let this whole thing sink in with all its ramifications to our lives.

Incomprehensible. Unbelievable. As the news slowly began to register, there were only more questions and uncertainty. What were my chances of having three healthy babies given my history of complications? In follow-up appointments, my doctor emphasized that this was an extremely high risk pregnancy. With every twinge, I expected trouble. But none came. We marked the pregnancy week by week until finally, at week 36, I had three very healthy babies without any unusual complications.

From the moment we heard the news to the day the babies were born, I braced for the worst. What we got instead was the best that anyone could hope for.

we'll be all right
Donna Patterson

History has to begin somewhere. In our family, the history of multiples begins with us

My husband and I didn't fall into any of the categories that would have made a multiple pregnancy more likely. There was no family history, and infertility wasn't an issue. I suppose that's why the news that I was pregnant with twins came as an absolute shock. Yes, even the prospect of twins sent me into shock. My head was spinning. I guess it was fear of the unknown. I'll never forget the drive home to my husband, Darryl, and our three-year-old daughter Alanna. Anxious and excited, I arrived at home and ran up the stairs and found them sitting together reading a book on Alanna's bed. When she heard she would be a big sister to not one but two babies, Alanna was thrilled and jumped up and down on the bed. Darryl sensed my concern right away and tried to reassure me. We'll be all right, he said. We'll be all right.

My gynecologist ordered a more thorough ultrasound just 10 days after the first. Unaware they were suspecting a third fetus, we were concerned something was wrong with the pregnancy. But then the technician confirmed what my doctor had suspected all along — a third fetus positioned low and near my spine. If twins came as a shock, you can't begin to imagine my reaction to triplets.

Darryl and Alanna were waiting in the hallway. During the wait, Alanna had fallen on the cement floor. She began to cry, and she cried loudly. Darryl remembers the anxiety as he came into our room. I was crying; Alanna was still crying. Darryl heard the word triplets and the colour drained from his face. Alanna didn't know what was happening and just continued sobbing.

Until then, I felt that Alanna was my whole world. How could we cope with three more babies? But Alanna had such a loving, mature outlook. Still aching from the fall, she said, "Mommy and Daddy, we'll be all right because we will each have one baby to take care of and we will do it together." I was so proud of her at that moment. At age three, Alanna had reassured me and helped me recognize just how wonderful this news was for us.

more than pregnant
Maureen Tierney

Just two days before we conceived triplet daughters, my fertility doctor informed me that I would probably have a multiple pregnancy. Apparently the size of my follicles indicated how many eggs I would release. I was stunned by this news. My husband and I really wanted children. We had had two miscarriages before the fertility treatments began. When I told my husband about our high chance of multiple pregnancy, he looked at me with the same blank look I had when I first heard this prediction. How many babies had the doctor meant? I didn't ask the question aloud because I was afraid to hear the answer. All I knew was I wanted a baby. I had always wanted three children, while my husband wished for two. Since we couldn't exactly split the difference at 2.5 children, I settled and planned for two.

When I called the clinic to see if I was pregnant after my first cycle I was totally and utterly thrilled to find out I was. I screamed when the technician told me my beta count was 4,000+. My husband and parents were away that Saturday so I cried my head off and tried calling everyone who might be home. No one was.

At the fertility doctor's request, I called on Monday for an appointment. On the phone, I mentioned to the secretary that my blood count was about 4,000+, which meant I was pregnant, right? She gasped and said, "You are more than pregnant, you're having several babies." I was taken aback, but not completely convinced. An hour later she called back saying the technician had made a mistake. My beta count was 400+ and not 4,000+. "Relax," the secretary said, "It's one baby." Relieved, I scheduled my ultrasound for one week later.

In the meantime, my mother told me that she had been severely ill while visiting her family in Ireland a month earlier. She was expecting test results from her doctor on the same day as my ultrasound. My heart sank. She had been hiding this news from me, concerned that I would become upset unnecessarily and discontinue my fertility treatments. On Monday morning, my parents and I went to her doctor's office to be told that a growth had been found in her colon and that she would be referred to a cancer specialist for surgery. I went to my fertility doctor that same afternoon and I told him what was happening. He was very supportive. My mother was in the waiting room while my father waited in the car. As my doctor performed the ultrasound, I saw two distinct sacs with two fetuses. "Twins," I said, thinking, "I can handle twins." He said nothing but continued the ultrasound. Then he pointed to the third sac. I was stunned. This I knew I couldn't handle — not without my Mom. I started to cry uncontrollably.

How could anyone cope with these two challenges?

What a wallop! Triplets and cancer. Life and death. Joy turned to horror. How could anyone cope with these two huge challenges? I wanted the children but I wanted to be there for my mother when she needed me. How could I cope with triplets without her help? How could I possibly do this? There was no easy answer. The doctor called his secretary who wanted to observe the ultrasound. She could not understand my grief. My doctor explained. Her look of sympathy still remains with me. Why was this happening to me? I couldn't deal with it. How was I supposed to carry three babies while my heart ached? My mother's surgery was not for another three months. How could I ever cope with this incredible stress? What if my stress resulted in a miscarriage or preterm labour? The questions went on and on in my mind. My husband's mother had died of the same disease within six months of her diagnosis. What a nightmare!

Our hearts were heavy in my family. I found myself feeling confident one day that all would go well, and the next day, feeling like I was in the depths of hell. These emotional swings carried on until my mother's surgery. The only way I felt I could cope and have some peace was to pray.

I was working full-time and felt quite nauseous and tired every morning during my first three months of pregnancy. Recurrent nightmares and constant trips to the bathroom turned nighttime sleep into a series of catnaps. Prior to my mother's surgery, I would wake up in the middle of the night in a terrible sweat after dreaming that she was dying and that I could not be at her bedside. I dreamed that I was unable to attend her funeral because I was confined to bed. I dreamed that my children would never know their wonderful grandmother. I had never met my own grandmothers.

One lived in Ireland and the other died before I was born. I wished with all my heart that my children would know their grandmother, especially one as wonderful as theirs. This ongoing nightmare became nearly unbearable. My new obstetrician told me that my worrying was jeopardizing the lives of my babies. I had been following all of his instructions for physical care, but my anxiety was putting the pregnancy at risk.

My mother's surgery went well. The doctor felt he had got all of the cancer before it spread any further. What a relief! From then on, I felt empowered; I could handle anything that would come my way. I focused exclusively on my pregnancy. I cannot express the joy I felt that day when the doctor said my mother would be fine. After surgery, she went through one year of chemotherapy. Six months into her therapy she became a grandmother for the first time of three granddaughters! Exceptional woman that she is, she, and my father, helped us with the night feedings until I hired help.

Writing about this personal experience was difficult for me. It was such an emotional time. I'm afraid that I do not have any great inspiring words of wisdom to offer people who are facing a multiple birth and a challenge as great and frightening as cancer. I endured it by living one day at time. It was the only way I could.

and baby makes five
Michael Quesnelle

It's not every day you find out you're going to be a dad three times over

The day is as vivid in my mind now as the day it happened. My wife, Diane, and I had been trying to conceive a child. After two and a half years of cool showers, boxer shorts, folic acid and temperature charts, we finally sought a little help from modern-day science.

After all the usual testing, blood work, sperm counts and motility tests, artificial insemination was recommended as our best chance at becoming pregnant. My wife was given drugs to help her ovaries release several eggs. We were on our way. Our infertility specialist advised us well in advance that the combination of being inseminated and having several mature eggs in wait could result in a multiple pregnancy. But the sheer thought of having a baby, let alone twins, was reason enough for us to go ahead with the procedure.

Success! We were pregnant. On the very first attempt, my wife conceived. Now it was just a matter of waiting for the first ultrasound.

During one of her visits to our family doctor we were told that her beta count was rapidly increasing. Only seven weeks into the pregnancy, an ultrasound was arranged. Around 11 a.m. on the day of the ultrasound, my pager went off at work displaying my wife's work number. I went to the pay phone to call her, expecting great news.

"Are you sitting down?" she asked. An eerie feeling swept over me. "We are definitely pregnant," she said. The phone went silent for a moment.

"Great!" was my reply. "Just how pregnant are we?" There was a long pause on the phone and then I vaguely remember the word — triplets.

"I don't think I heard you, honey."

"Triplets — we are going to have triplets."

I'm not sure what happened during the rest of the day. It's all just a fog to me. After all, it's not every day you find out that you're going to be a dad three times over!

Once the initial shock subsided, we enrolled in a prenatal class geared towards multiple births. In addition to all the usual things associated with a pregnancy, the instructor gave us a lot of information about what to expect with three bundles of joy. My wife and I were very lucky to have an instructor who was not only a registered nurse, but also a mother of twins, which in our case was one less than we were expecting, but still helpful to say the least.

By the end of the second trimester, my wife and I were feeling pretty good (well, I was anyway)

The first few months of pregnancy went by uneventfully. Regular checkups with the family doctor, prenatal classes and excursions to garage sales occupied much of our time. My wife stockpiled diapers, wipes and all the other goodies while I kept busy preparing the nursery. Living in a two-bedroom, one-storey house didn't leave a lot of space for the addition of three little ones, but we made do with what we had.

By the end of the second trimester we were feeling pretty good (well, I was anyway). I finished the nursery, somehow managing to squeeze three cribs into a 9- by 11-foot room, along with two dressers, a change table and several stuffed animals. My wife, on the other hand, was busy trying to squeeze three growing babies into a rapidly expanding tummy.

By now, everyone we knew (or our friends knew) were aware of our impending additions. I was amazed by the kindness, caring and generosity of so many people. Several co-workers at our office set up a large cardboard box in the cafeteria with a sign on it that read Donations for the Quesnelle Triplets. All sorts of things were dropped off — toys, sleepers and comforters, to name a few. I found myself lugging home bags of donations every week. Everything helped.

At 30 weeks, my wife was admitted to hospital for bedrest, not an experience she would enjoy. Her first two weeks in hospital were nerve-racking. Doctors had to intervene to stop labour with drugs and a decision was made to transfer her to a hospital with a higher level of neonatal care. The nearest hospital with beds available was an hour's drive away.

I didn't get much sleep the night before

By week 34 my wife developed toxemia, a condition that ultimately meant that a cesarean would take place within the next few days. I didn't get much sleep the night before. I was like a little kid on

Christmas Eve. The anticipation left me a little numb. Thankfully, I had Diane's mother and sister staying with me at the house that night. They were great company. At the hospital the next morning, I found my wife in better shape than I was, I think. After all the preparations were completed, she was given an epidural so she could be awake to greet our new additions at the same time as me.

May 31, 1995, at 9:31 a.m., our first baby, Haleigh, was carefully removed from a small incision and quickly whisked away after a brief stop to see her mom and dad. Okay, a girl. That's all right. Our next baby, Meagan, arrived at 9:33. Another girl. Still okay. Finally at 9:34 a.m. baby Garrett was born. Yahoo! A boy. Now don't get me wrong — three girls, three boys, or any mix in between would have been great. But I'm just glad we got a son out of it all the first time. I mean, I wouldn't want to risk a second triplet pregnancy.

It's hard to believe all of it happened two and a half years ago. Since then we've been through a lot. We knew they would be a lot of work, but I don't think anyone could ever be truly prepared for triplets.

From the first stages of rolling over on the floor to the first few tentative steps, life seems to have accelerated to a blur. Some days I sit back and wonder where the time has gone, but no matter how hard the day, I always find something that makes me smile. I know I've said a lot about how I feel about my kids, but it wouldn't be fair not be mention the person who has really been the "Rock." Diane has been a fantastic mom. Yet through all of the feedings, the diapers, the colds, and sleepless nights, she still found time for me, to be my wife and friend. So to all you guys out there, remember, don't just be a dad, be a husband, too!

honey, life is now
an adventure

Bracha Mirsky

I remember clearly the day I went for my first ultrasound. I was excited, but a little nervous as well. I knew something was unusual about my pregnancy but I assumed it was twins. (I had these dreams.) But at my previous visit, my doctor stated very clearly, "No, you are too small for twins." Measurements of my uterus indicated one baby. That was at 15 weeks, and I had been sick through the entire first trimester.

I remember my dear mother telling me that the only thing that made morning sickness tolerable was what you held in your arms at the end. But I did not have morning sickness. That would have been

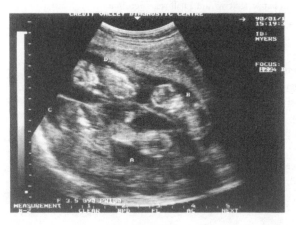

a treat! I had all-day sickness. I lost 8 lbs. in my first trimester and was passing ketones in my urine. My doctor said this was bad stuff and that it could harm the pregnancy, so he put me on medication at 15 weeks. By the end of my first trimester, I could finally hold some food down long enough to digest it.

Once I started eating, as you might imagine, my stomach exploded outward. I didn't really notice at first. But when people started guessing I was seven instead of three months pregnant, I started to worry. I realized the truth when I met a friend who was seven months pregnant — I was much bigger than she was! I have to admit that my doctor wanted to do a routine ultrasound at 12 weeks gestation. But I wanted as little intervention as possible in the pregnancy, so I told him no, unless he had a medical reason. Alas, the plans of mice and men, moms, parents ... Fast forward a few weeks and there I am, begging my doctor over the phone for an ultrasound appointment. "No, you don't have to have one," he says. "Please, I really do!" (He hasn't seen my humungous stomach yet.) My doctor finally agreed to order an ultrasound. I wasn't sure what to expect.

Ah, the ultrasound. What a lovely new experience for pregnant women of our time. For people like me who can barely tolerate four ounces of liquid in their bladder, drinking eight cups and holding it until someone gets around to you is a little uncomfortable. Then they expect you to keep on holding even as you're lying flat on a table and they're squeezing cold jelly onto your stomach. It will all be over soon, they assure me. The average ultrasound takes 15 minutes and one technician. So how come I'm still here 45 minutes later with two technicians and three doctors? (If anyone else comes in, I'm going to have to leave.)

"What's going on?" I say.

"Oh, nothing," they say.

"Do you always have so many people doing an ultrasound?" I ask, fishing around for some information. Let's face it, something was up.

"Oh yes," says the young doctor next to me, "we have to write the report."

I look him right in the eye, but he won't give an inch. What do they think — that pregnancy lowers the IQ? He really thought I bought it! If all five of them had not been smiling and obviously in a happy, relaxed mood, I would have freaked!

Well, I was finally re-leased and headed straight to the washroom (45 minutes, what can I say) and then to my doctor's office. I was sitting in the waiting room, when my doctor walked in and announced, "It's triplets." Uh, not even, "Good morning," or "Hi, how are you?"

"What?" I snapped.

"It's triplets. You're going to have three babies."

I blanked out and shrunk back into my chair. Then I started giggling. Three! I had waited so long for a baby and suddenly I had hit the jackpot. I couldn't stop smiling and left the office on cloud nine, running to tell the news to my husband — a man who had some trepidation about having one child.

As I was about to tell him about the three babies, I just smiled. And then I said, "Honey, life is now an adventure!"

2
a special care pregnancy

no one to turn to

Donna Launslager

Without much professional advice, having healthy quadruplets seemed a miracle 13 years ago

Hearing that we were about to have quadruplets was undoubtedly the biggest shock of my life. These babies were spontaneously conceived and there was no history of multiples in our families. In fact, my doctor had ordered an ultrasound to determine the likelihood of a fourth miscarriage. I thought I was losing another baby, not expecting four!

It was a very lonely feeling — we were the only family in our area going through this experience, and there was no one to turn to for advice or guidance. We couldn't find any special literature, and no one referred us to community resources or to a multiple birth association. Other than a prescription for prenatal vitamins, I went without appropriate nutritional advice. Professionals involved in our care offered us very little information, and considering my pregnancy history, surviving quadruplets just didn't seem like a very real possibility. But after dealing with the trauma of losing a baby at seven months gestation and then being blessed with one healthy baby boy, we felt we could accept whatever happened. Although I was determined to be optimistic, it took a lot of inner strength to deal with the emotional, social, medical and economic stresses we were facing. We took one day at a time and prayed that everything would be okay.

At 20 weeks I decided to take early maternity leave from work. With the support of a loving family and good friends, I managed to remain positive and relaxed throughout my pregnancy. Resting was possible with the help of neighbours, who took care of our one-year-old in the mornings, and a generous woman who agreed to clean our house once a week for very little money. In spite of the fact that I suffered from nausea, loss of appetite and was extremely uncomfortable, I sailed through the pregnancy without major complications. Fortunately, I was able to rest at home until 30 weeks, at which point I was hospitalized only because of the long distance from our house to the hospital. I was not restricted to complete bedrest and could walk around the hospital halls and go home on weekends until delivery. My doctors planned to let my pregnancy progress as long as possible; however, at 35 weeks, the decision was made to schedule me for a cesarean section.

It was a miracle. Our babies were born a week later — one boy and three girls — all healthy, with birthweights ranging from 2.5 pounds to just under 5 pounds.

Reflecting on our experience 13 years later, I know how very lucky we were to have four healthy babies considering the lack of specialized information we had. Since then, I have thought a lot about other families with triplets and quadruplets who were not so lucky and are dealing with the short- and long-term effects of their babies being born too early. According to current data, more than 90 per cent of higher order multiples will be born very prematurely.

Expectant parents are asked to place a great deal of trust in their doctor's skills and instincts, even though a general lack of awareness persists among Canadian healthcare providers about specific multiple birth issues. But many of the uncertainties that families face can be eased through connections: with peer support, and resource and referral networks. It is important to be proactive, to get involved in your pregnancy and delivery plans, and to develop good communication with your caregivers.

Expectant parents have to take it upon themselves to educate and prepare for all aspects of pregnancy, labour and delivery. While the lack of comprehensive information on multiples continues to be a problem, some principles are becoming known and accepted universally by experts the world over. In short, the chances for a healthy multiple pregnancy and birth increase with early diagnosis to ensure proper pregnancy management, excellent nutrition, adequate rest and peace of mind. And with peace of mind comes the inner strength that so many us need as we go through this experience.

exception to the rule
Suzanne Lyons

Multiple pregnancy management quite different

I always considered it absurd when I was pregnant with triplets that I was carrying so many babies but had so little specific information for ensuring they were born healthy.

Like many first moms-to-be, I spent a lot of time in bookstores scanning the pregnancy and childbirth sections. I looked at books that outlined typical stages of fetal development, duration of pregnancy, nutritional needs, tests to expect and what they should indicate, and precautions I should take. I even found a select few titles that specialized in twins. But at the end of the search, I walked away feeling less informed about the special needs of a higher order multiple pregnancy.

Pregnancy management and risks are markedly different from singleton pregnancies. There will be many tests, some the same as those ordered for a singleton pregnancy, others quite different or more frequent.

Here is a brief description of the kinds of tests and monitoring a woman expecting multiple babies may encounter throughout her pregnancy.

Abdominal Ultrasound

While an abdominal ultrasound provides useful information for any pregnancy, it is a particularly essential tool in a multiple pregnancy for determining a number of things:

• Diagnosing the multiple pregnancy and noting the number of fetuses and their sizes

• The number of placentas and their position

• Fetal chorionicity based on the number of chorions and amnions. Understanding the chorionicity of the fetuses from a very early stage of the pregnancy can provide some insight into additional risks to watch for in this pregnancy

• Fetal growth, condition and development at that particular moment of time

When? First ultrasound from week 5 to week 17

How often? Monthly to several times a week later in pregnancy

Referral to a specialized twin clinic

Once the multiple birth pregnancy has been diagnosed, many women are referred to a twin clinic that provides additional guidance on antenatal care, preterm labour prevention, fetal reduction, cervical cerclage (stitch) and other issues that are unique to their pregnancy. Clinic visits are a supplement to regular obstetrical care.

When? Referred from week 12 and onward

How Often? Usually four to five visits

Transvaginal ultrasound

Transvaginal ultrasounds may be performed to measure the length of the cervix and to detect cervical changes. Changes in the length of cervix can help your obstetrician predict when labour may occur. Experience shows that if a woman's cervix is less than two centimetres in length at week 24 of the pregnancy, the risk of delivery before 34 weeks is approximately 75%. Cervical assessment by transvaginal ultrasound may or may not be offered as part of ongoing care through the pregnancy.

When? Between 18 and 24 weeks when the test is most predictive of preterm labour

Genetic counselling

Generally offered to women age 32 and over when the chances of chromosomal abnormalities in multiple pregnancies increase. Following genetic counselling, some women may elect to undergo amniocentesis to rule out Down syndrome and open neural tube defects such as spina bifida. During the procedure, a thin needle is inserted through the abdomen into the uterus where some of the amniotic fluid is drawn from each fetal sac and analyzed. In multiple pregnancies, special care must be taken to collect fluid from each sac individually. Mothers carrying multiple fetuses may face higher risks of infection, rupturing a sac or triggering premature labour as a result of amniocentesis than do mothers carrying one fetus.

When? 16 weeks

How often? Once

Alpha-fetaprotein

A maternal blood test can measure the alpha-fetaprotein (AFP) produced by each fetus. An elevated AFP level in the mother can be an indicator of spina bifida in a multiple pregnancy because the fetal protein leaks into the mother's blood. However, the AFP test is not a useful screen for Down syndrome in a multiple pregnancy.

When? Between weeks 15 and 17

How often? Once

Glucose tolerance

With multiple pregnancies, there may be a higher risk of developing gestational diabetes, which is caused by pregnancy hormones that suppress the action of insulin in the body. To test for gestational diabetes, the mother drinks a glucose solution and waits for an hour before a blood sample is drawn and her plasma glucose tested. While the test is no different than screening performed in a single pregnancy, managing gestational diabetes through dietary control may require consultation with a dietician to ensure adequate nutritional intake for multiple fetuses while blood sugar intake is being controlled.

When? Between weeks 26 and 28

How often? Usually once

Urine tests

These tests can detect urinary tract infections, and the presence of ketones and/or protein in the urine. Protein in the urine can be an indicator of pre-eclampsia or kidney disease. Ketones in the urine may indicate that the mother is not getting an adequate amount of protein in her diet.

When? Every prenatal visit

Biophysical profile

A biophysical profile uses ultrasound and fetal heart rate monitoring to assess certain biophysical variables in each developing fetus. Providing more detail than an ultrasound, a biophysical profile helps to determine how each fetus is doing, and signals if one or more of fetuses are deteriorating or if the uterine environment has become hostile in some way.

Biophysical profiles may be performed frequently from week 32 onward. Complications during the pregnancy may prompt a physician to begin ordering profiles even earlier so that he or she can keep a continuous watch on the well being of the babies.

When? Typically from week 32

How often? Weekly to many times a week

With thanks to Dr. Jon Barrett

Professional Notes from the Obstetrics Nurse Specialist

warning signs and discomforts in a multiple pregnancy

Margaret Wood PhD Medical Science, R.N.

Pregnancy, especially a multiple pregnancy, presents unusual challenges to the body. Some discomfort is expected. Taken to the extreme, these discomforts can be warning signs that all is not well. How can you tell the difference between common discomforts and warnings? I will explain the differences and give you some guidance about how and when to help yourself and when to seek help from your healthcare professional. First, I will take you through the basics of the anatomy and physiology of pregnancy, and relate the symptoms to your bodily changes. Then I will advise how you can deal with those symptoms and when to seek help.

The chief hormone of pregnancy is progesterone. When ovulation occurs, the egg escapes from the ovary, leaving behind on the ovary the corpus luteum, or yellowish body. The corpus luteum produces both progesterone and estrogen, which prepare the uterus to receive the fertilized egg. Even if the egg is not fertilized, the effects of the progesterone are quite pronounced: bloating, swelling, increased appetite and a little weight gain and moodiness. If fertilization does occur, the egg implants in the soft, spongy uterus where the placenta grows and develops to support the fetus. The placenta quickly takes over the function of the corpus luteum, and produces the progesterone necessary to maintain the pregnancy.

The effects of progesterone are profound, and progesterone can be viewed as the culprit that causes most of the discomforts of pregnancy, and yet, as the saviour that is maintaining the pregnancy. Without progesterone, there would be no pregnancy. There would also be no constipation, swollen feet, heartburn, varicose veins, backache, or oily skin! Every organ and system in the body is affected by progesterone during pregnancy. Here's how.

The cardiovascular system

Some early changes in pregnant women involve the cardiovascular system. From early in the first trimester (one to 13 weeks after the last menstrual period) until late in the second trimester (14 to 26 weeks), the blood pressure decreases, and then rises until term, when it returns approximately to the woman's pre-pregnancy level.

Blood pressure is dependent on the pregnant woman's position: it is lowest when she is lying on her side, highest when she is sitting, and mid-point when she is standing. These positional changes can lead to what is called postural hypotension. Non-pregnant people may suffer from a drop in blood pressure when they suddenly stand up from a lying-down position, but for pregnant women, the opposite is true. Lying on her back, called the "supine" position, may dangerously lower a pregnant woman's blood pressure. Side-lying is the best position for resting or sleeping.

Since women with multiple pregnancies have a greater decrease in blood pressure in the second trimester than women with single-ton pregnancies, they may be at a greater risk for significant postural hypotension, or drop in blood pressure. It is important that women with multiple pregnancies move from one position to another slow-ly and deliberately to avoid sudden changes in blood pressure and feelings of dizziness or faintness. If these symptoms persist in spite of slow changes in position, advice from a physician is necessary.

In a singleton pregnancy the mother's heart rate increases about 15 per cent. In a multiple pregnancy, the increase is about 40 per cent. More oxygen-carrying blood is speeding faster around the mother's system — her heart pumps more blood more frequently. In fact, the output of the heart is increased by close to 50 per cent. Most of this increase occurs by the end of the first trimester, but the increase con-tinues until 32 weeks of pregnancy. Again, the mother's position has a significant effect on cardiac output. It is recommended that preg-nant women lie on their sides and not on their backs because the pregnant uterus can compress the vena cava, the major vein that returns blood from the body to the heart. Women with multiple pregnancies not only have higher cardiac output, their uterus is much larger and tends to compress the vena cava even more.

One of the noticeable effects of the increased volume of blood and progesterone is swelling. If your feet are swollen, make sure you lie on your side to encourage the flow of blood back to your heart from your legs. You will find that the swelling is reduced after a good rest on your side, or after a night of sleep. If the swelling does not go down at all after resting, or if you notice that you are swollen around your eyes or face, or that you fingers are puffy, tell your physician. This kind of swelling may indicate pre-eclampsia or high blood pressure (also known as "pregnancy-induced hypertension" or PIH), a potentially dangerous condition that must be treated. The incidence of pre-eclampsia or PIH is higher in twin pregnancies than in singleton pregnancies, and it is even higher in triplet and quadruplet pregnancies. The increased incidence may be the result of the larger placental mass of multiple pregnancy.

Less obvious swelling occurs in the gums. You may find that your gums bleed a little when you floss: this is a normal and expected occurrence in pregnancy. However, bleeding more than a slight amount is a warning sign that should lead you to seek medical attention. Dental hygiene is very important during multiple pregnancy. Try to brush with a soft brush using gentle strokes away from the gum line, and floss after every meal. Please see a dentist during your pregnancy. Gum infection is very difficult to treat and has potentially serious effects, including activation of the uterus leading to preterm labour.

Uterine changes

Uterine growth begins early in pregnancy. In multiple pregnancies, the volume of the uterus is about the same as it is in singleton pregnancies until the end of the first trimester. However, by the 18th week of pregnancy, the volume of the uterus is about twice as much for twin pregnancies as for singleton pregnancies, and far greater for higher order multiple pregnancies. In fact, for twin pregnancies, by the 25th week the uterine volume is equal to that of a singleton pregnancy at term!

Uterine activity increases in multiple pregnancies. From the 23rd week until term, women with multiple pregnancies have more contractions than women with singleton pregnancies. These contractions may be related to the increased size of the uterus (overdistention) or to other factors such as the increased activity of more than one fetus. The frequency of contractions increases until term. The increased uterine contractions may (or may not) lead to preterm labour, depending on the force the contractions exert on the cervix. Fluid leaking from the vagina should be reported immediately because it may be amniotic fluid, indicating a break in the bag of waters surrounding the babies. Known as "rupture of the membranes," it means a different plan of care for you, including hospitalization. Bleeding from the vagina must be reported as soon as possible — it is always a warning sign.

Your physician diagnoses preterm labour when there are uterine contractions and dilatation of the cervix. Fortunately, if it is diagnosed early enough — before the cervix reaches four centimetre dilatation — the likelihood of stopping the preterm labour is fairly high, at least for a few days. It is important to pay attention to contractions. Do not dismiss them as being "just" contractions that are expected. Remember that there is an unknown effect on the cervix, so inform your physician about your contractions so that your cervix can be visualized by way of a speculum or transvaginal ultrasound to see if it is dilating. Digital exams are not recommended because they can stimulate the cervix and introduce bacteria into the cervix

If you suspect you are having a contraction (it may not be a contraction at all, but the babies rolling and playing), follow these steps: (1) check the time of that contraction and the next ones (2) think about what you were doing when the contraction started (3) stop what you were doing and lie down for about half an hour if possible (4) drink two glasses of water or juice (5) if the contractions do not go away after that half hour and seem to be building in frequency or intensity, call your healthcare provider right away. If the contractions go away, be happy.

Endocrine changes

Progesterone is not the only hormone made by the placenta that is more elevated in multiple pregnancies compared to singleton pregnancies. The maternal progesterone and human chorionic gonadotropin (hCG) levels in twin pregnancies are double that of singleton pregnancies. hCG is largely responsible for morning sickness but its role in early pregnancy is to maintain the corpus luteum, which produces progesterone and estrogen until the placenta takes over. The human placental lactogen (hPL) levels are also much higher. So too is the maternal alpha-fetoprotein (MSAFP) level. These hormone levels are sometimes used as an indication of the well-being of both the mother and the fetuses.

Changes in the respiratory system

The volume of air breathed per minute increases by 40 per cent in pregnancy, amazingly, without an increase in respiratory rate. This is accomplished by an increase in "tidal volume" — deeper breathing made possible by higher levels of estrogen which relax the rib cage — greater in multiple pregnancies than in singleton pregnancies. These changes, which occur in early pregnancy and continue until delivery, are necessary to compensate for the 20 per cent increase in oxygen consumption in the normal pregnant woman. Although a certain amount of shortness of breath is expected, if you experience shortness of breath while resting, or any difficulty breathing, call your healthcare provider as soon as possible.

Progesterone has the effect of swelling the tissues, so it is not uncommon for pregnant women to have "sniffles" or the feeling that they have a cold. To minimize this symptom, keep a humidifier on in the bedroom while you are sleeping, protect the skin around your nose with a moisturizer, and blow your nose gently. Slight nosebleeds are also common if the air is dry and cold: heavy nosebleeds need medical attention right away. Antibiotics have absolutely no beneficial effect on viruses and should not be used to treat sniffles. Seek help if cold symptoms are accompanied by a cough, fever, chills, or painful joints because these signs of bacterial infection are treated with antibiotics.

Gastrointestinal function

Just as progesterone decreases the tone of the walls of the arteries and veins during pregnancy, it also decreases the tone of the sphincters in the gastrointestinal tract. One such sphincter, the cardiac sphincter, is at the bottom of the esophagus where the esophagus and stomach meet. When the cardiac sphincter loses tone, especially during pregnancy when the pressure within the stomach itself is increased, many women complain of the symptoms of gastric reflux, including severe heartburn and regurgitation.

To combat these symptoms, try eating many small meals per day rather than three regular meals, and separate food from fluids. After eating a meal, try to stay up rather than lie down for an hour or so. Hydration and nourishment in pregnancy are important for your well-being and the growth of your babies. The Globe and Mail (August 12, 1997, p. A18) reported a study carried out in Israel where it was confirmed that women who fast in their pregnancy are likely to trigger birth. One theory is that the deprivation of fluids causes stress in the adrenaline-producing glands and leads to early contractions.

Constipation is a common complaint in pregnancy. Again, we can blame this effect on progesterone, which decreases the muscle tone of the intestines. There is also increased water absorption from the intestines, compounding the problem of constipation. Eating bulk forming foods, such as foods with high fibre, will help control constipation. It is important to drink extra fluids, too. If you are constipated, do not strain while having a bowel movement. Straining can cause a sudden drop in the blood pressure and may also cause or aggravate hemorrhoids.

a special care pregnancy

Kidney function

The kidneys increase in size during pregnancy, probably because of an increase in blood flow through the kidneys and the extra work they have to do. The ureters, or tubes that carry urine to the bladder, dilate not only because of the obstruction caused by the enlarging uterus, but because of the relaxing effect of the progesterone. The symptoms of bladder infection include frequency (passing a small amount of urine frequently), urgency (the feeling that you can't wait), and a burning sensation as you are passing urine. However, urinary tract infection may be present even without these symptoms. Your physician will ask you for a mid-stream urine sample, which

System	Common	Warning Sign
Cardiovascular	Low blood pressure	Dizziness or faintness
	Swelling of feet and ankles	Swelling of face and eyelids; swelling that does not go down with rest
	Slight bleeding of the gums when flossing; slight nose bleeds in dry cold weather	Bleeding of the gums and nose that is a little more than "slight"
Uterus	Mild irregular contractions; mucous vaginal discharge	Mild regular contractions that may signal preterm labour; fluid leaking from the vagina; bleeding from the vagina, no matter how slight
Respiratory	Mild shortness of breath when walking; stuffy nose	Shortness of breath when resting; stuffy nose accompanied by fever, chills, cough, pains
Gastrointestinal	Hard stools; heartburn	Constipation that does not respond to simple measures; nausea, vomiting or diarrhea
Kidneys	Frequent urination	Frequency with urgency and burning, backache, unusual odour, chills, or other signs of infection
Muscles and Joints	Awkward gait; lower backache; muscle cramps	Unusual backache; pelvic pressure; headache; any pain

will be examined for bacteria. If bacteria are present, you will be treated with antibiotics because it is well-known that urinary tract infection, even without symptoms, can cause preterm labour.

Weight gain

A common recommendation is that mothers with twin pregnancies gain about 1.5 pounds per week during the second and third trimesters for a total weight gain of 35 to 45 pounds; that mothers expecting triplets gain 45 to 50 pounds by 34 weeks; and that mothers expecting quadruplets gain more than 50 pounds. There is no standard recommendation for the "ideal" caloric intake. Enjoy good food — one of life's greatest pleasures.

Muscles and joints

During pregnancy, and more so during multiple pregnancy, there is a noticeable change in gait and balance even before there is much weight gain or change in body shape. This effect is related to another pregnancy hormone, relaxin, that softens the ligaments and tendons. The joints are loose. Care must be taken while walking or performing any activity while standing to avoid falling or straining muscles and ligaments. Warning signs of difficulty include severe or unusual backache, headache, sacroiliac pain leading to sciatica, pelvic pressure, and radiating pain in any limb. The sacroiliac joint is between the hip bone and the sacrum. Normally, there is no movement in this joint but in pregnant women it becomes moveable. Movement of this joint may cause some discomfort, but not pain. If you experience these symptoms, seek advice from your physician.

The ligaments that support the growing uterus can cramp, causing sharp pain in one side of the abdomen or in the groin. An ice pack, such as a bag of frozen peas or corn, applied for about 10 minutes, should relieve this common discomfort. If the pain persists beyond an hour or so, contact your healthcare provider.

Nighttime cramps in the calves are also common, and may be related to either too much or too little calcium or to too little potassium or phosphorous. Standing on a cold floor, stretching your toes toward your knees, and massaging the calf will bring relief; however, if there is a hard vein or warm, reddened swelling in the calf, do not massage it. Notify your physician because those are signs of a deep vein thrombosis or blood clot.

Backache is expected as a pregnant woman's posture changes in response to the growing uterus, but severe backache accompanied by a tightening of the abdomen may warn of preterm or term labour. To minimize common back discomfort, perform pelvic tilt exercises slowly several times a day and pay attention to good lower back support when seated.

Warning signs in a multiple pregnancy are often discomforts taken to the extreme. Report warning signs immediately to your healthcare provider. Common sense approaches to the demands of a multiple pregnancy include: REST when you are tired; DRINK before you are thirsty; and EAT when you are hungry. Never ignore fatigue, thirst, or hunger. Best of all, enjoy life to the fullest.

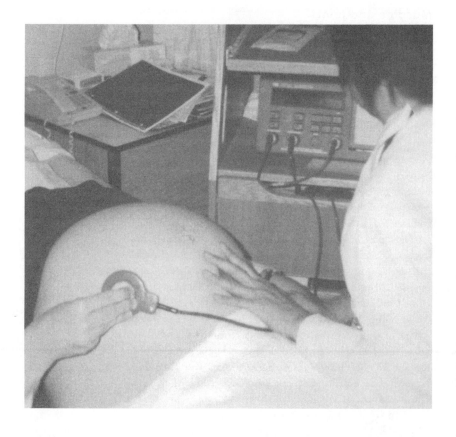

Common Terms and Definitions

Cardiovascular system: the heart and blood vessels

Cardiac output: the amount of blood that the heart pumps out to the body per minute

Corpus luteum: a yellow mass of endocrine cells formed after the release of an egg from the ovary

Esophagus: a muscular tube for the passage of food from the mouth to the stomach

First trimester: the first three months of pregnancy (one to 13 weeks from the last menstrual period)

Gastrointestinal: the system consisting of the stomach and the intestines

Ovulation: the moment the egg is released from the ovary. In women, ovulation normally occurs 14 days before menstruation

Placenta: the oval-shaped, spongy structure in the uterus through which the fetus derives its nourishment. The mature placenta is about seven inches in diameter and weighs about a pound. Following birth, the placenta is expelled (the "afterbirth")

Preterm labour: preterm labour has two components: dilatation of the cervix and uterine contractions. It occurs between the 20th week and the 37th week of pregnancy. Once the cervix reaches four centimetres dilatation, the woman is in active preterm labour. Active labour has little chance of being stopped, and the birth of the babies is imminent. Preterm labour diagnosed before the cervix reaches four centimetres dilatation has a greater likelihood of being stopped, though it is not always possible to do so. Drugs called "tocolytics" may be used to stop labour at this early stage

Progesterone: a female hormone secreted by the corpus luteum prior to implantation of the fertilized egg and by the placenta after implantation

Prostaglandins: a substance present in many body tissues; has a role in reproduction; used for inducing (artificially starting) labour. It has the effect of softening the cervix, preparing it to dilate, and causing uterine contractions

Second trimester: the second three months of pregnancy (14 to 26 weeks from the last menstrual period)

Third trimester: the last three months of pregnancy (from 27 weeks after the last menstrual period to delivery)

Ureters: the tube that carries urine from kidneys to the bladder

Urinary tract: consists of the kidneys, ureters and bladder. A urinary tract infection can occur in any of these places, sometimes without symptoms. The sign of a urinary tract infection is bacteria growing in the urine, visible under a microscope

Vena cava: literally means "hollow vein;" it carries blood to the heart where it is pumped to the lungs for a new supply of oxygen

---

Professional Notes from the Fetal Zygosity Specialist

---

zygosity matters!

Geoffrey A. Machin, MD, PhD, FRCP(C)
Fetal and Genetic Pathologist

In most pregnancies, a single fertilized egg becomes an embryo with its corresponding placenta. But with a multiple pregnancy, the cascade of events that unfolds in the very early stages of pregnancy is dramatically different. A multiple pregnancy occurs in one of two ways:

1) A single egg (zygote) divides at some point after it is fertilized. Each division gives rise to another individual. This is called a monozygotic twin or triplet pregnancy.

2) On the other hand, if more than one egg is released from the ovaries at a given time, and a sperm fertilizes each egg, there will be multiple zygotes created. There is no division of the zygote. This kind of multiple pregnancy is called multizygotic. More specifically, a twin pregnancy created by two different eggs fertilized by different sperm would be described as dizygotic. With triplets, it would be considered trizygotic and so on.

It's important to note that many higher order multiple pregnancies have mixed zygosity. Referring back to the example of triplets, it's entirely possible and quite common, in fact, for two of the fetuses to be monozygotic and the third to have a different zygosity, having evolved from a different fertilized egg.

Throughout this article, I will refer to infants who are monozygotic (MZ), which means developing from one zygote. I will also refer to infants who are multiZ, which means "developing from multiple zygotes." Contrary to common misconception, MZ does not mean identical. As every parent of MZ multiple birth babies knows, there is no such thing as "identical" babies. There are always some differences, and sometimes very distinguishing differences. Many parents mistakenly think that their babies cannot be MZ because they are not absolutely "identical."

If we do away with the concept of identical multiples and substitute "close similarity," the problem solves itself. My colleague, Dr. Fiona Bamforth of Edmonton, Alta., and I have offered zygosity testing (for a moderate donation) to parents of twins or more who did not know the zygosity of their children. An overwhelming 96 per cent of multiples tested turned out to be MZ, but not identical, remember. Parents of multiZ children can clearly see that they are unalike. A boy and girl, for example, cannot share zygosity. But parents of MZ children may also notice differences and mistakenly assume that they cannot possibly be MZ because they are not absolutely identical. Relax! MZ children are very similar, but never identical.

Frequency of multiple pregnancies

Two social trends have increased the frequency of multiple pregnancies:

1) Older maternal age has increased the number of multiZ pregnancies, since ovulation patterns can become more variable with age and more likely to produce more than one egg at a time.

2) Assisted reproduction technology (ART) has greatly increased the birth rate of triplets, quadruplets and more. Interestingly, in pregnancies resulting from ART, there is still a very considerable rate of MZ infants. This may come as a surprise to many parents, given the focus on producing and fertilizing multiple eggs in ART. The reasons for MZ infants in multiple pregnancies resulting from ART are unknown. But it is wrong to assume that all assisted multiple pregnancies lead to multiZ babies. Often there is at least a pair of MZ twins in the pregnancy.

In naturally conceived multiple pregnancies, the rates of MZ and DZ twins are well-known. But there is no extensive information on triplets or more. For naturally conceived twins, the rate of MZ twins per 1,000 births is constant all over the world, at a rate of about 4/1,000. The DZ rate varies greatly from place to place. The highest rate is in Nigeria, while the lowest is in Japan. In Japan, the majority of twins are MZ, but in Nigeria the majority are DZ. In Europe and North America, between 35 per cent and 40 per cent of naturally conceived twins are MZ, and 60 per cent to 65 per cent are DZ.

Zygosity and number of placentas

This is a confusing area, and a good deal of misinformation is often given to parents. A brief grounding in early embryology will help to clarify the picture.

a special care pregnancy

Very soon after an egg is fertilized, it begins to divide into multiple cells. Within two days, the cells that will form the placenta separate from the cells that will form the embryo. The proper term for the placenta and its associated membrane is the "chorion." Every fertilized egg that will form only a single fetus will develop a placenta and an embryo. Therefore, in dizygotic twins or trizygotic triplets, the number of placentas equals the number of embryos. The placentas may be separate or fused.

The situation is much more complicated for MZ twins, triplets, quads and quints. There can be many kinds of placental arrangements, depending on exactly when the multiple process happened. *(see Fig. 1)* If the division for MZ triplets, quads or quints happens very quickly, say, less than two days after fertilization, each fetus will have its own placenta. So, for example, triplets could be MZ, but have three placentas, if the division occurred very early after fertilization.

However, if the division(s) take place more than two days after fertilization, the outer cell mass that forms the placenta will have already separated from the embryos, and there will be an embryological plan for just one placenta even though there are three or more embryos. These types of MZ triplets, quads and quints will have a truly single (not fused) placenta. They are called monochorionic pregnancies.

For MZ twinning, the zygote only divides once into the twin individuals. For MZ triplets, one of those twins divides again. The situation is even more complex for MZ quads and quints. Since there needs to be successive divisions from MZ twins to produce

zygosity at a glance

MZ - monozygotic	Evolving from one zygote. Often referred to as "identical"
MC - monochorionic	A single (not fused) placenta
MA - monoamniotic	A single amniotic sac
DZ - dizygotic	Evolving from two zygotes. Often referred to as fraternal
DC - dichorionic	Two placentas
DA- diamniotic	Two amniotic sacs
TZ- Trizygotic	Evolving from three zygotes
TC – trichorionic	Three placentas
TA - triamniotic	Three amniotic sacs

multiple fetuses, it follows that some of those splitting decisions might occur at less than two days after fertilization (making two placentas), and others at more than two days after fertilization (producing monochorionic placentas). In this way, MZ triplets, quads and quints could have a mixture of placentas.

There is not an easy one-to-one relationship between the number of placentas and zygosity. Many parents are misinformed by their healthcare professionals.

Here are the simple rules (for twins):
1) Different-sexed twins are always dizygotic (DZ)
2) All DZ twins have one placenta each
3) Same-sexed twins may be DZ or MZ
4) Monochorionic twins must be MZ
5) But MZ twins may have two placentas (dichorionic, or DC) or a truly single monochorionic placenta, depending on how soon the twin splitting happens after fertilization
6) Not all twins with different placentas are dizygotic. This is the most common mistake made by healthcare professionals. I have met hundreds of parents of twins who have been misled. Their same-sexed twins are very similar. But since the pregnancy was dichorionic, their parents were misinformed that their twins must therefore be DZ

Same-sexed twins with two placentas (DC) may be MZ or DZ. The placental status gives no information about zygosity. Other tests are necessary if there is real, persisting doubt about zygosity.

About eight days after zygote formation, the amniotic membrane and cavity separate from the embryo. Therefore, if the MZ twinning happens more than eight days after zygote formation, the MZ twins will not only share a placenta but also the amnion. This pregnancy is called monochorionic and monoamniotic (MA). Only about five per cent of MC twins are MA. These twin fetuses are literally floating around in the same swimming pool. There is nothing to stop their umbilical cords from becoming entangled. Sometimes spectacular braids are made. There is a danger that these entanglements will be sufficiently tight to cut off the umbilical circulation of one or more of the fetuses. But the great majority of MC twins have one amniotic cavity each — they are diamniotic (DA) or tri-amniotic (TA) if they are triplets.

If twinning is delayed until about 13 days, the twins will be unable to split completely and will remain conjoined (so-called Siamese twins).

The importance of chorion and amnion number

The number of chorions and amnions can give some information related to zygosity. However, in themselves, the chorion and amnion numbers are very important because they shed light on the relative likelihood of major complications in the pregnancy. *(see Fig. 2)*

Pregnancies with just one placenta (monochorionic) have much higher risks than pregnancies with two or more. The reason for this is that the truly single placenta has divided loyalties and has great difficulty supplying the needs of twins or triplets. After all, one placenta usually does a good job for a single embryo. To ask a placenta to look after two or more embryos is sometimes too much.

However, the main difficulty posed by this kind of pregnancy is the possibility of blood circulations of the fetuses becoming mixed up. *(see Fig. 3)* A single placenta has no way of mapping out which blood vessels belong to which embryo. Blood flows to the placenta from the embryo in the umbilical cord via two umbilical arteries. When these vessels reach the placenta, they branch and run across the placental surface before dipping down into the substance of the placenta to pick up oxygen and nutrients from the maternal blood that also runs through the placenta. On their way back to the embryo, veins run across the surface of the placenta to the cord and then return to the embryo via the umbilical vein.

When there is a single (MC) placenta looking after the fetuses, two sets of factors can affect the efficiency of the placenta:

1) There may be competition among the embryos for the amount of placenta their blood vessels use. This can cause significant discordance in growth rates. To some degree, differences in the amount of placenta allocated to each fetus depend on where the umbilical cords insert into the surface of the placenta. When the cord reaches the placenta near the centre, vessels radiate out in a circular fashion. When the cord inserts into the edge of the placenta, it can only spread out in a semicircular fashion. With

two or more different cord insertions, one or two central and one on the edge, the central fetus will win out and "hog" the placenta at the expense of the others.

2) There can be major mistakes in the hooking up of vessels to the fetuses. For instance, one fetus may send an artery branch to a particular part of the placenta. But there is no absolute rule that says that the venous blood from that zone must return to the same fetus. The placenta is unable to determine which vessels belong to which fetus, and the vein might, by mistake, run back to the umbilical cord of the wrong fetus. This sets up the possibility of twin-to-twin transfusion, which is the most frequent and severe complication of monochorionic placentas in MZ twins. These artery-to-vein connections occur very infrequently in dichorionic placentas.

Other complications of an MC placenta include twin-reversed arterial perfusion and complications in the surviving fetuses if one fetus should die before birth.

Antenatal ultrasound diagnosis of chorion and amnions

Given the increased risks of MC multiple pregnancies, determining chorionicity is one of the most important issues to be tackled at antenatal obstetric ultrasound examination. The chorion and amnion membranes, when present, form a recognizable septum or line between the fetuses. When there are two or more chorions present, the membranous septum is thick and usually forms a tent-like wedge as it reaches the placental surface (the so-called "twin peak" "lambda" or "delta" sign). Chorion status is most easily recognized in early pregnancy, preferably in the first 10 weeks or so. When there is a single chorion, the septums between the amniotic sacs are extremely thin and may be difficult to see. However, there are other ways of determining the number of amnions:

1) Early in the gestation (at about six weeks) a yolk sac is present for each fetus except for monoamniotic (MA) twins/triplets, for whom there is only a single yolk sac.

2) If the cords are intertwined, the gestation must be MC and MA.

3) If the twins are conjoined, they are usually MC and MA.

4) If necessary, for instance when doing amniocentesis, a coloured dye can be injected into the fluid close to one fetus. When fluid

is withdrawn close to the other fetus, the presence of dye implies that there is a single amniotic cavity. If no dye is drawn back, the pregnancy is MC, DA. Other methods have been used, including the injection of sterile air bubbles instead of dye. Air bubbles intensely reflect ultrasound waves, and their extent within the gestation will indicate the number of amniotic cavities.

Although the number of chorions and amnions is a vital test that should be done at the obstetric ultrasound examination of multiple pregnancies, it is a matter of great concern that the test is not always carried out competently. This is partly because of pressure of time and money, and partly because some feel that ultrasound is not as useful a tool as has been supposed. So, for instance, many clinics only do a single ultrasound, usually at about 16 weeks. This is far too late to do the best job of determining chorion number. In an ideal world, every pregnancy would have an ultrasound at the first antenatal office visit. At that time, all multiple pregnancies would be detected and sufficient time could be allocated to be sure that chorion number is determined with complete certainty.

In addition, confusion is caused by the use of the non-specific term "sac," which means different things to different people. For instance, all dichorionic twins have two sacs, meaning two chorions and two amnions. Many monochorionic pregnancies also have two, three or four amnions, but the implication is vastly different, considering the high risks of MC pregnancies. Since a monoamniotic multiple pregnancy is very rare, telling an expectant mother that the fetuses are contained within their own sacs is to give her no useful information. The question is, "How many chorions are there?" Then the amnion question can be settled later.

Why does zygosity matter?

During pregnancy, considerations of zygosity take a back seat in contrast to the overwhelming importance of chorion and amnion number. However, the fact is that if the fetuses are MC, then they must also be MZ. Few parents are told this by their care providers. Suddenly, after birth, the parents realize they need information on zygosity, for their sanity if for nothing else. What is the first question they are asked as the babies take their first trip to the shopping mall in their stroller? "Are they identical?" Zygosity is a basic "right-to-know" issue for multiple babies and their parents. But the information is seldom available because zygosity determination is not paid for as part of routine obstetric care. Sadly, many parents of MC infants are not aware that their babies share zygosity.

What are the justifications for zygosity testing?

1) MZ twins are ideal transplant donors and recipients for each other. There is a great shortage of organs for transplantation, and MZ pairs will not reject tissues transplanted from each other. Transplantation is therefore cheap and effective because there is no need to monitor and treat the recipient for transplant rejection. Skin grafts and whole kidney transplants have been done successfully between MZ twin pairs.

2) If one MZ twin has a serious, chronic illness with a significant genetic component in its causation, there is a significant chance that the other twin will develop the same disease sooner or later. This applies to depression, schizophrenia, diabetes, asthma, rheumatoid arthritis and several forms of cancer. Intensive observation of the second twin will allow the earliest detection and treatment of the disease that has already developed in the first twin.

3) There is much discussion about the ability of twins, triplets and more to socialize with their peers when they have such an intense relationship with each other. The situation is probably more severe in MZ than DZ multiples. Whether to separate children in school as part of individuation is another topic, much more complex in triplets and quads.

4) There have been incidents in which twins have been misidentified and switched at birth. This would be less likely to happen if zygosity were routinely tested at birth. In one case, a pair of male twins (call them A and B) were born on the same night as a single male (call him C). Because the twin pregnancy was dichorionic, it was wrongly assumed that the twin boys were dizygotic. The three boys got mixed up in the newborn nursery. Twin A went home with the single male C as a twin pair. Not surprisingly, they did not look alike. Meanwhile, twin B went home with his happy parents as an apparent single boy. Twenty years later, C met twin B at college and noticed how similar he

FIG. 1

Triplets, zygotes, timing of splitting and number of placentas

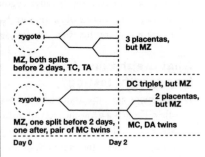

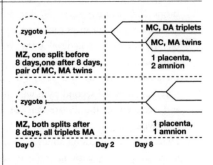

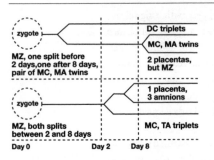

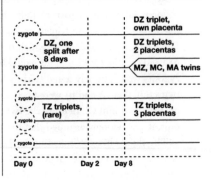

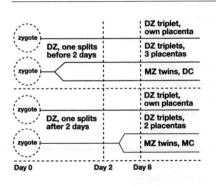

looked to his own "twin" A! Needless to say, zygosity testing showed that twins A and B were MZ. This could not have happened if zygosity testing had been done at birth.

Contrary to popular belief, zygosity testing is simple, cheap and reliable. If twins are monochorionic, then they must be MZ. To determine the zygosity of DC twins, simple blood grouping can be done as a start. Any detectable differences imply different zygosity. If no blood group differences are found, definitive testing can be done using "DNA fingerprinting." With this method, DNA taken from each individual is cut up into fragments of different sizes, which read out like a barcode. If no differences are found, the children are MZ. If differences are found, they are DZ. Naturally conceived triplets and quads usually include at least a pair of MZ twins, and are often completely MZ. Parents who would like to find out more about zygosity testing should get in touch with Multiple Births Canada.

The future

In my experience, many parents of twins, triplets and quadruplets do not know the zygosity of their children, or have been given false information based on misunderstanding of the relationship between zygosity and chorion number. One of the greatest tasks for these parents is to form an effective lobbying group so that zygosity testing at birth becomes a routine component of care in multiple birth pregnancies throughout the world. We should not be deterred by people who say it is not important, does not matter, will become obvious with time, or is none of our business. Zygosity does indeed matter.

FIG. 2

Chorions and Amnions

Monochorionic
monoamniotic placenta

TWIN A   monozygotic   **TWIN B**

Chorion (placenta and outer membranes):
Solid Line
Amnion (inner membrane):
Dashed Line

Monochorionic
diamniotic placenta

TWIN A   monozygotic   **TWIN B**

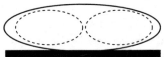

Chorion (placenta and outer membranes):
Solid Line
Amnions (inner membrane):
Dashed Lines

Fused dichorionic
diamniotic placentas

TWIN A   dizygotic   **TWIN B**
or monozygotic

Chorion (placenta and outer membranes):
Solid Black & Grey Lines
Amnions (inner membrane):
Dashed Line

Separate dichorionic
diamniotic placentas

TWIN A   dizygotic   **TWIN B**
or monozygotic

Chorion (placenta and outer membranes):
Solid Black & Grey Lines
Amnions (inner membrane):
Dashed Line

FIG. 3

Blood vessel complications in monochorionic twins

Unequal Sharing

TWIN A
2500g

TWIN B
3000g

The umbilical cord of TWIN A is inserted at the edge of the placenta, whereas the cord of TWIN B is close to the centre. Blood vessels running out from the cord of TWIN B have a much greater share of placental tissue than TWIN A. This can cause slow fetal growth in TWIN A.

Blood Vessel Connections

TWIN A
2500g

TWIN B
3000g

Most MC twins have blood vessel connections on the surface of the placenta. These may be direct artery-to-artery connections (continuous thick lines), or vein-to-vein connections (dotted lines).

Twin-to-twin Transfusion

TWIN A
2500g

TWIN B
3000g

Many MC placentas also have artery-to-vein connections, in which blood is actually transfused from the donor twin (left) to the recipient (right). This only happens in MC placentas, and is the chief reason why placenta (chorion) number should be diagnosed by an early ultrasound exam. Twin-to-twin transfusion can occur with MC twins or triplets.

Professional Notes from the Family Physician
---

in the circle of caregivers
Alice Bluemke, MD

Sharing the experience with parents expecting quadruplets

As a family doctor it is a privilege to witness the unfolding of people's lives. Each life tells a unique story that is filled with amazing tales, heroes and challenges conquered. I still remember being interviewed by a young couple in June 1988, pregnant with their first child, as one of several potential caregivers for providing obstetrical care. After being chosen for this role, it became the first of three pregnancies and deliveries I would have the honour of participating in with this couple and family.

From early on, the second pregnancy presented differently: a greater than normal fundal height for dates and hyperemesis with secondary weight loss. I questioned the possibilities of multiple gestation or a molar pregnancy. An ultrasound was booked. The day of the ultrasound was the first in my medical obstetrical career that I received an urgent page from an expectant father with a verbal report of the prenatal ultrasound, long before I heard from the radiologist: a spontaneous quadruplet pregnancy!

I can still remember hearing the shock and excitement in his voice and his concern for the well-being of his wife and the babies, and for the future financial provision for his family. For me, even though I had considered a multiple gestation, I was surprised by the number and knew that as a family doctor doing obstetrics, this was a once-in-a-lifetime experience. Since the pregnancy had become high risk, I consulted with an obstetrical specialist and made arrangements for the mother to be followed at a hospital in downtown Toronto where there was a high risk pregnancy clinic. Local referrals were also made to a dietician, public health nurse, social worker and for future home care and a consulting pediatrician. Although there were many unknowns, planning ahead for community resources was my primary role as a family physician throughout the pregnancy and thereafter.

a special care pregnancy

At 21 weeks gestational age, the mother was admitted to our local community hospital, suffering from gastroenteritis. Knowing premature labour and dehydration were risks, intravenous hydration and bedrest were ordered. Mom recovered quickly without complications. At 24 weeks, she was admitted to the tertiary care hospital downtown for bedrest and observation. During my visits with her, we talked about the size of her pregnancy, her breathlessness at times, and how each of the quadruplets was positioned. Our shared excitement about the pregnancy was realistically guarded by concern about the risk of premature labour and the outcome for the babies. However, we both knew that she was in a setting of optimal care for both mother and children.

At 27 weeks, contractions started, and despite attempts to stop labour, events progressed to the point where a cesarean section became the best course. I had made prior arrangements to attend the delivery. I recall an exceptionally large number of medical and nursing staff in the operative suite, partly because it was a teaching setting, but also because of the attending neonatology staff. Dad was present, and Mom was awake with epidural anesthesia in place. I watched with great anticipation as the usual lower uterine segment incision was made. Quadruplet A, a girl, was delivered at 11:47 a.m., followed quickly by a boy. Then another girl! And then another boy at 11:50 a.m. This was my live introduction to Alison, Harrison, Jessica and Kenny and it was a magnificent moment to share with their parents. I felt truly blessed.

Throughout the summer of 1990 I enjoyed my home visits with Alison, Harrison, Jessica, Kenny and their older brother Craig. Housecalls with weigh scale and immunization materials in hand became a much more practical approach to well-child care than office visits. These visits continued until 1992. Sometimes the visits were done when the children had respiratory infections and sometimes to celebrate birthdays. It should be noted that the quadruplets were also followed in the neonatal follow-up clinic at the downtown hospital and with a local pediatrician.

It was during the home visits, as I observed the volunteers and met with extended family, neighbours and professional caregivers, that I was repeatedly reminded of the old African proverb: "it takes a village to raise a child." Many letters were written and requests made for practical and financial support to community health agencies, charity clubs, pharmaceutical companies, insurance companies, local and regional government agencies. Some of the responses were exceptional; others disappointing.

Alison, Harrison, Jessica and Kenny are celebrating their 10th birthday this year. They, along with their parents and their two sibling brothers are the heroes of my story, having faced many obstacles and met the challenges, teaching the rest of us that to survive, family members must work together, take risks and make sacrifices for each other.

a special care pregnancy

fetal reduction

could you make the choice?

Donna Zidar

For five years, my husband and I rode the infertility roller coaster together, going through years of ovulation monitoring, several unsuccessful surgical procedures and five unsuccessful spermwash cycles. Like all infertile couples, we moved back and forth from days of great expectation and hope to days of despair.

After spending months on the in vitro fertilization (IVF) waiting list, we began our first IVF cycle. At this point, we were very enthusiastic. I attended an information session prior to the start of the cycle and recall being informed of the risk of multiple births. The risk was mentioned, but somehow it was minimized and not given the proper emphasis that it deserved. We never really gave it much thought. After all, I could not get pregnant with even one child; how could I possibly become pregnant with three or four? The possibility of having a multiple pregnancy was about as real as winning the lottery when you buy only one ticket. Having a multiple pregnancy was a fantasy, not a risk at all to us — or so we thought.

I proceeded through the IVF cycle and was absolutely thrilled to find out on day 27 that my beta count was 269. Most of the doctors and nurses felt that I was probably pregnant with twins. Our dreams of having a family were finally coming true. As in the past, though, our expectations and hopes were dashed when I started to experience bleeding during my sixth week of pregnancy. After an ultrasound examination, I was informed that one heart could be seen beating, but there also appeared to be another sac that was empty. I was told to come back the next week for another ultrasound examination.

Pregnancy was considered high risk

The following week's ultrasound showed two hearts beating, but one sac still empty. Again, I was told to come back the following week. The next week there were three hearts beating. And the week after that, four hearts were beating. At this point, excitement turned to horror as we were told that this pregnancy was considered high risk. We needed to consider the option of reducing one or two of

fetal reduction

the fetuses to give the remaining ones a better chance of developing and to lessen the risk of very premature delivery. By sacrificing two of our children, we would be giving the remaining two a better chance at survival.

I felt desperate. There was no one that I could turn to for advice or counsel. I was referred to two doctors by the IVF clinic. One of the doctors would perform the reduction procedure and the other doctor was a high risk obstetrician who had never actually delivered quadruplets, but had done some research on the subject and quoted us various statistics regarding quadruplet deliveries. While we appreciated the research information, the statistics did very little to help us with a decision. Yet, impossibly, the decision to reduce the pregnancy was needed quickly because the procedure had to be done soon or not at all. How could we possibly make this decision?

We were trying to conceive a child, not reduce a child

We tried to rationalize the situation. While trying to hold down a very stressful full-time job, I was experiencing bleeding, continual vomiting and extreme fatigue, and through it all, I was expected to make the most important decision of my life. We were trying to conceive a child, not reduce a child. How could we possibly reduce two of our children? Yet, what if all of our children should die? Would it be easier to reduce the pregnancy and avoid the stresses and pressures of having four children at one time? While we had never been parents before, we knew that trying to feed and dress four babies would not be easy. How would we afford to raise four children at the same time? What if they were to be born with health problems? Who would help us with the gruelling night feedings, diaper changes, bathing and doctor's appointments? And how would we possibly have time to give each of them the love and attention that they deserved? The prospect of having four children at the same time was terrifying. But could we live with ourselves if we reduced the pregnancy?

Looking for the answer, I went from one doctor to another trying to speak to someone who could help me make a decision with which I could live. I resorted to the telephone book and finally made an appointment for myself at the high risk pregnancy clinic in Toronto. When I was examined by ultrasound at the clinic, the technician took the time to show us each baby and to point out the little fingers and toes. A neonatologist gave me a tour of the Neonatal Intensive Care Unit (NICU) and showed me premature babies and what we should expect. Finally, the answer came to us.

These four little beings were no longer embryos or fetuses to us, but the children we had worked so hard to conceive and the family we had always wanted to have. Together, my husband and I decided to do all that we could to give each child a chance at life, but left it to God to decide which child would survive. We did not feel that we had the right to take the life of one child in order to help another. I guess it was at this point that we started to love each child as a separate and unique person.

We continually reflected on our decision
As the pregnancy progressed with various bouts of bleeding and complications, we continually reflected on our decision. Had we made the right choice? What lay ahead for us? Would our children live or die? Would they be born with enormous health problems? If I were to lose this pregnancy, would I ever become pregnant again? The stress during the pregnancy was almost unbearable. As I lay in hospital for nine weeks on strict bedrest, my days were spent agonizing over what the future held.

Finally, at 31 weeks, I gave birth to four beautiful, healthy babies — three girls and one boy ranging in weight from 2 lb. 13 oz. to 3 lb. 2 oz.

While I am eternally grateful for my beautiful children, my IVF experience has given me new insights into the infertility process. I now realize how important it is for couples to educate themselves before they become pregnant. It is the responsibility of each couple to listen to their doctors and be informed of the risks involved. The risk of a multiple birth is not a fantasy. It is a very real health issue and should be treated as such. It is the responsibility of healthcare professionals to ensure that their patients have access to plenty of information about the risks involved with IVF. It is also the responsibility of the IVF clinics to have a support system available to couples who are faced with the dilemma of having a multiple pregnancy. It is not enough to simply give them the choice to reduce. They must also provide patients with easy access to multiple birth support groups and be ready to refer them to the specialized high

fetal reduction

risk clinics at different hospitals. Finally, couples who are not willing to make the choice regarding fetal reduction should never have more embryos implanted than the number of children they feel they could safely bring into the world.

If we had been wiser and more educated before entering our first IVF cycle, we never would have put our children at risk of prematurity, breathing and feeding difficulties, low birth weight, bleeding into the brain, developmental delay, and especially, death. If we had had fewer embryos implanted, perhaps my pregnancy would have been a joyful experience and not the most stressful event of my life. The risks are real and too great to be ignored.

choosing reduction
Anonymous

For us, it was the only answer
to an impossible question

I was one of the many women who, after years of trying to conceive a baby, finally experienced the thrill of seeing a positive test. At the time, I was a patient at a fertility clinic in Ontario. Before I started therapy of combined fertility drugs, I recall being told about the high risk of multiple births that was associated with these drugs. But I consented to proceed nonetheless.

Soon after the blood test, an ultrasound exam confirmed I was pregnant — with twins. As advised by my doctor, I went for genetic counselling and amniocentesis because I had just passed the age of 35. The procedure was performed successfully and after 30 days, the test results showed two healthy fetuses.

About 21 weeks into the pregnancy, a follow-up ultrasound was performed, revealing news that would devastate me. I sensed there was a serious problem when the head of radiology came into the exam room. At some point in the past few weeks, one of the fetuses had died. The earlier ultrasound and amniocentesis had indicated all was well. How could this be? A complete scan of the remaining fetus indicated that everything else was perfectly normal. But through the remainder of the pregnancy, I was overcome with constant worry.

Finally, I gave birth to a healthy 6 lb. 1oz baby boy. It was very upsetting when the obstetrician removed the other fetus. And the procedure was difficult because the fetus had almost fused to the upper part of the uterine wall. Had it fused completely, a hysterectomy would have been inevitable. To this day, I am grateful for the expertise of the attending obstetrician.

Our attempts at pregnancy without drug intervention were unsuccessful

A year passed and my husband and I decided to plan for another child. Unfortunately, our attempts at pregnancy without drug intervention were unsuccessful. As before, I scheduled my appointment with my ob/gyn and shortly after, started back at the fertility clinic.

I proceeded with the same combined therapy of drugs and soon became pregnant. This time, however, I was shocked to hear I was pregnant with four fetuses. My head started spinning as I was lying on the ultrasound table. No matter how many times you go over the potential risks of conceiving multiple fetuses, your only goal is to get pregnant. Nothing else seemed to matter. Now, suddenly, everything else did matter.

My ob/gyn understood my confusion, shock and despair. There were two options: I could proceed with a quadruplet pregnancy, or explore the possibility of fetal reduction. Before making a decision, I discussed the pros and cons with my own doctor and a genetic counsellor in great detail.

Having to make such a decision, one that would profoundly affect the rest of my life and my family, was the most sensitive, emotional and ethical dilemma I have ever faced. We investigated fetal reduction further and eventually decided to do the procedure. Our decision was based on several issues. The first was my age. At 38, I was at risk of experiencing major complications in the pregnancy. Secondly, I worried about our history with the twin pregnancy — about one of the fetuses dying. I doubted my body would tolerate another multiple pregnancy. A third, very important issue, was our two-year-old son. I worried that our devotion to him would have been unintentionally compromised. To my husband and me, this would have been a tragedy in itself.

fetal reduction

Finally, I just didn't think I would have the necessary stamina for caring for triplets or quadruplets. I knew that I would shoulder the care by myself during the day with little or no help at all. I knew with my husband's busy work schedule, I would be kidding myself if I thought he could always be there when I needed him. Taken as a whole, the risk factors for our family were too high.

Many people will view my reasons for fetal reduction as being selfish. But they were honest. I don't think it is selfish to want the best for your children by being able to provide for them adequately in a healthy, nurturing and loving environment. That was first and foremost the reason we reduced the pregnancy.

I am happy to say that I gave birth to healthy twins, a boy and girl, and I have never looked back on the decision we made. Our children are the first priority in our lives and always will be. For those who are going through or are about to go through the same kind of experience, all I can say is that support and guidance are out there, but ultimately, the decision is yours to make based on careful thought. There can be no right or wrong answer. The decision should be based on what is best for you and the circumstances that surround you. No one should tell you otherwise — but they will. Ultimately, the choice is yours to make.

> **quote**
>
> **Many people will view my reasons for fetal reduction as being selfish, but they were honest**

multifetal reduction
Bev Unger

Words I wish I never heard

After four long years of trying to get pregnant, the fertility treatments worked! The results finally came back positive. We were pregnant!

We had gone through the tedium of keeping temperature charts, a dozen treatment cycles and a revolving door of doctors. There were numerous cycles of injections and artificial insemination, daily blood work, ultrasounds, endless needles, and long waits between each cycle — only to hear the negative results over and over again.

We tried "relaxing" (ha-ha). Then we tried in vitro fertilization, which didn't work. We were ready to give up. Along the way we investigated adoption as a possibility and decided for our own peace of mind that we could not give up having a child of our own until we tried everything possible. So we gave pregnancy one last shot (literally). Using a combined drug therapy and intrauterine insemination, we found the right combination. At long last.

But seven weeks into the pregnancy, my hopes dissolved. I spent an entire Sunday in bed bleeding, afraid to stand up, unable to move for fear of losing this long-awaited pregnancy. I called the doctor first thing on Monday in a panic. "You need to see me right away — I'm bleeding," I said, all the while thinking that I had already had a miscarriage. As we headed to the fertility clinic for an ultrasound, I prepared for the worst. Commotion and whispers among the technicians at the ultrasound seemed to confirm bad news. Then they told us about the four heartbeats. From there, we moved to the doctor's office down the hall. After scanning the report, the doctor told us about yet another sac, which had a weak heartbeat. If embryo number five was to survive we would know in the next few weeks.

Then we were introduced to multifetal reduction, a term my husband and I both wish we had never heard. Since the recommendation for a safe pregnancy was two embryos, our doctor told us that we needed to consider whether or not to reduce this pregnancy. In the span of a single visit to the fertility clinic, I went from thinking I had miscarried a single baby to having quadruplets, then quintuplets and then to the prospect of having to reduce the embryos.

We spent the next weeks wondering if I was carrying four or five. We had very mixed emotions — from ecstatic to fear to elation to worry — you name it, we felt it! In addition to trying to comprehend the possibility of carrying five babies, we also had to decide whether to eliminate some of them. It made the weeks that followed unbearable. If we decided to reduce, the procedure had to be done in week 12, just four weeks away. The doctor suggested that we travel to a fertility centre in the United States. Whatever our decision, our physician offered full support, which meant a lot.

These were the toughest weeks of my life. We thought the news of being pregnant would be the happiest news we could ever receive. Now the joy was replaced with feelings of uncertainty and sadness. I would never want to relive that emotional roller-coaster. The thought of reducing the embryos was unbelievably difficult, but we needed to face it, whether we wanted to or not.

a special care pregnancy

fetal reduction

We considered all of the options and all the risks: there was a high risk to each of the children if I carried all the babies. Would they all survive? How premature would they be? Would they all be healthy? Could we manage to give proper care to the children if one or more had a disability? Then there were the physical dangers and emotional stresses of carrying multiples. There were the long-term implications of prolonged bedrest, early hospitalization, the high cost of raising four or five children, the strain on our relationship and marriage, the difficulty and challenges in caring for and raising four or five children, the implications for our family and our way of life. The list of considerations seemed to grow every time we talked about it.

We had no idea how to make a decision like this. We spoke to families who had reduced, to families who had chosen not to reduce, to neonatologists at various hospitals, to a social worker from the U.S. clinic, to our very supportive families, to everyone and anyone we thought could shed some light on this difficult decision. But we could not find the answer. We wanted someone to tell us what to do. Finally one of the doctors we spoke with made it very clear. He said you have asked all the right questions, you have researched this as much as you possibly can, no one can give you the answer except you. He was right!

In week nine, I started to bleed again. The fear of losing the pregnancy fell over me again. A hastily scheduled ultrasound showed four very strong heartbeats. We were so happy and relieved the babies were fine. The fifth sac was empty. Realizing that I was carrying four babies and that all were fine and healthy made the whole situation easier to cope with.

We were amazed when we saw the four heartbeats. They were so real. So alive. For us, the decision not to reduce was made at that moment. We went with our hearts, with the gut feeling we had when we thought about losing one or more of the babies. Finally, we came to the conclusion — we could not reduce.

Once the decision was made, we could finally enjoy being pregnant and focus all of our energies on our four babies. We began the journey to make this multiple pregnancy the most positive and the healthiest pregnancy we possibly could.

nutrition

not a single bite
Diane Myers

When illness makes eating impossible

The idea of seeking professional help about food seemed a little odd to me since I consider myself quite knowledgeable about nutrition. But after a severe and prolonged illness during the first four months of my pregnancy, I knew I needed some advice.

The worst point in my so-called morning sickness, which would have been more aptly described as "round the clock" sickness, was around week 10 of my pregnancy. Still unaware I was carrying quadruplets, I had lost about 15 pounds. Maybe I should have suspected something because it was an entirely different experience from my first pregnancy, which was completely nausea-free. During this pregnancy, it seemed that I was constantly at the doctor's office, asking my family physician and a rotation of her colleagues what I should do about the vomiting. Their advice was always the same — take anti-nausea medication.

But I just did not feel comfortable following this advice given the risk of adverse effects to the baby. By week 15 of my pregnancy though, shortly after I found out about the quadruplets, I was hospitalized for malnutrition and given the medication intravenously along with lots of liquids. While the babies did not seem to suffer through all of this, I certainly did.

The upheaval and emotions in those early weeks after we discovered I was pregnant with quadruplets only exacerbated the effects of my nausea and took a physical toll. Being hospitalized for malnutrition was a dramatic slap in the face that led me to seek professional nutritional advice. Once I was discharged from the hospital, I asked for a referral to a nutritionist to stay on track and regain my strength and tolerance of food.

A cracker here and there

I was still unable to eat much — a cracker here and there. The mere thought of meat often sent me running to the bathroom. While the nutritionist had no experience with higher order multiples, she worked with what knowledge she had to try and get me eating and gaining weight. She put me on a high calorie, high protein drink,

nutrition

which I tolerated gradually. I remember initially only being able to manage a single protein drink through the day, sipping it slowly.

I visited the nutritionist twice a week in the beginning and then once a week after I started gaining some weight. Once I began to eat more regularly, I was placed on a 4,000-calorie-a-day diet. It is very hard to eat that much in one day. You almost always have to be chewing on something. We called it the ice cream and potato chip diet. The babies were using up all my fat reserves and we were trying to replace them.

My relationship with this nutritionist was also beneficial when I was admitted to hospital for bedrest at week 24 of my pregnancy. Even though I was on the high risk floor, my first meal there was pitifully low on calories. My nutritionist contacted the hospital's nutritionist regarding my special circumstances. The next meal was plentiful and palatable. In addition, I received two or three snacks a day and had access to more milk than I could drink in the patients' fridge.

I truly believe that the assistance I received from my nutritionist enabled my babies to grow large enough to survive the many complications associated with being born at 27 weeks gestation.

a tale of gluttony
Mary Anne Moser

I remember looking at a plate of food piled high in front of me and proclaiming to my husband that when this pregnancy was over, I was going to fast, just for the sheer pleasure and indulgence of not eating.

I was on an eating program like no other — 3,500 calories a day was my target. My understanding was that I needed to gain as much weight as humanly possible. I focused on healthy food, since every mouthful took up precious room in my stomach. Every morning to start, I would eat a massive bowl of Alpen, which must have packed on well over 500 calories, and perhaps closer to 1,000 calories with milk. Later, I would have breakfast, which consisted of eggs, toast with peanut butter, and fruit. Lunch came just a couple hours later.

I ate mid-afternoon and again at dinner — the most difficult meal of the day to swallow.

Over the course of the day, I drank three or four pints of skim milk and water when I was thirsty. My meals or snacks included half chickens, tubs of cottage cheese, nuts, avocado and fruit. Normally I eat little, if any meat, but during my pregnancy, I decided I needed the protein hit. Since turkey has the highest amount of protein of any meat, I ate it from the tin as a snack. It was the same with salmon and tuna. I also took a pregnancy vitamin. People were astounded by how much I could eat. Often, eating seemed an unpleasant but necessary task.

Once I was admitted to hospital at 27 weeks, I consulted a dietician. We agreed that I would check off double and triple portions of most items on the hospital menu. Another mother of triplets had warned me that she didn't get enough to eat in the hospital. I had three big meals a day, plus morning, afternoon and evening snacks. My visitors would also come with food and I would sometimes have two dinners. It sounds downright gluttonous to describe it now, but believe it or not, I did not get really fat. I think the bulk of it went to the babies and what was stored was absolutely necessary for breastfeeding! Breastfeeding seemed to use up the reserves at an almost alarming rate. In fact, six months after the babies were born, I had zero fat reserves and had to make a conscious effort to eat more so that I could continue to produce milk.

At one point, fairly early on in my pregnancy, a nurse told me that while I should try to eat well, I needn't make myself uncomfortable. Though this advice was well-intentioned, it was evident from the requirements of the three fetuses I was carrying that I would indeed have to eat to the point that it was uncomfortable, if I wanted the babies to grow. I gained almost 70 pounds during my pregnancy and delivered three healthy babies (4 lb. 12 oz., 4 lb. 12 oz. and 4lb. 10 oz) at 34.5 weeks. We were all discharged from hospital four days later.

Yes, eating so much was uncomfortable, but it was also temporary.

a special care pregnancy

nutrition

Professional Notes from the Dietician

---

great beginnings
Daphne Lucci R.D.N.

The unique nutritional needs of women pregnant with triplets, quadruplets or quintuplets have yet to be fully understood. More research is needed to determine actual vitamin, mineral and protein needs as well as weight gain requirements for optimum fetal growth. What is known is that women expecting multiples tend to experience more of every symptom of pregnancy, such as tiredness, nausea, heartburn and constipation, and also need more nutrients than a woman carrying one baby. Meeting nutritional requirements can be a challenge, but the effort is definitely worth-while. It is well known that women who eat a healthy, well-balanced diet and have a sustained weight gain throughout pregnancy tend to have babies with higher birthweights.

tip

Making healthy nutritional choices is important for moms expecting multiple babies

The food groups

Making healthy food choices and having a well-balanced diet are important to great beginnings for multiples. Eating to satisfy hunger is one of the better ways to determine if you are getting enough. Getting full quickly is common in a multiple pregnancy and often small, frequent meals work best. Energy (or calorie) requirements are highly individual. Extra calorie requirements are estimated at 300 kilocalories daily in the second and third trimester for single pregnancies. It is unlikely, however, that 300 kcal extra is needed for every fetus a woman carries, partly due to reduced activity or bedrest.

In your first trimester, evidence suggests that nutritional needs do not increase significantly with the important exception of folate (see vitamin/mineral supplements for more details). Nausea can affect appetite and dietary intake, but this often resolves itself by 16 to 17 weeks, when nutrition becomes especially important to the growth of your babies. In the second and third trimesters, nutrient needs increase and it is wise to have a healthy, well-balanced diet. Serving sizes in each food group are an estimate, and unless your weight gain falls below the target set by you and your doctor, you are probably getting enough food.

The dairy group

Twins/triplets   Quads/quints
4-5 servings daily   5-6 servings daily

Examples of single servings — choose a variety
- 250 ml milk or buttermilk (1 cup)
- 250 ml calcium fortified soya or rice milk
- 50 g cheese (3" x 1" x 1")
- 2 slices processed cheese
- 250 ml cottage cheese (1 cup)
- 175 ml yogurt (3/4 cup)
- 125 ml evaporated milk (1/2 cup)
- 75 ml instant skim milk powder (1/3 cup)
- 60 ml Parmesan cheese (1/4 cup)

• Choose lower fat milk products (skim, 1%, 2%) more often.
• Choose at least three of the five to six servings daily as fluid
  milk, or fortified soya milk, instant milk powder or evaporated
  milk, as they are the only choices which provide vitamin D.
• New dietary intake standards for Canada indicate a woman
  with a single pregnancy does not require extra calcium above
  non-pregnant needs (three servings daily). Until more is
  known about actual calcium needs in a multiple pregnancy,
  it would be prudent to add extra calcium for each additional
  baby carried.

The protein group

Twins/triplets   Quads/quints
3 servings daily   4-5 servings daily

Examples of single servings — choose a variety
- 50-100 g of cooked meat, poultry or fish (about the size of a
  deck of cards)
- 1/2 - 1 can tuna/salmon
- 50-100 g cheese or 175 ml cottage cheese (3/4 cup)
- 1-2 eggs
- 125-150 ml cooked dried beans, peas or lentils (1/2-1 cup)

a special care pregnancy

nutrition

- 100 g tofu (1/3 cup)
- 30 ml peanut butter or tahini (2 tbsp.)
- 60 ml nuts or seeds (1/4 cup)

• Choose leaner meat, poultry and fish and dried peas, beans and lentils more often.
• Include protein foods such as beans, peas, lentils, tofu or nuts in your diet daily if you are avoiding meat, poultry, fish and eggs completely.

The fruit and vegetable group
8 to 10 or more servings daily

tip

Remember that serving sizes in each food group are an estimate, and unless your weight gain falls below the target set by you and your doctor, you are probably eating enough

Examples of single servings — choose a variety
- 1 medium-sized vegetable or fruit (potato, carrot, tomato, peach, apple, orange or banana)
- 125 ml vegetables or fruit, fresh, frozen or canned (1/2 cup)
- 60 ml dried apricots, prunes or raisins (1/4 cup)
- 1 small bowl of salad
- 125 ml juice (1/2 cup)
• Choose dark green and orange vegetables and orange fruit more often.
• Choose AT LEAST three vegetable and three fruit servings daily.
• Choose raw fruits and raw or lightly cooked vegetables more often.

The grain group
8 to 10 servings daily

Examples of single servings — choose a variety
- 1 slice bread
- 175 ml cooked cereal (3/4 cup)
- 175 ml ready-to-eat cereal (3/4 cup)
- 1 pancake or waffle
- 1 tortilla or roti
- small bannock or scone
- 4 graham wafers
- 6 soda crackers

Examples of TWO servings:
- 1 hamburger or hot dog bun
- 1 roll or muffin
- 1 bagel, pita or English muffin
- 250 ml cooked pasta or rice (1 cup)

• Choose whole grain and enriched products more often
  (examples include whole wheat bread, bran muffin, oatmeal).

Vitamin and mineral supplements

Your dietary intake is your best source of vitamins and minerals, but it is a good idea to supplement your diet when you are carrying multiples. In your first trimester, the only supplement you need is 1 mg of folic acid whether you are carrying twins, triplets, quadruplets or quintuplets. Your doctor may suggest more folic acid if you have Type I diabetes, if there is a history of neural tube defects or if you are on certain medications. Your doctor may have suggested a prenatal supplement. Prenatal supplements usually contain adequate folic acid (1 mg) but they can sometimes aggravate symptoms of nausea or constipation, which are common in the first trimester. In this case, it may be better to delay taking the prenatal supplement until your second trimester when it is likely to be better tolerated.

In your second and third trimesters a prenatal supplement containing 60 mg of elemental iron, 1 mg of folic acid and 15-30 mg of zinc is adequate for twins and triplets. It is probably a good idea to take an additional iron supplement (i.e., one ferrous gluconate) if you are expecting quads or quints. Your doctor may suggest more iron if you are anemic. It is better to take small doses of iron spread out over the day than one large dose of iron. For example, ferrous gluconate, which contains 30 mg of iron, is much better absorbed when taken two times daily compared with one dose of ferrous sulphate, which contains 60 mg of iron.

If you are not consuming sufficient dairy products for a multiple pregnancy, calcium supplements are required. Take the calcium supplement separate from your prenatal vitamin for best absorption. For every dairy serving you miss, take 300 mg of elemental calcium (equivalent to one extra-strength Tums®). Ensure your prenatal supplement contains vitamin D if you are taking less than three cups of cow's milk or vitamin D fortified soya or rice milk daily.

nutrition

Weight gain

Weight gain guidelines have been developed for twin pregnancies but not for triplets and higher. Women expecting twins who were a healthy weight before they became pregnant can expect to gain between 16 and 20.5 kg (35–45 lb.) with an average weight gain of 1 kg per week in the second and third trimester. One would expect slightly higher weight gains with each additional baby. Since there is limited research on triplets, quadruplets and quintuplets, you should observe how you are feeling (overfull or hungry) and also where you are gaining weight. If you notice significant weight gain on upper arms, thighs or buttocks, it is most likely excessive. If you notice thinner arms, legs, buttocks or face, it is a sign of inadequate weight gain. Fluid retention, often noticed in the feet, hands and face, does cause extra weight gain that is lost within days of delivery.

Women expecting multiples may experience decreased appetite in the late second or third trimester. Since weight maintenance or weight loss at this stage has been associated with low birthweight babies in a multiple pregnancy, steady weight gain should be the goal. A visit with a dietician may be helpful if gaining weight becomes difficult.

Managing nausea

Nausea is very common in the first trimester for women carrying multiples. Try eating small, frequent meals of foods and drinks that are appealing to you. What appeals to you at this point may be different from your usual food choices. Do not worry if the only foods you seem to tolerate are "unhealthy foods." By your second trimester, you will probably be feeling much better and will be able to make healthier food choices when nutrition really counts.

- Do not force yourself to eat foods that are unappealing.
- Discontinue your prenatal vitamin as a trial. Make sure you take 1 mg of folic acid.
- Try to get some fresh air. Avoid smells that are nauseating to you (common culprits are perfume, smoke, cooking smells).
- Get plenty of rest. Stress and fatigue can aggravate nausea.
- If your nausea is severe and you are losing weight (greater than 5-10 lb.) or if you are concerned, talk to your doctor and ask for a referral to a dietician. You can also ask your doctor about medications for alleviating nausea and vomiting.

• Review other resources, such as the book No More Morning Sickness by Mirian Erick.

Eating and bedrest

Bedrest is often recommended for women expecting higher order multiples. Be sure to accept offers of prepared items such as casseroles, muffins and salads from people who would like to help. It is a good idea to have plenty of "no preparation" food items on hand such as yogurt, milk, puddings, crackers, cheese, peanut butter, nuts, whole grain crackers, fruit, dried fruit, juices and frozen entrees. Some women keep a cooler close to their bed or couch. Bedrest affects different women in different ways. Some notice indigestion, constipation or loss of appetite with bedrest. The following suggestions may help ease some of those symptoms.

Constipation
• Maintain a high fibre diet by including bran, bran cereals, whole grains and plenty of fruits and vegetables.
• Drink 8-10 cups of water per day.
• Have 3-4 prunes or 1/2 cup of prune juice daily.
• If constipation is still a problem, discuss it with your doctor. There are medications that are safe during pregnancy that can help. Also, discuss the possibility of reducing or discontinuing iron supplements for a while until constipation is under control.

Indigestion/heartburn
• Try small, frequent meals. Avoid large meals and have fluids separate from meals.
• Sit upright following meals.
• Avoid foods which seem to aggravate indigestion or heartburn.
• Some medications are safe during pregnancy. Ask your doctor about them if other strategies do not work.

Loss of appetite/poor weight gain
• Depending on your condition, fresh air (open windows or sit outdoors in a comfortable chair), bedrest, and/or safe exercise (ask to speak to a physiotherapist) may help stimulate your appetite.
• Energy dense foods such as nuts, milkshakes, yogurt shakes,

nutrition

pudding, trail mix, juice, avocado, cheese, and canned or dried fruit may help you gain weight.
• Ask to speak with a dietician.

As you know, being "the nutrition provider" for multiples is an important and sometimes challenging job. Find support through your local multiples group and through friends and families who kindly offer to shop or prepare food for you. Remember that you can seek help from a dietician if you are concerned about your nutrition or have any questions.

housebound
Gillian Borowy

It took a month for me to let go of work emotionally

Before I became pregnant with triplets, I had a well-paying job with a terrific company. I controlled my own hours, I travelled, and my boss was in another country, so I could work independently. In short, life was great.

When I announced my pregnancy at 11 weeks (I was already in maternity wear and had to go public) I cut my hours to part-time. I was tired and frequently left work early to have a predinner nap. My concentration was not what it used to be, and it was affecting my performance. My co-workers teased me about my failing memory and my constant yawning. I am the kind of person who enjoys putting 120 per cent into my job. To be at less than my best was aggravating.

I planned to stop working at 27 weeks. I had the ideal situation: flexible part-time hours, and no standing or physical demands. I thought everything was going well. Then, at 22 weeks, my doctor told me to stop working — immediately. "But I still have three major reports due!" I cried. "Can't I work a few more days?" My doctor calmly asked if these reports were worth risking the health of my babies and myself. Of course they weren't. The next day I went on disability leave.

I felt like a child who had been unfairly grounded

For two weeks I wandered the house aimlessly. I would get up and shower as if I were going to work, and then after my husband left, I would sit and stare out the window. All I could think of was work. How were they doing? What changes would they make in my absence? Would my replacement do a good job? Do they miss me? I felt like a child who had been unfairly grounded.

Once I stopped feeling sorry for myself, I noticed how much more energy I had. I hadn't realized how tired work was making me. In the office, I would get caught up in my work and not eat for hours. But at home, I was quite bored and ate frequently, which

bedrest

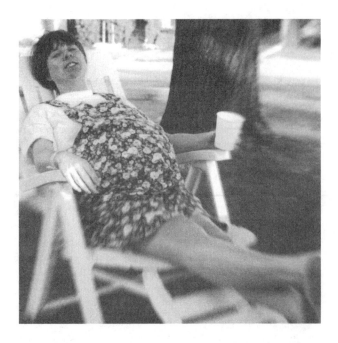

was good. I also slept better at night after stopping work.

It took me a month to let go emotionally. I had concentrated on my career for 12 years. It defined who I was, and I was afraid of losing that identity. I wasn't yet a mother, and felt I was in limbo, simply waiting, waiting, waiting.

This was also the first time in my adult life I felt dependent on others. It was extremely hard for me to let others drive me to my doctor's appointments and do the grocery shopping or the housework.

It is important to understand exactly what a doctor means by "rest." I listened to my body carefully and to my doctor's advice, then followed whichever was more conservative. I could still shower, make it to the living room couch and on most days, walk to the end of the street and back. I could not vacuum, do laundry, climb stairs and toward the end, cook or do dishes. I found it too difficult to reach the stove, cupboards or sink. If I dropped something on the floor, I either picked it up with my toes or it stayed there until my husband came home.

bedrest

My anger at our changing lifestyle made me question whether I would be a good mother, and this scared me

I was mad at the pregnancy, mad at the doctor, mad at my body and mad at my husband for worrying so much about me. I wanted my independence back! I wanted the freedom to come and go as I pleased! I wanted people to stop asking me how I felt! The depth of my anger at our changing lifestyle made me question whether I would be a good mother, and this scared me.

As boring as it was to rest so much, I'm glad I did. I now realize how important it was to the babies' health and to my ability to take the pregnancy so far along. When I checked into the hospital at 36 weeks, my days became even more sedentary, dramatically reducing the frequency of the abdominal tightenings I had been feeling. I never did go into labour and had a scheduled cesarean section at 38 weeks.

I had a very healthy pregnancy and owe much of it to the good advice of my doctor and to the determination of my husband to make me follow that advice. My message to other women expecting triplets or more is to rest more than you think you need to, and allow other people to take care of you. No one will think you are lazy. Your body is working harder than anyone else's. Relax, put your feet up, have a snack.

i'm sorry, but i can't
Joyce Mortimer

When others frown on inactivity

It can be hard for people to understand why you are taking it so easy when they have never been through a multiple birth. But the more your workplace and family knows about the risks and potentially tragic consequences of pushing yourself too hard, the more likely they will understand your need to withdraw from certain activities altogether and rest as the pregnancy progresses.

I tried to be patient with others and provided sound information and articles from expectant mother's packages, which went a

bedrest

long way to increasing that understanding in others. Starting with my husband and my sister (who bounced through her pregnancies), I recruited my physician's help in giving my husband a pep talk about taking bedrest seriously. My husband very quickly became my strongest advocate, protecting me against myself and others, especially at times when I felt psychologically too weak to say "no" to people who asked me to do more.

Once others have heard the evidence that supports the successful outcome of bedrest, ideally, they can begin to support and accommodate your need to rest, rather than working against the all-important effort to have healthy babies.

bedrest at home and hospital

Shelley Johnson

I started taking it easy the moment I found out I was carrying four babies. Then, under recommendation from the doctor, I stopped working soon after I heard the news. Instead, I channelled my energy into making a project out of my pregnancy. I was as relaxed as possible and, most importantly, tried to keep a positive outlook.

At home I would do something every day, but I never pushed past the limit. If I felt tired, I would listen to my body and take breaks. When I shopped, I never rushed or stayed out longer than two hours at a time. I knew there were many more days to fill and my four unborn babies to think about. My husband took care of the vacuuming and washing floors as I prepared for the babies by gathering and organizing clothes and equipment by phone. I tried not to stand too much to minimize any pressure on the cervix.

By 22 weeks, I looked full term and was tiring more easily every day. I often put my feet up in the afternoon and slept when I felt I needed it. This was easy for me, since I had no other children to care for. At 24 weeks, I was hospitalized 45 minutes away from my husband, Ken, and my friends. Here a few tips I picked up from my experience in the hospital.

a special care pregnancy

bedrest

- My husband visited usually every second evening and on the weekends. If I needed him more often, he was always there for me. On the off nights, he finished projects like the nursery at home and picked up baby furniture from friends. When we saw each other, we enjoyed working together on letters to companies requesting help and sample products. We also had lively discussions about baby names and pored through books on premature babies. On alternate evenings, my friends would try to visit and sometimes bring in take-out food, which was a wonderful treat compared with hospital fare.

- Every day, I showered and got dressed because it made me feel like I was still part of the world. Since I had a very limited selection of clothes that would fit by that time, Ken always arrived with one set of clean clothes and left with one bag of laundry.

- A small cooler by the bed was great for keeping a few drinks and snacks within reach. My husband would bring new ice packs, and rotated them when he came to visit.

- Personalizing my bedside helped. I had my own pillow, pictures and blankets, which made the hospital feel a little more like home.

- Since I was so far away from home and friends, I subscribed to a flat rate package for long distance calls. Chatting on the phone with friends helped to pass the time without costing a small fortune.

- When a friend or Ken would visit, occasionally they would push me outside in the wheelchair for a breath of fresh air or some ice cream. It was a refreshing change of scenery since I only ever got up for the bathroom or shower. There were times when I could not stand my room any longer.

- I stayed in a hospital ward with up to three other patients at a time and enjoyed the company for the most part. I made a dear friend there, who had triplets. Near the end of the pregnancy though, I grew tired of all the commotion as different patients came and went, and I craved some solitary peace. By this point, I looked post-term and felt physically drained. I came down with a cold and just wanted to focus on putting in time to help the babies. Each day became a struggle, but it was also gratifying to know that every single day was good for the babies. My doctor was able to assign me to a private room at no extra cost because I was developing toxemia and the pregnancy was at greater risk. The private room was nice and had an overnight cot in the room so Ken was

bedrest

able to stay over on the weekend. Once the babies were born, Ken stayed in the room and helped me as I recovered from the cesarean. With him there, I could access the breastpump, get up and move and go to the nursery any time to see the babies.

Now I find it hard to believe I stayed in the hospital for seven weeks on bedrest. But somehow the days went by, between doctor's visits, ultrasounds, meals, snacks, naps and visitors. There were even some days when just a shower felt like a day's work.

I remember the day I was discharged. Teary-eyed, leaving my babies behind, I felt as if I had never seen the outdoors. It was summer when I was admitted and autumn by the time I left. My first day out was an absolutely beautiful day. But as I look at our four children, I know why I made the sacrifice and would do it all over again.

a painful experience
Louise Redgers Bonnycastle

When I became pregnant with my first child, I was concerned about aggravating a back injury I had suffered in a car accident. After the accident, I had managed to live relatively pain-free as long as I exercised. The orthopedic surgeon I saw while I was pregnant recommended that I not gain more than 25 pounds and continue to exercise on a modified routine as I got larger. I did this successfully and got through the pregnancy virtually pain-free except during labour.

Now I was pregnant with quadruplets. I was told to expect an average weight gain of 60 to 80 pounds. I was told to expect an extended period of confinement to bed at home and perhaps in the hospital to prevent preterm labour. All of this terrified me as I thought about the return of chronic back pain that I had worked so hard to keep under control. Now I was about to lose control. The pain was sure to be excruciating and it would heighten my risk of going into labour early and losing the babies. My solution at about

bedrest

nine weeks into the pregnancy was to continue my exercise routine using lighter weights and gentler stretches, and hope that being fit and determined would carry me well into the pregnancy.

It seemed to be working. I was feeling pretty good except for the endless morning, noon and night sickness. I watched my diet, ate healthy foods and forced myself to eat when I would rather pass. I lost some weight during the first 12 weeks and then slowly started gaining. The back was feeling good too. It all seemed to be working. Then at 19 weeks, the doctor told me to stop exercising. I figured he knew more than I did about a multiple pregnancy so I had best listen. I stopped going to the gym.

For the first couple of weeks, I was fine. My weight increased, as did my size. Gradually though, the back pain returned. It started with little twinges in the morning as I tried to get out of bed. Gradually I would find myself waking with pain in the night, as I had in the past. Then it would subside after I had been up and moving about for several hours.

At 31.5 weeks, I was instructed to go on bedrest at home. I worried that without my only source of pain relief — the ability to move — I would begin to suffer again. The details of bedrest were never fully explained to me. I wasn't sure if it meant lying flat on my back all the time, or if I could sit up in bed and do things with my three-year-old son. Regardless, it became necessary to spend much of my day sitting up in bed so that I could do everything from puzzles to plastecine with my son. We read, did crafts, watched movies and endless children's programs to keep him amused throughout the day. The time dragged on endlessly for both of us. We had lunch and dinner at the table to give some semblance of family and to avoid toddler spills in bed. I'm certain that my doctor never experienced bedrest with a toddler to look after all day!

As the laundry piled up, I would sneak out of bed like a criminal to do a little at a time

The longer I stayed in bed, the more frequent and sharper the pain became. By 33 weeks, I was grumpy from the pain, as well as the confinement. It was okay to drag my aching body downtown twice a week to check for contractions and to waddle to the doctor's office, but not to walk around the house. As the laundry piled up, I would sneak out of bed like a criminal to do a little at a time.

> **quote**
>
> **I worried that without my only source of pain relief — the ability to move — I would begin to suffer again**

bedrest

The frustration was building with both the pain and the doctor. Finally, he decided that he would just take the babies at 34 weeks. Charlie, the smallest baby, had not been gaining weight, and I wasn't adding to my 20 pounds of weight gain.

At 34 weeks, Jenny, Heather, Charlie and Megan were born, small, but healthy. I had a spinal anesthetic to avoid the dangers of an epidural after spinal damage. I was certainly not prepared for the next few days. The back pain was horrendous. After spending the first 15 hours in bed, I was told to get up and walk down to the nursery after my catheter was removed. I could hardly feel my feet. My body was like jelly after spending so much time in bed. A walk just down the hall seemed like miles. I was exhausted when I got to the nursery and fell asleep in a rocking chair watching the babies. Mercifully, the nurses in the Neonatal Intensive Care Unit could not have been kinder.

Having someone spend the first few days in the hospital with you would be an invaluable help. You need somebody to fetch the breast pump and accompany you to the nursery, and even to the bathroom, and just to be there as you shower. You will have diminished muscle tone from the combination of the pregnancy, the bedrest and any pain medication you might have required. Your spouse will need to get some sleep in a real bed, so ask a friend or relative to give you a few hours of their time as their gift to you and your new family.

By the time the babies were five weeks old, they were all home from the hospital, and my back pain eased. Once I was eight weeks post-surgery, I returned to the gym and, within two weeks, most of the pain was gone except around the area of the spinal injection, which was still tender. After six months, my back pain was totally under control again.

counting the cost of bedrest

Serena Reynaud

Every book I read about multiple pregnancies supported the idea of taking it easy and putting your feet up twice a day. But not a single book supported hospital bedrest as being an essential step of pregnancy care. I write this to tell you why I do.

To credit my obstetrician, she did stress the importance of resting often. So, pregnant with triplets and toddler at home, I tried to rest often. My obstetrician warned me to do as little as humanly possible, to hire help even, but there was always one more chore to do. I consider myself a good researcher. Since nothing I found advocated hospital bedrest, the doctor's promise to put me in hospital if things looked questionable seemed a little excessive. I believed I was resting enough because I did not feel worn out at the end of the day. As well, bedrest would mean being separated from my husband and daughter because the only hospital that could accommodate me was two hours away. The hardship involved seemed unmanageable. I couldn't let it happen.

At 25 weeks, though, there I was in a hospital bed, resting. I was frustrated because I had been feeling great physically and mentally through this pregnancy. But Maria, my baby C, was not growing past the 10th percentile. I had learned, almost too late, that bedrest is not resting when you are tired. It is about your body needing every ounce of energy you can spare to properly nourish those babies inside. To give our daughters a fighting chance, they needed me to be on bedrest.

The terms of my bedrest

- I was allowed to sit up to eat
- I was allowed to go to the washroom myself
- I was allowed to flex my feet while lying down
- I was allowed to let my husband take me to the courtyard by wheelchair when he visited (which my doctor knew was only every two and a half weeks)
- I was allowed to lie only on my left side

bedrest

No sitting up to watch a show or do a craft. No sitting when visitors came. No sitting to play with my daughter. No puttering in my room. No showers, just baths. No sitting up to cry. No getting my own snack at night. If not for prayers, television and books, I would have gone insane.

And if it wasn't for such a strict, loving doctor, I may not have had three babies.

I stayed that way, far away from my husband and daughter, for 12 weeks. On the first day of week 37, I had three healthy girls.

I confess I strayed from these rules a few times. I often sat up when my daughter came to see me (which was every two or three weeks). I even paced for almost an hour late one evening, but most of the time, I did nothing but lie there.

What did it accomplish?

• All the babies were breathing room air within eight hours of birth
• Chantel (A) and Laura (B) were in regular cribs in four days and discharged from the hospital after just eight days
• Maria (C) gradually gained weight over 21 days and was discharged, with two apnea (breathing interruption) episodes behind her
• Breastfeeding and bottlefeeding began for all the girls in 24 hours
• No bilirubin lights
• No operations
• No transfusions
• No complications

The Neonatal Intensive Care Unit staff were astounded!

I would do it again and I would do it for twice as long. I fully believe if my doctor had not been as strong an advocate of bedrest, I would not have Maria, for things could have only gotten worse for her. As it was, Maria subsequently had to endure double-hernia surgery, a common complication in premature babies.

Doctors who send moms home when they have triplets or more babies growing inside should take note. While I'm sure strict bedrest is not a cure-all for every possible complication, it is arguably an excellent means of preventing myriad problems. I believe the medical community should acknowledge its value to a much greater extent. In my situation, bedrest put a stop to complications that were like dominoes falling onto each other.

I thank God my doctor had a stronger will than I did, and forcefully recommended bedrest. He just may have saved a life. For me, the cost of bedrest is negligible when I look in to the eyes of my three little girls. What is that worth?

Watching the clock and waiting — as long as it takes

Counting the cost of bedrest

On Floor 2C in Room 3, the walls are pale blue. I see this as a funny reminder that I am pregnant with three girls. My husband would find it amusing if I told him the meals served in this room are much tastier than most things I cook at home. Room 3 is filled with legend — I am not the only woman pregnant with triplets to have stayed here.

Every Monday is step-on-the-scale day. The rest of the afternoon my mind is filled with images of a postpartum me on a stairclimber. Tuesday is ultrasound day. From week to week, I get blatant proof of how every day spent lying down matters to these babies. Wednesday is only the day before Thursday. Thursday is TV night when I get to satisfy my curiosity about being a doctor watching ER™, and bond with a character who is also pregnant with triplets, on Friends™. The rest of the week passes with anticipation for Monday.

I understand the seriousness of why I am here. These babies cannot come this early. It is less painful missing my family when I remember I am nurturing a family inside of me. After being here for seven weeks, with eight more to go, I still hear a tiny voice asking, "Will I be pregnant tomorrow?"

When I think of this experience in its entirety, I am humbled. I could never have prayed for such an outcome. I didn't expect our 20-month-old daughter Jill to not only adjust, but flourish, at her grandparents' farm. (How can I compete with a tractor?) I didn't expect the people in our community to reach out to my husband so generously. I didn't expect to learn that the reason I am happy here is because my happiness is not dependent on my circumstances, but on my faith.

It is amazing to me that I lie here full of babies! I am living in the pregnancy time-vacuum, where every day crawls by. I have spent more time in Room 3 than in the home we bought in June. But every day pregnant is a miracle and I am blessed to have come this far.

bedrest

my first night in hospital
Maureen Tierney

Not exactly five-star accommodation

In my entire life I had never stayed in hospital, so when I was admitted for bedrest at 34 weeks, I didn't know what to expect. But I imagined it would be lovely. By that time, my energy was dwindling and I could hardly walk. I figured I could use the rest, a little pampering and meals in bed. What could be better? I had waited for this all my life!

I was assigned to a semi-private room with no roommate. Great! Total privacy. I was delighted when the nutritionist handed me a stack of daily menus to fill out. This would be like dining in a restaurant three times a day. And the staff was exceptionally nice. Since this particular hospital was unaccustomed to triplet births, I was getting the royal treatment. Oh boy, how I would soak up every moment of it. On the first night, my nurse did everything she could think of to ensure I was comfortable. She hunted down an egg-crate foam mattress that was guaranteed to give me the best sleep ever. After leaving me for the night, the nurse pulled up the bed rails and bid me good night. Just as my mother would.

I felt great. Snug as a bug
— until I had to go to the bathroom

I felt great. Snug as a bug — until I had to go to the bathroom. I shook the rails but they wouldn't budge. So I pulled the toggle to call the nurse. I waited five minutes ... 10 minutes ... 15 minutes ... I started thinking about all the talk that our healthcare system is going down the tubes. Is this what they meant? By this time, I was feeling pretty uncomfortable. How long does it take for the nurse to come? What if I had a heart attack? Out of desperation I shouted for help for 10 or 15 minutes. Surely someone would happen to walk by. No such luck. I kept pulling on the toggle. Did they forget about me? At this point I was ready to burst. What was I going to do? There was no bedpan in sight. I had not wet the bed since I was five years old ... and if I did, I would ruin my special egg crate mattress ... the last one in stock. Enough! I decided to take action.

I tried lifting my legs over the bed rails, but I was so large, and the distance from the rail to floor was too great. The only possible solution was to try and reach for a chair a few feet away beside the bed and crawl out. How to do this? I stood up on the bed and caught hold of the rail hanging from the ceiling that held the curtain around my bed. I used the rail for support and gingerly lifted my leg out over the bed, snaring the back of the chair and dragging it over to the bed. What a spectacle I must have made. Hospital life certainly wasn't shaping up as I had imagined. Finally, I managed to crawl over the bed rails and RUN to the bathroom. What a relief!

Of course, now I had to attend to the small matter of why I had been abandoned. Complaining, I went to the nurses' station. The nurse returned with me to the room, insisting they had not received a distress call from my room. The toggle wasn't connected.

That first night in hospital was the last night the toggle wasn't connected.

a three-month rest is no holiday
Patricia Harber

Bedrest was very hard on me psychologically because I consider myself very independent and active. Learning to rest was a process for me. I had to learn to ask my husband, daughter and the people around me to do things that I used to do for myself. Instead of being a wife and mother, I became the dependent patient. It was a tough role to fall into at times.

Bedrest also placed a lot of stress and responsibility on my husband's shoulders. After working all day, he would come home to prepare dinner, do the shopping, attend to the needs of our teenage daughter, clean the house and take care of the many other little things that were suddenly beyond my capabilities.

My daughter also faced many challenges. Her family was about to change dramatically. And the mother who was always there for

bedrest

her — and only her, for 15 years — was now the mother who spent her days lying on the couch.

When I was hospitalized at week 26, the strain wore on our family. I was farther away, removed and detached from their lives. Even though we talked on the phone, the distance affected our relationships. One of the hardest things about bedrest in the hospital was the feeling of isolation that came with it. Most of my family and friends didn't see the need to visit me because I wasn't sick. There were many long, lonely days. I "adopted" the nursing staff as my new family, enjoyed their company and became close to many of them.

To combat depression, I would often read about birth and fetal development to remind myself about what was happening inside me and why I was in the hospital. I also made lists, organized and planned what I needed for our layette, the equipment and clothing. As I pondered our new lives, I called many other triplet moms for their opinions on breastfeeding, equipment and house set-up. The local triplets club was always within reach by phone. I also kept in touch with another woman who was pregnant with triplets to discuss and compare our pregnancies, and so we could keep each other's spirits up.

It's amazing to think that three months of bedrest — of rest and relaxation — could be so tough. It was. But it was also productive, considering I carried the babies for 34 weeks. When I look back, the isolation and strain I felt in those months are fading memories made all the more distant by my three very healthy baby girls.

preterm labour

did i have all
the information?

Christine Marshall

When I was pregnant with triplets, I did everything I was told to do, and avoided everything I was told to avoid. I was careful to stop and rest during the day. I never overexerted myself. I lifted nothing heavier than a telephone book. I watched my diet faithfully and ate the maximum number of servings in each food group that I could manage every day.

But even after all my precautions, I went into labour at 26 weeks. Looking back after six years, I wonder if there were ways of preventing my labour, or if it was simply inevitable. I wonder if I had all the information I needed to prolong this pregnancy. Since my triplets were my first pregnancy, I had no experience with obstetricians. Our first meeting didn't take place until I was 25 weeks pregnant. After our first appointment, my family doctor called to ask how I felt about the meeting. I said that everything seemed fine and that I wouldn't be seeing the obstetrician until I was 32 weeks.

Insisting that schedule of care was inappropriate for a high risk multiple pregnancy, my family doctor intervened and ensured that I would be seen again by the obstetrician in two weeks — not four. A date was set, but I never made it. My babies were born before the next appointment.

The day before I went into labour, I had an ultrasound. I remember the technician commenting how difficult it was to get a clear picture of one of the babies since her head was positioned so low toward my cervix. "Is that a warning sign?" I asked, not aloud but to myself, assuming someone would call to alert me if it was.

That night, I spent many restless hours awake and uncomfortable. My mother called the next morning and despite my protests, insisted that I go to be checked. At the hospital it was confirmed — I was in labour and three centimetres dilated.

> ## quote
>
> **I wonder if there were other ways to prevent labour at 26 weeks**

preterm labour

Inside the ambulance,
I waited and counted contractions

Through all of this, my husband was making his way home from a business trip, unaware that I was en route by ambulance to a Level 3 hospital an hour away from home. I still remember the trip as if it were yesterday. It was the Victoria Day weekend and traffic was very heavy on the highway. In fact, the ambulance actually had to stop at an accident before passing to be sure no one involved required immediate medical attention. (Apparently, ambulances are required to stop at an accident if they are first on the scene.) Meanwhile, inside the ambulance, I waited and timed contractions with a nurse who, like me, was growing increasingly agitated about the idea of delivering three babies on the side of the road. I didn't think we were going to get to the hospital in time, and even if we did, I worried that my husband and my family wouldn't make it. I felt so alone and scared and couldn't imagine how I would be able to go through this by myself. I felt like it was the end of the world. How could this be happening to us, after all the care I took of myself?

Once I arrived, I was wheeled into labour and delivery. While one doctor checked me, another came in to talk to me and my mother, who had just arrived at the hospital. I couldn't believe, nor will I ever forget, what he told us. He said that since it was so early and a multiple pregnancy, the babies would be very small and their chance of survival was between 15 per cent and 40 per cent. Still in shock, I prepared for surgery. My husband arrived with his parents only 10 minutes before the birth. My world was falling apart, but with my husband and family with me, I found some strength and comfort. We were all going through the experience together.

My son Aaron and daughter Rebecca were born at two pounds each. My other daughter Trisha was just 1 lb. 5 oz. Considering their prematurity, their birthweights were the best we could have hoped for. (I wonder if all of those extra calories made a difference?)

I'm happy and delighted to say, although the next three months were heartbreaking, with many ups and downs, my three beautiful babies came home remarkably healthy and very close to their original due date.

preterm labour

trust your instincts
Paula Silva

I am lying in bed with insomnia, 27 weeks pregnant, reading and watching my husband sleeping soundly beside me. I glance at the clock. It's 1 a.m. as I rub my stomach trying to feel the babies, who have just recently started to kick. Suddenly my stomach feels harder than normal, then it quickly becomes soft again. Just my imagination? No, there it goes again! I can't feel it tighten inside, but the exterior feels harder to the touch.

It happens a few more times before I wake my husband. "What do you mean you think you are in labour?" he asks. It's true — I have no pain and no other symptoms. Still, I have read enough and have been told many times (not by my doctor, but by other mothers of multiple babies) that preterm labour can be painless. I make a call to a Level 3 hospital in downtown Toronto and they recommend that I go to the nearest hospital to see if I am in fact in labour.

At the community hospital, I spend about an hour describing the situation and trying to persuade the medical personnel to examine me. Please. The doctor concludes the tightenings are nothing more than Braxton-Hicks contractions and I am told to go home.

tip

If you suspect preterm labour — you are probably right

Any kind of contraction is serious. I know this and I will not go home

No, at 27 weeks pregnant, any kind of contraction is serious. I know this and I will not go home. At 3 a.m., we pull up to the emergency entrance of the downtown hospital. An examination confirms what I have feared all along. I am three centimetres dilated and then, too quickly, five centimetres dilated. When the obstetrician arrives at 11 a.m. he informs my husband and me that labour cannot be stopped and the babies must be delivered. We cannot believe it! I just saw my obstetrician two days ago! During that visit, I had expressed some concern that I thought the babies were coming soon. I had felt them drop, and a lot of pressure. The doctor shrugged it off, saying these things were normal. "What do I know?" I thought. "I've never been pregnant before." Then the doctor added casually, "Besides, if you do go early into preterm labour, I will give you something to stop it."

a special care pregnancy

preterm labour

If that was true, why am I in a hospital hearing that my babies have to be delivered so early? Why do we have to risk their tiny, fragile lives? I keep asking myself, "How could this happen, when my doctor said it could be stopped?" We are so worried. The neonatologist from the Neonatal Intensive Care Unit comes into our room to prepare us for all of the potential risks facing preterm, low birthweight babies. All we can do now is pray.

Thankfully, Thomas (2 lb.10 oz.), Austin (2 lb. 4 oz.) and Andrew (2 lb. 7 oz.), arrived in this world amazingly free of any major health problems. However, they did experience more than two months of the medical ups and downs that often come with prematurity — tests, jaundice, infections, tube feedings, oxygen assistance, blood transfusions, hernias, eye exams and many medications. But they are now at home doing very well and are a joy to all the lives they touch.

I realize now how important it was to have an experienced obstetrician that would listen and act on my observations. My experience shows that through reading and talking to other parents who had gone through a multiple pregnancy, I became my own expert. At the very least, that knowledge gave me the confidence to seek treatment elsewhere when my labour started.

preterm labour

a healer without limits
Bracha Mirsky

The doctor did everything medically possible to stop labour. All I could do was pray

I was 22 weeks pregnant, when at a regular checkup, my doctor announced, "We are going to admit you." He had noted signs of premature labour. I was expecting triplets, and even though premature labour is not uncommon, I was not expecting this — not this early.

Caught completely off guard, I was too stunned to be afraid. I was in denial. There were no contractions, or pain of any kind. My doctor was just being cautious. I was sure of it. So I laid around in the hospital on complete bedrest for two weeks. Then the pain began. Suddenly, I was in active labour, and quickly rushed to the labour ward where medication and IVs were started. A monitor was strapped around my stomach. Labour slowed and stopped and started again — over and over — all day.

The next day my doctor comes to me. "I am doing all I can," he says. "If there is anything you can do …" He lets the thought trail off. Anything, I can do? What I can do, but pray? Doesn't he know that's all I've been doing! Then he makes a big mistake. No doubt trying to cheer me up, he excitedly tells me that he was just at a conference where they discussed a case about a woman expecting triplets who went into labour very early. The first baby was born and died, but after that, the doctors managed to stop the labour and save the other two babies.

I am not cheered up. I am not happy. He leaves, and I cry. Not for the first time. Tears come from my eyes as easily as water from a tap. God, oh God, how could you bring me this far and abandon me? Please, I know all children come from you, your blessing, and I have prayed for these children. Please, please let them live and be well! You made them, but you also made me and you know my soul is bound with theirs. I cannot endure this, I beg you to save them.

My prayers went on for hours and my tears were constant, until at last I accepted, to the best of my ability, that the fate of these children was out of my doctor's hands and out of mine. But my prayers for them never ceased.

preterm labour

The situation continued for one week until finally, my contractions quieted, and labour stopped as mysteriously as it began. Soon I returned to the regular hospital ward, where I remained on bedrest until my three children came into this world at 36 weeks gestation, healthy and strong.

early arrivals
The Perinatal Partnership Program
of Eastern and Southeastern Ontario

Premature births are never a surprise in a multiple pregnancy. The only question is when
Every couple should know the signs and symptoms of preterm labour, but it is especially important for families expecting higher order multiples. Triplets, quadruplets and quintuplets rarely reach full term (between 37 and 42 weeks) before they are born. According to data compiled by the Triplets, Quads and Quints Association, the average gestation for triplets born in Canada is 33 weeks. For quadruplets, the average is 30 weeks.

Aside from multiple fetuses, there are other factors that have been known to increase the risk of preterm labour or birth. Here are some of the risk factors:
• Previous preterm labour or preterm birth
• Smoking
• Drinking alcohol
• Being underweight
• Not eating sufficient servings of recommended food groups
• High stress with little social support
• A vaginal, cervical or bladder infection
• A short cervix

Women who are pregnant with triplets or more are at a particularly high risk for preterm labour. They will spend significant time with their healthcare team discussing ways of preventing and identifying signs of preterm labour and what they should do if it happens.

preterm labour

Lower the risk of preterm labour

Here are some ways that may help prolong your pregnancy:

- Start seeing an obstetrician, preferably one with experience in managing multiple pregnancies, as early as possible in the pregnancy.
- If you smoke, try to quit or cut down significantly.
- Ask your doctor for clear instructions about appropriate activity levels. If you continue to work, ask when you will have to quit. Get an explanation of the benchmarks, such as weight gain, blood pressure and general well-being, that your doctor will use to assess your condition and whether you can continue to work as the pregnancy progresses. Find out the specific terms of your bedrest and follow them.
- Pay attention to your body. Stay off your feet, lie down and sleep when tired. Activity tolerance changes quickly. The flight of stairs you climb today may be impossible the following week.
- Notice when things feel "different" and talk to your healthcare provider about it.
- Ask for nutritional advice from a registered dietician or nutritionist, preferably from someone who has experience with higher order multiple pregnancies.
- Talk to your healthcare provider and local multiples support group about how to manage and reduce stress in your life.
- Minimize stress by organizing childcare for older children, assigning housework and other tasks before you are placed on bedrest or hospitalized.

Preparing for premature births

The best way to prepare is to learn the signs and symptoms of labour and develop an action plan for you and family if labour begins. You should also know in advance your hospital's capabilities for delivering and caring for your preterm babies. Level 1, or community hospitals, are not equipped to care for infants that are more than mildly premature. Level 2 hospitals can generally accommodate babies born after 34 weeks. However, if the babies experience complications and require high level medical intervention, such as a ventilator for breathing, they will need to be trans-

preterm labour

ferred to a Level 3 hospital for care in a Neonatal Intensive Care Unit (NICU). These facilities have the equipment and specialized staff to care for infants born with various health complications often seen in babies born under 34 weeks.

Warning signs of early labour

Many women carrying triplets or more experience silent labour, which is painless and free of cramping or contractions. They may dismiss some signs of labour, such as intermittent backache, as being routine occurrences of the second half of pregnancy. That's why it is important to know your own body and learn the signs of preterm labour. Recognizing the early signs can help you to obtain necessary medical intervention quickly, which can either prevent an extremely premature birth or better prepare the babies and hospital for their early delivery.

tip
Some women may just feel that "something is not right" or "different" in some way

The most common signs of labour

• Increase or change in vaginal mucus discharge
• A sudden gush or constant slow leak of vaginal fluid
• Vaginal bleeding
• Contractions
• Menstrual-like cramps or stomach pains with or without diarrhea that do not subside
• Lower back pain/pressure or a change in the nature of the lower backache
• Pelvic pressure, feeling full or heavy, or that the baby is pushing down

Fever, chills, dizziness, vomiting, a bad headache, sudden or severe swelling of your feet, hands or face are all important warning signs of other potentially dangerous complications, such as pre-eclampsia, and should be reported to your healthcare provider.

Preterm labour contractions feel different from "tightenings" that many women feel in the second half of pregnancy. True labour contractions are often distinguished because they:

• Grow more frequent and intense over time
• Won't subside if you move or lie down
• Accompany other signs, such as fluid leaking from the vagina or pelvic pressure

a special care pregnancy

preterm labour

What to do if you think you are in labour

• Stay as calm as possible

• Notify your obstetrician

• Go to the hospital, preferably the hospital where you are planning to have the babies, if the symptoms get worse. It is important to get to the hospital early if you are in preterm labour. Keep in mind that very premature babies (born before 33 weeks) will probably require the services of an NICU in a Level 3 hospital

• Understand that if you are in preterm labour, your body may delay labour on its own for a few weeks

• Don't blame yourself

What will happen at the hospital?

• If there are no changes or only very small changes in the cervix, you will probably be monitored in hospital until it is certain that you are not in labour or are about to go into premature labour

• If your cervix has started to open (dilate) or shorten (efface), doctors may try to delay labour with medication or they may deliver the babies based on your condition and the condition of the babies and your gestational stage

• If you have not already received a steroid injection to help the babies' lungs to mature, you may receive the injection

• If doctors suspect that you will give birth soon and you are not already at a hospital that can care for your children, you may be transferred at this point

tip

Tightenings of any kind should be discussed with a doctor regardless of whether other signs of labour are present.

Husband/partners may feel isolated

A complicated pregnancy involves not only mothers, but their partners as well. When complications set in, dad's concerns, needs and feelings are often forgotten, with most of the attention focused on mom and the babies. Dad is asked endless questions about his partner's condition, while often left alone to deal with his own feelings. The situation is frightening for both partners — dad has been dealt an equally poor hand.

Stress on everyone

Preterm labour is difficult for mom and dad and anyone else who is close to the family. In addition to existing responsibilities at work and household tasks, fathers may face a long list of other responsi-

preterm labour

bilities that mom used to carry out. Dad will likely have to assume most parenting responsibilities such as waking, feeding and preparing children for school, and especially, helping them to cope with fears about mom.

He will become the main link between mom and the outside world. As they deal with depression, isolation and fear that they may lose the babies or that something terrible might happen to mom, dad will be called upon to be extra sensitive and patient.

Because of the special circumstances in some pregnancies, a bond may occur between the expectant mother and her care provider. At times, dad may feel left out, uncertain, and his needs should be acknowledged and accommodated.

Information

Dad is the mother's prime advocate and, as such, should be fully informed about the potential choices they may have to make down the road. It's helpful if he can become involved in the medical care of mom and his unborn children by attending doctor's appointments and ultrasounds as often as possible.

Understanding

Dad will be afraid for the safety of the mother and the unborn children, but may also feel angry and frustrated. On a subconscious level he may even blame himself for what has happened. A father may experience anger because the mother is turning her attention inward to the children while he is turning all his attention outward toward his wife. Remember that dads need support and understanding through the pregnancy as well.

am i contracting?
Maureen Boyle, MOST
(Mothers of Supertwins) Inc.

How will you know if you are having contractions? It's possible to detect subtle contractions if you have taken note of how your abdomen feels when it's relaxed throughout pregnancy. As early as the 18th week, spend some time in the morning and in the evening with your feet up and your hands positioned on either side of your belly. Through the weeks, you'll get accustomed to knowing how your relaxed belly feels through touch. If you feel a tightening on both sides of your belly at the same time, this could very well be a contraction.

Since your belly will probably be quite firm by this point in the pregnancy, it may be difficult to feel the subtle difference between a contraction and relaxation. In fact, if your hands were not placed on your belly, you might not feel contractions at all. For comparison, bring your fingers to your face. First touch your cheek and then your forehead. Compare the difference in firmness between your cheek and your forehead. The difference between a contraction and complete relaxation may be just as subtle.

3

getting organized

preparing for fatherhood

Brian Borowy

My new life as a dad started the moment we heard the news

My wife, Gillian and I are the proud parents of three beautiful six-month-old baby boys. As an expectant father, I played an important role in helping my wife through a potentially difficult part of her life. The following is a summary of what I did to help Gill, and myself, through the first phase of parenting — pregnancy.

Gill and I received our wonderful news about three weeks prior to Christmas in 1995 during a scheduled ultrasound visit at the doctor's office. Aside from the obvious elation and joy that we were going to be parents, there was the sobering reality that I had no idea about how to be a parent or how we would manage Gill's pregnancy, let alone how we would cope once the babies came home. My head was swimming with worries and concerns, such as:

getting organized

- Is Gill's health at risk?
- What stresses will she have to endure during the pregnancy and birth?
- When is the "highest risk" period of the pregnancy?
- How can I help Gill during the pregnancy?
- What will the babies be like?
- How will our lives change during the pregnancy and after the birth?
- How will our relationship as a couple change?
- Will I be a competent parent?
- How will we be able to afford three babies?
- Who can I turn to for help and to ask questions?

Many of these questions are unique to individual circumstances. For me, however, it was possible to come to terms with most of these concerns by reading everything I could find on multiple pregnancies, by dedicating myself to Gill and the pregnancy, by planning and preparing for the babies' arrival, and by being a smart consumer.

Reading

The first item on the "to do" list was to research everything that has been written on multiple pregnancies. There is a growing collection of books on multiple pregnancies and an abundance of general materials on parenting and family life in bookstores and libraries. It's amazing how quickly you can assemble a personal reference library, which is a good idea considering the path you are embarking on. Any book given to you is worth keeping since some never go out of date. Even the older references will give you different perspectives for comparing modern thinking.

Get involved in the pregnancy

There are many ways of getting involved in the pregnancy. Here are some suggestions that worked for us.

Take care of your wife. Until Gill got pregnant, each of us took our health for granted. Now, with so much riding on Gill's health, I wanted to make sure I was doing everything within my abilities to keep her and the babies as healthy as possible.

Eat, Eat, Eat! Whenever I had the chance, I would ask Gill if she wanted something from the kitchen. If she declined, I would bring something anyway. Cookies were my favourite; however, I also brought her apples, cheese and the occasional sandwich.

Drink, Drink, Drink! The doctors and the literature all say, "Drink plenty of fluids." Whenever I woke up at night, I would always bring Gill a tall glass of milk. Pamper your wife! Do whatever it takes to help her relax and rest.

Take over as much of the housework as you can. As soon as we realized that we were pregnant with triplets, I refused to let Gill use any cleaning chemicals or do any physically demanding chores around the house. Tasks like bending over to fill or empty the dishwasher, vacuuming and carrying the laundry up and down the stairs put unnecessary strain on your wife's body.

Do fun things as a couple. Gill and I had been married for about two and a half years prior to our great news. In that time, we both worked and saved money and had never taken much time for ourselves since our honeymoon. We decided that we better enjoy ourselves as a couple while we still could. We went out for dinner at least once a week until Gill could no longer fit into the chairs or booths of our favourite restaurants. When Gill didn't feel like going out, we occasionally ordered food in.

We also bought an inexpensive stethoscope to listen to the babies' heartbeats. It was both fun and reassuring.

Go to doctor's visits. When you are there, listen to the doctor. Listen to what your wife asks the doctor and ask your own questions too. Your presence and input demonstrate to your wife that you are interested and supportive, and allow you to meet the doctor who will deliver your children before you get to the delivery room.

Maintain a positive attitude. As the supportive husband, you will have the responsibility of maintaining your wife's sense of well-being. There are times when she will really struggle with the changes her body is going through. Her self-esteem may waver — consider how you might feel if you gained five to 10 pounds per month, outgrew all of your clothing, got out of breath just by climbing the stairs and spent many restless nights because you couldn't roll over. Whenever Gill was down about what was happening to her, I reassured her by reminding her that the changes were only temporary. I told her that I loved her more than ever, that she was going to be a great mom and that all the sacrifices were helping to ensure the babies were born as healthy as possible.

Keep a sense of humour. When you are out in public and people gawk or ask embarrassing questions, laugh it off. Often people act shocked when you mention triplets to see how you react. My favourite line was, "Yes, only triplets, we were hoping for quads or quints," as if nothing could be more normal in the world.

Plan and prepare for the babies' arrival

There are many ways of preparing for your new lifestyle. The more things you can do in advance, the more relaxed you will be when the babies arrive.

Join a support group. By joining a group, you become part of a community of special families with special needs. You will find the people you meet in the group to be friendly and supportive. The advice and guidance you can receive from people who have already made it through your current situation are invaluable.

Visit a family with multiples. Gill and I visited a triplet family to see firsthand what it is like to have three little babies running around the house. We were so impressed. The children were chatty, energetic and fun. The parents were so proud and answered all of our questions. After the visit, Gill and I felt confident that we too could be successful parents of triplets and that everything would be all right.

Have confidence in yourself. In this way, parents of multiples and single babies are no different. You want children so much, and then as you realize it's going to happen, you lose your confidence. Do not underestimate your own abilities. Your instincts take over right away and you never look back.

Be a smart consumer

It's unfortunate that we get so hung up on the cost of everything, but face it, money is important and most people will agree — we never have enough. The key to stretching a budget is deciding between what you need and what you want. Once you have made this decision, find the least expensive way to obtain what you need.

Make a list of items. Ultimately, only you can decide what is essential, but in the process, use your judgment, talk to other parents, get advice, and read up on what is generally recommended. Sit down with your wife and make a list of everything you think you will need with a cost estimate for each item and then prioritize.

Purchase the priority items as far in advance of the expectant birth date as possible. Gill and I agreed that the only truly necessary items were adequate transportation, car seats, sleepers, diapers and a washer and dryer. We purchased car seats on sale long before the boys arrived, and we bought a previously loved minivan in the last few weeks of the pregnancy.

When you begin to make purchases from your priority list of items remember to:
• write to companies and find out what freebies are available
• learn the pricing of what you need and wait until the items go on sale
• shop at stores that offer discounts when you buy three or more items
• use coupons
• consider buying used items

We were amazed at the number of people who responded to our needs with donations. Accept all gifts graciously.

Gill and I were three times blessed with the arrival of our boys. Michael, our firstborn was 5 lb. 14 oz., David was 6 lb. 10 oz. and Ken was 6 lb. 8 oz. I know my wife did 99 per cent of the work carrying and nurturing the boys during the pregnancy, but I also played a role in our success.

By educating ourselves, treating my wife the best that I could, creating an atmosphere that was relaxed and happy at home, and purchasing most of the important items we needed in advance, Gill and I had nothing to do but wait for the arrival of the babies in the last few weeks of the pregnancy. We were still anxious and excited and nervous, but we were also as prepared as we could be for our new life.

what on earth do we need?

Patricia Harber

When it comes to baby equipment, drawing a line between what is essential and what's "nice to have" varies from one parent to another. However, for parents expecting their first babies, compiling that list of equipment can be a mystifying challenge. You may be wondering if you need three, four or five of everything. The answer is a resounding NO! You may not have the finances, let alone the space, for three baby swings or four bouncy chairs. Of course, for certain items, such as car seats, there's no room for flexibility.

The following list assumes that you are equipping your nursery with many of the usual items that you would typically find in a baby's home. Keep in mind that it is only a guide and that you can certainly do without many of the items.

Also, keep in mind these assumptions:

1. At least one load of laundry is done every 24 hours

2. Bottle needs calculated on six feedings per child in a 24-hour period (if on a four-hour schedule)

3. Bottle preparation is done once every 24 hours

EQUIPMENT	TRIPLETS	QUADRUPLETS	QUINTUPLETS
Cribs (can use 1-2 for first few months)	3	4	5
Crib mobile	3	4	5
Bed wedges (can use rolled up receiving blankets)	3	4	5
Car seats	3	4	5
Baby bathtubs/baby bath pillow support	1	1	1
Baby monitor (per room)	1	1	1
Change table (dining room table works!)	1	1	1
Triple or quad stroller	1	1	1-2
Double/single stroller	2	2	3
Highchairs/boosters	3	4	5
Baby seat/bouncer (Infant car seats work)	3	4	5
Swings	1-2	2-3	3-4
Upright activity seat	1-3	2-3	3-4
Activity/musical gym	1-2	1-2	2-3
Breastfeeding pillow	1	1	1
Rented breastpump* (heavy-duty double)	1	1	1
Bottle sterilizer (some use dishwasher)	1-2	1-2	1-2
Safety gates (depends on need)	2-4	2-4	2-4
Cool mist vapourizer (per room)	1	1	1
Large diaper bag or backpack	1	1	2
8 oz. bottles and nipples	18	24	30
4 oz. bottles and nipples	6	8	10

Freezer bags for storing/freezing expressed breastmilk with labels for dates are also available

Cribs are essential for the months ahead. Baskets, bassinets and portacribs are useful for the early months. Many parents find the cost of bassinets and portacribs to be a little high when buying three or more. When the babies are small, two or three babies can be placed in one crib. Most people put their children in their own cribs when they begin to wake each other up and/or when the children become too big to share the space.

Car seats are a must if you plan to travel in a car with your children. Some parents have been able to rent infant car seats — a helpful option since the children may grow out of these seats quickly. But keep in mind that infant car seats are often used as baby seats in the home and may be worth purchasing. Some full-size car seats can be adapted for both newborns and children up to 40 pounds. See the article on child safety restraints later in this chapter for more detail.

Stroller decisions seem to be one of the most agonizing. Some parents prefer one stroller that seats all of the babies, while others have managed with two strollers. Consider how often one person will be caring for all the babies, whether the stroller will fit into your vehicle, and how much money you have to spend. Buying a used triple/quad stroller through the multiple birth association can cut the cost dramatically.

Swings seem to be one of the most popular pieces of equipment for families with triplets, quadruplets, and quintuplets, although very few parents have one swing per child. There are many varieties that can be purchased. Some of the features that parents have reported to be useful are battery powered (not wind up), adjustable and dual-purpose seats. Some swing seats can be reclined to allow the baby to sleep more comfortably in the swing. Other swings have seats that can be removed from the stand and used as a baby seat.

Highchairs or booster seats (with trays) are not a necessity during the early months, but you will need one per baby (hungry little ones do not stand for taking turns patiently) when they begin to sit up and eat food. Many parents like the booster seats that simply attach to kitchen or dining room chairs because they take up less room, cost much less and their portability makes them ideal for travelling.

Activity seats are not recommended by many pediatricians for babies who have not mastered standing. But if you decide to use them, it is important that the children are able to place their feet flat on the ground. The best place for children to play, to encourage natural movement and development, is on a clean carpet or blanket on the floor.

Formula is something that most of us have in our homes at some point during the first year. If you are not breastfeeding at all, you will be buying formula by the case. Newborns will need about 12 ounces per day, building up to 32 to 40 ounces per day per child. There are many ways of purchasing formula — powder, concentrated liquid or ready to serve.

CLOTHING	TRIPLETS	QUADRUPLETS	QUINTUPLETS
Sleepers/flannel nightgowns	12	16	20
Undershirts	9	12	15
Bibs	18	24	30
Hats	3	4	5
Sweaters	3	4	5
Snowsuits/ bunting bags	3	4	5

Toiletries and miscellaneous

- Cotton swabs
- Binders/clipboards and charts to keep track of feedings, bowel movements, diaper changes, medication
- Rubbing alcohol
- Diaper wipes
- Baby bath soap (unscented)
- Baby clothes detergent & stain remover
- Diaper rash cream

- Petroleum jelly
- Bottle/nipple brush
- Cotton balls
- Baby lotion/cream (unscented)
- Soothers
- Baby thermometer
- Feeding spoons & bowls
- Baby scissors/clippers

Diaper needs vary. Most newborns go through 6-8 disposable diapers per day. Don't buy too many in the very small sizes, however, because the babies may grow out of them quickly. Babies using cloth diapers tend to need changing more often. Diaper services (cloth) are available and can recommend how many you will need to meet your requirements. Using this service has financial and environmental advantages worth considering.

LINENS	TRIPLETS	QUADRUPLETS	QUINTUPLETS
Plastic/quilt change pads	2	3	4
Baby washcloths	12	16	20
Hooded bath towels	6	8	10
Receiving blankets	12	16	20
Head holders (per piece of equipment)	3	4	5
Burp shoulder pads	6	8	10
Nursing bras	2-3	2-3	2-3
Nursing pads (reusable)	10	10	10
Crib sheets (fitted)	6	8	10
Light blankets	6	8	10
Warm blankets	3	4	5
Diaper pail	1-2	2	2-3

how are we going to pay for everything?
Maureen Tierney

A little research and creativity can add up to big savings

When we told family and friends that we were going to have triplets, clothes and equipment donations poured in. Still, at some point, every family will face the expense of having to buy some items, and the costs can be staggering.

If you are buying new items for three or more babies, don't hesitate to ask for a discount. You can also look in the "gently used" stores that are sprouting up all over the place. As well, local newspapers often run "equipment needed" or "for sale" notices in the children's classified sections.

I shopped at the spring and fall sales of the local twins and triplets clubs, where the prices are always excellent. The Triplets, Quads and Quints Association is an excellent resource of companies which are willing to donate goods. I contacted families who had triplets within the last year or two and inquired about any equipment, clothing and supplies they still might have. I also asked where they purchased diapers and formula. You may feel uncomfortable calling people you have never met, but in my experience, members are very willing to share their knowledge, experience and support.

Contrary to popular belief that companies provide ongoing supplies of diapers and formula, you can expect a one-time gift, often provided that you send copies of birth certificates as proof. Next time you shop, take note of companies that produce or import products that are not national brands and contact them. I found a good supply of baby wipes this way. I contacted a U.S.-based company that sent free packages along with the names of their Canadian distributors that sold at prices far below retail price.

Buying in bulk from retailers will often yield a better price, not to mention savings in time. I buy baby wipes by the case. If you ask, stores may give you samples of their products for cost and quality comparisons. If you are a member of a multiple birth association, show the store your membership card as proof that you are expecting three, four or more babies. You may wonder how you can compare the costs of formula before you have the babies and don't know the type you will be using. Since all baby formulas on the Canadian market must meet certain government standards, my pediatrician said they were all acceptable. I noted several regular formulas as well as "lactose-free" varieties in case we experienced this problem. Not surprisingly, I found that the more popular brand-named formulas were the most expensive.

Another option is to check grocery warehouses. Often listed in the phone book, these stores buy from other stores that have gone out of business. There are some real bargains to be found. Also, consider contacting diaper companies to see where they ship second quality products. I found the diapers were fine and an excellent price. The only potential problem is supply — it is best to call ahead.

There are some real bargains to be found

Try to be creative when thinking about how you can cut costs. While I was pregnant, a mother of triplets told me that she had received a year's supply of free diapers in exchange for participation in a market research survey about diapers. The focus groups can be very selective about age groups, so timing is everything. Try calling market research companies listed in the phone book or the classified section of your newspaper for information.

If your child has special needs and the costs of supplies are prohibitively high for you, consider contacting the insurance company where you have benefits, the social worker of the hospital, the Ministry of Health or your local politician. These organizations and people may have a solution, or they can certainly look into the matter on your behalf. If diapers and formula are going to put great financial stress on you, ask for these as gifts at your baby shower, or ask for cash instead.

Cutting costs is a challenge when you are expecting three or more children. But it can be done. It will take time and patience, particularly if you are not accustomed to comparing prices, but the effort will most definitely pay off.

clothing tips
Mary MacCafferty

• Ask people to pass on only those clothes they don't want back. It can become almost impossible to keep track of a treasured outfit that someone wants returned. I was always nervous about keeping those clothes in a decent state. (Formula can leave dark stains on some fabrics if it is not soaked before washing.) The hassle of watching out for someone else's favourite outfit was just not worth it.

• If people offer a large bag or box of baby clothes, ask them to help with sorting while they're still at your house (if your relationship with them can handle that situation well). That way, you can take what's suitable and ask them to take the other items back. Keeping clothes that will never be worn is taking up premium storage space. And finding someone or some place to pass clothes along to takes precious time. If you are sorting on your own, there are some charitable organizations that will pick up recycled clothes from your door.

• If you don't need the clothes right away, try to at least throw them into a garbage bag with other same-sized clothes or seasonal items. You can easily forget about those nice size 3 snowsuits if they're mixed with size 4 shorts and tank tops. Using clear bags for storage can help you navigate as you search for a certain bundle.

• If you are fortunate enough to have a lot of donated clothes, try keeping only those clothes you definitely know you would like to see your children wearing. I held on to bags and bags of "maybe" clothes. I even rationalized that some things would be fun for dressing up in. Unless you have lots of room, hoarding adds to the clutter and may prevent you from getting to the clothes you really want.

cotton service versus disposable diapers?

Gillian Borowy

I used a cotton diaper service until my three boys were seven months old, then switched to disposables. Here are the pros and cons of each option as I saw them.

Cotton diaper service

• I found the service very helpful for determining and then modifying the diaper quantities we needed. Initially they suggested 210 diapers a week for triplets, but after five days it was obvious I didn't have enough to make it to delivery day. I left them a panicky message at 2 a.m. saying, "I need more diapers and I need them now!" Seven hours later, 90 additional diapers arrived by courier, at no charge.

• For us, the cost was $32 a week for 250 diapers and a supply of burp cloths. There was also a set-up fee, an extra-large diaper pail to purchase for $12 and the vinyl wraps to buy to hold the diapers in place. We had to buy vinyl wraps to hold the diapers in place since pins aren't used. They were available from the service, but we found less expensive supplies at a few discount retail stores.

• Dirty diapers are picked up and clean ones are delivered once a week, saving time that would have been spent shopping for them.

• Aside from their versatility as burp cloths and mattress pads (which the service also cleans), cotton diapers are highly absorbent (not surprisingly) for mopping up spills. But they aren't ideal for household cleaning since they tend to leave behind a great deal of lint.

• The service did not require us to do anything with the dirty diapers other than drop them in the garbage bags that were provided.

• The worst thing about using cotton diapers was washing out the wraps. They can go in the washer if they are just wet, but if a loose bowel movement escapes the diaper and gets into the wrap's elastic, it has to be washed out by hand. It only takes a minute, but I was doing between two and six wraps a day, until the boys started solid food. The wraps fit very well, however, and protected the boys' clothes.

• We had no troubles with diaper rash. I used petroleum jelly at every

132

change, and zinc at the first sign of redness, which was rare. We also had fewer leaks with the cotton diapers overall than with disposables.

Disposable diapers
• Depending on the brand, disposables can be two to three times more expensive than cotton.
• They are less bulky, however, and take up less room in the diaper bag. Baby clothes may fit better when disposables are worn.
• Dirty disposables can just be thrown away, an especially appealing alternative to carrying dirty diapers home after an outing. Since most municipal garbage gets picked up once a week, like the service, there is no difference in the unpleasant smells produced. And, in certain communities, there are recycling programs for disposables.
• At seven months my largest boy was 22 pounds and growing out of his vinyl wraps. I had to decide whether to buy a new set of larger wraps or switch to disposables. At this point I was only using between 105 and 125 diapers per week, and the savings are less dramatic as the quantities dropped. We decided to go for the disposables, primarily for convenience.
• For us, the savings in the first few months were worth any minor inconvenience associated with the cotton diapers. Once we were using fewer diapers and the boys and I were getting out more often, convenience had a higher value.

some things can't be organized
Diane Myers

Until I was ready emotionally, the nursery remained empty
At 12 weeks into our pregnancy, the doctors told us that our chances of bringing four healthy babies home were very slim. The fear of losing our children was with me every day. How was I going to decrease the risks of this pregnancy, think positively and get ready? I felt that I should be doing something, getting ready … we would need so much stuff. At the same time I felt that I could

not get ready; what if something happened to the babies? How could I possibly take the nursery apart if something did happen? For me, fears of loss made it impossible to collect and organize clothes and baby equipment.

We had many generous offers of cribs, highchairs, clothing and extra hands, but I found myself unable to accept the offers completely. Many people would wonder why I didn't want to organize everything. They would cheerfully remind me that we needed to get ready. It was very difficult for me to explain my feelings. I didn't want to sound negative. I needed to be positive. I needed for others to be positive too, yet I could not allow anything in the house. Soon, family, neighbours and friends began to realize that the best way to help would be to collect the things we would need and store them for me. One neighbour began to collect donations of clothing in her garage. My family borrowed and collected bassinets, another neighbour organized the cribs, and a local sorority began to raise money to purchase a stroller and car seats for us.

At week 24, I was admitted to the hospital for bedrest. At that time there was nothing new, used, pink or blue in the house for the babies. At 27 weeks, Alison, Harrison, Jessica and Kenny came silently into this world. They were too small to breathe. Too small to let out the lusty cries that most parents hear when their babies are born. This was another hurdle for all of us. Twenty-seven weeks was early, maybe too early. Politely people asked if we were ready to set the nursery up yet. Quietly, I said no.

As the weeks passed, the children seemed to catch every virus floating around, but they were able to fight off the bugs. A month passed and the children were doing well. It was time to get started. We built a room over the garage, painted it and finished the basement. Our families brought in the bassinets, neighbours brought over clothes to sort. The house began to fill with baby stuff. We began accepting offers of help, volunteer charts were created, and baby schedules were organized.

At 36 weeks (nine weeks after their birth), Alison, Kenny and Jessica were ready to come home (Harrison was ready a week later). But we weren't quite ready for them. We raced through the next few days, finishing the nursery, along with a list of other household tasks, while the children waited in hospital.

The few weeks before the children came home were very busy,

and some might say that it would have been more practical to have done most of the work beforehand. Yes, it would have been sensible. But I just could not.

a few pointers from one mom to another
Sheree Goodman

Above all, trust your intuition

As I look back on the early years of parenting triplets, many suggestions come to mind. If you are a parent-to-be, especially if you are a first-time parent, take advantage of the free time you have together as a couple. Enjoy those romantic evenings out, those leisurely strolls, and explore those uniquely adult-friendly, but not stroller-friendly places. This is not to frighten you, but is just a gentle reminder that your lives will change in a dramatic way. Moms can attest to all of these changes, but few of us really appreciate them until after the children arrive. The mere sight of a triple (or a quadruple) stroller attracts crowds and the strollers make ordinary places quite inaccessible, by virtue of their size. I used to take leisure time for granted, but no longer.

After having three babies, the organizational side of my personality revealed itself. I discovered that I could be an incredibly organized person, when I had to be to survive each day. It helped me to minimize the state of turmoil in our lives during those early months. Articles offer all kinds of advice on scheduling baby feedings, sleeping, waking hours, chores, bathing and so on, but the bottom line is, babies don't read schedules. Do what works for you, and organize the rest of your time in whatever way allows you to get adequate sleep and nutrition.

If at all possible, try to get your spouse, mother, friends or helpers to accompany you on doctor's visits. If you can, prepare a list of questions and concerns ahead of time. There's nothing like the sound of a crying baby to distract you from your next question. If possible, you or your helper should also write down the doctor's comments because by the time you reach home, you can forget just what was said about each child. If you can manage to time your visits one at a time, with someone watching the other children, the stress, and confusion factors will be reduced dramatically. It may seem like more work, but the visits are much faster and smoother this way.

Your babies will take up most of your time

You've heard it before, but don't refuse any offers of help. Even if someone wants to sit and watch your babies while you grab a half-hour nap, it's worth it. If time and money permit, try to get some help with household chores. A volunteer can run errands to the supermarket or drug store. A neighbouring teenager who is not yet able to babysit can be of help sorting, or doing laundry, or mowing the lawn for a nominal fee. You are the only one who can breast-feed your children, but many chores can be delegated. Many local high schools have co-op programs where a student will work for you in exchange for academic credit. Community colleges also have similar programs. Research these ahead of the babies' birth when you'll have time to interview potential candidates.

Keep your housekeeping expectations realistic. Do not expect to have gourmet meals every night (unless someone else is cooking for you) and perfectly shined floors. Your babies will take up most of your time now, and friends who come to visit will only look at the children anyway. You'll be lucky if they think of you other than as the babies' parents.

Try not to be intimidated by the high costs of diapers, equipment, clothing and formula. Much of the infant equipment is used for just short periods of time. A lot can be borrowed from friends, relatives, or purchased at triplet/multiple club sales for far less money. You will be amazed at the people who come forward with gifts, or offers to loan items, when they learn of your pregnancy. Yes, formula and diapers can be costly. I would urge anyone who would have breastfed a single infant to consider breastfeeding triplets or more, too. This may seem impossible, but many have been successful and you can be too. All you need is a very positive attitude, some good breastfeeding assistance and some helpers to hand you the babies. Best of all, it costs you no money, and requires no bottle ster-ilizing or warming in the wee hours of the night. If you intend to pump and leave milk for someone else to bottlefeed while you rest, you will need a supply of bottles. I breastfed two babies at a time while the third had a bottle of formula usually, and rotated each feeding. One of my children did not take to bottles for the first two months and was breastfed at every feeding. I only weaned her at nine months when I was given a surprise weekend away. Diapers can often be bought on sale in large quantities. Often individual store managers will give you a deal if you approach a store where you normally do business. Check out the various diaper factory outlets, where the only compromise in quality is a reversed design or misprints on the packaging. These diapers are usually sold in large bags of 150 to 200.

You know your babies best

The best advice I can give is to trust your intuition. You know your babies best. All the medical books give good advice, but the advice can be general and will not always apply to multiple babies, who are sometimes slower to achieve milestones. Try to relax and enjoy your children since it goes by very fast.

Sleep any time you can and if you can't, go for a walk. That old saying that a change is as good as a rest worked for me on those days when naps just didn't seem long enough (theirs or mine).

The bottom line is that you will survive, but yes, there will be rough days. Everyone has those, no matter what age and number of children they have. Try calling your local multiple birth association or group for support before and after the babies are born. It really helps to talk to others who are going through the same stages as you.

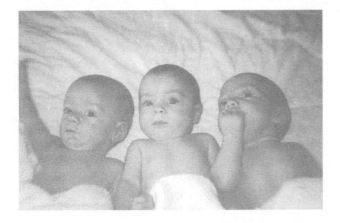

staying mobile

car seat safety

*The Infant and Toddler Safety Assn/Eastern
Ontario Car Seat Coalition*

What every parent should know

Before they take their first car ride home from the hospital, every baby must have a good quality car seat that suits their medical needs and size.

The basics of protection

• A car seat must be the right size, an especially important consideration for infants under 5 lb.
• The seat must meet Canada Motor Vehicle Safety Standards (as indicated on the back or side of the seat)
• It must be used correctly, with baby fastened into the car seat, and the seat secured into the vehicle
• It should never be positioned in front of an air bag

How to be safe and secure in an infant car seat

• Babies up to 9-10 kg (20-22 lb.) should always ride facing the back of the car
• Their bottom and back should be in contact with the bottom and back of the car seat
• Rolled-up diapers or small receiving blankets placed along the sides of the seat, around the head, and in the space between their crotch and the crotch strap can help make a better fit
• Car seat pads must have slots in the back so that car seat straps can be fed through without twisting. There should be no padding behind the baby's back or under his/her bottom
• The seat should recline at an angle of approximately 45-degrees. If the seat slopes and the baby's head flops forward, parents should tilt the seat back just enough so that the baby's head rests comfortably without falling forward. To do this, a firm roll of cloth can be placed under the front of the car seat below the baby's feet
• Shoulder straps must be in the slots at or below the infant's shoulders for rear-facing seats, and the harness must be snug and the chest clip at armpit level

staying mobile

Before choosing a car seat

• Parents who already own a car seat may be able to use it to transport small babies depending on the model and fit. Remember that used car seats must meet current standards and pass the used car seat safety checklist (See sidebar.)

• Parents who are purchasing new seats should look for models that accommodate small infants comfortably. Car seats with shoulder harness slots positioned fairly low on the back of the seat will fit a small baby better. Call car seat manufacturers for recommendations on specific models that might be more suitable

• Household carriers or feeding seats will not protect a baby in a vehicle

• For smaller infants, it's wise to purchase a restraint with a harness system rather than one with an overhead shield. Overhead or T-shields may come in contact with the infant's face in a collision

Transporting special medical equipment

An apnea monitor, portable oxygen tank or other equipment must be anchored to the floor of the car or under a seat, to ensure they don't fly around in a collision and injure car occupants.

Infant car beds

Infant car beds accommodate the special needs of infants who weigh less than 2.2 kg (5 lb.), and other medically fragile infants. Your doctor may recommend that your baby lie down while travelling in a car. In Canada, car beds are available through medical supply stories.

For current information on safety standards and car seat models, contact Transport Canada Road Safety.

staying mobile

used car seats
The Infant and Toddler Safety Assn

To help ease the financial constraints of purchasing three, four or five car seats and other items at once, donations often pour in from friends and family and the community at large. While most families are grateful for the help, it remains important to stay up to date with current safety standards to ensure donated items such as car seats will provide the best protection if an accident occurs.

Car Seat Checklist
If you answer no to any of these questions, the car seat may not be the safest choice.

Is the seat less than 10 years old?   ☐ Yes   ☐ No
Look for the date of manufacture or expiry date on the label of the seat. Eventually, the plastic on a child safety seat weakens with continuous exposure to the sun and cold. Be aware that some manufacturers consider a 10-year expiration period to be too long.

**Does the seat meet Canada Motor
Vehicle Safety Standards?**   ☐ Yes   ☐ No
Every seat sold in Canada must have a label saying that it meets a specific CMVSS for the model. Child safety seats manufactured and sold in the United States may not necessarily meet the more rigid Canadian safety standards and should not be used.

**Have you checked for a recall
on the seat?**   ☐ Yes   ☐ No
Many child safety seats have had public notice or warning issued. To find out if the seat has been recalled, contact any of the following with the make, model number and date of manufacture: the manufacturer, Transport Canada, the provincial Ministry of Transportation, or the Infant and Toddler Safety Association (ITSA) in Kitchener, Ontario.

Do you know the history of the seat?   ☐ Yes   ☐ No
Find out from the previous owner if the seat has ever been in a collision. If so, there could be hairline cracks in the plastic shell, not

readily visible, which could cause the seat to break easily in another collision.

**Do you have a copy of
manufacturer's instructions?**   ☐ **Yes**   ☐ **No**
The instructions provide detailed, illustrated information on how to correctly install and use the seat. Without them, errors can be made. Since more than 75% of parents use car seats incorrectly, it's important that you obtain a copy of detailed instructions from the manufacturer.

**Does the seat appear new and
have all of its parts?**   ☐ **Yes**   ☐ **No**
The condition of the seat is important. Be sure to look for these warning signs:
• Cracks, chips and any white or grey patches or lines in moulded plastic
• Warping, rust or broken rivets in the metal frame
• Cuts frayed edges or broken stitches in the harness straps
• Tears in the padding
• Harness, bucket or chest clip are not intact

Is the seat the right size for your child? ☐ **Yes**   ☐ **No**

Does the seat fit into your vehicle?   ☐ **Yes**   ☐ **No**
If there isn't a separate tether anchor bolt (required for all forward-facing restraints) already installed in your vehicle for each car seat, contact the vehicle manufacturer for instructions.

before you buy a new or used vehicle
Eastern Ontario Car Seat Coalition

Many parents find it necessary to purchase a larger vehicle to transport their enlarged family. As you are shopping for a new or used vehicle, keep in mind that it will need to accommodate many car seats at once. Tether straps of car seats must be anchored to specified points of the vehicle. Locations can vary from one model of vehicle to another.

New vehicles

In most cases, the vehicle owner's manual will indicate the location of predrilled holes in newer vehicles. From the 2000 model year and onward, tether anchorage bolts or similar attachment systems must be installed at the factory for passenger cars. Vans, light trucks and sports utility vehicles will be required to have factory-installed tether anchors for the 2001 model year onward. In certain models of older vans, trucks and sports utility vehicles, you may find that the anchor hardware has already been installed. Check the vehicle manual for details. Each car seat must be tethered to a separate anchor in the vehicle, unless the manufacturer specifies otherwise.

Older models

For older models without predrilled holes, contact vehicle manufacturers for the appropriate anchorage locations. The manufacturer can provide you with anchorage hardware specific to their vehicle if a position is available. You will need to have the hardware installed for each car seat as specified by the manufacturer.

Another method of tethering a forward-facing restraint is called "temporary tethering." When no tether anchorage is available, the latchplate or anchorage used for rear seatbelts in the vehicle can be used as the tethering point. This method can only be used if the vehicle manufacturer recommends it.

If you have any questions about car seat installation, check with the manufacturer or Transport Canada-Road Safety.

the big stroller dilemma
Ken Johnson, Maureen Tierney, Ineke Zigrossi

Purchasing a specially designed triple or quad stroller may be a costly investment and a bulky piece of equipment, but many parents can't imagine life without them. Others say they manage quite well without. Here's a rundown of the most common pros and cons.

staying mobile

Advantages

Independence. Almost invariably, families purchase a triple or quad stroller to ensure the parent or caregiver can leave the house and venture out with the babies alone. Maintaining some degree of independence can be especially important to a parent who stays at home full time to care for the babies.

"I appreciated the sense of freedom of being able to take my children out anywhere I wanted," says Maureen Tierney, mother of three girls. "With the triple stroller, I was never housebound and isolated. I didn't always have to rely on others. I didn't have to wait until my husband came home in the evenings to run some of our errands or to take the girls to the park."

Outdoor maneuvering. One of the surprising advantages is how easy the strollers are to move. "Our Runabout™ quad stroller was great," says Ineke Zigrossi, mother of quadruplets. "With its heavy-duty large rear wheels and one smaller one in front, we found it to be easier to maneuver than any of our twin strollers. For camping and hiking, it was the stroller of choice since it was manageable on any road or trail."

> quote
> ___
> The challenge is choosing the right stroller(s) for your family and lifestyle

Disadvantages

Lack of portability and maneuverability in tight places. Transporting the stroller is one of the most common disadvantages heard from parents. "We had to buy a large van since the quad stroller wouldn't fit into most minivans and didn't fold down to a compact size," says Ineke. "And we knew we would need the extra size van to accommodate everything else we needed with us on a trip."

Indoor environments, where corridors can be narrow, are tough to navigate. "Escalators are impossible, and we couldn't fit into most passenger elevators with the quad stroller," Ineke adds. Triple strollers will fit into most elevators and minivans. However, they may need to be dismantled to fit into some minivans.

Cost. A couple of extra seats in a stroller can add up! Many parents find the cost of a triple or quad stroller prohibitively high,

staying mobile

particularly when they are facing so many other expenses. Not surprisingly, stroller registries in multiple birth associations are a thriving marketplace for families buying and selling second-hand. If cost is a real obstacle, Maureen Tierney suggests telling co-workers, friends or family members (if they ask what they can purchase for you), to start a cash collection towards a stroller. Remember that well-maintained strollers will fetch a high resale price.

A stroller for every occasion

There are always times when a family splits off in different directions, so it may be essential to have a combination of single and double strollers in addition to the triple or quad model. Ken Johnson, father of quadruplets, wanted to avoid having so many strollers. "We didn't want to start our own stroller shop, with a variety of makes and models, so we decided to stay with two doubles," he says. "After we felt more at ease taking the children out at once by ourselves, I fashioned a linking bar so that either my wife or I

staying mobile

could hook the two double strollers together and take all of the babies out at once. But it was tough taking this monstrous stroller out anywhere other than around the neighborhood. Finally after they turned two and didn't seem to want to sit in a stroller very much anyway, we sold both strollers and found it easier to have them walk with us or to use our wagon and caboose."

Centre of attention
Described by Ineke as "a giant people magnet," quad and triple strollers will undoubtedly attract the attention of people in public places. "I thought I would scream if I heard one more 'You must be busy…'"

Suitability for early weeks/months
Some models are not suited for small infants, since the seats don't fold down into a lying position completely and there is little head and neck support. Maureen used a large second-hand pram for all the babies until they grew into their triple stroller.

4

reaching out for help

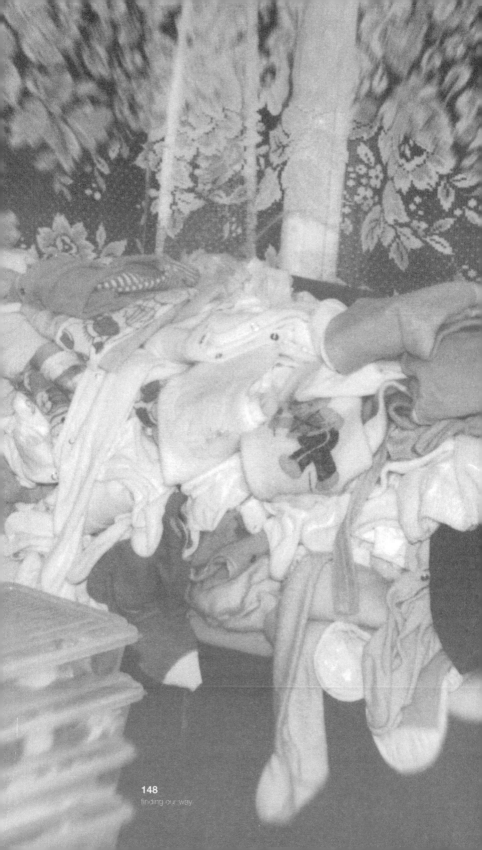

HELP! we need it

Maureen Tierney

Finding help — both paid and unpaid — is a big issue that faces parents expecting triplets or more. Contrary to popular belief, there is no government agency that will sweep into our homes and help. Since health problems prevented my parents from helping out as much as we needed, my husband and I looked to the community for support.

I thought it would be better to organize volunteers before the birth of our daughters. And I was right. There was no time after they were born, and I certainly needed help. I spent a great deal of time during the last three months of my pregnancy preparing for the babies.

As a starting point, I always accepted help from friends, family and neighbours. We found some teenagers in our neighbourhood who were very eager to help us. Since multiple birth children are often premature and therefore require more attention and medical care, your company's health insurance plan may pay for nursing care if your doctor signs the request.

I contacted the principal at the local elementary school where my children would eventually attend. The principal agreed to run a few lines in the school newsletter letting parents know that I needed help. One of the teachers told her friends about us and found two more volunteers. That's networking! Grade 8 students in the local Catholic school were expected to do volunteer work as part of their confirmation. Two students contacted us. I also got in touch with the local Catholic high school and discovered that the senior students were required to do 40 hours of community work. Two more students contacted us.

For the night shift, we looked for paid help

If your local health department runs a volunteer program, it might be able to find someone on your behalf. Be sure to ask how it screens potential volunteers. I also contacted my church, and the priest agreed to run a notice in its bulletin requesting volunteers.

For the night shift, we looked for paid help. It became too much for me to manage when my husband returned to work. For paid help, I tapped into my "contacts" at the Triplets, Quads & Quints Association. One mom recommended a nanny who had looked after her quadruplets. I was relieved to find someone who not only came highly recommended, but who also had experience with multiples. At first, it was nerve-racking leaving my children with the nanny at night, but knowing she came highly recommended by another mom helped me to relax.

Other options are advertising for paid or unpaid help at any local college or university with early childhood education or nursing programs. I asked about student placements in my home but discovered that colleges no longer offer their students this option. Of course, you could also call any of the many nanny agencies in the phone book or place an ad in a local newspaper.

In the process of interviewing assistants and volunteers, it's very important to know the right questions to ask to determine who you feel most comfortable having in your home. If you don't have experience interviewing people, as I didn't, talk to people who conduct interviews at work as well as to other mothers who have hired babysitters. What questions did they ask?

Overall, our experience with helpers was very positive. I was amazed at how everyone became so fond of our children and how they really looked forward to seeing them each week. It was a great relief every time they came to the door.

if we could do it again
Suzanne Lyons

While I was pregnant, my husband, Rick and I spent much of our time focused on prenatal care and very little on developing a plan for getting help after the babies were born. Neither of us had had firsthand experience with babies. Our response to the question everyone hears, " How will you manage?" was lighthearted and vague. We'll just manage, we thought. We were determined. Triplets? How hard could the whole thing be, really? We wanted to stay positive and not preoccupy ourselves with concerns about how we would cope through long days and sleepless nights. We made the assumption good-natured offers of help would somehow fall into place. We also believed that we could care for the babies by ourselves at night, as most parents would.

tip

See the value of having help

We did care for the babies ourselves and we managed. But we also suffered. And so did the babies. Not in a physical way, but emotionally. At the time I didn't see it. I didn't see how the practical, constant demands of feeding and changing diapers left so little time and energy for cuddling our babies. I didn't see how sleep deprivation was affecting my judgment and eventually, my health. Recurring illnesses I could never fully shake weakened me further.

While my husband was at work, I had help from my mother during the day and from volunteers sporadically on other days. At night, Rick and I slept in shifts. But if the babies were unsettled, as newborns can be, everyone was awake for many long hours. Those first six to eight weeks took a toll. I stole time to sleep, often in two- to four-hour stretches. Even as the babies napped during the day, two loads of laundry were always waiting, bottles had to be made, dishes needed washing and on and on.

Looking back, I wish we had recognized that we needed more

help and stretched our resources somehow to hire someone to care for the babies at night, even for just two or three months. We could have avoided the added stress of extreme fatigue and, more importantly, we could have enjoyed the babies more at this time. To be honest, I don't look back at the first two months with many fond memories. Since these boys will be our only children, it saddens me knowing that we sleepwalked through this part of our sons' lives and our lives as parents.

Caring for multiple newborns without hired help is tiring, but we are living proof it can be done. I also realize now that having that kind of help in place would have had immediate and possibly long-term benefits. Unfortunately, it took us too long to recognize that. While we were coping fairly well, we could have been doing a whole lot better.

I once remarked to a friend about how rarely I found the time and energy to pick up and hold one of the babies, just to cuddle and focus on him — not because he was crying — but because I simply wanted to hold him. The sympathy in her eyes surprised me. Distracted by tasks and trying to hold things together, I wasn't aware that I was missing something. Having extra help could have given us a chance to experience a few more of those moments, and I would grab that chance today.

do you need volunteers?
Tina Spigarelli

First understand your needs

My husband and I made some misguided assumptions about help before the babies were born. We thought our insurance would cover the costs of a private nurse once the babies came home. We also assumed that our families, who were supportive during the pregnancy, would come around to help. We were wrong on both counts.

Soon after the four babies arrived, we filed an application with our health insurance company and found that we didn't qualify for paid assistance because the babies were discharged from hospital very healthy. That was the first shock. The second was that our families, who had promised to help, came up empty-handed when we needed them. So we were alone with four babies and two older children to care for and no backup plan. Friends and neighbours assumed that because we both had families, there would be plenty of help.

In the hospital there was a wonderful group of volunteers who would go to the nursery to feed the babies for us when we could not be there. The founder of the group, Mary, was the sweetest woman I had ever met. She would always ask how things were going. After I had three babies at home for three weeks and was doing everything on my own, it was clear to the nurses that I was looking very tired and was absent from the nursery, where one baby still remained. They told the volunteer group that I was not getting help, and soon Mary called.

Being very private people by nature, my husband, Pino, and I were used to doing things for ourselves. We discussed getting help but our fear of losing our privacy and allowing strangers into our home held us back. The babies were born so tiny and premature that we also feared people coming in with airborne viruses would put the babies at risk for respiratory infections. We weighed the pros and cons but decided that we were just not able to take care of the babies on our own.

When Dylan, the last baby in hospital, was released, Mary offered to come over with another woman named Anita. By this time, both Pino and I welcomed the help. Our two helpers began coming two days a week for a couple of hours, which gave us time to take a walk or catch up on some sleep. We felt very comfortable with these two elderly women and soon adopted them as the children's grandmas.

After a couple of weeks, things were going so nicely that we decided to bring in other people to help out. This was a mistake. Before I knew it, there were 15 women coming over five days a week, morning and afternoon. I started to feel uncomfortable with having to share the babies with everyone and began to resent them being there. After a few months, the babies started coming down with colds, and I felt like I was always taking someone to the doctor. I was beginning to feel depressed and inadequate and that I no longer had control of my own home. My personality is somewhat timid and I didn't feel comfortable asking volunteers to do things

quote

There were 15 women doing 15 different things at the same time

the way I liked to have them done. So there I was, with all these women doing 15 different things at the same time.

I have always taken pride in being organized and began to feel overwhelmed with having to have the house cleaned for inspection. I felt as though everyone was grading me and that I was failing. I am sure now that I was not being judged, but this dramatic change in my life made me feel like I was losing my grip. Blaming others, I think, was my way out.

After five months at home, the babies all came down with a severe respiratory virus called RSV (respiratory syncytial virus). Pino and I felt responsible because we were allowing the babies to be exposed to so many people. I took this as a sign and decided to take action. I told everyone except Mary and Anita that I wouldn't require their help anymore and took on the responsibility of taking care of the children and the house myself. We kept our two "grand-mas" and had them come once a week on Pino's day off so that we could sneak away for lunch. These two very special women have been coming to our home for the last 15 months and have made Fridays our special day.

Sure, taking care of the babies on my own was very difficult and sometimes nearly impossible, but the control and peace of mind I felt while doing it made it worthwhile. I bonded with my children naturally and the babies learned to be patient and understand that there is only one of me and four of them. Of course, I was very lucky to have two older children, aged 10 and seven, who became our two busy helpers and resident experts on feeding. They accepted and bonded with the babies as much as we did. They adore their siblings and quickly became very protective.

Handling things essentially on your own is possible, but don't be afraid to ask if you need help. Looking back, it would have been better to tell the volunteers what we needed and what they should expect from us — all in advance. I would also emphasize the importance of not coming to the house if they felt ill at all, or if they had been in contact with anyone who was ill. Having people over to help is fine, as long as they are helping. If you feel threatened that you are losing control, you need to change the arrangement to better suit your needs.

The other day while I was driving Mary and Anita home, Mary asked if the reason we asked them to stay was because we felt comfortable leaving while they were there on Fridays. That way, there was less chance of us stepping on each other's toes. I was relieved they understood the kind of people we are and that we needed time away and privacy. And I also understood why they were the right volunteers for us.

lend a helping hand
Diane Myers and Linda G. Leonard

Ideas for helping multiple birth families
A family member, friend or colleague is expecting triplets or more babies. What do you do? If you are like many people in the situation, you may be concerned about the health and well-being of the mother and her babies. You may also feel that you would like to help the parents cope with some of the challenges in some way. But how?

All families are not created alike
No two multiple birth families are alike in their willingness to ask for or accept assistance from others. Assistance can take many forms, from providing household help to cuddling babies to helping parents reach an important decision. Balancing the need for privacy and the need for help can be difficult. There are differences among parents as to the amount of control they want regarding who helps, and how, when, and what assistance is provided.

Some mothers and fathers are clear about what they need and find it easy to request and receive support from family and friends. There are families who want help but don't know who or how to ask. Others prefer to manage on their own, and some will accept only certain types of assistance. A few parents have had a difficult time becoming pregnant or are afraid that something will go wrong with the pregnancy; they may postpone making preparations for the babies' arrival until they feel more confident. There are parents who think they should be able to do it all by themselves and equate needing help to personal inadequacy. Others don't know what kind of assistance they will need because they are feeling too overwhelmed, or because it is hard to imagine what life is going to be like with three or more babies.

Ways you can help

Family, friends, neighbours, community organizations and business-
es can do a lot to support multiple birth families during pregnancy
and after the births. Here are a few suggestions.

- Ask the family what kind of assistance they think they would like.
  In most instances, it is important not to take over but to bring
  information or ideas to the family and let them make the decisions. The parents' opinion of what they feel they will need may
  change once the children are born and later as their children
  grow, so keep the communication lines open.

- People are usually very willing to help, but sometimes they need
  to be invited to become involved. With the family's permission,
  "invite" other people to help.

- It may be helpful to have a volunteer coordinator if several people are helping the family.

- Reduced activity or bedrest at home or in hospital may be prescribed during a multiple pregnancy. Help may be needed to
  arrange the babies' room and assemble equipment such as cribs
  and supplies in one or more areas of the house. Some parents find
  themselves moving to accommodate their larger family: help with
  packing and unpacking may be needed.

- Pet feeding and walking, plant sitting and mail and paper collection is often needed, especially during periods of bedrest at home
  or in hospital.

- A calendar posted on the back of the front door will allow volunteers to sign up for their next visit before they leave. The parents can also use this calendar to let helpers know of special dates
  or appointments, when they will need extra help.

- Grocery shopping and meal preparation is helpful. Volunteers can
  drop off a freshly prepared meal (or arrange it with a local restaurant), or deliver a meal that can be frozen.

- Household tasks such as vacuuming, laundry, folding baby clothes,
  preparing bottles, unloading the dishwasher and cleaning bath-
  rooms are a big help. Posting tasks and directions on how to operate appliances such as the temperamental washing machine saves
  time and the need to ask the mom. Certain things, such as laun-

tip

*Mary
MacCafferty*

**One of our
friends asked a
few neighbours if
they wanted to
help us by cook-
ing a modest
meal and bring-
ing it to her to
keep in her
freezer. Each
evening she
delivered a meal
to our door for
the first three
weeks after the
babies came
home.**

dry and bottle preparation, can be done at the volunteer's home.

- Find out the costs and availability of homemakers, nannies and social services. Don't forget to use the local multiples club, Multiple Births Canada and the public health nurse as information sources.

- Many local, national and international companies provide free samples, coupons or discounts for baby products or equipment. Many require proof of the births (physician's note, photocopies of birth certificates, etc.) Organize a telephone/letter/e-mail blitz to investigate possibilities, and once the babies are born, provide the requested information. Check multiple births web sites or your local club for lists of companies that offer freebies.

- Great gifts include a stroller, cribs, car seats, swing seats, diaper service, disposable diapers, baby clothes and homemaker services. Some stores offer discounts with multiple purchases and some may donate one of the items for triplets or more. Ensure that used items meet Canadian Safety Standards.

- Free babysitting enables the mother to do something special for herself, and lets the parents go out, spend time with an older child, or run errands. Since all babies may not come home from the hospital at the same time, the parents may need someone to care for the babies or siblings at home while they spend time with the hospitalized infant(s).

- Provide an overnight nanny. If friends and family can contribute toward the cost of a nanny for the first three months, it will give mom and dad a chance to enjoy their babies during the day while more rested.

- "Borrow" a baby for the night. One mother of infant triplets could cope with two at night, but not three. Each weekend, her mom and dad took a different baby home for one or two nights.

- Invite an older sibling or siblings over to your home for a play date when the babies are napping can provide the parent with a bit of a break and is a special treat for the older children.

- Expectant and new mothers of multiples can quickly become isolated in their homes and often crave the opportunity to talk with another adult. Home visits, telephone calls or e-mails help reduce loneliness and can build confidence.

- The cuddly part: help with baby care, feeding, and consoling babies is appreciated, and especially if a mother is breastfeeding, is

tip

Mary MacCafferty

One of our neighbours decided that her gift to the babies would be to prepare their formula for the first three months or until we no longer needed to sterilize bottles. My neighbour kept the sterilizers at her house with a double supply of bottles. Her husband would collect the bottles and deliver them back to us the next evening in exchange for the second box of empties.

ill, or if one or more of the babies has higher care needs.

• Simple outings require an effort which can seem equivalent to preparing for a weeklong camping trip. An extra set of hands is welcome when a mother (or father) needs to get the babies to a physician's appointment or wants to take the babies along to a multiples' or breastfeeding support group or to the local mall.

• Emergency care: arrange for someone to be available on short notice to care for babies or older siblings in the event of an unscheduled doctor's office or emergency room visit.

• Photographs and correspondence. Put together photo albums and keep them updated, hire a professional photographer who will come to the family home to take a family portrait, assist with thank-you cards and Christmas/holiday cards, and ensure that family and friends are getting updated pictures of the children.

• Go through donated clothing on a regular basis to see what is usable, sort it into sizes and remind the parents that there is a whole bag of clothes ready for the next stage.

• Fund-raising ideas: after the first year, the family will have stacks of baby clothes and equipment. Assist in the preparation of clothing and equipment for a garage sale. Organize a family or neighbourhood fund-raising party — a street party to raise money for the larger items (stroller, car seats, a van) is lots of fun and a great way to encourage community awareness and support.

• Please remember, if you are ill with a cold or flu, it is easier for the parents to care for their children on their own for a few days than to care for two, three or more children who are sick for many weeks. Please call the family and tell them you will return when you are well.

• Remember to take time to care for yourself if you are providing sustained support to a parent of multiples.

When people can no longer help

Mothers and fathers with multiples regard their helpers as lifelines and may feel that they are being abandoned when assistance is withdrawn. Parents note that support from people tends to wane after a few months. This can happen because the parents seem to be coping well and the helpers believe that the parents no longer need the support, the novelty of multiple babies wears off, the helpers' energy levels drop, or the demands of helpers' lives take precedence. If you are unable or do not want to help any longer, try to give advance warning to the mom and dad so that they have time to adjust or arrange alternate plans if help is still needed.

The generosity of family, friends, neighbours and others has a profound impact on multiple birth parents and their children.

5

the big moment

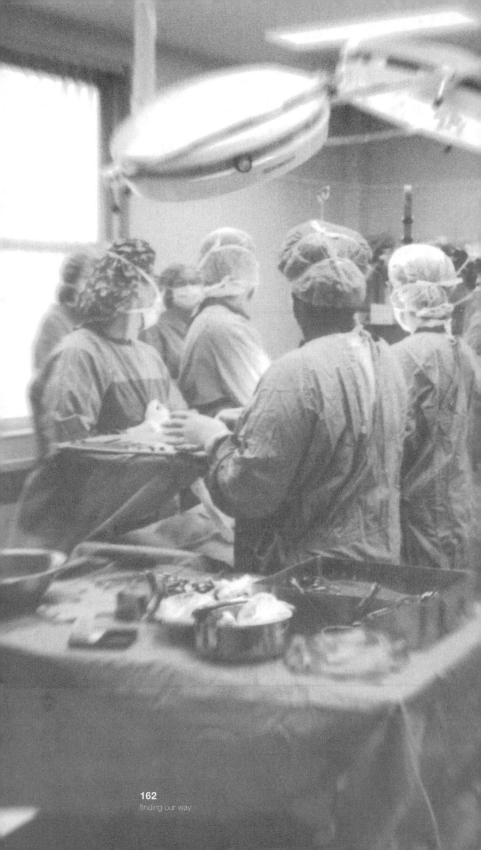

the hospital experience

Jeanette Niebler

From admission to delivery to recovery, what every parent of multiples can expect at the hospital

Packing

Aside from the many typical items most pregnant mothers take to the hospital, here are a few ideas about what you may find especially useful:

- Your phone list (you'll be surprised by the numbers you'll forget) and your calling card, which is a less expensive alternative to charging the calls to your room.
- A laptop/palm pilot for sending e-mails.
- A calendar so that any visitors who offer to help once you are home with the babies can write down their names for certain dates right away.
- Makeup, curling iron, other toiletries. You may not want them, but they're nice to have in case you do.
- Ear plugs or a portable radio to drown out the hospital noises. If you are wear-

ing ear plugs, be sure to let the nurses know in case they try to wake you up and panic because you don't hear and respond to them.

- Lipstick or moisturizer as well as some type of throat drops or suckers — hospital air is very dry.
- Robe, slippers, nursing nightgowns — they will be more comfortable than anything the hospital has for you.
- High-cut underwear that will fit over your incision with room to spare! Men's boxer shorts work very well.
- Your own sanitary pads. The hospital will provide you with some, but if you will be more comfortable with your own brand, take them. Tampons should not be used.
- Pillows, an egg-crate mattress, or a large duvet that you can throw over the hospital bed can all help you feel more comfortable.
- Planning on pumping or breastfeeding? If you have long hair, take something to tie your hair back.
- Nursing bras and pads, and a nursing pillow if you have one.

For the birth
- A video camera to tape the birth (and the babies while they are in the hospital). It's a good idea to discuss the possibility of videotaping the birth with your doctor prior to the delivery. You don't have to tape all of the actual birth sequence unless you wish, but it does give you the option of seeing what actually happened later on.
- Your own music to play during the delivery. (Check with the doctor first.)
- A Polaroid or digital camera. If you're not able to see your babies right after they're born, ask your husband or family members to take lots of pictures of the children in the Neonatal Intensive Care Unit (NICU).

If babies remain in the NICU
- A disposable camera for each baby if they need to stay in the hospital for a period of time. Write their names on the cameras and leave them by the isolettes. That way, you or the medical staff can take photos and you'll always know which baby is in the picture. As you're taking pictures, consider positioning an object beside the babies for perspective that shows their size. (Hands work well.) The time will fly quickly and you'll soon forget just how

little they were.

- If your babies are going to be in the NICU for a long period of time, tape recorders for their isolettes are a good idea. Tape soothing music or the voices of mom, dad or other family members to play for the babies. You will have to check whether the hospital allows tape recorders, since they sometimes affect the functioning of hospital equipment. Cell phones are usually not permitted in the NICU because they can interfere with the equipment.
- A small, safe toy (something soft and colourful that makes soothing sounds) to place inside each isolette. Medical staff will need to ensure the toy is safe.

What will happen during the cesarean delivery?

If you have any fears or concerns, tell your anesthesiologist or your nurse so that they will know how to help you. Nothing that you say is going to sound ridiculous since they've been through many, many deliveries.

Here are the steps you can expect leading up to the birth of your babies:

- An intravenous will be started in your arm prior to surgery to provide you and the babies with lots of fluid.
- If an epidural or a spinal anesthetic is scheduled, a nurse will help you to remain motionless during the procedure. This is a good time to use relaxation-breathing techniques.
- Receiving an epidural or spinal may be slightly to moderately uncomfortable. A few women have found the epidural painful, but it is the only way the doctor can perform the cesarean without putting you completely under anesthetic. To minimize any discomfort or pain, an area of your lower back is injected with a small amount of local anesthetic. You may feel a slight burning sensation with the injection. An epidural needle will then be inserted into the numbed area. At this point, most women report a feeling of pressure on their lower backs. Be sure to report if you feel other sensations, such as pain or strong tingling sensations in your hips or legs. Once the epidural is inserted, a small soft catheter is inserted through the epidural needle and the needle is removed. The catheter is taped to your back, and you should then

tip

My daughter's SAT [oxygen saturation level] improved noticeably when very low volume music was playing. She also loved to hear stories with a heavy rhythm or pattern. I taped my voice reading some books and asked the nurses to play the tapes when we weren't there. A tape recorder is necessary for each isolette because there is a risk of spreading bacteria if the tape recorders are shared

be able to lie comfortably on your back. When the anesthetic is injected through the catheter, you may feel a cold sensation down your back. Let your nurse or anesthesiologist know how you are feeling during the procedure.

• Once the epidural takes effect, your blood pressure may drop somewhat, which can make you feel light-headed or nauseated. The fall in blood pressure is rarely serious and can be easily treated by the anesthesiologist. Again, let your anesthesiologist or nurse know exactly how you are feeling.

• The hospital staff will have warm blankets to cover you if you shake or feel cold after the epidural.

• An anesthesiologist will stand by your head with your partner/support person and possibly a delivery nurse. You will be monitored carefully and will never be alone. All of these people can answer questions for you. Let the anesthesiologist or nurse know if you feel claustrophobic, since it may be possible to move the curtain between your head and body further away from your face.

• You may be able watch the surgery using mirrors if you wish.

• The tugging and pulling during the cesarean delivery may feel rather odd, but you will not feel pain. You will be completely numb from your breasts to your toes. If not, tell the anesthesiologist.

• The actual birth will only take a short time (usually no more than five minutes). Sewing the uterus and closing will take about 45 minutes. If you can arrange it, have a support person there to talk to you during this time.

• You may be extremely emotional, or you may even fall asleep. Both reactions are completely normal.

• Let your obstetrical team know if you and your partner would like to see each baby after each has been delivered. You can usually get a quick glimpse of each of them before the neonatologists or pediatricians assess them. If your babies are healthy and breathing well, you and your partner will likely have an opportunity to spend some time with your babies as the surgical team completes the surgery.

What to expect in the recovery room

• Most mothers experience shaking to some degree from the epidural anesthetic. Don't be alarmed. Although it can be frightening not to have control over your body, it will go away fairly quickly. The cause of shaking is unknown. However, this side effect can be treated with a medication administered by the anesthesiologist.

• You will probably be wrapped in warmed blankets to help you feel more comfortable.

• Expect to be given a sponge bath to wash off any blood from the surgery. Tell the nurse if you are feeling hot or cold so that you can be treated accordingly.

• Expect to spend at least an hour in the recovery room before being taken to your room. Your partner will be allowed to remain with you. Your doctor may recommend that you wait until the next day before going into the nursery. Your partner can visit the NICU or you can always phone the NICU to check in on your babies. Not to worry; if there are concerns with the babies, the doctors will let you know. For now you need to sleep.

• A partner or a support person in your room can help to get whatever you need and can talk to the nurse or doctor on your behalf if you wish. If you are experiencing pain, do not be afraid to ask for and accept pain medications. You will be able to move better and recover faster.

• If your mouth is dry, ask for some ice chips. Usually, you need to wait a couple of hours before you are given the okay for drinking fluids.

How can you best manage pain and discomfort?

• It is important that your pain is under control so that you can move, visit your babies, and feed and care for them. Pain medication works best if taken on a regular basis and will not usually harm the babies through the breastmilk. But it's best to verify the safety of medication with your doctor prior to beginning breastfeeding.

• Ask the obstetrician about applying TENS electrodes adjacent to the cesarean incision immediately after the repair is complete. TENS is a modality used frequently by physiotherapists for other types of pain.

• A sanitary pad placed horizontally over your incision will prevent your underwear from rubbing against it.

• Ask the physiotherapist to measure and fit you for TED stockings, which are worn early in the morning within a few days postpartum to decrease painful swelling of the legs and feet (edema) that can result from fluid accumulation during the pregnancy. This facilitates the elimination of excess fluid via urination and results in the quick resolution of painful edema, which can be even more marked after the birth than during the pregnancy.

• Take care with how you move. Your abdominal muscles will be so weak at this point that you can overcompensate, strain your back muscles and end up with strains and pulled muscles. Don't be afraid to ask for assistance, especially with sitting up. One way to sit up without assistance is to lie in the fetal position on one side. Use your arms and pillows to slowly wedge yourself upright, and drop your legs over the side of the bed so that you are sitting side-wise on the bed. Practice sitting up while someone is with you so that when you are alone, you can manage on your own.

• Expect a lot of gas in your abdomen. Your abdomen may become bloated and move as if the babies were still inside you. You may have shoulder and neck pain from the gas. Walking around and rolling on the bed may help relieve some of the gas. Constipation after delivery may be a problem. To alleviate constipation, drink plenty of fluids, maintain a fibre-rich diet, walk as often as you can and use a prescribed stool softener (which will not affect the babies through the breastmilk) if necessary.

tip

Be cautious when you begin to walk. Your legs will be weak if you have spent time on bedrest

• Expect to remain on a mainly liquid diet for one or perhaps two days while your digestive system recovers. When you begin eating solids, you may feel odd. Cramps and flatulence are completely normal. Uterine after-pains or menstrual-like cramping, especially while you are breastfeeding, may be troublesome. Try relaxation breathing and ask for some pain medication if necessary.

• Oversized sweatsuits or loose-fitting clothes are more comfortable to wear than street clothing following surgery.

• Carry a small pillow with you in case you have to sneeze or cough. Holding the pillow over your incision as a brace will reduce the incision pain.

• Some mothers have used a tummy "belt" in the hospital. The belt is about eight inches wide and fastens together with Velcro. It is a great tool for supporting the abdominal muscles and preventing clothes from shifting and irritating the incision. Ask your nurse about obtaining one.

• If you are breastfeeding, ask for assistance from a lactation consultant or nurse on how best to position the babies for your own comfort as well as the babies' comfort.

Body changes

- Don't expect your stomach to flatten out right away. You will probably still look pregnant when you leave the hospital. Give yourself a
break — after all, you've just given birth to three, four or more babies!
- You can expect to bleed a lot (like a heavy menstrual period) as
you shed lochia, which is blood and mucous from the uterus. Ask
the nurses about it if you are concerned. Bleeding will last longer
than in a singleton pregnancy and a small amount of bleeding two
months after the delivery is not uncommon.
- After 24 hours, the catheter in your bladder will be removed. The
removal is painless. You may need to urinate frequently after the
birth and may even sweat more. This is your body eliminating a lot
of the extra fluid that you accumulated during the pregnancy.
Watch for and report burning on urination or feeling as if you have
the flu. Bladder infections after a cesarean are not uncommon.

Getting rest

- If too many visitors or telephone calls are becoming problematic,
try putting a note on your hospital door that says, "New mommy
sleeping. Do not disturb." Turn the ringer off your hospital telephone. Keep an update of your situation on your home answering machine, so that family and friends can find out how you are
and leave their warm wishes. Ask your partner or a friend to make
the necessary calls to family and friends. Tell everyone the best
times for visiting.

Spending time feeding and cuddling your babies

- If your babies are in the NICU, your most important task is to get
yourself healthy so that you can care for your children when they
come home. Eat and rest and listen to the nurses. If they tell you
to take a day off from visiting, seriously consider it. Soon, you will
be totally responsible for your children's care.
- Most parents of higher order multiple birth children find that a
feeding schedule rather than feeding on demand makes life at
home easier. Learn what your babies' schedule is in the hospital
and adopt it once the babies are at home. If you would like to
have your children eating all at the same time or at different intervals, discuss this with the nurses in order to work out a schedule

that can be easily followed at home after discharge.

Your emotions

- Be aware of the signs of the "baby blues" and postpartum depression (PPD). It's not uncommon for new mothers to experience some degree of depression or sadness. However, research seems to indicate that depression may be more common and extreme in mothers of triplets, quadruplets or quintuplets. You will have a lot of hormones floating around your body and these may lead to more intense emotions than singleton mothers can experience.
- Make sure that those around you, especially your partner, know the signs of postpartum depression because it usually requires medical attention. (Refer to Depression and Anxiety by Linda Leonard in Chapter 9 for details about postpartum depression.)

Going home

- Before going home, with or without your children, make sure you are in touch with other parents of triplets or more and ensure that the ongoing hospital and community supports have been established.
- If you are breastfeeding and pumping, try to arrange for the delivery of an effective breastpump (prior to delivery, talk to a lactation consultant and other parents of multiples about recommended breastpumps).
- If you are going to be using formula, check with your neonatologist about recommended formula and ask a family member or friend to arrange for its delivery.
- You should not drive for a few weeks after surgery because your ability to react may be compromised by the anesthetic, previous bedrest (there may be some muscle atrophy), and fatigue. Arrange rides for hospital/doctor's appointments.
- Once you get home, you may find it easier to sleep on the couch until you are able to move with less effort. Couches may be easier to get in and out of since they tend to be lower than beds.
- If you have a pet that likes to join you in bed, you might consider locking it out of the bedroom for awhile. The last thing you need is Rover or Kitty jumping on your stomach in the middle of the night.

> ## quote
>
> I had overwhelming feelings that I wasn't equipped to mother three babies, that I had to be crazy having my mom stay with me, that God had somehow mistaken us for a couple that could handle this ... I wasn't really incompetent — I was just hormonal. This feeling cleared about 10 days after they were born, which was, coincidentally, the day they came home from the hospital.

Acknowledgements to Lynda P. Haddon, Linda Leonard,
Dr. Elizabeth Bryan and Diane Myers

unexpected delivery
Monika Buzanis

What do you mean I am in labour and fully dilated?

I assumed that since my triplet pregnancy was progressing so well, I would be able to carry the babies longer than the 34-week average. But at 27 weeks, I found myself bleeding one morning and was soon admitted to the hospital with a ruptured amniotic membrane. How did it happen? I will never know.

Each day in the hospital, the bleeding continued slowly and I started having mild contractions. So these were the infamous Braxton-Hicks that everyone talked about. As the days wore on, the contractions grew stronger and more intense, and my husband and I became increasingly worried and scared.

By the third night, the contractions were so painful that I couldn't sleep. Just as I would doze off, another contraction would hit. After a long, restless night, the contractions eased a little during the next day and I managed to sleep for a few hours.

I spent much of the fourth night awake, with contractions every 15 to 20 minutes. After an early morning internal examination, I was given a shot of morphine to help ease the pain. Although I had been very reluctant to take any drugs throughout my pregnancy, I was quite willing to compromise in this case. Aaahhh ... no pain ... mmmm, sleep.

Doctor described the contractions as "not that intense"

On the fifth night, the contractions started again, this time in 10- to 15-minute waves. To ward off another sleepless night, I was given a sleeping pill at 11 p.m., which helped. An hour later though, I was awake again. Blast those contractions! The nurses described them as an annoyance, but I was beginning to feel frustrated with their intensity and regularity (about 5 to 10 minutes apart). After three hours of watching television in a fruitless effort to take my mind off the pain, I finally telephoned the nurse and complained that I still couldn't sleep. They checked the three fetal heartbeats and confirmed the babies were fine. The doctor on call came in to assess the contractions and described them as "not that intense." He decided against another internal and recommended a shot of morphine if I was having trouble sleeping.

But on this night, things were different. The morphine didn't take the pain away as it had the night before. In fact, the contractions kept getting stronger. I had to concentrate on deep breathing — on not screaming — and on counting through the contractions to try and find some relief. I had no idea that the contractions were about two minutes apart at this point because in between the contractions, I would almost drift into sleep, which was induced by the morphine shot.

After an hour of contractions that were "not that intense," I was at my wit's end. I telephoned the nurse again. The doctor came in — again. The fetal heartbeats were checked — again. An internal was done — again. Suddenly, all was quiet. Then the doctor instructed the nurse to move me to the case room immediately.

"You are fully dilated and I just saw the head."

"Wait a second! Is this it?" I exclaimed.

"Yes!" the doctor said. "The baby has lots of hair."

"Wait! Let me phone my husband!"

The whole time I was in active labour and didn't realize it. My experience was not typical, since cesarean section is the standard procedure for delivering triplets. It's believed that the risks associated with very preterm vaginal deliveries, especially those that are breech, outweigh the benefits. Since we believed from the very beginning that I would have a c-section, we never attended prenatal classes that covered labour and delivery. And since I had never experienced labour, I didn't realize that this was the real thing.

With me, a c-section was not possible because our son Nolan was so far down. Doctors and nurses scrambled to prepare the case room while urging me not to push. I was given an epidural in case the other two babies had to be delivered surgically. Nolan was then delivered vaginally. With the two remaining babies' heartbeats showing no signs of distress, the doctors decided that a vaginal delivery would be the best. Nolan was the biggest of the three (a bruiser at 2 lb. 6 oz.) and he eased out rather nicely. The doctor was able to deliver our other son Jeremy (1 lb. 13 oz.) two minutes later, and our daughter Emily (1 lb. 15 oz.) three minutes after Jeremy — both feet first.

Given the small size of the babies and because I experienced no delivery complications, the vaginal birth actually turned out to be better for the babies and for me. The physical trauma of the delivery was so modest that later the same evening, my husband and I attended a session at the hospital on premature babies. We were the last couple to introduce ourselves and the introduction caused a few jaws to drop. "Hello, my name is Monika and this is my husband Mike. We had triplets, two boys and a girl — this morning at 6 a.m."

We understand that the contractions and movement through the birth canal were beneficial for helping to squeeze fluid out of the babies' lungs. Overall, the doctors felt that the vaginal delivery was better for our premature babies' lungs.

On the other hand, we were extremely fortunate that the babies did not suffer any injuries given their tiny size, soft heads and breech deliveries.

wrong place at the wrong time
Denise Mori

Delivering triplets in a small community hospital away from home wasn't my plan

I was 28 weeks pregnant when my mother and I hopped into a car to visit my sister, who lived in a small community in Ontario. I had just stopped working that week. But with the exception of some recent swelling and insomnia, I had felt great through my entire pregnancy. Prior to taking the two-hour trip, I consulted my doctor about the risks of going into labour. He was sure I was five or six weeks away from delivering. "Have a good time," he said, "and be sure to stop and have a bite to eat if you feel tired at some point during the trip."

Off we went. On the second day after arriving at my sister's house, contractions started at 4 a.m. My sister called the nearest hospital, which was half an hour away and told them to expect a mom who was about to deliver triplets. Fortunately, our call came in the midst of a shift change and personnel from both shifts stayed that early morning waiting for our arrival.

In spite of the extra hands, I remember all the effort that went into getting us transferred out of this community hospital and into a facility with a Neonatal Intensive Care Unit (NICU) that was equipped to care for very premature babies. While the numbers of medical staff were adequate, they didn't have a whole lot of experience or equipment among them. The doctors frantically called hospitals from Kingston to Niagara Falls to no avail. One hospital in Ottawa could accommodate the babies, but could not deliver them. Just as the medical personnel didn't want me to deliver the babies at this hospital, I was just as anxious to leave. Being in a small community hospital wasn't the plan. I was supposed to be in a larger hospital with close access to an NICU if necessary. And it was clear that we would in fact need this level of care.

In the meantime, my husband, Dave, was barreling along the highway from our home two hours away and got caught by photo radar going 123 kilometres an hour. (Incidentally, he managed to talk himself out of a ticket considering the circumstances.)

Finally, delivery became inevitable. Derek was born first weighing 2 lb. 13 oz.; then Amanda at 2 lb. 11 oz.; and Jason at 3 lb. The delivery went well. Immediately after they were born, the babies were dressed and flown by helicopter to a Level 3 hospital in Ottawa. They were on respirators and feeding tubes. Heavily drugged, I remember peering at them through the incubators before they left. I waited another four days in the hospital recovering from surgery — my bladder had been nicked during the c-section — before I saw my babies again. Dave and I drove to Ottawa. When we arrived in the NICU, it was like I was seeing the babies for the first time. I had seen premature infants on a tour of a nursery before, but I had never seen babies that little. It took my breath away, their little chests were pumping so hard, they were so small, so thin, so fragile-looking and hooked up to so many wires and machines. I was scared for them and wondered if they would survive.

Within one week, the babies were stable and flown to another Level 3 hospital nearer our home. Soon they moved again by ambulance to a Level 2 hospital just a half hour away. Week by week, they looked bigger and stronger. After the early weeks, my husband and I recovered from the shock of seeing them as small, fragile infants and began to see them simply as our babies, and ourselves as their parents.

finding room for everyone
Jeanette Niebler

Until the 11th hour, not a single hospital could accommodate us together

After I found out at 15 weeks that I was pregnant with triplets, my medical care went into high gear. I was immediately referred to a high risk obstetrician who had experience delivering triplets. With frequent cramping and nausea, I was confined, for the most part, to the house for the duration of my pregnancy.

I went into labour at 28 weeks. This was the fourth time I had been in the labour and delivery ward at the hospital to have contractions monitored. I knew how important it was to be monitored whenever I felt contractions, or even in those times when I felt like something was different. I also knew that it is not uncommon for pregnant moms to be unable to feel contractions, since the uterus becomes so large and active with three or more babies.

As was the pattern with me, I was having five or six contractions an hour on this particular day. This time, when the contractions didn't slow down, the doctor did an internal exam and found that I was dilated by two centimetres. Since our local hospital was not equipped to care for three babies born at 28 weeks, I was sent to a hospital in downtown Toronto.

As soon as I arrived, I was given the first of a series of steroid shots to help mature the babies' lungs. The doctors were very positive, telling me that the babies had an excellent chance of survival if they were born then. They gave me a shot of morphine to relax me. My contractions gradually stopped, and I remained in hospital on strict bedrest for the next week.

After a week in the hospital and much begging and pleading on my part, I was released with strict instructions to stay off my feet, and to go to the hospital immediately if I felt even a twinge. I had two wonderful days at home before I began contracting again. This time, I was sent to a hospital in Hamilton.

When I was admitted there on a Sunday evening, the contractions were uncomfortable, but not painful. The next series of steroid

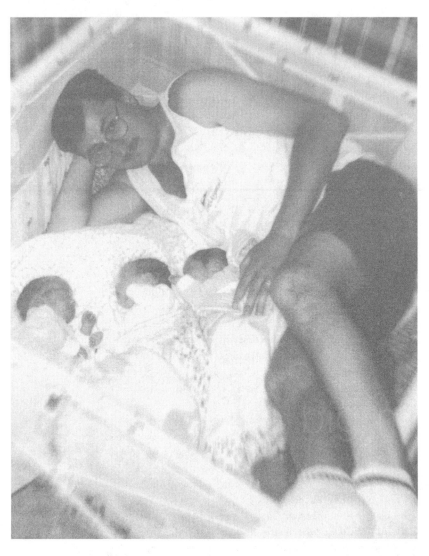

shots were injected for the babies' lungs and I remained in hospital under observation. After waking the next morning, I was still having mild contractions, but not enough to create a stir. The next internal exam was about 2 p.m., when they found I was seven centimetres dilated, and Rachel's head was moving down quickly.

Arrangements were made to take me by air to another hospital two hours away

The NICU was short of ventilators so arrangements were made to take me by air to another hospital about two hours away. The transfer soon became impractical because it was believed that I would probably end up delivering in the air. Arrangements were made then to transport the babies to different hospitals because no one facility could accommodate all of us at once. At one point, it looked as though I would be in Hamilton, with a baby in London, one in Toronto and the third in Ottawa. Fortunately at the 11th hour, they managed to clear enough beds in the NICU so we could stay together.

At about 7 p.m. that night, the doctors decided to deliver the babies by c-section. Rachel's head was poking through my cervix even though my water hadn't broken. I was very lucky that my husband, Chris, and my mother were allowed to come into the operating room with me. We also had three doctors and two nurses handling the delivery, a student anesthesiologist and her supervisor, two nurses and one doctor per baby, and assorted other hangers-on, including a class of medical students watching from the gallery.

The delivery itself was fairly easy — I was awake but feeling rather nauseous, so I didn't pay that much attention to what was going on around me. Rachel Erin was born at 2 lb. 15 oz., Kirsten Margaret was born at 2 lb. 13 oz. and Dylan Charles was born at 3 lb. 4 oz. Dylan had thoughtfully wedged himself under my rib cage and was lying in such a way that the doctor didn't have anything except his slippery back to grab on to. After rearranging my internal organs a bit, the doctor was able to get him out, and Dylan entered the world kicking and screaming.

Neither of the girls could breathe room air at first, so I was not able to see them in the operating room. One of the nurses brought Dylan to me so that I could see him before they whisked him away to be assessed. Within 24 hours, all of the babies were breathing room air and we began to experience life in the NICU.

step by step
Linda Kawamoto

Preparing and recovering from a c-section

A few days before my babies were delivered, I went to the hospital for a question-and-answer session with the anesthesiologist and to have some blood work done. I prepared quite a list of questions since it seemed like detailed information wasn't always offered until I asked.

Finally the big day arrived. I had survived just over 34 weeks of pregnancy — the last three months of which were spent mostly lying down. By that point, I was experiencing fainting spells and had some difficulty breathing and moving around. I was admitted to the hospital at 7 a.m. Once I was on the ward and wearing a hospital gown, my temperature, blood pressure, pulse and breathing were checked. The nurse started an IV and I waited to be wheeled down to surgery. While I waited, three medical students asked permission to observe. I agreed, but the nurse in charge refused, saying the room would be too crowded and that only senior students were allowed inside.

When it was time, my husband put on his surgical gown and met me inside the operating room. My IV arm was tied at a 90-degree angle to my body to allow drugs to be administered as necessary during the surgery. But I wish I had asked for a more relaxed position of, say, 45 degrees, because my shoulders hurt later. The pain may have been caused by the unnatural position of my arm for a prolonged period, or perhaps it was due to the drugs that were administered.

The babies' grandparents were happy to be able to share in the joyous occasion from the viewing room, where they could see the birth. A nurse stayed with them during the entire procedure and stipulated that any complications would mean the viewing area would have to be closed off.

A large green sheet was draped in front of me so that neither the family nor I could see the actual surgery. However, we were all able to see the babies as soon as they came out. Matthew (4 lb. 10 oz.), Jessica (4 lb. 1 oz.), and Ellen (4 lb. 5 oz.), were delivered to the waiting arms of three nurses who immediately examined their assigned patient. Tom, my husband, videotaped the babies as they entered the world. I enjoyed watching this later, since the whole experience happened so quickly.

I didn't see the babies again until that evening when my brother took me over to the Neonatal Intensive Care Unit (NICU) in a wheelchair. Coming back to the room, I felt very sick. I was cautious about taking painkillers with codeine since they can cause constipation and vomiting.

I was also warned that there might be a lot of gas afterward and to move as soon as possible. With this advice in mind, I tried to walk, but my shoulders ached and my feet started to swell. I was glad to have slippers that stretched to wear at the hospital since I wasn't able to fit back into my shoes right away.

After three days, NICU beds were in demand and our babies were transferred to another hospital, where they stayed for two and a half weeks to establish feeding. I pushed to be discharged that day as well so that I could be at home with my five-year-old Stephanie, and Tom, and see the babies at the other hospital.

Before being discharged, my incision had to be checked and the staples removed. Ouch! (You may want to have someone shave the area where the incision will be made prior to the surgery; otherwise, hairs as well as staples will be removed.) Unfortunately, just as the staples were being removed, there was a power failure and only emergency lighting was available. It was difficult for the nurse to properly clean and dress the incision.

A week after Matthew, Jessica and Ellen were born, my feet were still swollen and the pain remained in the area of the incision. The public health nurse who visited us at home checked my incision and suggested that I see my doctor or go to a hospital emergency department to have it treated. The incision had become infected, and I went through the additional ordeal of cleaning it, changing the dressing and having antibiotics applied twice daily. Someone I knew who had stitches seemed to heal better than I did with staples. While everyone's situation may be different, I would recommend discussing the options with your doctor.

Once I was home, I gladly accepted all offers of help. I had to arrange to be driven back and forth to the hospital to see the babies since it was several weeks before I was physically capable of driving. Meal preparation, housework and care for my other child were other ways people helped. I learned not to be a martyr and accepted all offers of assistance willingly and gratefully!

becoming a mom
Veronica Lanz

Through a haze of tears and uncertainty

I was in hospital on bedrest, 33 weeks pregnant and patiently waiting for the day when my triplets would be born. One day around dinnertime, my doctor came into my room, confidently predicting that I would carry the babies for another two or three weeks. At 8:30 p.m. that night, my water broke. Evidently, the babies had other

plans. Baby A had flipped over toward my other hip, and broke his sac. I pulled the cord to call the nurse and sat on the toilet sobbing. I was terrified. I did not want them to come yet — I wasn't ready! I wanted more time!

The nurses said that the water breaking did not necessarily mean that the babies would be delivered and they encouraged me to stick to my normal routine, which included a 9 p.m. snack. My doctor arrived 15 minutes later and decided that he was going to deliver the babies, but since I had eaten, he said we

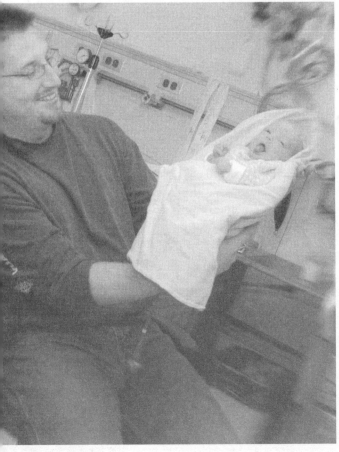

Courtesy of Mississauga News

would need to wait six hours. I phoned my husband and family — the big day had arrived.

Once my husband arrived, I moved to the high risk delivery room, and at about 11 p.m., started early labour. I was totally unprepared to deal with contractions. Since there was never any question that I would have a c-section, I knew nothing about labour and how to breathe. I took rapid, shallow breaths, which only worsened the pain. Two hours passed before someone enlightened me about breathing techniques.

At around 1 a.m., I was given a spinal to remove the pain completely. The only thing I can remember about the spinal was that it was a momentary pain that relieved a much bigger pain. The next two hours were relatively uneventful as we waited for six hours to pass so the c-section could begin.

Many people were present during the operation. Two doctors performed the surgery, my family doctor assisted, an anesthesiologist monitored me, a pediatrician and nurse stood by for each baby, a host of other nurses milled about, and my husband was there, of course. We occupied two operating rooms and created a lot of overtime for medical personnel at 3 a.m. on a Sunday.

As soon as the first baby was removed and I heard the words, "It's a boy," I started to cry and continued crying through the rest of the operation and in the recovery room afterwards. Giving birth to my son and two daughters was such an overwhelming experience. My tears expressed happiness as well as fear.

My recovery from the c-section was slow and painful, exacerbated by the many weeks of bedrest that preceded the birth. On the third day after the babies were born, I started to cry again, and basically cried for three days. I was walking hormones. About this time, I started to get night sweats and had to change clothing and bedding several times a night. The night sweats lasted for a few weeks, but it took a full six weeks after the birth to really feel like myself again.

The weeks that followed the birth were the most difficult in my life. All the joys, fears, uncertainties, sleeplessness and struggles blended into a continuum from which I emerged a mother. Thinking back, the c-section is just one of many memories of which there is hardly a scar.

quote

All the joys, fears, uncertainties, sleeplessness and struggles blended into a continuum from which I emerged a mother

grandparent power
Chris Picoulas

The day that our daughter Donna delivered her triplets, Grandmother Joan, who has been sort of a mother hen to her children, once again rose to the occasion, only this time, much higher.

Our home is 80 kilometres from the hospital where Donna was giving birth to the babies. We hopped into our "reliable" jalopy and took off. It's amazing how a little thing like triplets entering a new world can affect some people. For example, my wife, who has criticized me for driving too fast for the past 50 years, all of a sudden finds that I'm driving too slow! Too slow at 130 kilometres an hour!

Maybe the high speed was too much for the old car, but just as we came within a few kilometres of the hospital, it quit and sputtered to a stop right on the highway. My wife jumped out, without any idea of how she would get to the hospital or how much money she was carrying. Now my wife is not the hitchhiker type, nor is she a marathon runner, but fortunately, a taxi approached. She hailed it — yes, on the highway — and headed for the hospital, declaring, "This girl of mine cannot give birth to triplets without me being there!"

So what was I to do? Well, the car situation was resolved shortly, thanks to a tow truck. I then arrived at the hospital in time to see my three precious granddaughters lying peacefully in their incubators. It is without prejudice, of course, that I say I found them to be indescribably beautiful. And they still are today.

the first year

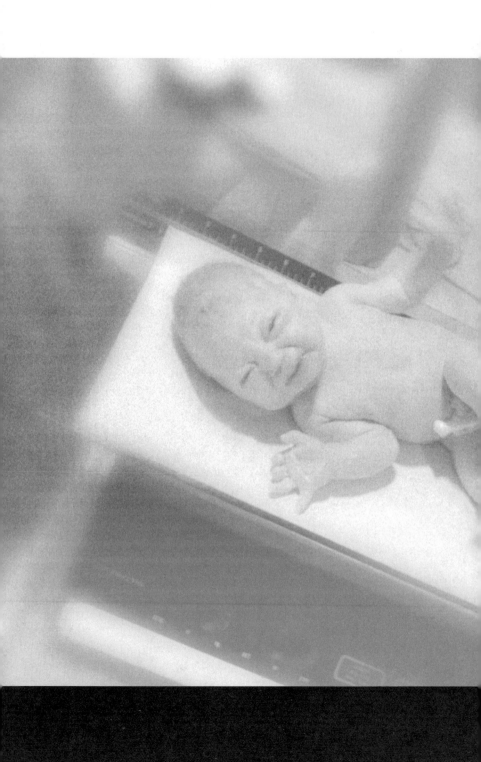

6

fragile lives -prematurity

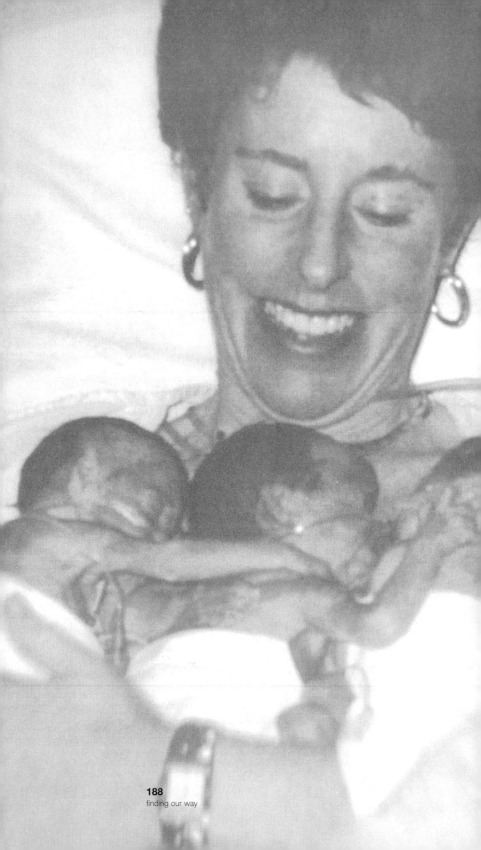

sights and sounds of the NICU

Diane Myers

Since your babies may be born early, it's highly possible that you and your children will begin life together inside a Neonatal Intensive Care Unit (NICU). Also known as a Level 3 facility, the NICU is designed for infants whose survival depends on having immediate access to the most intensive and highest level of specialized neonatal care.

Some families spend weeks, even months in these facilities, while others may be there for a period of hours. Many families bypass the NICU altogether and move straight to Level 2 care. Very premature infants (those delivered earlier than 32 weeks) require admission to an NICU. Since there is no way of knowing for certain what the needs and condition of your babies will be until they are born, it is helpful to have some sense of what to expect in the NICU, who works there and what equipment you will encounter.

Many families, typically after they reach the 23rd or 24th week of pregnancy, tour an NICU with a social worker, doctor or nurse. Tours are casual and flexible so that they address your specific needs and concerns. On our tour, my husband John and I started by washing our hands and putting on hospital gowns over our clothes. Strong emphasis is always placed on handwashing for everyone entering an NICU. We later found out that it is also wise to wash your hands between babies. If one of your children is sick (you may not know it yet) you can easily pass it along to the other children. Washing your hands and changing your gowns can prevent some of the transfer of viruses and bacteria.

Neither John nor I had ever seen a premature baby before. Although I was nervous, I was also very interested to see what was behind the curtains of the NICU. Throughout the tour the nurse seemed to be the one asking all the questions to get a sense of what we already knew. She showed us a child that had been born a few weeks earlier at 25 weeks gestation. The tiny baby, she said, was doing very well. He was attached to all kinds of monitors and wires. The nurse carefully explained the purpose of the wires and monitors, but I didn't remember a thing she told me. The message that I heard was that this baby, born so small and early, was doing well.

To mimic the uterine environment as much as possible, the NICU is designed to be dark and quiet for the babies. The nurses will try to cluster necessary treatments and tests to allow the babies to sleep. There will be babies lying inside plastic isolettes or incubators where the temperature is regulated. Some will be bundled and kept in the fetal position for muscle development, while others inside the isolettes may only be wearing diapers and hats to maintain body temperature. On occasion, a child will be taken to a different part of the hospital in his or her isolette for special tests or treatments that cannot be performed in the unit.

The practice of cobedding (placing two or sometimes three) infants in the same isolette has been known to help stabilize the babies' breathing and heart rate. Some NICUs are reluctant to cobed infants citing a risk of cross-contamination among the babies. Since there have been no studies on cobedding, the risks and benefits are anecdotal at this point.

Some isolettes will have stuffed animals on top and pictures all around. Items placed inside the isolette may be in plastic bags if they cannot be washed. You may see moms and dads sitting in front of the isolettes with their hands on their child's body or holding their baby's tiny hand through the portholes in the side. Other parents will be talking or singing quietly to their baby, or feeding drops of breastmilk through tubes that run through their baby's nose or mouth to the stomach. Some moms will be in rocking chairs holding their child(ren) and breastfeeding or bottlefeeding. Many NICUs now practice kangaroo care, so you will see parents holding children skin to skin on their chests.

Some NICUs cannot provide privacy for families while visiting their children, while others do have the capacity. There may be siblings of all ages visiting their new brothers and/or sisters. All the while there are nurses and doctors caring and watching out for each newborn. Monitors will be beeping and buzzing as nurses rush over to see if the baby is having some difficulties or if the connecting lead has just shifted from its proper position. There is constant movement, all of it directed toward giving your children a chance to grow, heal and be comforted.

The NICU and transitional care units

For the most part, your babies' medical and parental care will take place inside the NICU until they are ready to graduate to a transitional care unit (TCN). While they are still considered part of the NICU, TCNs (also called Care-by-Parent Units), care for babies who are no longer critical. Because they are an extension of the NICU, TCNs differ from Level 2 nurseries, which care for babies who have grown and progressed even further.

The bells and whistles

Various monitors help the medical team track and evaluate a baby's body temperature, oxygen levels, heart and breathing rates. These are the main indicators of your child's present condition and progress.

Incubators have automatic monitoring systems to regulate the internal temperature of the incubator so that it remains between 32C and 37C degrees. If the child's temperature rises or falls, the environment inside the incubator will either adjust automatically, or an alarm will sound.

There are several other events that might cause an alarm to sound:
- An interruption in breathing (apnea).
- A respiration rate that has dipped below or exceeded the average range for the gestational age and health of the baby.
- A heart rate that has fallen below 100 beats per minute (brady) or gone above 200 beats per minute (average or acceptable range for a preemie is between 110 and 160 beats per minute).
- Leads have disconnected.

Common terms and abbreviations

This list is intended as an introductory reference, but it is not complete. There are a number of very good books that will explain the terms and equipment in more detail. Always remember to ask and ask again if you have not understood what you are being told.

For breathing

APNEA - A pause in breathing. Since premature babies have immature respiratory centres in the brain, sometimes they forget to breathe. The baby may need physical stimulation (a tickled foot), medication, CPAP (see below), or the baby may resume breathing without any intervention at all. Apnea episodes will subside as the baby matures, usually between 35 and 40 weeks.

ETT - Endotrachial tube, a long breathing tube that goes down the trachea (windpipe) and to the lungs, but not into the lungs.

NPT - Nasopharyngeal tube, a short soft single breathing tube inserted toward the back of the nose.

ALLADIN - Short double breathing prongs that are placed just inside the nostrils and secured by ties and a hat.

CPAP - Continuous positive airway pressure, which can be delivered by an NPT or ALLADIN.

LF - Low flow, a tiny double prong which rests just inside the nostrils and delivers oxygen or a combination of oxygen and air.

O_2 - Oxygen, which is described as a percentage when the baby is on a ventilator (ETT, NPT or ALLADIN) and as cc/min or ml/min when the child has progressed to low flow.

O_2SAT - Oxygen saturation measures the percentage of hemoglobin saturated with oxygen. This indicates how well the hemoglobin is carrying oxygen to the tissues. Normal oxygen saturation is between 88 and 92 per cent. This will vary depending on the infant's gestational age, condition, etc. It is used to determine whether the oxygen should be increased or decreased and delivered by another method. O_2Sat levels are obtained by a light-censored probe attached to the baby's toe or finger. This sensor does not cause any discomfort to the baby, and the light does not generate any heat.

For the heart rate

BRADY - Bradycardia occurs when the heart rate drops below 100 beats per minute and the baby requires stimulation (physically or with medication) to boost the heart rate.

DIP - Describes a situation where the heart rate drops briefly below 100 and recovers a rate above 100 without stimulation.

BP - Blood pressure, which can be taken with a small blood pressure arm cuff or internally via the UAC. (See below.)

For medication and fluids

IV - Intravenous, which can be in the hands, feet, arms, legs or on the scalp.

LONG LINE - An intravenous line inserted into a large vein, which can be left in place for an extended time period. It is also referred to as a PICC line – for peripherally inserted central catheter.

UAC - Umbilical arterial catheter, a line that goes into the artery in the bellybutton, through which blood can be taken, and fluids and medication administered.

UVC - Umbilical venous catheter, a line that goes into the vein located in the bellybutton from which blood can also be taken.

For feeding

TPN - Total parenteral nutrition, an IV solution, typically yellow in colour, that supplies the baby with vitamins and minerals until feeding is fully established.

LIPIDS - The white IV solution that supplies fat to the baby until full feeds are established.

NGT - Nasal gastric tube, a feeding tube that goes down the nose and esophagus and into the stomach.

OGT - Oral gastric tube, a feeding tube that goes down the mouth and esophagus and into the stomach.

NPO - Nil per os, means nothing by mouth; the baby is not being fed orally.

EBM - Expressed breastmilk (pumped).

FORT - Human milk fortifier, a powder supplement used in breast-milk to add extra minerals, proteins and vitamins.

ML - Micro-lipids, a fat supplement added to breastmilk and formula.

q2h (Q2H) - q means "every" h means "hour" - q2h means every two hours, q4h means every four hours. Feedings and medications are given on this type of schedule.

Tip - A glycerin tip suppository is used to help the baby have a bowel movement.

CBC - Complete blood count that includes: **HGB** - Hemoglobin, which may detect anemia **WBC** - White blood cell count, which may help determine if the baby has an infection. **DIFF** - Differential count, used to determine the number and variety of different white blood cells and may further indicate infection.

C&S - A culture and sensitivity is taken to determine if an infection is present. The sensitivity indicates which antibiotics the infections will respond to best. The C&S can be performed on different body fluids or parts such as blood, mucous, spinal fluid, any discharge, or a skin rash.

MBR - Micro-bilirubin, measures the bilirubin or jaundice level in the baby's blood. Jaundice is a common condition in premature babies, characterized by yellow or orange skin.

'LYTES - Electrolytes measure sodium, potassium and chloride in the baby's blood. The results may determine the type of IV solution or medication the baby receives.

PHOTOTHERAPY - A form of light treatment used to treat babies with jaundice.

GAS, ART STAB, CAP GAS, BLOOD GAS - A blood sample taken from an artery using the UAC or the artery in the wrist or ankle. Results of the cap gas (capillary sample taken from the heel) help determine the respiratory and metabolic status of the baby.

Some conditions seen in premature infants

Abbreviations are often used in the NICU to describe conditions seen in some premature infants. Here are the few of those abbreviations and the full terms. Please use this as a starting point for inquiry with the doctor and for your own research.

ROP - Retinopathy of prematurity

IVH - Intraventricular hemorrhage

PVL - Periventricular leukomalacia

PDA - Patent ductous arteriosis (heart murmur)

NEC - Necrotising enterocolitis

BPD - Bronchopulmonary dysplasia or chronic lung
or lung changes

CLD - Chronic lung disease

RDS - Respiratory distress syndrome

RSV - Respiratory syncytial virus

Medical personnel in the NICU and TCN

Neonatologist
A pediatrician with specialized training in newborn intensive care.

Neonatal Fellow
A pediatrician in special training in newborn intensive care, a future neonatologist.

Resident
A doctor in pediatric training.

Clinical Nurse Specialist/ Neonatal Nurse Practitioner
An advanced practice neonatal nurse who has extensive, specialized training in the medical care of NICU babies.

Registered Nurse
The person (people) who you will have the most contact with during your babies' stay in the NICU. Your babies will likely be assigned to a primary nurse who will most frequently take care of your babies. He or she will develop a nursing care plan and teach you to care for your babies. You might have a primary care nurse for each child.

Primary Charge Nurse/Team Leader
A nurse with extensive experience in the NICU who coordinates all NICU activities to ensure the unit runs smoothly.

Social Worker
Your counsellor and contact for accessing community resources such as accommodations and home help, stress relief, and emotional support for you and your family during and after your babies' hospitalization.

Registered Respiratory Care Practitioner (Therapist)
A person with special training, which focuses on your babies'

breathing, respiratory system and the equipment used to assist and monitor breathing. He/she also obtains and interprets blood results used to assess and monitor your babies' respiratory status.

Pharmacy Services

Pharmacists work with the doctors to choose the best medication for your babies. The pharmacist can also provide parent education for those whose babies may be discharged home on medication.

Dietician

The person who specializes in the nutritional management of the infants in the NICU. This includes TPN (see above) as well as oral feeds your babies receive. He/she is also available to counsel about maternal nutritional needs and concerns.

Pediatric Occupational (OT) and Physical Therapists (PT)

People who specialize in the assessment and treatment of certain musculoskeletal and neurological conditions. They also provide staff and parent education in developmental care and milestones for babies.

Lactation Consultant and Breastfeeding Team Leader

People who provide individual and staff counselling on breastfeeding or pumping.

Primary Care Coordinator

A person who assists the nurses with preparations for the babies to go home. He/she may provide individual counselling for parents on certain aspects of discharge or draw together other resources to help with the discharge and provide referrals to outside resources.

Infection Prevention and Control Practitioner/Nurse

The person who monitors the NICU to ensure procedures are carried out with the least amount of risk for the babies, families and staff.

Hospital Chaplain

The hospital-based religious support person.

Depending on the health of your children you may or may not encounter the following specialists:

- Cardiologist for heart
- Neurologist for brain and nervous system
- Nephrologist for kidney (urine)
- Gastroenterologist for intestinal and nutritional concerns
- Endocrinologist for gland and hormones
- Hematologist for blood
- Ophthalmologist for eyes

fragile lives-prematurity

• Audiologist for hearing
• Speech and Language Specialist for sucking and swallowing and later speech and language delays

Keep in mind that this tour is only an introduction. If you wish to know more, ask questions, read the reference materials that are available, and then ask more questions. Although I consider myself a very inquisitive person who enjoys research, I sometimes found that reading about prematurity and its complications didn't provide me with any comfort. In fact, it just scared me.

Understand your comfort level with information and let your healthcare providers know when you have had enough. When circumstances arise that make it necessary for you to know more about some of the issues related to prematurity, then it would be worthwhile to have already collected some good books and web site addresses so that you can begin to find the answers you need.

With special thanks to Donna Wilson, Clinical Nurse Specialist and Marion Deland, RNC, NICU Nurse Educator.

apgar
Apgar is a series of tests done when the babies are born to assess their general condition.

score	0 points	1 point	2 points
Appearance	Blue or pale bluish extremities	Normal skin colour	Normal skin colour
Pulse Rate	Absent	Less than 100 per minute	Above 100 per minute
Reflex *(response to irritating stimulation such as nose being suctioned)*	No response	Grimace	Sneeze or cough
Activity *(muscle tone)*	Limp	Some arm	Active motion and leg flexing
Respiration	Absent	Irregular, weak cry	Good strong cry

Professional Notes from the Perinatal Social Worker

---

you are not alone
Annette Bot

So, you have had triplets, quads, or maybe even quintuplets! You are probably experiencing a range of feelings right now: excitement about the births, concern over adjusting to such a large and sudden increase in family size, and uncertainty about the extraordinary changes that will soon affect your lifestyle.

As a social worker in a perinatal regional centre in a large urban community, I have worked with many families over the years that have had triplets and quadruplets, sometimes prior to delivery, but most often following the birth of their babies. I have watched parents go through many stages of adaptation as they prepare for the births and then take over their new role as parents. As you move through this process, it is helpful to be well-informed about the many resources that can provide much-needed education, practical help and emotional support.

Parents are usually apprehensive about how they will manage the care of several babies all at once. In many instances they have already connected to a multiple births association before being admitted to hospital. I have noted that this connection provides these parents with valuable support and education around practical issues related to parenting triplets, quadruplets or quintuplets. For parents who are not aware of this resource, one of my early goals in providing assistance to families would be to help them make this connection.

While most parents are aware of many of the practical, organizational issues related to the care of multiples, they are often not prepared for the emotional implications of premature births. This is often a very stressful time for parents, who must deal with their infants' passage through prematurity, which varies according to the babies' gestation, weight, respiratory needs and other medical considerations. Parents should be prepared for the high possibility of premature delivery and acquire as much information as possible beforehand.

Soon after you discover that you are expecting multiples, check out the specific services available in the hospital where you will deliver. Very likely it will be an advanced care maternity centre, offering a variety of services to assist you. Some centres have special programs with nurses assigned for individual counselling and teaching. This information could be available to you several months before delivery and might alleviate some of your concerns. For example, valuable information on premature labour, aspects of prematurity, nutrition, breastfeeding, and resources that you may need after delivery, could be very useful to you prior to the birth of your infants and help you prepare for what's ahead.

If your babies are hospitalized, it is important to keep in mind that, as parents, you are essential members of the healthcare team. You will be encouraged to spend as much time as possible with your babies in order to bond with them and participate in their care.

Your familiar voices and special touch are unique to each of you and represent consistency in your babies' lives during this critical period of hospitalization.

That's why you may need to look at local accommodation options if you don't live near an advanced care hospital. Long distance travel to and from the hospital will take a toll, and deprive you of valuable time with your babies or opportunities to rest. A perinatal social worker at the hospital should be able to help you find accommodation. Some perinatal centres have specially designated parent rooms or offer access to economically priced residences in close proximity to the hospital.

If you had intended to breastfeed your babies, it's still possible to do so even if they are born very early. By pumping breastmilk to feed your babies during the early stages of prematurity, you can maintain your milk supply until the babies are mature enough to go to the breast. Often, parents find it psychologically rewarding to provide nourishment to their hospitalized babies. It can help parents overcome feelings of detachment and helplessness in a high-tech setting where their babies are in the care of doctors and nurses. Many hospitals have breastfeeding centres that provide individual consultation and assistance with breastpump rentals, and instructions on how to operate the pump and store the milk. Look to the breastfeeding centre for ongoing support throughout your babies' hospitalization and afterward.

A parent group can normalize the experience of prematurity

Many hospitals across Canada have special support groups for parents of preterm and sick infants. A parent group can help you to normalize the experience of prematurity while providing education and support during the hospitalization period. In these groups, parents can learn techniques for enhancing their interaction with their babies and learn about the normal stages of growth and development related to prematurity. With the support of other parents in similar situations, they may also find a way to cope.

Financial management

Often a major area of concern for parents of multiples is the financial management of their suddenly expanded families. If either parent has extended healthcare insurance coverage, explore the extent of coverage. Some plans include nursing care that may be available to assist you in special circumstances. In some situations, it's a good idea to have a financial assessment completed by your local social services branch. These new additions to your family, along with the extra help that is required for you to manage, may put you in an income category that entitles you to financial assistance.

Getting help at home

Before your infants are discharged you may want to inquire about home care services. There are essentially two kinds of care. Homemaker or home support services are available in most Canadian communities. Home nursing care may be available to you under your provincial health insurance plan and is usually dependent on the medical needs of the infants and/or mother. In certain situations, these services may be subsidized by the government or by private insurance coverage. However, there are very specific definitions for qualifying for subsidized home support.

In Ontario, it may be possible to access help under provincial coverage if your babies have medical needs that require professional supervision and monitoring after discharge home. In some situations, the babies' mother may qualify for coverage if she has a medical condition that requires nursing care in the home. However, if the mother is granted care, it does not imply that funding would include care of the babies. In these situations, the family should arrange for alternate care, such as a nanny, at their own expense.

Each case is assessed differently. But in all cases, applications for home care — be it provincially or privately funded — must be strongly supported with letters from the pediatrician (for the babies), the hospital social worker, a family physician and possibly, the obstetrician. The more comprehensive the documentation, the greater your chances of accessing subsidized care. If you have insurance coverage through your employer, human resources personnel can represent your needs very effectively with the insurance company. Union members may also find valuable support through their association. If you are able to pay for home care help, certain agencies, particularly in large urban centres, have specialists in premature infant care.

Your district public health nurse will also be an extremely valuable resource for you. She will not only provide you with much-needed support and education in matters related to your infants' care but she can also be an important link to community resources. For example, I was able to connect a sole-support mother of triplets to a whole range of resources through her community health nurse. This parent was linked with a variety of volunteers, including early childhood education students as well as the local church group, who provided round-the-clock assistance to help her survive that very difficult first year.

By taking advantage of the many supports offered both in the hospital and the community, your transition to the world of triplets, quadruplets and quintuplets will be greatly eased.

we never looked back
Candi Cuppage

After 101 long days in hospital, our babies began their triumphant journey home

Taulea, Colton and Sheldon came into this world just 25 weeks after they were conceived, weighing just 1 lb. 9 oz., 1 lb. 5 oz., and 1 lb. 7 oz. at birth. My labour was triggered by an infection that I was never aware I had until after the babies were born. En route to the hospital, I was given a steroid shot with the hope of stimulating the babies' lung development. However, we knew that it was better if the steroid is given at least 24 hours prior to delivery. Our babies had to be delivered sooner. Given the combined set of circumstances — extreme prematurity and sudden labour — we knew they would need life support if they were to survive.

I remember my first look at our three new babies. They were lying very still in open isolettes, beautiful, yet almost inhuman. Tubes were inserted into their tiny mouths, lines ran to their belly buttons, and machines surrounded them, always beeping and ringing. They were so tiny that a facecloth beside them seemed the size of a blanket. We were bombarded with mountains of medical information, but the most important underlying message was that the next 48 hours would be the most critical.

One of the priorities was to give the babies medication to help close their heart and lung valves. Taulea and Colton required more medication than Sheldon. Eventually, surgery was discussed as a last resort for Taulea, but fortunately, the problem resolved itself.

Hours turned into days. I remember looking at Colton and wondering whether he could sense that he was living outside of the womb. Distressed by direct contact, Colton seemed more comfortable hearing my voice muffled through the plastic barrier of the isolette, as he might have heard it through my body. I moved from one isolette to another, talking to each of the babies through plastic barriers.

After a few days, they had lost more than 200 grams. Two had jaundice and needed phototherapy. Once they had their first bowel movements, my breastmilk was introduced. We started with a tiny drop (1 cc) of milk and, as their tolerance increased, so did their feeds.

As the weeks passed slowly, there were many upheavals and

uncertainties. The babies' tiny feet were constantly poked for blood to monitor their blood gas levels and to check for infections. They each needed three or four blood transfusions, and I prayed after each transfusion that it would be the last. Sometimes, they would stop breathing and their hearts would stop beating. Through these episodes, their oxygen levels swung up and down dramatically.

It is difficult to describe my first experience of holding these tiny babies who were connected to tubes that branched off in countless directions. Most of their weight came from the machines and blankets.

With their oxygen dependency came many other potential problems, including the effects on eye development. Since their eyes had not yet fully developed, and it was unclear how the oxygen would affect their development, it became important to minimize their dependence on machines. After 32 weeks, doctors performed eye exams weekly to check for retinopathy of prematurity or retina detachment. What appeared to be the beginning of a detached retina in Taulea mercifully corrected itself.

Two airplane trips and a dozen transfers by ambulance

It seemed like there would be a few days of good news and one day of bad. Taulea and Sheldon reached the kilo club (2.2 lb.), while Colton seemed to take forever. We felt such great relief when he finally reached that milestone, only to see him develop a blood infection. Colton took a giant step backward and moved into an open isolette again where medical personnel could access him quickly for emergency treatment.

My husband, Paul, and I took two airplane trips and travelled by ambulance a dozen times with the babies in special transport isolettes. Sheldon and Taulea graduated to Level 2 care and moved to another hospital a two-hour drive away, only to suffer a setback and return to Level 3, this time in a different hospital. In all, our babies moved to three different hospitals, which meant new routines and different nurses. At one point, we faced having three babies in three different hospitals. I lost it at that point and refused the separation of two.

In one of the hospitals where Taulea and Sheldon stayed for a short while, the nursery became contaminated with the chicken pox virus. Paul and I were considered a risk since we had been exposed. During the 18-day incubation period, we couldn't come in contact with Colton, who remained in Level 3 care. Thankfully, Colton had a great team of caring nurses. Through videotapes and tears, we watched him achieve steady gains. There was never a dull moment in our lives.

It was great to see them change, grow and slowly become newborn babies. Exactly 101 days after they were born, two of our babies were ready to come home. Our hearts broke at having to leave Colton in hospital, but he followed nine days later and our new life finally began. The hospitals, the machines, the needles and tests were finally behind us. I remember leaving the hospital without any fear of caring for the babies at home. I just wanted them to be able to leave, to be at home and comfortable. With a triumphant, "We're outta here!" we left the hospital and didn't look back.

Taulea, Colton and Sheldon are now typically rambunctious five-year-olds. Paul and I rarely speak of the early stresses we experienced. But the journal and memories I keep will always remind us how delicate and blessed their lives really are.

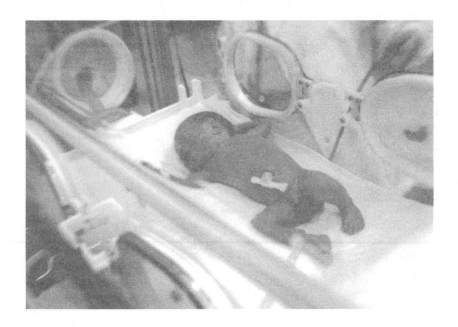

kangaroo care
Susan Quenneville

Early in 1999, our triplet girls were born at 26 weeks gestation, all under 2 pounds. I went into labour at home and was raced by ambulance to the hospital where an emergency cesarean section was performed.

For the first three weeks of their lives, our girls were on ventilators and couldn't be picked up and held. All we could do to bond with our babies was gently touch and talk to them, which we did, every day. When the girls came off the ventilators but remained on oxygen and connected to monitors, we began to take them out of the incubators. That's when we experimented with kangaroo care, or skin-to-skin contact.

The girls were 23 days old when I held them all together for the first time. They each weighed about 890 grams. The nurses helped to settle me into a reclining chair with my top and bra removed. Then they placed the babies across my chest and covered their backs with blankets. It was an amazing experience, being able to wrap my arms around all of them, hearing their sweet noises and feeling their skin on mine. I cried.

Skin-to-skin contact helps with bonding, stabilizing the baby's body temperature, improving the digestion and settling sleep. It is the most warm and loving therapy for parents and babies. My husband (the first man to do this in the NICU) and I practiced kangaroo care with the babies daily. At first, we held the babies together and then gradually, one at a time. They thrived, feeling our love and comfort every day.

After our daughter recovered from a near-fatal bowel infection and caught up to her sisters' development, the girls all grew at the same rate. They started to bottle and breastfeed without difficulty. Many of the doctors and nurses believe that kangaroo care was part of the reason our babies did so well. After 88 days in hospital, we finally took our girls home, where they are now living happy and healthy. While my husband and I have been blessed with three miracles, we believe that kangaroo care helped them get where they are today.

quote

Feeling a parent's love and comfort through skin-to-skin contact

baby steps
Diane Myers

Tiny and fragile, our 27-week newborns grew into little babies in the NICU

Heading into my 27th week of pregnancy with quadruplets, I was feeling remarkably well, considering I was the size of a 46-week pregnant woman. Every time I rolled over in my hospital bed, it felt like an exercise in parenting the unborn. As I turned, the children took their time following. Come on guys, time to move now, let's go!

My labour began very early one morning. I knew the signs since I had been in labour before with my eldest child, but I waited a short time just to be sure. After an hour had passed, I rang the bell at 4 a.m. to alert the nurses. There wasn't a sound in the hallway. Were they sleeping? Then suddenly, I heard footsteps running down the hallway and nurses calling out: "That's Mrs. Myers! She never rings for us! Hurry!" They may never know how comforting those words were to me. I needed them, and they ran to help me.

The head nurse reached me first (she must have been a sprinter at some point in her life). "Are you okay?" she asked. Calmly, I responded that I felt that I was in labour. That's when the action really started. An internal examination showed that I was three centimetres dilated. Next came a call to my husband, John, and countless other calls to assemble the surgical and neonatal teams.

As I lay on a stretcher in the hallway waiting for John and the dreaded epidural, the full meaning of what was about to happen became clear. My babies were going to arrive three months early! I remember crying and saying, "It's too early," over and over again. I thought of nothing else — not that the babies might not survive or that they might have health problems in the future — but simply that it was much too early.

John arrived for the fun part, the epidural. He had been stuck in morning traffic but was able to bypass the tie-ups and get to the hospital with a police escort. The anesthesiologist instructed me to bend over and grab my knees. A questioning look crossed my face. I guess she assumed I hadn't understood the instruction because she repeated it. At that point I couldn't help but say with no small hint of sarcasm, "I have not seen my knees for at least two months; I cannot imagine how you expect me to grab them." The rest of this procedure did not go smoothly. Eventually, the epidural was inserted, even though I pleaded more than a few times to "just put me out." In hindsight I am glad the nurses were persistent. They kept telling me that it was better for the babies if I remained awake. It was also better for me emotionally and physically to remain awake.

With the epidural in place and the drugs flowing, we headed into the operating room. The delivery went quickly and smoothly. Alison, Harrison, Jessica and Kenneth were born within one minute of each other close to noon that day. The surgeon announced the children's sexes as they were born and then the NICU team designated to each baby whisked their new charge away. The delivery had gone as well as it could have. Immediately, the babies were given surfactant, a steroid to loosen the lungs, and were connected to breathing supports and headed into the first day of their lives.

I was sent to the recovery room, where I immediately started shaking in reaction to the pain medication. Our family doctor had attended the delivery, spending her time by my head talking to me throughout the delivery, and then in recovery. She told me "the shakes" were common but went to talk to the nurses to change my medication. I responded similarly to another codeine-based medication. Switching to medication without codeine seemed to reduce my reactions.

While in recovery the nurses brought me a picture of each baby, while John and our family doctor took turns visiting the babies and reporting back to me. The information was helpful, but I truly did not know what all the terminology meant. I just wanted to hear that the kids were fine. I could not take in much more.

On the way to my room from recovery, the nurses wheeled me through the NICU on a stretcher to see each baby. I did not appreciate until the next day what a navigational feat that was. The babies were in two different rooms filled with equipment and monitors.

Information overload

Intubation, apnea, bradycardia, jaundice, oxygen levels, gavage feeding, RDS, CT scans, and blood gas were just a few of the many terms I began to hear. I felt bombarded. The second day, I heard that my babies had something, were doing something, or needed something. And oh yeah, here's the breast-pump you requested.

My mind was still clouded by pain medication and now it was overloaded with words and diagnosis and prognosis that meant nothing to me. On the day after surgery, I called the nurse to ask for help to go and see the babies. Fortunately, I had taken a tour through the NICU before the children were born so I knew what kind of environment and equipment to expect. But reality hit hard when the nurse wheeled me to see my Baby A, Alison. She was covered in wires. Can I touch her? I could place my hand on her body. I looked back at the nurse. What can I do to help her? Nothing.

As time passed though, I began to realize there was a lot I could do. As parents, John and I had very important jobs: being there, becoming educated about our children's conditions, being their advocates, and most importantly, loving them. The last point may seem like the easiest, and most obvious, but for me, bonding was not immediate and did not seem to come as naturally as it did with our firstborn.

The next few weeks were a constant blur of the medical ups and downs that are often seen with very premature babies. Alison suffered a brain bleed, Jessica lost too much weight, Kenny was doing well and Harry was doing poorly. After another week passed, all of the children contracted a blood infection called sepsis. Antibiotics were given all around. Harrison had barely recovered before he was set back again with a different infection that required another round of antibiotics.

After two weeks in the NICU, Kenny, Alison and Jessica were ready to be taken off their intravenous lines. That meant they needed to survive as other babies do — on breastmilk and formula. Through naso-gastric tubes, which ran internally from their noses down into their tummies, John and I spent each visit gavage feeding the babies precious drops of breastmilk that I had conscientiously pumped. After feeds we placed our hands on each child's torso and talked to him or her quietly. When Harrison eventually joined the gavage team, we directed most of the breastmilk to him, since he was the weakest. The medications helped and the children's growth and health curves began to head upward.

Holding my babies

In their first two weeks of life, our babies experienced the world as a busy, painful, sterile place. One day, just as I walked through the doors of the NICU, I saw Alison being taken out of her incubator.

I had never seen any of the babes anywhere but behind the plastic walls of an incubator. The nurse, not knowing that I had never held any of the babies, said, "Great to see you; could you hold Alison for a minute while I straighten her bed?"

I felt so out of control. Yes, of course, I wanted to hold her, but how? Is she okay, out here? What should I do about the wires? How do I hold her? I need to sit down! All of these thoughts were running through my head as the nurse passed my little one over to me. It never occurred to me that I could hold my babies. From that point on, I always asked, "Can I hold Kenny today? Can I hold Jessica today? When can I hold Harrison? I was able to hold Kenny and Jessica at my next visit, but I was not able to hold Harrison until he was about a month old. That was very hard for me. He was the one who needed me most, and I really needed to feel him close to me.

Taking a first breath

Kenny came off the ventilator first. Then came Jessica. Alison was not taken off the ventilator in a planned, conventional way. I remember visiting her one afternoon and seeing that the tubing in her nose had disconnected from the respirator machine at the other end. Tangled lines were lying on the floor. As cautioned, I did not touch anything that was on the floor, but I was fairly certain that these tubes belonged to Alison. Experience had taught me that if Alison were in distress, alarms would be sounding off by that time. So I nonchalantly approached her nurse and told her about discovering the tubes on the floor. She felt bad. I simply said, "I think Ali's ready to breathe on her own now." The nurse agreed, got the doctor's permission to keep her off the ventilator, and monitored her carefully for the rest of the day. Alison never needed any help breathing again in those early days in the NICU.

Harrison was, and still is, the type of child who seeks forgiveness, not permission. He ripped out many, many tubes. Many were reinserted quickly but some were left out until Harrison began to demonstrate that he was not ready to go it on his own. As time passed, Harrison seemed to know what he could do without and took it upon himself to disconnect from the machines. If he remained stable, the tubes were not reinserted.

Moving to transitional care

I arrived in the NICU one day to find only three babies. Where's Kenny? Is he okay? A nurse, seeing the panic across my face, approached me. "We just tried to call you," she said quickly. My heart stopped. "Kenny has graduated to transitional care." Take a breath. I knew transitional care was our next step, but I was not prepared. I heard myself blurt out a bunch of questions about where I could find him, if I could visit and is he okay? The nurse giggled, saying Kenny was more than okay, which was why he moved upstairs to transitional care. The rest of the children took their turns graduating. Of course, Harrison was last — although he moved to transitional care before he was completely ready because the doctors and nurses felt that he would cope upstairs in his incubator, and that it would be easier for John and I to visit. Harrison was still having apnea and bradycardia spells in transitional care, and he was also still on low flow oxygen.

Once they were out of the NICU, the focus changed from survival to growth in a nursery that encouraged more direct parental involvement. John and I fed, bathed, changed and cuddled the children. Before our eyes, our children became little balls of baby — much different from the tiny beings that came into this world a month earlier. They eagerly awaited each feed. I tried to schedule my visits around feeding time. As time passed, the nurses helped to schedule Alison, Jessica and Kenny's feeds at the same time. Harrison was still on his own schedule — a behaviour pattern that continues to this day. The children seemed to be getting so big. The reality check came when John's sister Joan and her husband, Wayne, saw the babies for the first time on a visit from Montreal. Joan came to the hospital to help me feed the children. Just as I was about to pass our biggest baby, Kenny, to her to feed, I saw the anxiety cross Joan's face. When I asked if she wanted to feed Kenny, she said, "Oh yes I do, but he is so small." In my mind, I was thinking that he wasn't small. He was nearly five pounds and almost ready to go home.

Big brother

Through the two and a half months that I spent going to and from the hospital, pumping, talking to the NICU nurses, reading about what the doctors had just told me and recovering from my c-section, there was Craig. Craig was 17 months old when the foursome

---

tip

As time passed, I began to realize there was a lot I could do. As parents, John and I had very important jobs: being there, becoming educated about our children's conditions, being their advocates, and most, importantly loving them. The last point may seem like the easiest, and most obvious, but for me, bonding was not immediate and did not seem to come as naturally as it did with our firstborn

was born. I went into the hospital 24 weeks pregnant. So for the last three or four months, Craig and John had survived on their own. Once the children were out of immediate danger, we tried to include Craig in our visits to the NICU. When Craig joined us, the visits were cut very short. The NICU was no place for Craig. After a two or three-minute whirlwind visit with his brothers and sisters, he was ready to leave. During the day, with Craig in a home day-care program, I visited the babies. As they moved to transitional care it was much easier for Craig to visit. The nurses welcomed Craig, though we still kept his visits very short. It must have been a hard time for him, but when asked, he doesn't remember life without his siblings. I believe his young age, strong family support and his easygoing nature helped him through what I know to be the toughest year of our lives.

The big day

This day was mixed with joy and sadness. Two weeks before their due date we were getting three children home, but not our entire family. Kenny, Jessica and Alison were very ready to come home, but Harrison still needed to go 48 hours without an apnea spell. Harrison was ready five days later and he was welcomed and squeezed into our new life of diapers, bottles, breastfeeding and sleep schedules.

Overall

I never thought that our children would not survive. I also never let myself really understand how sick our babies were. This was probably my way of coping. If I did not think the worst, the worst could not happen. The first year of our quadruplet's lives was the hardest one so far. Their prematurity had lifelong effects: Harrison has a severe hearing loss which requires him to wear bilateral (two) hearing aids and Alison has mild cerebral palsy. All of the children are still at risk of learning disabilities.

What does that mean to them and us? It means life may be hard. John and I have now lived in "hard" for 10 years. We have come to the conclusion that hard is just fine.

our path to survival
Joanne March

With faith, family and friends

My husband and I met as we graduated from high school, and it seemed like we had a perfect life. I had always thought things would just keep rolling along perfectly — two kids, a dog, a small house with a white picket fence — that kind of thing. Then we hit the first of what were to be many curves on a bumpy, tortuous, and often very dark road in our lives.

In one year, my husband and I went from a tiny apartment where two people standing in the kitchen was one person too many, to a house filled with all kinds of people and three premature babies.

This road began when I became pregnant with triplets. We were thrilled — a little nervous — but thrilled just the same. Things, I thought, would just keep plodding along as expected. Then midway through week 22, I started to bleed. After rushing to the hospital we discovered Baby A's sac had prolapsed. I was immediately put on antibiotics and tipped back into a trendelenburg position, best described as being essentially upside down in bed. The plan was for me to stay in that position for the next 12 weeks. I felt safer that way. The next morning, I was airlifted to Vancouver, still in trendelenburg, too afraid to sit up. There, doctors tried to push Baby A's sac back in ... but it broke. We were all devastated.

The hospital gave us a private room so that we could grieve. The pastor came to see us and suggested that we should start thinking of funeral arrangements. We just lay there together and cried.

Determined to do all we could to give our babies a chance

I have always been a positive person I think, and I know that together with a wonderful support network of family, friends and mentors, things began to take a small, but definite turn for the better. We watched the clock as everyone waited for my body to reject Baby A and begin the process of labour. But my husband and I were still determined to do all we could to try and give our babies a chance. I was pumped full of a cocktail of antibiotics and other drugs to settle my uterus down.

I never got out of trendelenburg, having only sponge baths in bed and using a bedpan. How embarrassing! Slowly my private, quiet self gave way to a new me. Imagine trying to go to the washroom upside down in bed and realizing that you can't quite slide the pot under in time because these babies are pushing down on your bladder. And when you really have to go, you really have to go! At that moment, the specialist walks in — without knocking of course — flings the curtain open only to ask, "How you are doing?"... And ... well ... there you are!

Then there were meals in bed (literally), transfers to a trolley to wash my hair in a hallway sink, and many, many questions, exams, and then more questions! It was a teaching hospital. I began to realize that if I were to survive these daily experiences, I would have to change my outlook and personality. And so I did.

Slowly we marked off the days. Then one week. Then another. And then a few more. I was weaned off some of the drugs. I was determined to prolong the pregnancy and acquired as much knowledge as possible. But I could never have done it without all of the help and support I received. My husband and my mom took shifts so that I was never alone. There were always lots of doctor's appointments, ultrasounds, other tests and, of course, meals to look forward to. Visitors helped chase away the boredom and bad thoughts. This was so important. It helped me to look at the bright side of things too — we still had a chance!

Then at 27 weeks, Baby A was born. A team of 15 doctors and nurses, plus the whole school of interns, I am sure, were all present and waiting. The expectation was that all three babies would be born, but they weren't. Immediately after Baby A was born, I was again pumped with more drugs and a new batch of antibiotics. I spent two days in total darkness in a quiet room down in the delivery ward — back again in trendelenburg. Total silence, total darkness, my legs lifted: it was the only way that I could keep from contracting. Even whispering a few words to my husband was enough to trigger my uterus.

Meanwhile in intensive care, Baby A started his new life. But it soon became too much for his tiny premature lungs to handle and his condition quickly began to fail. As my body began to settle down on the third day after delivery, I was stable enough to move back to the maternity ward. On our way upstairs, we were able to stop at the special care nursery to see Baby A for the first time. He was so tiny and frail looking, fighting for his life.

The next days and weeks focused on survival. Just as the doctors were reaching the end of what they could do medically for Baby A, he started to pull around, and showed signs of pulling through. Now it was my body's turn to fail. By this time, I was almost 34 weeks. No one was certain about what should be done because a pregnancy like this had never happened before where all of the babies had survived. So, six weeks after Baby A was born, the decision to induce labour was made, and in June 1993, babies B and C were safely delivered. We had done it. We could now hold each one. We cried again.

Five days later, I was discharged from the hospital. The story of such a unique birth had travelled globally, covering the front pages of newspapers here in British Columbia, as well as in France, England, South America and Australia. Even people in the Antarctic and China knew about us! Three offers came in from California asking for television profiles. We declined all of them. We agreed to do a few interviews for the CBC in Canada and to assist those associated with universities and other institutions wishing to investigate our case for the purposes of research. Our story was followed by many people, and in some ways, influenced the thinking toward delivering multiples.

I give the trendelenburg position great credit, among many other things, for prolonging the time between delivering Baby A and Babies B and C. Until 34 weeks, I remained in that inverted position as best as I could. Toward the end, the bed was levelled a little, but I remained head down. On the morning of our planned delivery day, I was not dilated. But after 20 minutes of standing in the shower and moving around a bit, I was eight centimetres dilated and events quickly started to roll. It made me wonder what would have happened if I had gotten up to use the washroom or have a shower like everyone else on "bedrest?"

As we were packing to leave the hospital, Babies B and C were doing well and would stay in the hospital for approximately three weeks to gain more weight. Baby A was still struggling, but he was a fighter. I was sure he would make it.

Then on that day, the road took another U-turn. As my husband and I were about to leave the hospital happily, with me in my wheelchair, a girdle, and a huge bra (the biggest Vancouver had, but still two sizes too small), a specialist stopped us. He showed us into a small room. I was sure he was about to congratulate us on how well things had turned out. But he didn't.

He explained that Baby A had severe periventricular leukomalasia (PVL), the effects of which were significant damage to areas of his brain, leading to advanced cerebral palsy. To what extent, they could not exactly tell us. He would have vision problems, gross and fine motor dysfunction and likely a whole range of other conditions which, by that time, I was not really hearing. We were devastated. We sat and cried together yet again. More people came and went but I didn't really notice. Did I mention, this was also my 30th birthday?

My husband and I left for two days of solitude at a small bed and breakfast in the Gulf islands where there was no radio and or television. Nobody knew us, and we were all alone. Our babies were safe. We needed some time. Some time to be together, some time to think, and some time to readjust our outlook on life. That trip was one of the best things we could have ever done. We came back ready to start again — down a new road.

Baby A, Clayton, was to spend the next nine months of his life in the hospital. We stayed when we could and commuted the nine-hour return trip from Kelowna to Vancouver on weekends. It was a rocky road for Clay, but he kept hanging on. During those months, Baby B, Tanner, and Baby C, Amanda, were home, and doing very well. For us, the days were long, and the nights short. Very short.

Today that mountainous road is starting to level out a little. We measure our life by the days and try not to be consumed by the unknowns that lie ahead. We have also come to appreciate little things more in life, such as a small step, a string of funny words, even just a smile. We appreciate how much a strong family and good friends can mean, too.

Our children are now four. They are typical, energetic, fun-loving, "Dennis-the-Menaces" ™ who just love to swing, dig in the dirt and catch bugs. The only difference is that one of them has cerebral palsy. Having some difficulty getting around alone can have its merits though. Clay is the envy of all young children when he rides his new bike around. In all, he has three very cool chairs: one electric wheelchair, one manual wheelchair, and one ski chair! Clay's supplemental oxygen ended last year, and he is now completely off the 12 medications he needed at one time.

We are very proud of all of our children. Looking back we never could, and still cannot survive alone — not without our friends, relatives, family, and especially, not without one another. Each of us tries to always be there for the other, sometimes to laugh and sometimes to lean on. I am glad that we changed our way of being and that now we can embrace our new life with love and the excitement of living.

Sometimes we look cautiously into the future and know that if we turn our heads to face the wind, our love, strength and courage will give us all that we need to walk down that bumpy road together and win.

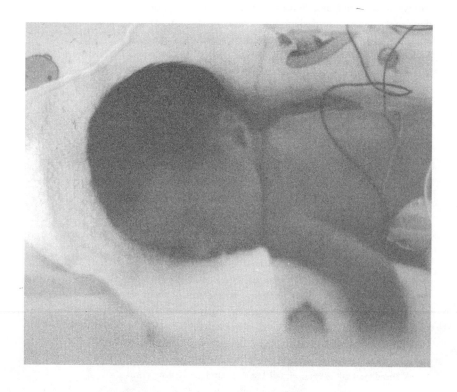

small miracles
Jodi Kerr-Taylor

Physically they were weak and struggling, but in spirit, our 28-week-old newborns found their strength

Looking back, it's hard to believe that our sons are over a year old now. They entered this world so abruptly, and had such a rocky start, that I sometimes can't believe how far they've come since that day.

The story begins just before the boys were born. My last doctor's appointment had gone as usual. My cervix was a little soft (whatever that meant) so the plan was to admit me to the hospital for bedrest the following week.

A few days later, I awoke one morning after a long night with a very upset stomach. My husband was scheduled to be the master of ceremonies at his cousin's wedding that day, and was all set to head out for a morning golf game with the wedding party. I thought that it would be a good idea to go to the hospital to be checked out before he left. I didn't think anything was wrong with the babies; I just thought that I had a mild case of food poisoning or something like that.

When we arrived in the emergency department at the hospital, I was immediately sent to labour and delivery to be checked out. Once they had done the examination, the nurses told me I was in labour and dilated by two and a half centimetres. I was in shock. "No, it's too soon," I said. That was it. I didn't think any more about it, or about the fact that my babies were about to be born 12 weeks early. Not another negative thought entered my mind. After calling our families, my husband left to pass the wedding speech and music over to someone else. Then the obstetrician on call arrived and arranged for me to be taken by ambulance to a hospital in Toronto.

Our sons Shane (3 lb.5 oz.), Matthew (2 lb. 9 oz.), and Bradley arrived (2 lb. 8 oz.) that day — September 16, 1995. We heard a very faint, almost inaudible cry from each of them before they were taken to the NICU. After some time in recovery, the nurses wheeled me through the NICU to see my sons. They were so tiny, so helpless.

At 3 a.m. on the first night, the phone at home rang. My husband immediately knew something was wrong. The nurses needed his permission to give Shane a blood transfusion. When I heard of the transfusion, I panicked. I thought they meant a complete transfusion, not just a "top up" as we came to refer to it.

I spent some time sitting beside their isolettes, watching as they slept

The next day when I saw my babies I was a little more "with it" than I had been the previous day. I spent some time with each of them, sitting beside their isolettes and watching as they slept under the lights (for jaundice) and connected to countless machines. There was a ventilator to assist breathing, an oxygen monitor to check saturation, and IVs to feed them and to give blood. Every time I moved, it seemed another alarm went on. There was constant buzzing and beeping. One of the doctors explained that they would all be getting a head ultrasound done, which was a routine test for premature babies. I asked if they could postpone Shane's ultrasound to let him recover from his blood transfusion. But they advised against it and scheduled it for the afternoon. Later that day another of the babies got a blood top up.

The next day, one of the doctors spoke to my husband alone while he was in the NICU. I knew when I was ushered into a private room that something was terribly wrong. Shane had had an intraventricular hemorrhage — a bleed in his brain. There was some permanent damage, but they couldn't tell how much. His motor skills would be compromised without question, and there was also a possibility that his intelligence would be affected. The neonatologist was not able to tell us exactly what would be wrong with Shane. Another ultrasound was scheduled for the next week to determine if there was any more prominent damage. Then they gave us what seemed to be an almost unthinkable decision. Did we want Shane taken off his ventilator? NO, NO, NO! This couldn't possibly be happening. Was I going to lose one of my babies?

We briefly talked about what the doctor had just told us, but it wasn't until that night after my husband had gone home that I really thought about it. If Shane were a single baby, it wouldn't matter to me. I would spend all the time in the world with him. But could I with triplets? How much time would I have for him and for his brothers? I went back into the NICU and spent most of that night just staring at Shane sleeping, barely moving. He had such a pained look on his face; if only I could take some of his pain away. I hadn't even been able to hold him. What if my baby died without ever being held?

The next day, the doctor told us that if we were going to take Shane off his ventilator we had to decide now. He gave us an hour. My husband and I shared our thoughts, our concerns, and we cried together as we decided to let our son make the decision for himself. We would unplug the ventilator and see what Shane wanted to do.

As the doctors went in to disconnect the ventilator, I went back to my room and sat with David and cried until the doctors came back to our room. I expected the doctor would be carrying the body of my son, but he wasn't. Shane had been taken off the ventilator for five minutes and nothing had happened. He went on breathing until it was plugged in again. But now the doctors were concerned about the effects of leaving him off too long, which could lead to more brain damage.

Shane had decided. He wanted to stay.
Our son wanted to stay with us

David and I went back to NICU with the doctor, who showed us that Shane's heart rate remained strong when the ventilator was unplugged. That was all we needed. Shane had decided. He wanted to stay. Our son wanted to stay with us. From that moment on, I decided that we were going to do everything to help Shane. We would make him comfortable and get him strong and well.

Over the next week we made what I thought was a lot of progress. When the boys were only five days old, I was discharged from the hospital. All along, I knew that I wasn't going to be taking any of my babies home with me that day, but it didn't lessen the feeling of emptiness.

Once at home, I continued pumping breastmilk and made the trip down to the hospital each day. When he was a week old, Bradley developed an infection, and required antibiotics, and then a blood top up. Then Shane got the infection, only his was worse. He didn't seem to respond to the antibiotics. Breathing became very difficult and by day 12, he was back on the ventilator. Those are the ups and downs of prematurity. Just as you think you are making some progress — boom — a setback. By the third day, Shane had developed cysts on his neck, which the doctors thought was the infection coming out. I took this as good news, but then the doctor came to talk to us. Results of Shane's head ultrasound showed that the size of his ventricles in his brain had enlarged. The cerebral spinal fluid was collecting in the ventricles of his brain, instead of circulating up the spine and through the brain in a continuous motion. The doctors wanted to see if they could open the blockage and get the fluid moving.

After three attempts, they contacted a neurosurgeon at another hospital, who said that Shane required immediate surgery since the fluid was putting pressure on his ventricles and potentially causing more damage to his brain. Again my tears started to flow like a river. Why was this happening? I thought that maybe the doctors in the NICU were trying to prepare us for the worst. Maybe the situation wasn't as bad as they had first told us. So I asked the neurosurgeon for his opinion. "You are going to have a severely neurologically damaged child." I can still hear those words ringing in my ears. Again the tears began to flow. Shane was prepared for transfer to the other hospital for an operation.

With the surgery came another setback. The doctors planned on inserting a device called a shunt into the ventricles, a long tube that runs down through the neck and into the stomach where the fluid would be absorbed by the body or eliminated as urine. But they couldn't insert the shunt because of the infection in Shane's neck. The tube would have to run right through it. Yet he desperately needed something to take the pressure off the ventricles. So instead, the doctors inserted a reservoir that collected the excess fluid, which would need to be drained with a needle periodically.

The surgery was performed when Shane was approximately three weeks old. The surgeon told us that he had been steady as a rock through the surgery and that he would be able to return back to be with his brothers later that day. When we arrived back at the NICU, the nurses were so excited to have Shane back so soon. We were glad to have all our sons under the same roof again. Matthew and Bradley were doing very well, both gaining weight and increasing their tolerance of food. Occasionally, they still needed a blood top up. The nurses observed differences in the boys' personalities right from the beginning. Matthew liked to be left on his own, Bradley was a bit fussy and Shane was easygoing. This still holds true today.

One of the most terrifying moments for me was one day when we went in to see the babies, and when I looked to where Bradley was, there must have been a group of at least 10 doctors and nurses surrounding his bed. A screen was up around it so we couldn't see what was going on. OH NO, I thought, what now? What now! We had been making so much progress. I ran through the unit in near hysteria, asking what had happened to my baby. One of the nurses came and grabbed me and apologized for not calling us at home to tell us, but they had moved Bradley to the other end of the unit. He was asleep in his new spot. This time there were tears of joy.

At long last, I held Shane in my arms

After Shane's surgery, everyone could see the difference in him. He was starting to open his eyes (something that he hadn't done much of), and within five days, he was off his ventilator completely. Shane and his brothers moved from their isolettes to cots. And then, at long last, I held Shane in my arms. Our first cuddles together were so special. Soon my husband and I were allowed to care for the babies ourselves more and more. We fed them, changed them and even bathed them, and we enjoyed every minute of it. We were getting to be old pros. The alarms still rang off, but we were accustomed to turning them off and resetting them ourselves. The boys were six weeks old and finally, we were able to have regular contact with them. We finally felt like we were playing an important role.

The progress we saw from that point was unbelievable. We introduced bottlefeeding to Bradley and Matthew, and they did quite well. David and I were so proud of our boys. By Halloween they had graduated to a transitional care nursery, where we were expected to take a more active role in their daily care, which we were happy to do. Shane's reservoir hadn't needed to be drained for 10 days and it looked like he may not need the full shunt after all. Things were looking up until ... On the second day of transitional care, we went in to find Matthew missing. Overnight, his heart rate had sped up to over 300 beats per minute and he was sent back down to the NICU so they could keep a closer eye on him. No damage showed up on an ultrasound, but they had called in a pediatric cardiologist to look at him anyway. Within three days he was back up with his brothers. The cardiologist saw nothing to be concerned about when she did tests on Matthew. We just had to keep an eye on him.

We started to discuss with the doctors and nurses a plan to get ready for sending the boys home. It would be two or three weeks yet, but it seemed a miracle that we were even talking about it. The plan was to send Bradley and Matthew home together, and Shane would follow. We were ecstatic ... and then. The fluid came back in Shane's head, just when the doctors told us the shunt wouldn't be necessary. He looked dazed all the time, became very sleepy, and was throwing up his feeds when we moved him the slightest little bit. Matthew's heart rate raced again and now required medication. Poor Bradley just stayed in his little cot, happy for our visit at suppertime, and stayed out of the way the other times. Shane was scheduled for the surgery to finish off his shunt. The nurse, David and I took Shane across the street by taxi to the other hospital for surgery.

We knew it wasn't over, but we were almost there

Once again, Shane came through with flying colours, and the results were amazing. Within a couple of days, we could see the difference in him. On November 28, 1995, Bradley came home with us. Matthew and Shane were to be transferred to a local hospital since winter was setting in and the 90-minute trip downtown was getting to be too much, especially with one baby at home. As we left the hospital that day with Bradley in tow, we were the happiest parents alive. What a long time we had waited, what a journey it had been. We knew it wasn't over, but we were almost there. Shane was still having difficulties feeding and we were trying to get the right combination of medicine to control Matthew's heart rate.

Bradley and I visited his brothers in the hospital every day and went back with Daddy at nighttime. On December 12, 1995, Matthew came home with us. On December 16, 1995, exactly three months after he was born, Shane, our last baby, came home. Finally we were a family — a happy family.

I thank all the doctors and nurses who helped us through these trying times. In the first few months, all the doctors would have to do was look at me and I would start to cry. These people cried with us and laughed with us and in the end, gave us the most precious gift, our babies to bring home.

all is well
Patricia Lumsden

Thriving with 31-week-old quadruplets

Wouldn't you know it! The night I went into labour was the night of the staff Christmas party in the hospital, leaving just a skeleton crew on duty. On the way back from a 3 a.m. washroom visit, my water broke. While I knew that delivery at 31 weeks was early, I didn't want to panic. I was moved to the labour and delivery floor as staff frantically prepared to monitor my contractions. Early morning calls went out to my husband, Martin, and our doctor. Since the contractions were not terribly intense, I drifted back to sleep. Then at 6 a.m., I was given a steroid shot to help develop the babies' lungs. If delivery could be prolonged 12 more hours, the plan was to give me another shot.

By noon, the contractions had worsened, and the doctors decided to move me by ambulance to a hospital with a fully equipped NICU. Once there, I was hooked up to an IV, and my legs were elevated to reduce the pressure on my womb. Contractions became extremely severe, and very near 6 p.m., the decision was made to operate.

Martin came into the operating room to observe the c-section along with a crowd of others including, the anesthesiologist, his assistants, four doctors (including ours, who made the trip with us), a surgical nurse, a pediatrician for each baby, a nurse to assist each doctor, plus the intern I requested be there so he could have the experience.

Several hours later I woke up to find we had four little girls. Mary Elizabeth was 3 lb. 8 oz., Caroline Dawn was 3 lb., Jennifer Lee, 3 lb. 6 oz., and Patricia Ann weighed in at 2 lb. 6 oz. Caroline had a collapsed lung, and required immediate surgery. As soon as I was able, the nurses wheeled me down to the NICU on a gurney, and three incubators were brought out before me in the hallway, one at a time. I reached in and touched three of my babies! I was amazed at how they looked — they were small and thin, but so soft. Their fine hair was shaved in small sections to run IV lines, blood had been taken from their heels and they were receiving oxygen through their noses. I cried, thinking they were the most beautiful things I had ever seen. But I was so anxious about the second born, partly because I hadn't seen her. That night, because she was hooked up to so much equipment, and because my gurney wouldn't go through the door of NICU, I relied on Martin to keep going back into the unit to check on her.

The next morning, as soon as I was awake, I walked down to the NICU and saw my second baby, and the other three. Things were looking good for all of them. They were a little jaundiced and still taking a bit of oxygen, but compared with some babies in the NICU, ours were doing remarkably well.

We learned that at 31 weeks, a baby's sucking instinct has yet to develop, so our girls had to be tube fed. Watching the procedure bothered me at first, but after a few times, the babies opened up their little mouths in anticipation, just like baby birds, waiting for mother bird to feed them, as milk was poured down the tubes and into the tummies. It became a normal part of life.

After a day or so, the hospital conducted genetic tests on the babies to determine their zygosity. The tests showed the girls were, in fact, identical (monozygotic). Once the news spread about the "identical quad girls," the media became very intrusive and relentless. One newspaper wanted to run a day-by-day series, which we refused to do. The babies were still in such a fragile state. Extra security guards were assigned to prevent photographers from sneaking into the NICU for that first picture. One newspaper sent a potted plant with a letter asking for a story and picture that same day! The hospital issued several news releases, and our doctor held a press conference with the hope of appeasing the curiousity.

For our part, Martin and I decided to wait until we were sure all the babies would survive before granting any interviews, although the pressure to surrender was great. Finally the hospital insisted we allow a photo. It was like a stampede! That picture ran in just about every major newspaper in Canada.

Two weeks after their birth, the babies were doing well enough to be transferred back to our original hospital, where they would stay for approximately one month. They were still connected to monitors, which would alert us if they had forgotten to breathe. An alarm would send a nurse rushing to the incubator to give the baby a nudge to start her breathing again.

With freshly scrubbed hands and wearing a hospital gown, I went into the special care unit and spent hours feeding, rocking, touching. The process was like this: open the incubator portholes, unhook the monitors and dress the baby in a little shirt. The babies were kept in diapers only inside the temperature-controlled incubators. (At first, Patty Ann was too small for even a preemie diaper and wore a doctor's surgical mask on her little tiny bottom.) Next, I would wrap the baby tightly in a blanket, open the top of the incubator and take the baby out. Then I held her, rocked her, bottlefed and burped her before reversing the procedure. I would gently place the fully wrapped baby back in the incubator, close the top and, working through the portholes, remove the blanket and shirt and reattach the monitor apparatus. Then it was on to baby two, three and four.

I was so thrilled with them. I could tell them apart in a day. It was easy — Patty Ann had a birthmark on her chest. Mary Beth had a red mark on her eyelid, and as she grew, two dimples appeared on her cheeks (where the others have just one). Carrie Dawn's complexion was pale compared with the others, and she also had the scar from her operation. Jennie Lee had much more hair, and one of her ears stuck out just enough to make a difference.

I couldn't wait until they were all home! We prepared a beautiful nursery for them, and arranged the whole house around their care. We allowed the local newspaper to take a family photo, and we did other interviews for radio, newspapers and magazines, but soon began refusing more requests than we accepted. It wasn't long before our baby girls showed us that they needed every bit of energy and focus that we could spare.

accepting our reality
Lois Haighton

Severe complications at 35 weeks
changed our image of early parenthood

My husband, Andrew, and I are the proud parents of three beautiful little girls, Amethyst, Emerald and Topaz, who were born at 35 weeks.

My pregnancy progressed uneventfully until 28 weeks when an ultrasound indicated some resistance to blood flow in the umbilical cord of triplet B. Fortunately, the blood flow normalized without any further problem. Otherwise, I was very healthy during the pregnancy, suffering only from shortness of breath and some minor discomfort with the 53 pounds I had gained. I even managed to work until I was 32 weeks along. Finally at my 35-week appointment, the doctor informed me that since triplet C had not gained much weight from the previous appointment, they would deliver the babies the following day. From the ultrasound, the technician estimated the weights of the babies to range from 3 to 4 pounds I was happy that the babies would all be over 3 pounds and, although I was a little nervous about the c-section, I was also excited that the day had finally arrived.

A couple of weeks earlier during a visit to an NICU, I had been given a chance to observe babies that had been born at 32 weeks. My understanding based on research and conversations with my doctor was that the chances of complications in babies born after 32 weeks were fairly minimal. And the excellent prognosis for these premature newborns in the NICU seemed to confirm it. I expected that my own children would be small but otherwise healthy at 35 weeks. After a few short weeks in the hospital, I was confident that they would be ready to come home.

Our babies were born weighing 3 lb. 15 oz., 3 lb. 6 oz. and 2 lb. 15 oz. I saw each girl briefly before they were whisked away to the NICU. All appeared normal and I could not wait to be fit enough to see them again and hold them. A few hours after I was admitted to a room, I began to hear about the first set of problems with my triplets. Two of the babies were diagnosed with respiratory distress syndrome (RDS). The babies were put on a ventilator and given a steroid called surfactant. Surprisingly, my smallest baby, Topaz, the one I had worried about most during my pregnancy due to her small size, was remarkably strong and able to breathe on her own.

The day after the birth of my triplets, there were so many new problems that I started to doubt that they would ever make it home. Amethyst and Emerald had a heart murmur due to Patent Ductus Arteriosus (PDA), a condition in which the duct that shunts blood away from immature lungs in the fetus does not completely close at birth. Also, grade 1 intraventricular (brain) hemorrhages were detected in Amethyst and Topaz. In addition to all this, Amethyst and Emerald both needed blood transfusions. Unfortunately, neither my husband nor I could donate blood. His blood type was A+ while the girls were O+. Although I was O negative (universal donor), I had received Rhogam to prevent the development of antibodies against the Rh antigen and was therefore ineligible. Although the PDA was expected to be treatable with drugs alone, and the doctors did not consider the hemorrhages to be an immediate concern, taken as a whole, all of these complications, which could lead to potentially severe problems in the future were extremely upsetting.

Fortunately, the next day, there were no new problems and I was allowed to hold Topaz for the first time, which gave me an emotional boost. Over the next few days the only new complication was jaundice, which was successfully treated. By the end of the first week, things had greatly improved. Both Emerald and Amethyst had been removed from the ventilator (Amethyst had pulled hers out) and I had the opportunity to hold each of them. Also by the end of the first week, our mighty little Topaz was tolerating full feeds and no longer required IV supplements.

A few days later I thought that the worst was over, Emerald had also reached full feeds (although she did not tolerate formula well) and Amethyst was also close to reaching full feeds. The children were even included in a television feature on multiple births. The day after the interview, my parents visited their grandchildren for the first time. Everything seemed right on track.

Amethyst's abdomen looked suspicious

That night the doctor called us at home to tell us that an x-ray of Amethyst's abdomen "looked suspicious" and they would be stopping feeds and putting her on antibiotics. The next morning, (Day 12), the doctor called again to say that Amethyst had an intestinal perforation (a hole in the bowel) and that they would continue her antibiotic treatment and watch her closely for 24 hours. If the bowel did not repair itself, she would require surgery. The last of this conversation had to be relayed to me by my husband. After hearing about the hole in her bowel, I was too upset to continue listening to the doctor. I was sure his next words were going to be that Amethyst would not survive.

Amethyst suffered from Necrotising Enterocolitis (NEC). I quickly consulted my medical book and discovered that this condition was fatal in about 30 per cent of cases. NEC generally affects very low birthweight and very premature babies, both of which Amethyst was not. We were totally unprepared for this.

I keep the picture as a reminder
of how far we have come

When we reached the hospital an hour later, the nurses were already preparing Amethyst for transfer to another hospital for surgery since her condition had worsened. We could not accompany her in the ambulance, so Andy and I walked the short distance to the children's hospital. The walk was very difficult. I sobbed all the way there and Andy, who is usually very optimistic, looked very distressed and walked in silence. After the operation, the surgeon informed us that Amethyst had survived and fortunately needed just a small section of her bowel removed. The doctors did not expect any long-term effects. For the short term, she would require a colostomy. Our dear little Amethyst looked extremely frail with so many tubes attached to her body. A photo taken by the women's auxiliary sat beside her incubator. It is a most disturbing picture, as she appears lifeless in it. I keep it as a reminder of how far she has come.

NEC was the last major hurdle for Amethyst in the hospital; however, there was some concern that Emerald, who had exhibited feeding intolerance, was at risk for developing NEC as well. Although the causes are unknown, there is some speculation that feeding intolerance is a precursor of NEC. There were also a few frightening instances where x-rays of Emerald's abdomen also "looked suspicious" warranting temporary discontinuance or a reduction of feeds. As a result, Emerald needed to be supplemented with IV solutions again. She was very close to needing a long line since so many of her peripheral veins had collapsed. On one occasion, it took the nurses over 40 minutes to locate a new IV site. Like most parents, I could never remain in the room when such procedures were being performed, so on that day, it was extremely upsetting to return to the NICU after two 20-minute absences to hear my little Emerald still screaming.

Amethyst also was very close to needing a long line since foods were started very slowly. On a few occasions it was necessary to use the veins in the scalp for the IV sites. On one of these occasions a nurse refused to let me hold Amethyst and Emerald since she was concerned that the IV would become dislodged. Instead she told my husband and I to take turns holding Topaz and not bother Emerald or Amethyst. This was one more obstacle keeping me from getting close and bonding to my two sicker babies. Not to be denied, I would wait until shift change, when another nurse would bundle up Amethyst and Emerald for me to hold. For a couple of weeks I lived in fear that Emerald would also develop NEC and that Amethyst would suffer a recurrence and I would lose them both. I even had a very irrational fear that one of the doctors or nurses would accidentally drop Topaz and I would end up losing all of my babies. Finally, at about three and a half weeks after their birth, all three of my babies were transferred to transitional care, where I was allowed to fully participate in tending to all their needs including feeding, bathing and, in Amethyst's case, colostomy changes.

Our little Topaz was released home first almost five weeks after her birth, with Amethyst following three days later. Emerald, who was still on low flow oxygen, her condition now considered chronic lung disease (CLD), was transferred to the local hospital when Amethyst was sent home.

Emerald was not discharged until she was a full seven weeks old. During her stay in the local hospital, she picked up a fungal infection in her mouth (yeast/thrush) and a severe case of diaper rash that required direct oxygen saturation treatment. Since I was incorrectly informed that washing between breastfeeding was sufficient to prevent the spread of yeast (an antifungal cream must also be used on the mother's nipples and any bottle nipples or pacifiers must be boiled for 20 minutes), I passed the infection on to my other two girls. Although minor ailments in comparison with the NEC and CLD, thrush was one more thing to deal with.

Emerald seemed so lonely — it was frustrating that I could not take her home

Even though Emerald was in a hospital closer to home, it was very difficult to spend time with her now that we had two babies at home to tend to. I could only manage to get to the hospital to feed Emerald once each day. She seemed so lonely and it was very frustrating that I could not take her home. It took a very long and agonizing time for the doctors to wean her off the oxygen. The local hospital also seemed to set her back in other ways. When she left Level 3 care at the other hospital, she had been breast and bottle-feeding and sleeping in a cot. At the local hospital they put her back in an incubator (although only for a couple of days) and started feeding her through a tube again. Also, the doctors expected that

Emerald would be home within a few days of transfer. Instead it took two full weeks. Other things about the local hospital bothered me. I was particularly disturbed that the nurses wore jewelry. At the other hospital in the NICU, jewelry was strictly forbidden. It was also irritating when on more than one occasion the nurses would ask me when Emerald would be going home. I thought that this was information that they should be providing to me.

In the beginning I felt cheated

Now that the girls are home and healthy, things are much easier and Andy and I are able to enjoy our family a lot more. However, in the beginning I felt cheated that, even though I had drunk gallons of milk, eaten tons of fruits and vegetables, taken vitamins and the prescribed steroid shots, and carried the babies to 35 weeks, my children were not as healthy as most triplets born at 35 weeks. But I have long since stopped feeling sorry for myself and started counting my blessings. My beautiful babies did not die, and there are no lingering ailments except for a few scars that Amethyst will have to bear and possibly a few more colds that Emerald may have to endure. In every way (physically and mentally) they are normal little girls, and they are very wonderful, loving and lovable. And I realize that I am very fortunate indeed.

three big boys
Gillian Borowy

My three boys were born by scheduled c-section, one day short of 38 weeks gestation. They weighed 5 lb. 14 oz., 6 lb. 8 oz., and 6 lb. 10 oz. While I stopped working at 23 weeks, I was not hospitalized until 36 weeks because I had healthy blood pressure, no protein in my urine, lived close to the hospital, and had plenty of help available at home.

Contractions were strong from 30 weeks onward, but they never settled into a regular pattern so I never pushed the "this is it" panic button. There were plenty of nights, however, when I would be up at 3 a.m. or 4 a.m., timing contractions, writing notes on what was happening, desperately trying to listen to what my body was telling me. Was this labour? Contractions would be six minutes apart three times in a row and then disappear. Then they would come back in eight-minute intervals, then two minutes, then I would fall asleep, and in the morning all would be calm. I was afraid of not recognizing the early signs of labour. When I asked my doctor how I would know for sure if labour had started, he just smiled and said, "Don't worry, you'll know." Intended to be reassuring, his remark only served to intimidate me and, in effect, put an end to my questions.

Every week that passed felt like a major accomplishment. By 36 weeks, I was asking to be checked into the hospital. I was exhausted, suffering from constant cramps and nausea, and had difficulty finding the energy to feed myself. Turning over and walking were very difficult. Hospital bedrest reduced the contractions and cramps and I gained more weight under the guidance of a nutritionist. An examination at 37 weeks showed that I was three centimetres dilated, and the boys were born two days later. The doctor asked if I had felt any contractions, and I think he was surprised when I said no. I had no idea anything had changed.

After the operation, the boys were in better shape than I was. One of them was jaundiced and needed phototherapy for a day, but otherwise, they were 100 per cent healthy. The pediatrician said they were ready to go home on the third day, but I was nowhere near ready. I couldn't even walk at that point. I had spent the first 24 hours after the operation on painkillers, IVs and ice chips. My husband was torn between showing the boys off in the nursery and taking care of me.

The boys were born on a Friday, and my husband had to return to work on the Monday. For those five days until we went home the following Friday, I was on my own caring for the babies because they didn't require specialized medical care or monitoring. I cried most of those 120 hours! The nurses were pushing me too fast to have the boys in with me. I needed to concentrate on my own recovery for a few days first.

It was very hard on my body to take the pregnancy to 38 weeks, and we all suffered for it. I was beyond exhaustion from day one and was expected to fully care for three hungry babies on my own. The nurses would take one baby if I begged them, but it was obvious they felt that I should be caring for them on my own. My body was too tired to produce breastmilk, and I certainly did not enjoy motherhood for the first few months. But knowing the health risks that come with prematurity, I would not have had it any other way.

Professional Notes from the Staff Neonatologist

neuromotor development in your premature baby's first year

Dr. E. Asztalos, Medical Director,
Neonatal Follow-up

When a baby is born before the expected due date, new parents are flooded by emotions surrounding the early birth. Soon after, questions begin to arise, one of the most common being, "What will my baby be like as he/she grows older?"

There is no doubt that with prematurity comes a risk of problems or delays in neuromotor development. Two to three decades ago, those risks were higher, especially among babies in younger gestational age groups. Today, with the advances in both obstetrical and neonatal care, the chances for survival and healthier outcomes have markedly improved.

For most infants, the objective is to go home when they reach 36 to 38 weeks corrected gestational age; in other words, two to four weeks before the expected due date. Most infants are able to go home once they achieve independent feeding and adequate growth.

During the first four to six months at home all preterm infants, regardless of how preterm they were, have two major tasks to accomplish: to grow in both muscle and fat, and second, to strengthen their new muscles.

Full-term infants already have a certain amount of muscle bulk and will be able to curl up in a position developed in the last trimester of pregnancy, called "physiologic flexion." In this position, an infant brings the hands and feet to his or her middle.

Preterm infants have less muscle bulk and floppier muscle tone, so they have more difficulty pulling to the curled up flexion position. Consequently, it's important to help them build abdominal and upper shoulder muscle groups to facilitate hands and feet coming to the middle.

Motor development in the preterm infant will usually occur along the same milestones as a full-term infant, but at a slightly different rate or pace. Motor development also tends to follow corrected age. As the infant grows and gains more muscle strength and control, especially in the trunk and abdomen, the gap between corrected age and chronological age narrows. In general, catch-up will occur between 12 to 24 months so that by the age of two years, a child's preterm distinctions will become far less apparent.

Growth stages

0 to 4 months corrected age. The greatest rate of growth can take place in this time period. As a result, it is not unusual for babies to have voracious and insatiable appetites. They need frequent feedings, but adding cereal to a bottle will not help them sleep through the night sooner.

Midline head control is the primary objective at this time. The infant needs to learn to keep his/her head centred and should be able to move the head side to side and then return to the middle. Parents can place rolled towels beside the baby's head as support until he or she can accomplish this alone. Car seat head supports themselves are not enough to provide midline head support. Rolls placed inside the head support (when it is not being used as a car seat) will provide necessary additional support for keeping the head centred and for bringing the shoulders forward so that hands are positioned in the middle.

Also during this stage, infants start to learn about their body by bringing hands to the mouth and bringing legs and feet towards the abdomen.

Lying on the abdomen is a crucial activity for building strength. Being on the tummy is difficult for an infant at this stage, but it's essential for upper shoulder muscle strengthening. The infant can build stamina in this position two or three times a day, so that by four months corrected, he/she will be able to maintain a nice upright head position for two to five minutes.

> **quote**
>
> Corrected age is the time the babies should have been born, and not their actual birthdate

The emphasis in this time period is on strengthening the trunk, so there is really no obvious gross motor milestone achievement. Deliberate rolling may occur around four months of age, or soon after. Before that, rolling is usually the result of a "flipping over" action that is seen when the infant tightens the back muscles.

4 to 8 months corrected age. From four to six months, the focus remains on trunk strengthening. As this is taking place, the infant will want to sit upright to interact with the environment. Upright positioning in an adult's lap will provide the opportunity to have this experience and begin playing with simple toys. By six or seven months, most infants are ready to sit in a highchair. Sitting independently should be achieved by the end of eight months.

During these months, the baby will become more mobile in the tummy position and should be encouraged to move around in a circle. Toward the end of this period, some may progress into a crawl position on their hands and knees.

8 to 12 months corrected age. This period focuses on achieving mobility and transition. The infant learns to move from a sitting position to the abdomen and to crawling. With further strengthening of the abdominal muscles, the skill of switching from a crawl back to a sitting position is mastered.

Although many infants want to stand during this time period, most are not ready, especially if they cannot pull themselves up to stand without assistance. Until the infant is ready to pull up to stand, he/she should be encouraged to spend more time developing skills in sitting, going into and out of sitting and crawling.

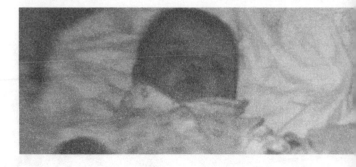

As the infant starts to show readiness to pull to a standing position, he/she should be encouraged to go up on the knees first, and then to stand on one foot, and finally, to pull up. Using the arms only and keeping the legs straight is not effective and should be discouraged.

Once upright, cruising around furniture is an easy next step. In the standing position, the feet should be flat. Transient standing on the toes is acceptable as long as the infant goes back to flat feet.

Independent steps may or may not take place soon after. If not at this point, steps will follow within the next six months.

Baby equipment

Many parents ask what equipment they should get to help their infants with neuromotor development.

There is only one strong recommendation: do not invest in a jumper or walker. These two items do not promote a normal sequence of neuromotor development. Although the infants love them, there is too early and too great an emphasis on the legs rather than the abdomen and trunk. These items encourage more pushing of the legs and standing on the toes. Contrary to popular belief, they do not promote earlier walking. A few new items have come into the market: the exercise/activity seat and the treadmill. The treadmill is promoted to encourage early walking, which is not necessarily valid. When standing is achieved, most infants will want to be mobile, not remain stationary on a treadmill. The stationary exercise centre has come in to replace walkers on the market. Most parents find it a blessing to have as somewhere to place the infant for a few minutes. If an exercise centre is used, place the seat height at the lowest level so that the feet are flat to discourage pointing of the toes.

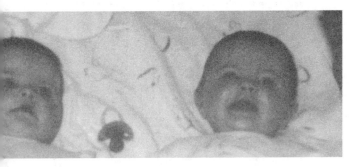

The floor is the best playground for your infant since much can be accomplished by spending time on the tummy and back.

Shoes are not mandatory. Babies need to learn about their environment from their body. The infant learns to adapt to a position by weight shifting and exercising the small muscles in the feet. When shoes are required, the best are sturdy running shoes that provide support as well as flexibility. The fancy "walking booties" are not ideal because they tend to be extremely rigid and have no traction on the soles.

Warning signs

Between 30 and 40 per cent of preterm infants need some professional input to monitor and provide guidance on their development. Often they have low muscular tone but want to learn to move quickly. As a result, these infants may experiment with a variety of compensatory movement patterns to achieve certain goals. Tightening of the muscles in the arms, legs, and back (called fixing) is the most common compensatory pattern, especially in the first four to six months. As the trunk and abdominal muscles strengthen, this "fixing" becomes less prominent. There maybe muscle tightening periodically as new skills are acquired, but once mastered, the tightening will subside.

The following clues should signal whether an infant's motor patterns should be evaluated:

• If by six months corrected age, the infant cannot bring legs, feet and hands to the middle or start rolling
• Sitting is not achieved by eight months corrected age
• The infant tends to pull himself/herself up to stand using the arms and not bending the knees
• Standing on the toes is frequent

All preterm infants, particularly those under 32 weeks gestation, should have vision and hearing assessed in the first year, because both contribute significantly to neuromotor development and how an infant interacts with the surrounding environment.

The preterm infant who was very immature (born earlier than 27 weeks) is prone to various eye disorders, and careful monitoring, both in the nursery and during the first year, is vital. Infants who were also very ill will likely have more than one assessment as well. Those born before 32 weeks should be screened in the nursery for retinopathy of prematurity (ROP). They are at higher risk of developing changes consistent with ROP. Once a pediatric ophthalmologist has started screening an infant for ROP, he or she will determine the frequency of subsequent assessments until final resolution. When ROP is no longer present (most ROP is completely resolved by four months corrected age), the infant should have an assessment for visual acuity by the first birthday and then again every one or two years later for monitoring.

All infants, term and preterm, should have a baseline hearing assessment to rule out any hearing difficulties. Hearing is important for language/communication development. Too often an assumption is made that the "child is hearing fine." Preterm infants are at higher risk of hearing deficits than the general population, but unlike vision, no clear pattern has been established. Some of the risk factors being considered include medications, noise, oxygen loss and cerebral insult. Preterm infants should have hearing assessed at least once before 8 to 12 months corrected age. Many experts are recommending a test called auditory evoked potentials (ABR) before four months corrected age, while some are advocating screening in the newborn period. These are possible if the necessary equipment and facilities are available. A soundfield hearing assessment is valid later in the first year because it assesses middle ear function. The important message is that hearing needs to be assessed. Most preterm infants found to be hearing impaired do not necessarily have the classic findings and their condition would easily be missed. Hearing impaired preterm infants can hear some sound but not necessarily all sounds.

What is the neurodevelopmental prognosis for infants of higher order multiple pregnancies? Generally good. A recent review of triplets, quadruplets and quintuplets delivered at two perinatal centres in Toronto suggests that long-term developmental problems in infants born after 28 weeks were significantly lower than in those born earlier. Neonatal health problems become even less prominent after 30 weeks gestation.

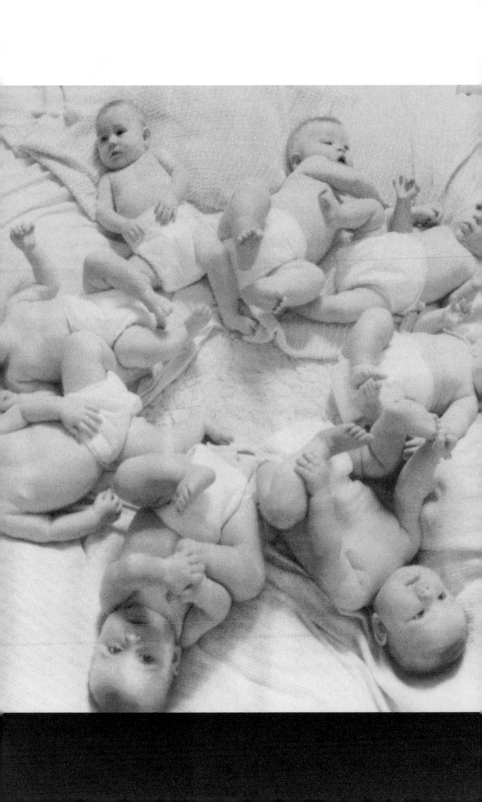

7

many mouths to feed

babies,
breastpumps
and bottles
Jeanette Niebler

Putting it all together for breastfeeding

When Rachel, Dylan and Kirsten were born at 30 weeks (2 lb.15 oz., 2lb. 13 oz., and 3 lb.), I thought it was very important that they receive all the benefits of breastmilk. After talking with my obstetrician during prenatal visits, as well as to other mothers of triplets, I was convinced that it could be done. A body can adjust to meet the triple demands for milk, and breast size doesn't seem to matter. On a good day, I'm an A cup, and I managed.

I started expressing breastmilk using a double electric pump on the day after the babies were born. For the first four or five weeks, our babies were fed milk that I had pumped since they had yet to develop the sucking reflex to breastfeed. Make sure that you have a nurse show you how to arrange the cups and the suction properly because your nipples can easily become damaged or sore from too much suction or from cups that are positioned incorrectly. The more relaxed you are, the easier it is to pump, especially at first. Sometimes just looking at a picture of your babies helps with the letdown reflex. When the babies are strong enough to leave their isolettes, holding a baby while you pump can also help stimulate milk production. The most important thing for building up milk production is to pump regularly and drink plenty of fluids. I was eventually pumping both sides for 15 to 20 minutes every two to three hours. If you are going to pump for triplets, you will need an electric pump which can be adapted to pump both sides at once. We rented a pump from the hospital pharmacy and paid about a dollar a day (we also got a discount for having triplets — don't forget to ask!) When you start pumping, you will not get very much milk, just small amounts of rich, high protein colostrum. Literally every drop of yellow-coloured colostrum is like gold to your babies — even if it is only one or two drops. Be sure to take it to the special care nursery for your babies. If you have problems producing enough milk, there are medications you can take under a doctor's supervision that can help.

Pumping can also get boring after a while. While it's gratifying providing desperately needed milk to your babies, and it is a part of their care that only you can provide, it is also rather tedious being hooked up to a milking machine for a large part of the day. Put your pump somewhere where you will be comfortable, and make sure that you have a large drink of something with you. For the last few months I was pumping, I had my machine set up in front of the computer — you can type, and even play a video game while you're hooked up.

When the babies were about three weeks old, we decided to try breastfeeding. Rachel was still being fed intravenously because she couldn't digest any type of food, so we started with Kirsten and Dylan. Kirsten latched on well the first time she got near my breast and never looked back. She became known (not so affectionately) as "jaws" for her endearing habit of grabbing my nipples in her gums and shaking her head like a dog with a bone.

Dylan was another story entirely. The minute he was near my breast, he would fall asleep. We tried everything from undressing him to tickling his bare feet to washing his face, but there was no way of keeping him awake to nurse. It's possible that there was just too much stimulation for him to handle, and he would just crash. After a week of trying, and one successful breastfeeding session, Dylan developed an intestinal disease and all of his oral feedings were stopped for 10 days. When he was finally allowed to eat again, I don't think that he cared where the food came from — he began nursing as if he had been doing it all his life.

When Rachel was finally able to digest food, I started breast-feeding her immediately with no problems. This meant we had to manage the logistics of feeding three babies. All of the babies had been supplemented with preemie formula for times when I could not pump enough milk. We decided that the best way to feed them was to nurse two at each feeding and give the third a combination of breastmilk and formula in a bottle. There were no problems (luck-ily) with nipple confusion. According to our nurses, there is rarely a problem alternating bottle and breast, particularly in the very early stages. It's possible that multiple birth babies adapt since they are often exposed to both breast and bottle while they are learning to latch. But experience varies from one family to the other.

Although I would occasionally nurse two at a time, with one on each side, I found that I preferred nursing one at a time. That was the only time that I could guarantee one-on-one cuddle time with a baby. Occasionally, I would breastfeed two and prop the third with a bottle beside me on the couch. Tandem nursing is definite-ly much faster. When things were going well, I could feed two babies in 12 to 15 minutes.

I nursed and supplemented with formula until the babies were four and half months old. Being very underweight to begin with, and never finding enough time to eat well and keep up my milk production, it all became too much of a strain on my body. Many women continue breastfeeding their triplets until they are well established on solids, but for me, the time had come to stop.

I believe that breastfeeding the babies was the very best thing I could have done for them.

against the flow
Gillian Borowy

Everyone around me was a self-proclaimed expert on breastfeeding. But who was right?

My experience with breastfeeding was not what I expected, but I'm glad I did it. While I was pregnant, I was looking forward to breast-feeding, and wanted to try to exclusively nurse all three boys. The first thing I realized was that I would have to be very strong and determined about it. Other people's reactions were almost always negative: "You won't have enough milk. You'll be too tired. There's no way you can nurse all three." Etc., etc., etc. I knew it had been done before, however, since I had spoken to two of the other moms of triplets who had done it. I wanted to try.

To prepare, I read all I could find on breastfeeding, I attended a breastfeeding clinic at the hospital, I arranged for the lactation consultant to visit me the day I gave birth, and I spoke to my husband about it — a lot. I knew I would need his encouragement and support.

During the first two days after the boys were born at 38 weeks, I was too weak. I couldn't even lift my head, much less hold a baby in my arms. My husband tried to hold a baby to my breast for me, but I wasn't interested — I felt like I had been run over by a truck.

On the third day I felt better and started to breastfeed. The nurses had been very cooperative and had not introduced the babies to bottles since I had been told that breastfeeding would be easier if the babies were not introduced to bottles before the breast. The babies seemed to latch on well and I thought I was off and running. I breastfed almost every hour for two days instead of building up gradually, and my nipples paid the price. I was so sore I would cry out and burst into tears every time a baby latched on. It upset my husband to see me in pain, and he couldn't understand why I was putting myself through this, but he wanted to be supportive.

I did not feel it was going that well, but the nurses and the lactation consultant all told me that the babies were latching on properly. They had no suggestions for improvement. I was frustrated because the babies would nurse for over an hour and still be hungry — wasn't I producing anything? Were they feeding properly?

The only advice I received was to try breast compression by hand and squeeze a shot of milk into the baby's mouth to wake him up and make him keep sucking.

The nurses showed me and my helpers how to cup-feed and sent us all home when the boys were one week old. I still wasn't sure if I was producing enough milk, or if things were really going well. People would ask how the nursing was going and I would say, "I don't know — is this what it's supposed to be like?" I was very uncertain. To reduce the nipple soreness I restricted myself to one baby per feeding and applied lanolin ointment. The soreness was gone in two days.

Cup feeding was a difficult process that gave the babies gas and frustrated my helpers. After only two days at home we switched to bottles and everybody was happier, including the boys. There was no nipple confusion. In fact, we were using three kinds of nipples as well as breastfeeding, all with no problems! If a baby is hungry it will suck on anything. The only problem that arose from bottle-feeding was that it was faster and easier than breastfeeding, and we could tell exactly how much the babies were getting. Breastfeeding quickly lost my husband's support.

The people helping us were so eager to feed the babies every time they cried, I had to ask them to let me breastfeed! I felt I was going against the flow of the household, and some days I just did not have the strength to do it. I found I was breastfeeding less and less, and I confess that it was easier on me that way.

I thought I would try to pump milk, so that I could do it when I wanted to, and we could see how much the boys were eating. I first tried a portable pump. It hurt! The larger mechanical pump was much better because I could control the suction. Sometimes it took me 40 minutes to pump two ounces, and sometimes it took 20 minutes to pump four ounces. I had to increase my milk supply, which meant pumping or breastfeeding more frequently.

Everybody around me was a self-proclaimed expert — my mum, my sisters, other mums, the nurses. What was upsetting me was that they were all telling me different things. Who was right? It took me far too long to realize that they were all right. What they did worked — for them. I had to do what was right for me, and stop worrying about what anyone else said.

The first time a baby was satisfied and slept four hours after a nursing session, I felt so good! A real accomplishment! Unfortunately it didn't happen that way very often. The babies seemed to want to nurse all day, whether for food or comfort I don't know, but I didn't have the energy or resolve to do it.

Breastfeeding became a major source of stress for me. When I breastfed I became tense because it was taking so long and the babies were not getting enough to eat from me. Yet the thought of stopping breastfeeding also upset me. My husband called it a "female macho thing" and began to lose patience with me always wanting to talk about it.

I persevered with partial breastfeeding until the boys were two months old. At that point I was on my own during the day with them and it was easier to bottlefeed. I wasn't exclusively breastfeeding, so if I was going to sterilize and fill 10 bottles with formula, it was no more work to do 20. I could do several things at once while a bottle was propped for a baby, while breastfeeding was all-consuming. The babies were two months old and healthy, I wanted to stop breastfeeding, and yet I had real difficulty letting go. I couldn't put my emotions into words. Was it pride? Was it embarrassment at admitting failure? (It was not failure, but I couldn't see that at the time.) Was I afraid I would lose the bond between baby and mother? Was I striving to fulfill some image I had of myself? Maybe my husband was right — maybe it was a female macho thing.

Stopping at two months was the right decision for me. It wasn't what I had originally planned to do, but so what? My babies got the benefits of breastmilk when they needed it most, and I also did what worked for me. My boys will only be relaxed and happy if I am. I cannot tell anyone else what to do or how to handle the issue of breastfeeding. All I can do is tell them to really listen to their own emotions, and follow what feels right. Please yourself, and you will please your family.

mama moo
Patty deLaat

One of my many nicknames as a mom breastfeeding triplets

One of the first thoughts to cross my mind, after overcoming the shock of hearing I was expecting three babies, was the idea of breastfeeding. How in the world could I breastfeed three babies at the same time? Could I produce enough milk to sustain three babies? How much help was I going to need if I wanted to attempt this very worthwhile undertaking?

I had always planned on breastfeeding, although the original plan was for one baby at a time. But I was not going to allow the fact that I was expecting triplets to change those plans. I knew that breastmilk gives a child the absolute best start at life. My antibodies would be passed on to my babies through colostrum and milk to boost their immune systems. I didn't want my children to miss out on this good start. The incentive was especially strong since my triplets, like many others, were likely to be born prematurely.

During my 12-week stay in hospital on bedrest, I asked to meet the breastfeeding specialist, who, naturally, was happy to hear that I was planning to breastfeed. The specialist stressed that a mother's body usually produces as much milk as is requested of it, so production wouldn't be a concern. The real concern was the amount of time it would take to feed the babies. Some babies need only a few minutes to get their fill of milk, while others can take hours. She stressed how important it would be to have many family, friends and home care workers who could help me with other tasks as I concentrated on feeding the babies.

Once the babies were delivered, seven weeks early, several days passed before I was able to hold them. Though this time period was very disheartening for me, I spent the time expressing breastmilk using an electric pump, and bringing the milk to the NICU in small containers. At first, there was such a small amount, just the protein-rich colostrum and a bit of watery milk to start, but it was adequate to sustain all three babies. The NICU doctors reassured me, explaining that since the babies were small and their tummies imma-

many mouths to feed

ture, they were unable to process very much milk anyway.

One of my babies, Rachel, along with many other babies in the NICU, became sick with a bacterial infection the first week after she was born. But through the illness, she was given breastmilk, and was able to fight off the life-threatening infection. I believe the breastmilk may have contributed to her recovery. Although I was not able to breastfeed Rachel until almost six weeks after her birth, I still pumped enough milk to feed her, while I breastfed her brother, Stephen, and her sister, Samantha.

Latching can be one of the biggest hurdles to jump with premature infants. Full-term babies have the natural instinct to latch on and suck, but the tiny mouths of premature infants have to be taught how to open wide. Without a proper latch, breastfeeding can be a very frustrating experience for the baby and a very painful one for the mother. The breastfeeding specialists accompanied me into the NICU many times to ensure the babies were latching well and to offer tips on holding the babies. The "football" hold seemed to be the best position for us. By placing the baby's body at my side with only the head positioned at the front (like a football being carried up a field), my other arm was free to take another baby to position on the other breast. This double-arm position was a bit uncomfortable at first. Then I discovered a wonderful invention called a breastfeeding pillow, which supported the weight of the babies better. I became more comfortable, and soon, more confident with the whole process.

Stephen and Samantha were released from hospital three weeks before Rachel. At home, the three of us became very well acquainted with each other. We found a routine of feeding that satisfied them, and didn't greatly tire me. My sister became a live-in helper who learned to finger-feed the babies while I was at the hospital visiting with Rachel. To avoid nipple confusion that sometimes happens when bottles are introduced, the babies suck breastmilk through a tube taped to a helper's baby finger. Our public health nurse was an unending supporter of breastfeeding, and was very helpful with teaching alternative methods for feeding.

I could now feed "twins," but the real test would come when Rachel joined the rounds. Once Rachel came home, I began to rely on my helpers to bring the babies to me to be fed and to burp them. I spent most of my time either sitting down feeding the babies, or standing at the change table, changing them. I found that about 60 per cent of my time was spent feeding the babies. Stephen was a fast eater and took just 10 minutes to feed, Samantha was finished after 15 minutes generally, and Rachel took as long as half an hour. But by the time Rachel came home, Stephen could eat and be satisfied for six-hour stretches. There were no times when everyone demanded to be fed at once.

If I hadn't breastfed, I would still have had to spend the same amount of time bottlefeeding. When I did introduce bottles of formula after nine months, the difference I found between breastfeeding and bottlefeeding was the amount of time sterilizing (my husband insisted on continuing) and measuring. Breastfeeding didn't require the 20 minutes spent boiling bottles and nipples, nor an hour a day measuring and filling those same bottles. The expense of bottles was very low for me because I only used them for water, juice and pumped breastmilk. The expense of formula was not a factor for us because we received free cases of formula, which we didn't need until after nine months. Soon after the nine months, we began to introduce cups and other methods of feeding, including bottles, because breastfeeding had long been established.

I can say with heartfelt thanks that the triplets were healthy, happy and very contented, and I feel that the closeness I developed with them during our feeding and cuddle times has carried on to this day. I will never regret the time that I spent breastfeeding my children because it truly was one of the most amazing parts of being a mother that I have experienced so far. As the sole source of food for my children, I was an essential and crucial part of their early existence.

bottlefeeding was one tough choice
Keri Tabet

Deciding whether or not to breastfeed is an intensely personal decision that can take an abundant amount of research, both in literature and through personal contact with other mothers and healthcare professionals. As a first-time mother expecting quadruplets, I began my research soon after I found out I was pregnant and ultimately decided to feed my children formula.

I began my research by reading all of the breastfeeding and bottlefeeding sections in mother and infant care books. Quickly I realized that the conventional thinking suggested "breast was best." Admittedly, in all of the dreams I had of becoming a mother, bottlefeeding had never entered my mind. However, quadruplets had never entered my mind either!

There is not a great deal of material available on breastfeeding multiples, but in the articles I read, it seemed that many mothers were successful either supplementing or exclusively breastfeeding for the first three or four months. These mothers were very committed to providing this nourishment to their infants; however, they also said they were often exhausted and felt tied to their houses, especially if the babies would not take a bottle at all. The mothers enjoyed the closeness and bonding that breastfeeding provided as well as the knowledge that breastmilk is the best source of vitamins and nutrients for developing infants. Breastfeeding was also touted as being affordable and convenient since there are no bottles of formula to prepare.

After reading all the advantages of breastfeeding, I seriously wondered whether there were any benefits to bottlefeeding. I was especially worried about bonding. However, I read that giving a baby a bottle can also be very nurturing and there were other bonding methods, such as skin-to-skin contact, or "kangaroo care." I reasoned that with bottlefeeding, my husband could also be involved equally and develop a closeness with all of our children. There would be no restrictions on my diet if we chose to bottlefeed and possibly, my husband and I would have more freedom to spend time together as a couple (although, having four children at once changed our relationship forever).

After all that research, I was left still debating the choices. Both methods had pros and cons. The biggest con to bottlefeeding was that it seemed selfish. But after much discussion with my husband and other mothers, I found the strength and reassurance I needed to support a decision to bottlefeed. For the most part, healthcare professionals supported my choice and I was never made to feel less of a mother for doing so.

The decision was right for me

After the babies were born, it quickly became apparent that the decision was right for me. One of the major benefits was the fact that I had an adequate amount of recovery time after giving birth by c-section. I had never had surgery and was very nervous prior to the delivery. But I have a high pain tolerance and knew that I would get through it. However, I was unprepared for the post-operative effects, such as heavy bleeding, extreme fatigue and acute pain from the incision. Perhaps if this had been a normal pregnancy with an uncomplicated delivery and recovery, I would have been in a better position to breastfeed. But during the last trimester of my pregnancy (from 18 to 31 weeks), I was confined to my home and restricted from any physical activity. Of course, bedrest was in the best interest of the babies. But after they were born, I found it a struggle to walk any distance. It was 10 days before I could comfortably walk to and from the car at the hospital and up the stairs to see the babies in the special care nursery. I soon realized that my health was as important as that of my infants since I would be their primary caregiver once they came home from the hospital.

I was told to expect significant discomfort when my milk supply came in. Thankfully I did not suffer from engorgement or pain at all, although I have been told this is the exception and not the norm. But the prospect of physical discomfort didn't discourage me from choosing bottles, and the nursing staff was ready to provide some advice on managing the engorgement if it became a problem. Once my choice to bottlefeed was made clear and accepted by those caring for my children, I was never questioned about my decision.

Bringing our newly expanded family home from the hospital was exciting, although my two daughters and one son came home first and our smallest son followed 10 days later. The news that our family was home spread quickly through our extended families and church. A schedule of help and meal preparation was developed quickly among family, church friends, school friends and neighbourhood volunteers. I was rarely alone during the week and was grateful for all the support.

Being an outgoing person, I had no trouble with friends and strangers constantly in my home; however, I did not feel comfortable with the thought of breastfeeding or breastpumping in front of them. I would not have liked going off on my own as I enjoy the adult company. I have also been blessed seeing the joy other people experience as they feed the babies.

This is especially true of their grandfathers, who have had a chance to experience more of the nurturing and closeness they may not have had when my husband and I were babies in another generation. I must admit I was concerned that other people feeding the babies could jeopardize my bonding with them as their mother, but soon it became apparent our bond was very strong regardless.

I would be remiss if I said that breastfeeding never entered my mind again once my foursome were all home. Sometimes I would see a baby at the mall or on television snuggled up to their mother and feel envious. However, I think the envy had more to do with the freedom and conveniences of having one baby versus four. These mothers never seemed to be tied to their homes and had the freedom to do everything they wanted whenever they wanted. Having four babies at home changed my life and the adjustment did not happen overnight. Bottlefeeding allowed my husband and I to take breaks outside the house together from time to time to restore ourselves. There was no need to keep an eye on the clock, knowing our capable helpers would tend to our babies. Looking back, I am grateful for those times when my husband and I could take our breaks.

We were very blessed with four healthy infants although they were nine weeks premature. At two days old, they were transferred to our local hospital for Level 2 care, where they only needed time to grow. At 34 weeks, they all took bottles, although some faster than others. Each of the babies was fed the same formula, which made bottlemaking easier once we came home. Yes, formula is certainly expensive, but we took full advantage of all the coupons and free offers that came our way and in the end, had to purchase very little ourselves.

We have not experienced any health issues as a result of bottlefeeding and I do believe that all the commercial formulas do contain the essential vitamins and nutrients to ensure healthy growth. (Although, on the advice of our pediatrician, we supplemented vitamin D over the winter.) The best advice I can offer expectant mothers is to research all of the alternatives, and remember the choice is a personal one. Do not feel obliged to make decisions based on societal pressures. Do what is right for you. In the back of my mind, I may always wonder if I could have breastfed my foursome, but I do not regret my decision to bottle-feed because it was best for my situation. Bottle or breast is up to you — but I hope that you will find support regardless of the method you choose.

enough for four?
Louise Redgers Bonnycastle

Yes, you can breastfeed quadruplets

For me it was an emotional issue. I had breastfed my son and found it so rewarding that I was determined to do it again for our next child. Little did I know that our next child would be three girls and a boy! When I found out I was having quadruplets, I was in a state of panic trying to figure out how we would cope.

I knew it was possible to breastfeed twins because I had seen it done at a local breastfeeding clinic while waiting for a friend who was having some difficulties with her baby latching. I called the clinic and they assured me that I could breastfeed quadruplets but probably not exclusively. I could settle for that. Discussions about breastfeeding never came up with my doctors in prenatal care. It was as if the issue of breastfeeding quadruplets did not exist. The neonatologist I met before the babies were born didn't mention it and I confess I never asked him how the babies would be fed while they were in incubators. Issues such as prematurity and health risks seemed to be more pressing. We focused on the medical care they would likely need — but not on what they would eat to survive.

The big day arrived. The babies were delivered by c-section at 34 weeks and quickly held up for my husband and I to see before they were whisked away to the NICU. Jenny weighed 3 lb. 12 oz., Heather 4 lb. 1 oz., Charlie 2 lb. 7 oz. and Meagen 3 lb.13 oz. I was patched back together and taken to the recovery room, anxious to see my babies. My husband was given a full report that all were doing well and that I would be taken to see the babies on the way to my room later. I remembered putting my first-born to the breast shortly after he was born, encouraging him to latch and cuddling him. With the quadruplets, I felt so empty without that connection.

The nurses wheeled me on a stretcher to see my babies in the NICU, pointing out each one and then exiting to take me to my room. I wanted to scream! I wanted to stay! The next morning the nurse came in and explained that I could make my own way down to the nursery and that later, if I desired, they would get me a kit for a breastpump that was out on the floor somewhere. Like any mother, I made my way to the nursery. I placed my hands through the small porthole doors of the incubator and had my first touch contact with the babies. The NICU nurses were great. They explained that each baby would have a feeding tube and that if I collected breastmilk and brought it to them, they would refrigerate it and try to split it among them. I was determined to get the breast-milk flowing so I spent the next few days searching out the breast-pump and trying with little success to get any quantity of milk. I was exhausted and stressed.

By the time the babies were a day old the nurses were encouraging me to hold the feeding tubes while the babies were being fed small quantities of breastmilk. Soon I was able to hold the babies for five minutes at a time to snuggle and try to get them to latch. I was finally beginning to feel like a mother. The little boy seemed to have a natural instinct to latch. I was thrilled!

When I was ready to go home, I rented a breastpump from the breastfeeding clinic so that I could continue to collect my milk, store it in the containers provided and bring it to the hospital everyday. Then when the babies were four days old, they moved to a Level 2 facility because they no longer needed intensive care. The second hospital assumed that I wanted to give the babies breastmilk. They gave me a kit to use while at the hospital and carefully explained how to store and label the milk. There was also a quiet area for feed-ing and I tried to breastfeed each child at least once each day.

My girls were not eager to latch onto the breast. At that point, when all of the babies were being supplemented with formula, my nipples were cracked and sore and I was tired, it would have been easy to give up. It took all of my resolve and the presence of my healthy happy three-year-old to make up my mind to continue.

When the naso-gastric tubes were removed, bottles were intro-

> ## quote
>
> Nurses encouraged me to hold the feeding tubes while the babies were fed small quantities of breastmilk

duced. I was worried about nipple confusion and would have preferred to stay with alternatives like finger-feeding where the baby
sucked from a feeding tube taped to a small finger. But there weren't
enough resources or time at the hospital. And the priority was to
get the babies eating and gaining weight. I spent my nights attached
to the breastpump every two hours and my days feeding one child
at a time on the breast and then pumping out what remained in
order to increase my supply. Often the nurses felt that after 20 minutes of sucking in stops and starts, the baby might not have had
enough and so they would also provide a small bottle of formula as
a supplement. The girls were growing and were soon discharged
from the hospital. But my little boy was not doing as well.

Once the girls were home, I was torn. I felt that they needed to
continue to be breastfed during the day, but I needed to be at the
hospital too. The boy was failing. He could not seem to digest formula and was losing weight. I decided to give him all the breastmilk
that I could pump or feed for the next few days and trust that I
could get the girls back on breastmilk after the crisis was over.
Charlie thrived! He gained a little weight and the doctors were
amazed. They suggested that we put a powdered supplement into
the breastmilk to increase the calories and top him up with a bottle of that after each attempt at the breast to see if he would gain
even more weight. It worked. The crisis was over. Now it was time
to get the girls back on the breast.

I was determined to persevere

There was enough milk for at least two babies each feed at that
point. But the girls decided to give me a hard time, refusing to latch
after an absence of several days. My husband suggested I give up and
just feed the boy. I was determined to persevere. I spent a great deal
of time coaxing them to latch one at a time. It took a few days and
they were back in the habit again, perhaps more interested in being
cuddled by their mom. Once they were all effective latchers again,
I began to feed two babies at a time. I would sit either in a large
rocking chair with the huge breastfeeding pillow stretched across
the arms or in the middle of the bed supported by all the pillows I
could find. It was wonderful.

Since there was no way of covering up or breastfeeding two
babies discreetly, friends and relatives either became accustomed to

or avoided feeding times. Our little boy came home and joined the fun. I continued to use the pump after each feed and stored additional milk for about four months before sending the pump back. I even froze some, which turned out to be a blessing when I came down with flu and could produce very little. Typically, I was able to produce enough breastmilk to feed two and sometimes three babies at a time. Formula would make up the difference.

Leaving the house was a challenge. I would only breastfeed one baby at a time so I didn't offend anyone. We would give the others formula in those situations. I would rush home uncomfortable and pump out. We did not go out often in those early months.

At home, breastfeeding went well. Two at a time was standard and we alternated each feed. When my husband was available, he bottlefed the other two, holding them in his arms in a rocking chair so they still got their cuddle. When I was on my own, things were more difficult. Of course, all too often, the babies wanted to be fed at once. We borrowed a second breastfeeding pillow, which allowed me to loosely prop bottles for two babies on the floor. Then I would sit on the floor as well and breastfeed the other two. It wasn't easy but it worked. My three-year-old was a great help at retrieving dropped bottles for hungry babies and if he was inclined, I would encourage him to feed one. He was terrific, and has a special bond with the babies because he felt a part of the flurry of activity.

Burping had to be done one at time, so somebody always had to wait. But things got easier as they gradually moved from two-hour feedings to three and then four. They slept through the night as early as four months, after a day filled with activity and little napping. I continued to feed them until, one by one, they decided to wean themselves between 13 and 15 months. I hated to see them stop but they had teeth, not to mention personality! But they were off to a great start and I felt very good about the whole experience.

Breastfeeding is natural, but like motherhood, it does not automatically kick in every time. Don't be afraid to ask for help or even just to check with the local breastfeeding clinic to make certain latching and sucking are progressing correctly. This will help to ensure that breastfeeding is a great experience for both you and your babies.

"successful" breastfeeding not always exclusive
Carol Molko

Just knowing there was at least one other mother of triplets who was able to exclusively breastfeed her babies was all I needed to know in order to try. If she could do it, then so could I. What's more, I had the added confidence of experience since I had exclusively breastfed my first daughter, Sharice, for six months. My goal was set — I would successfully breastfeed my triplets, exclusively.

Well, goals are ideal. Then, the babies are born, and reality kicks in. After six months, my definition of "successful" breastfeeding relaxed. It had to. I learned that successful breastfeeding doesn't necessarily mean exclusive breastfeeding, especially where triplets are concerned.

Jeremy, Shawn and Alyssa were born prematurely at 29 weeks, weighing between 1078 and 1170 grams. I began pumping breastmilk immediately so that I could establish a good steady supply for them. I wanted only what was best for the babies and I was determined to keep up my supply of milk with their increasing demand.

The first eight weeks of their lives were spent in the hospital, five of those weeks in the NICU. I visited my babies every day in the hospital and pumped around the clock. At first, I used a double breastpump to minimize my pumping time. After about a month, however, I gave the pump up altogether. My nipples were getting just too sore and tender. For me, it was more convenient, faster, easier and completely painless to just express by hand.

To this day I am extremely grateful that all three of my babies learned how to breastfeed easily and early on. This was our sweet "success" and I was very proud of it.

However, I let this early success become overshadowed by the growing realization that I was simply not able to produce enough breastmilk to feed all three babies. In fact, at best, I was only ever able to produce enough milk for just one baby, which of course, I divided equally among them. Formula feeds eventually made up the majority of their feeds. Chalk it up to a very hectic and demanding schedule, inadequate rest, inadequate fluid intake, and/or just the plain physical impossibility of me being able to produce that much breastmilk. It just wasn't going to happen. I envied the other moms of triplets at the hospital who were able to store up freezer loads of breastmilk containers, when I could no longer even keep up with my babies' daily requirements.

My friends and family continue to ask me whether I am still breastfeeding the triplets at six months. They are amazed when I say yes, although I explain that each of the babies may only get the equivalent of one breastfeeding session per day, and the rest, formula. With all the work and very little rest in caring for triplets and a three-year-old preschooler, most people think that it is just wonderful that I still manage to find the energy and time to nurse my babies, even if only a little bit, each and every day. And do you know what? So do I.

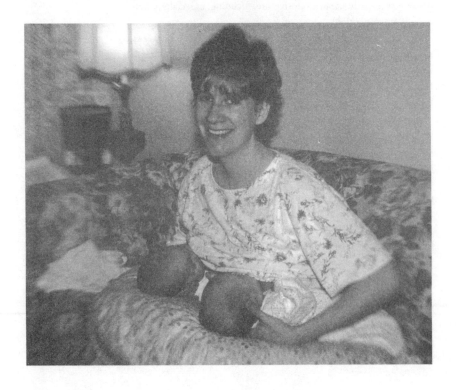

open and serving
24 hours a day
Maureen Tierney

Fast-food baby feeding

Within a week of coming home from the hospital with triplets, we
had a "staff" of five: my parents, my husband, Peter, Peter's cousin,
Marion and me. Peter had taken four weeks of vacation and Marion
stayed for five weeks. Believe it or not, I had not given much thought
to how we would handle the feedings and the sleepless nights, probably because I was a first-time parent. But we quickly learned.

Initially, I assumed all of our feedings would be scheduled
like clockwork. I imagined I would sleep in between the feedings as we did while in the hospital. I could handle that. But on
the first day home, the feeding schedule we followed while in
hospital apparently had stayed, well, at the hospital. And the
thought of continuously feeding around the clock was mind-
boggling to me. We were already getting a sense of how different the girls were in temperament. One of my daughters,
Monica, would take about an hour and a half to feed because she
sucked so slowly with her eyes closed and insisted on being held.
Thinking she was asleep, I would try taking the bottle away only
to hear her piercing screams of protest. It took one person to
feed her while another person fed the other two if they were
awake. Lorraine was the smallest of the three. She ate less, but
more frequently than her sisters. After she had breastmilk once a
day, she needed to be fed again sooner since breastmilk did not
satisfy her for as long as formula. Jacqueline sucked more than
she could swallow! We had to be careful to burp her after she ate
three or four ounces of formula and no more or all of her bottle would come back at us!

We all found it best to pre-schedule ourselves for 24-hour duty.
Marion was available during the day, while the rest of us took turns
on the graveyard shift. Nighttime was definitely the most difficult.
It was hard to sleep well during the day or in the evenings to
refuel for the night ahead. I was sleeping in four-hour stretches at a
time and then up again. It really took a toll on all of us. After seven

many mouths to feed

weeks, I managed to hire a wonderful nanny to do the night shift until the girls slept through the night.

Handy to have an emergency supply of bottles ready

We prepared 18 to 21 bottles of formula to last about 24 hours. I used a sterilizer that could accommodate eight bottles at the same time. The bottlemaking process took a total of 90 minutes. Initially we used four-ounce bottles since the babies were eating smaller amounts in the early days. I remember times when one of the girls would suddenly go through a growth spurt, unrecognized by us at the time. After drinking a full bottle of formula, the baby would continue to cry. We would try everything to please her before considering if she just wanted more to eat. Behold, another bottle solved the problem. In those situations it was handy to have an emergency supply of extra bottles ready. As the babes grew and the amounts increased, so did the time between feedings. It was helpful to keep a log of each child's eating habits until they were six months old. We kept track of the time they ate and the amounts of the feeding, which helped us to anticipate who would be feeding next.

How did we feed the babies? For the first 10 weeks when there was no real schedule, we fed the babies in our arms one at a time. That was fine until Peter returned to work and Marion went home. Thankfully, they did not demand to eat at the same time all of the time. If two were hungry at the same time, I would put one on each side of me on the couch and give them their bottle. If another became cranky, I would put her in the battery-operated swing. I found the swing to be an absolute must for the first four months. The babies also sat in their car seats a lot of the time, which I could rock with my foot if one was fussing. I also used the breast pillow when I breastfed, which I did once or twice daily with one baby.

When our night help arrived, she taught me an invaluable trick, which I hadn't considered. She propped the bottles on a thick towel as the babies sat in their car seats. I could now feed all three girls right in front of me. This became the main way to feed the girls, especially when I was alone. Feeding triplets all at once on your own can be incredibly frustrating otherwise. Feeding two at once often took 20 minutes or more, not to mention time for burping. All the while, a poor baby would be left screaming for a bottle and attention. When I finally did reach her, she would be inconsolable and full of gas from crying. Propping was the best way I could manage.

Now it was time to get them on a schedule so they could feed at the same time. Non-scheduled feedings were unpredictable and left me feeling as though all I was doing was feeding babies day and night. I needed a break away from feeding, not to mention time to do other things like laundry, prepare meals, and even chat with a friend from time to time. The only glitch in my schedule was Lorraine, my smallest, who ate less than her sisters. Lorraine needed more feedings. From our charts I could see that Lorraine would start crying to eat about 45 minutes ahead of her sisters. My solution was to try and delay her bottle for as long as possible by playing and walking with her. After about 20 to 25 minutes, I would feed all the babies. It took a while for this to work, but it did eventually.

While getting the girls on a feeding schedule took some maneuvering in the beginning, it was worth the effort. And once I did manage to get it going, I never looked back.

Use Caution when Propping Bottles
Open and serving 24 hours a day

Propping a bottle on a towel in front of your babies as they're seated in infant seats will allow them to feed without an adult having to hold the bottle. Doctors discourage the practice because there can be a risk of choking for babies who are incapable of pulling away when they have had enough. If you do prop, never leave your babies unattended while the bottles are propped and always ensure the bottles are well positioned so the babies can comfortably reach the nipple without disrupting airflow to the nose.

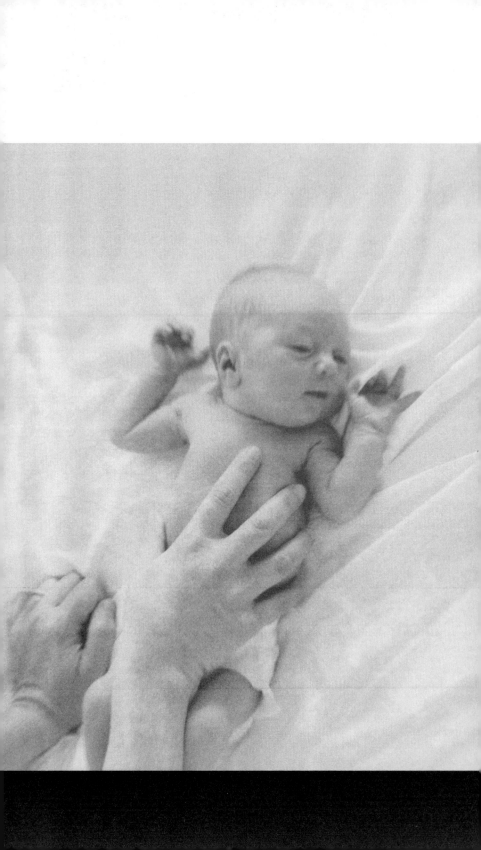

8

early days at home and hospital

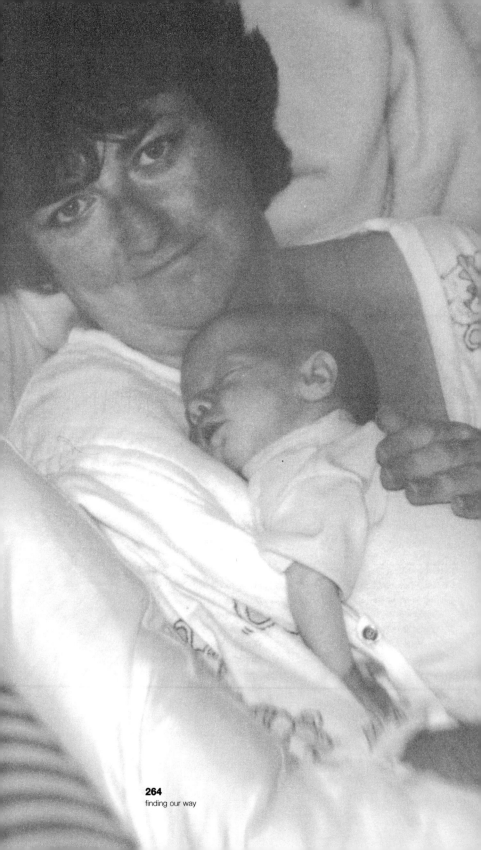

what is love to a baby?

Bracha Mirsky

Aharon, the smallest of our triplets, was 3 lb., 3 oz. at birth and had to gain another 2 lb. before he could be discharged from the hospital.

It was hard leaving Aharon all alone in a hospital so far away from home. Since I was recovering from a cesarean, had two newborns at home and couldn't drive, my visits with Aharon were always a weekend event. Fortunately, my husband worked only a few blocks from the hospital and spent every lunch hour and an hour after work with our smallest son for those two months. Aharon stayed in an incubator for the longest time. He gained weight very slowly. But we contacted the nursery every day and heard he was a fine and active little fellow.

Finally the day came when we could take Aharon home. I called the nursery to speak to his nurse, wanting to know his routine. His brother and sister were on schedules, with wakeful times and sleep times. Imagine my

delayed bonding

shock at being told, after two months of daily contact with staff, that he had no schedule and cried around the clock constantly. I couldn't believe it. Why hadn't they told us?! My husband was there every day! That afternoon, when we picked up Aharon, I looked into his small face, and for the first time noticed how tense he looked. Even his skin seemed tight. His little hands shook. As for crying, they were right, he cried constantly unless held.

My husband and I talked it over. What was wrong? Why did he shake, why did he cry? My husband, who spent a great deal more time in the hospital nursery than I had, told me what he had observed. As he sat there holding our son, he would see the nurses rotating from baby to baby. If another one began to cry they would sometimes call out, "It's not your turn yet." After all, they had only two hands. Three nurses for 20 babies. It never occurred to my husband that our son's experience for the first two months of his life would have such an impact. If it wasn't Aharon's turn for a feeding or bath, then he was not touched except when my husband or I were there. To me, that was the essence of the problem. He had been fed, changed and washed, but he had not been held.

What does a baby know? Tell him you love him, he hears, but does he understand? His universe consists of only himself and how he feels. Hunger, cold, wet, warmth and being held. So I embarked on a tactile comforting campaign to restore what he had been deprived of most — human contact. I held him almost constantly, except when he slept. I put him on my stomach when I slept or in my arms until he slept. His bassinet was beside my bed at night, and I never let him cry. At the first whimper I was there.

My poor shaking, trembling child. If I kissed you a hundred times today, would you know you are loved? Now you can feel that love in a way you understand, with your body pressed close to mine. You are not alone anymore.

I continued with this, with the help of my husband, for one month. After the first week, Aharon stopped shaking and after two weeks, he started to smile. Soon he would wake up and lie in bed content for a little while. After a month of healing, we started to ease him into the family routine. He soon responded similarly to his brother and sister, and I felt that we had successfully embraced him into our family through the all-encompassing magic of touch between a baby and parent.

delayed bonding

leaving babies behind
Tina Spigarelli

When home is hundreds of miles away

I wish I had magic words of wisdom for parents, but it seems there are very few universal truths about our experiences. Every situation is different. For example, some parents live close to the hospital and feel very connected to their babies. I, on the other hand, lived 500 miles away from my quadruplets.

While my husband and I gathered and read as much information on premature babies as we could, I still wasn't prepared for seeing and relating to our own tiny, helpless children. I realize now that although I may have put many of the fears and anxieties that come with prematurity behind me, the guilt remains about losing all those weeks of precious bonding time.

Born at 30 weeks, my four babies were placed on ventilators for breathing in the first few days. While the prognosis for everyone looked favourable, our doctor reminded us that nothing was guaranteed. Four days after my c-section, I was discharged from the hospital, and although I hated to leave my babies, I was happy to say goodbye to what had become my temporary home for the last five weeks of pregnancy. I cried a lot in those weeks while I was in Toronto, hundreds of miles from my husband and two other children, aged nine and seven. My husband and I stayed in Toronto for 10 days until the babies were out of danger and stable, and then left for home to be with our two other children. I couldn't stand another minute without seeing Ty and Britt. I was torn. I missed my kids, but leaving the babies so far behind ... I knew it would be difficult to travel back.

Then once I was home and saw that Ty and Britt were no worse for my prolonged absence, I started to miss the babies desperately. At first I didn't want to sleep because I felt guilty sleeping as they fought to gain strength. Then I felt angry and torn for not being able to be in two places at once. I was fighting off depression — the worst feeling of all. It was hard going into the babies' rooms and seeing empty cribs and wondering if they would ever be filled. I couldn't bring myself to finish the decorating in fear that I would jinx their arrival. I moped around the house all day watching the clock for my time to call the hospital. I called twice a day, once in the morning and

delayed bonding

again at night. The darkest moments came when we heard bad news about medical setbacks and felt helpless and distant.

Three weeks went by before two of the babies were well enough to be transferred to our local hospital. Since there were just two beds available to babies needing special care, our other two babies, Dylan and Riley Rose, had to wait back in Toronto until the first two were ready to come home. We lived like this for a month. Once two babies came home, the others were transported from Toronto to the local hospital. But visiting them was nearly impossible. It couldn't be any other way, but with no help and four children, and soon, five children at home, I am ashamed that I could only visit Dylan three times the entire time he was in the hospital. For the last week, he was alone, although my husband went every day after work.

It is an awful feeling to be too busy to think about, let alone see, your tiny baby in hospital. To this day, I honestly don't feel the same connection with Dylan as I do with the other three quadruplets. I think I try to overcompensate sometimes. I do love him without a doubt, but he is closer to his dad, even though I am his primary caregiver.

While the babies were in hospital, I found strength in my family, friends and in my faith. Also, I took an active part in my babies' care, by keeping up to date on their medications and keeping a daily journal of events. It allowed me to look back and see their progress or regression.

After my experience, I learned to stop comparing myself with others because each situation is unique. Later, I found comfort in giving others support and I remembered to lean on my husband from time to time. I knew I wasn't going through this experience alone and that my husband could shed tears as well.

delayed bonding

waiting to feel
like a mom
Jeanette Niebler

I didn't really feel close to my babies until shortly after I brought them home from the hospital when they were nine weeks old. Looking back, I think there were many factors that stopped me from sharing a bond with my children at first.

To begin with, let's face it — premature babies look nothing like rosy-cheeked, plump babies. While I felt fortunate that each of our babies had hit the three-pound mark, they were still incredibly small and thin. They had no fat deposits on their bodies at all, their genitals and ears were not fully developed, and they were covered in fine hair. More than anything, they looked like little old people. Looking in their faces, it was impossible to envision what they would look like as mature babies. Their faces were scrunched and their bodies were tiny. Rachel's arm was about the size of one of my fingers. Because they were so small and delicate, I was sure I would inadvertently hurt the babies if I held them. Although I overcame that fear relatively quickly, I didn't feel very maternal worrying about wires and monitors and breaking my babies! And with all of the life support equipment, it was difficult to see these little creatures as people.

I remember my first experience holding one of the children. Dylan was two days old when the nurse handed him to me swaddled tightly in a blanket, with a large hat pulled down just above his eyes. I could barely make out his face underneath the wraps. He opened his eyes, took one look at me and stopped breathing. Not the kind of reaction that instills boundless confidence in your mothering skills! Fortunately he recovered quickly and, as the days passed, his apnea attacks (breathing lapses), which are quite normal in preemies, began to subside.

It was also difficult feeling like a real mother when the medical staff were in charge of everything, particularly during those first few critical days. For as long as our babies remained unstable, my husband and I were not allowed to hold them for very long. Instead, we sat by the isolettes, staring at our children, feeling powerless. Our nurses were wonderful and later encouraged us to par-

early days at home and hospital

delayed bonding

ticipate in the babies' care as much as we could. But those early days of not being able to change diapers, feed, or hold the babies, were enough to make me hesitate. In the many weeks that followed, I would stop and ask the nurses if I could take the babies out to be held or bathed or changed. The nurses kept insisting that they were my babies and that I should do what I felt should be done, but I never really felt like I was in control of them.

The one department that I did have absolute control over was milk supply. I always ensured that I pumped enough breastmilk for the babies when they were gavage (tube) fed and to maintain the production when they were ready to breastfeed. For me, pumping was difficult because I resented all the time it took and it involved yet another mechanical device. About three weeks passed before the first of the babies developed a sucking reflex that was strong enough to try breastfeeding. Once that happened, I felt much more confident as a mother and knew I was finally doing something for the babies that only I could do.

It's not that I didn't "love" my babies while they were in the hospital — I did, if love means thinking about them constantly, worrying about their progress, and missing them when I couldn't be there. But I did feel disconnected from them. I would go to the Neonatal Intensive Care Unit and look at them, even hold them and feed them, and still not feel as though they were actually mine. I think that part of this detachment might have happened even if they had come home right away. There were three babies, and there was very little time to spend cuddling each one.

Still, once we were home and I was responsible for their care, I began to feel like a real mother. Soon I couldn't imagine life before them and I began to accept that all the warm and fuzzy feelings of emotional attachment are not always instantaneous. The bond grows stronger over time. And with every day that passes, I love them more, despite our uncertain start.

delayed bonding

falling in love with
my babies
Diane Myers

Will I ever love you the way a mother should?

When our four babies were born, one of my concerns, aside from the medical issues, was how to bond with these children when I wasn't even allowed to hold them. For our first child Craig, everything seemed to fall into place so nicely. I was in total control of my new baby almost from the first minute.

But things were different with my second birth. Each baby was rushed away by his or her special team to be ventilated and cared for by medical personnel, while I was dispatched in the opposite direction to the recovery room after the c-section.

The hospital staff tried diligently to connect me with the children on the first day. While I was in the recovery room, the nurses brought pictures of the children to me. Then on the way back to my room, they wheeled me on a stretcher through the Neonatal Intensive Care Unit (NICU) to see my new babies.

As the days passed I still had little control over my children's care. I would sit beside the incubators occasionally putting my hand on a baby's back. This seemed to go on forever. Then about two weeks after their birth, I was allowed to hold Alison — briefly. As time dragged on I began to change and bathe all the children except Harrison, who seemed to catch every bug in circulation. The first time I held Harrison was one month after his birth.

When did I bond with my quadruplets? Tough question. Now that they are age 10, I know I dearly love them as I do my other children. But I'm not exactly sure when I fell in love with them. There were many feelings of guilt, caring, love and rejection all through the first year. And I was so tired I wasn't sure if I had bonded with them at all. If one of the children was having a bad day, week or month, it was easy to pass that child along to a volunteer. At times I thought, "What kind of a mother am I? I don't have the same connection with these children as I had with my first baby. What am I doing wrong?" Eventually my fears were relieved. I am normal and I do love my children. I may not like everything they do every day but I do love them. And I realized that I needed breaks

delayed bonding

so that I could see past the bad days and enjoy my children.

Thinking back, I think there were several factors that stopped me from bonding with my babies in the early weeks.

Personal illness. Recovering from the c-section was especially difficult after the prolonged immobility of bedrest.

Emotional instability. I needed time to balance my hormonal system again.

Fear that the children might succumb to illness. I tried to fight off thoughts that the babies' lives were at risk, but deep down, I knew that it was true.

Lack of personal contact in hospital. Their fragile medical conditions prevented me from holding, feeding, bathing or consoling my babies.

A colicky, perpetually fussy baby at home. I felt that I was spending too much time with one child and not connecting with the others.

Fatigue. I couldn't think clearly or sort, describe or analyze my emotions rationally.

Boredom. The first six months were extremely busy but not very intellectually stimulating.

Volunteers taking over the care of the children. A necessary thing in my household, but it left me with a feeling that the children didn't really need me. They were happy with anyone who would feed and cuddle them.

How did I deal with these feelings? To be completely honest, I am not sure if I did deal with them. Some days, I would declare, "Today I will spend less time with Alison (who no one else could settle and feed) and more time with Kenny." But as the day progressed, I would find Ali in my arms and Kenny playing happily with a volunteer. Hindsight tells me that I could have done a lot of little things differently. But the only real thing that would have comforted me was for someone to tell me that my feelings were normal. I was not a bad mother because I had all of these conflicting feelings. I was a person in a very hard situation who only needed to know these short-term feelings of inadequacy with my children would give way, almost imperceptibly, to love as strong as ever.

getting to know our babies
Pino Spigarelli

Dad takes parental leave

When they think of bonding, many people think of the strong connection between mother and baby. But what about the bond between father and child?

In the 10 long and painful weeks our newborn quadruplets had to stay in a hospital 500 miles from our home, I too felt the emptiness that comes with being separated from our babies. When they were strong enough to finally come home, I felt that I needed to be with the babies more than just after work. That's why I took parental leave from work for seven weeks.

I would not trade these seven weeks for anything in the world. Waking up every day to feed and cuddle my babies was priceless. Undeniably, these were tough and trying times. I would get up during nighttime hours mostly, while my wife took charge in the daytime hours. Since we didn't have much help at first, we lived and breathed babies 24 hours a day. But it was a very important period for me as a father bonding with my children, especially given our separation for the first two months.

I cannot overstate the benefits of taking parental leave for any father. A baby learns to recognize your voice, senses how you smell and very quickly knows who you are. These days, my job takes me away from the house about 13 hours a day. Yet when I arrive home after work, our eight-month-old babies smile and feel comforted when they hear my voice and I pick them up. I'm not saying this does not happen to a father who does not take parental leave, but I do think the bond between father and child can be much stronger if it is established in the early months.

Of course there are other reasons to be at home — sharing the incredible workload in the early days is reason enough. But after looking at how quickly my two older children have grown, perhaps I realized that children are small only once and I am determined to share the joys of the early years as much as I can.

home at last

ready, set...wait
Maureen Tierney

Leaving the hospital sooner or later
Our daughters were a week old when we left the hospital for home. At the hospital the girls were all eating at the same time like clockwork. My husband, Peter, was staying overnight with me the first week. Together we would wake up in the middle of the night, feed and change the babies, and then it was lights out. A nurse came in to help with the third baby. I was feeling very confident that all would go as smoothly as it had at the hospital. But I forgot the nurse was not coming home with us!

I started to get a good sense of what life would be like without our nurse the day we left the hospital. That morning, my father and Peter must have made 15 trips to the car to move all of my things out of the room. Between my mother, Peter and I, we continued to feed the babies as the cars were being loaded and for an eternity afterward. Just as we would say, "Let's go!" one or two or three of the girls would start crying to be fed. This went on for a few hours. We just couldn't get out of that hospital. Finally I said, "That's it — we're going!" Sometimes, you just have to take matters into your hands. Just as we pulled into our driveway, Jacqueline threw up every last ounce of formula we had just given her.

Home sweet home.

home at last

long road home
Mary Anne Moser

Just hours after the high drama of a near vaginal birth in the operating room, we were told to prepare for our babies to spend several weeks in the hospital. Our triplets, delivered at 34 weeks, weighed 4 lb., 12 oz.; 4 lb., 10 oz.; and 4 lb., 12 oz. So it came as a surprise when, 24 hours later, all of the babies were in the regular hospital nursery and murmurs began about our impending discharge. The hospital was busy, and the nursery full, so our bulk delivery was a strain on resources. However, since I had spent the past two languid months at that hospital, contracted an infection in the operating room, and was overwhelmed with having three new babies (shock, hormones, lack of sleep), the idea of leaving seemed like a distant goal.

But there they were, the day my fever abated, unhooking my IV and discussing our discharge for later that day. They could just as well have said, "We'll be operating to remove your head this evening," and my response would have been the same. "All right."

I had spent four days hobbling about, feeling not good with the infection, but good because the babies were all healthy. Not good because this breastfeeding business was not at all straightforward but good because people were trying to help me. Not good because of my hormones but good because of my hormones. Not good because I didn't know which way was up and I didn't think I would ever sleep again but good because the nurses said if they weren't too busy they would do one of the night feedings for me. Not good because my hospital gowns were covered in body fluids and I was a wreck but good that my family was around and I was allowed to be on my feet for the first time in three months. But not good because it hurt to stand with all that weight on my stomach and no muscles to support it. All in all, it was an incredible emotional tug of war that I still find difficult to believe, let alone describe. And in the midst of everything, we were all going to be sent home.

Fortunately, the pediatrician assigned to our babies hesitated for a moment. "They are small and a bit jaundiced. Maybe we are pushing them too soon. Let's see if we can move you to a less crowded hospital for a few days."

When it was time to transfer the babies to another hospital, I

home at last

cried my heart out, as though I would never see them again. This instinctual protectiveness surprised me. Although I had no experience of being a mother, and I knew that the doctors and nurses were much more experienced with babies, it physically hurt to be separated from them. Trite as it sounds, the umbilical cord most certainly persists long after it has been physically cut. But off they went by ambulance with very qualified attendants, and I was assured they would be fine for the few hours they would be out of my sight.

In fact, I'm sure they were better off. One look at me and I'm sure they would have been traumatized. In my naive optimism, I had packed a big baggy summer dress to wear home. It wasn't a maternity dress but I always thought it could have been, since it was so loose. I slipped it over my head and there it stuck. After pulling it down, I looked like a clown gone wrong. A dress that hangs loosely on a slim frame looks like a colourful tight bag on a bloated postpartum mother of triplets.

At any rate, after a few days of feeding, sleeping and recovering in a quieter hospital, we were ready to try it on our own. Having lost a bit of weight after birth, all of our babies were discharged weighing a little over 4 pounds, even though the car seats are not designed for babies under 5 pounds. It was a little unsettling but we were at a loss for alternative ways of getting them home.

Not having had the time to shop for a vehicle that would accommodate three car seats at once, we had to rely on grandparents to take one of the babies in their car. The babies' heads were falling forward, the seats much too big, and we worried, checked, rebundled, lurched and panicked for 48 kilometres home over bumpy detours because, of course, the highway to our house was under construction. As both sets of the grandparents later attested, it was the most nerve-wracking trip ever. And with every bump, my incision reminded me that there was still some recovery to do.

But there we were, safely home (or so others assumed — I for one wasn't sure if irreparable brain damage had been done). We settled in, panic and excitement beneath the surface, and tried to pretend all was normal. I didn't actually find the first night to be very different from daytime, and we lived for the visit from the health nurse the next day. Every hour ticked by like it was a million years.

home at last

The next day the need for a minivan sunk in. Our first visit to the doctor was in three days and we had no way to get us all there! So my mom and I sent my husband out with a shopping list: milk, peanut butter, twist ties (for pumped breast milk), minivan. Almost without pause, he got everything on the list. And we've been as efficient ever since. Of course.

getting into the baby routine
Vera Holtvluewer

The first four months

I am convinced that it's essential for moms with three or more babies to develop a time schedule for feeding and napping. This is especially true for those who have older children as well. I found that once I strayed from a schedule, everything else started to fall apart.

When our babies came home from the hospital, they were on a four-hour schedule, and we tried as much as possible to stick to it. If the babies wanted to eat more often, we would try to get them to eat more at each feeding instead. With triplets, the four-hour feeding schedule allowed me to organize my time so that I could feed one baby after the other. For example, if you feed Baby A at 8 a.m., Baby B at 9 a.m., and Baby C at 10 a.m., theoretically you would have about one hour left to do other things before the routine starts all over again.

The way you choose to handle things will depend on the amount of help you have at home. If you have full-time day and night help, you may want to feed two of the babies at once and the third or fourth later. If you just have day help, you may want to feed them one at a time — day and night. When help arrives during the day, you may be able to catch up on some sleep at that point.

Once you have figured out a basic feeding routine, you can then work in a bath schedule and other things that need to be done. It worked for me to pick one day to do our household laundry (baby laundry was almost every day in the beginning). Another day would be chosen to clean each of the rooms, buy groceries and so on. In

home at last

the very early stages, many of these things were only done if and when we had the time. Eventually our lives ran more smoothly and everything had its own place and time.

The Art of Triplet Time Management

Once the babies started sleeping longer at night, our days began to look something like these sample routines.

*4 Months (3 months corrected)	7 Months	9 Months
6:00 a.m. Bottle	6:00 a.m. Bottle	6:00 a.m. Bottle
10:00 a.m. Bottle	6:30-8:30 Nap	8:00 a.m. Pabulum
2:00 p.m. Bottle	9:00 Bottle & Pabulum	9:00 a.m. Bottle
6:00 p.m. Bottle	9:30-11 Nap	9:15-11:15 Nap
9:30 p.m. Bottle	12:00 p.m. Lunch veg/fruit	12:00 p.m. Lunch
11:00 p.m. Bottle	1:00-3:30 Nap	1:00-3:30 Nap
12:00 a.m. Bedtime	5:00 Pabulum	4:30 Dinner
	7:00 Bottle	6:00 Bottle
	8:00 Bedtime	7:00 Bedtime

*At 4 months of age, our babies didn't have scheduled naps, but slept for the most part between feedings

parents take note!
Deb Muenz

My husband and I kept detailed notes that showed exactly when and how much our babies ate, when they were changed and how long they slept. Taking notes was especially helpful during the early months. Here are a few of the ways our notes were put to good use:

Doctor visits

We could report how much and how often the children were eating and whether or not they were having normal bowel movements. Parents of single babies and caregivers may be surprised to hear we couldn't remember all the details. Parents of triplets or more will nod and understand. If the children were sick, we also kept track of their temperature, when medication was given and the type of medication administered. Both of our girls are allergic to certain penicillin-based drugs, so we've kept careful records of their reactions to these drugs. And it helps us to ensure we don't give them this medication again.

A tool for helpers

Our helpers found it useful to have written schedules to follow. There wasn't a need to spend time asking a lot of questions since they could easily determine the time of the last feed and estimate the time of the next one. Bath times were scheduled and any medications were administered and noted at the proper time, and most important, given in the proper dosage.

Feeding time and quantity

In the early days, our children were fed every three hours. As they began to grow and eat larger quantities, a record helped us figure out which bottle could be cut. If the babies started drinking only a few ounces at one of their feeds, we tried to stretch the time before the next bottle by about 20 minutes to half an hour.

Solid food introduction

We found the records valuable when solid foods were introduced. If a certain food wasn't tolerated well or caused a diaper rash for one or all of the babies, we removed it from the diet for a while.

> ## tip
> Record-keeping can be a benefit when chaos turns the house upside down

home at last

Sample Nursery Record
Patricia Harber

BABY NAME:		
	Date	Time
Sleep		
Breast milk (# of oz./ml)		
Formula supplement (# of oz./ml)		
# of burps/spit up/vomit		
Bowel movement (Y or N)		
Wet diaper (light or heavy)		
Bath (Y or N)		
Vitamins/Medications		
Care giver initials		
Additional information		

shift duty
Patricia Lumsden

During the early weeks after our foursome was born, the babies were released not at once, but in shifts from the hospital. Jennie Lee, the first baby home, had a few days all to herself, getting spoiled with love and attention. With every squeak and peep, she had us up and running. Then, over the next few weeks, her three siblings began arriving home in shifts. With the foursome home, Jennie must have wondered why her parents were suddenly so slow off the mark. Nonetheless, it was a huge relief when everyone was finally home since arranging hospital visits while caring for one, then two, and then three babies at home, while one still remained in special care in the hospital, was tough.

For the first year, we had a nanny who worked from 9 a.m. to 5 p.m., five days a week. When the babies first came home, they were fed every two hours, then every three, and then every four hours. On the week nights I managed the feedings alone, and on weekends, my husband, Martin, would take over. Since I have always found it difficult to sleep during the day, I didn't get much sleep through the week. I believe I ran on adrenaline that first year.

I kept a chart for the first three months, recording feeding times and amounts, bowel movements, baths and vitamin drops. We stuck to a scheduled routine for the first two years since any disruption always led to chaos. The entire morning was taken up with feeding, a full bath for everyone, diaper changing, more feeding, a clothing change and housework. In the afternoons, we would take a long walk in two double strollers, and work in the

usual feedings, diaper changes and often, another change of clothes. Fussy time at our house was from 4 p.m. to 6 p.m., without fail. Many, many meals were eaten while holding a baby, or with two rocker chairs at each foot, rocking away. All it would take was a single cry from one baby to start everyone off, and it always happened in that two-hour timeframe.

In the evenings, there was another feeding and a quick wash, and bedtime at 8 p.m. For the first nine months, when the babies were waking at night, I always went to bed no later than 10 p.m. Martin took care of the feedings until he went to bed around midnight, or as near to it as he could arrange a feed and change for all four. Then it was my shift for the night.

When one or two babies woke at once, I held and fed them both at once. If three or four woke at the same time, as often happened, I had to sit them in their rocker chairs and prop the bottles with a small blanket. I knelt on the floor in front of them all, burped them in rotation, fed some more, burped again, changed their diapers in rotation, rocked them a bit, then put them back in their cribs, and went back to sleep until the next wake-up call.

survive and thrive
Sara Salter-McLean

A few ideas for making life easier and more fun with three babies at home

Getting babies to sleep

Establishing consistent sleep habits was one of the biggest challenges we faced, but something we have had great success with so far. After three months, two of the three babies slept from 9 p.m. to 6:30 a.m., with only occasional blips in the middle of the night. Our little boy was the toughest. He enjoyed his bottle, cuddle and "playtime" too much to go back to bed and sleep for another three hours. By the time he was five months old, he also slept through the night — a blissful night we will remember for a very long time. Now, at 11 months old, the babies go to bed at 8:15 p.m. and usually sleep peace-

home at last

fully until 7 a.m. in the morning. Nothing is totally perfect. My husband and I still get up once in a while to find a soother, replace a cover, find a hand that has been tangled inside a sleeper, or to reposition their special toys.

How did we do it?

• We tracked each baby's sleep patterns and arranged the timing of nighttime and morning bottles to maximize their sleeping time.

• For the first two months, we woke them every four hours for a bottle. We kept the lights very low, changed them quietly in the almost-dark, barely spoke to them and put them back to bed immediately. In other words, we kept the stimuli to a minimum.

• In month three, we started progressively waking the babies 10 or 15 minutes later for the middle of the night bottle. For example, for three or four nights, we would wake the babies and give them a bottle at a certain time. Then, for the next four nights, they would be fed that bottle 15 minutes later. The following week, we would wait another 15 minutes, and on and on until we gradually expanded the time between bottles by more than six hours. As time went on, we started noticing that they were more sleepy than hungry. We continued delaying their bottles, and they began to trust that we would wake them to eat.

• If they did wake up crying, we did not automatically feed them a bottle. The delay was not an issue with the girls, but it was with our son. At first, we tried to console him and over time, it worked. We also increased his nighttime bottle by one ounce and reduced his middle of the night bottle by the same amount. We realized he was not crying out of hunger but out of a need for comfort.

• If we knew he was not hungry and consoling him did not work, as a last resort, we would let him cry. After three minutes of his crying, I would go back into the room to reassure him and then return every five minutes and then every seven minutes until he stopped, which was usually after 20 to 30 minutes. Fortunately, we only had to repeat this routine for three or four nights before he realized something was different. This approach may seem very cold and unloving but, in fact, it is the opposite. Personally, I feel it is extremely important that babies have the confidence to "self-calm" and ease themselves back to sleep without a bottle or cuddle.

home at last

- We taught the babies "self-calming" techniques during the daytime naps that they could apply at night. My theory was that if we could get them to nap well during the day on their own, they could then apply the experience when they woke at night and were alone. Some tools for self-calming were attachment items such as a blanket, stuffed animal, or a thumb. Even helping them find a certain position that they found relaxing was helpful. For one of my girls, we played soft music and if times got tough at night, we would turn it on. But the music never became an essential part of her bedtime ritual. Additionally, everyone followed exactly the same routine, including my nanny and grandparents. Consistency was extremely important.
- We put them in two rooms based on their sleep patterns. For the first four months, everyone stayed in the same room, but as the sleep habits changed, it made more sense to separate them.

Staying on schedule

I'm not sure if we could have survived without a schedule. The trick, I believe, is to first develop a schedule and modify it as the babies' needs change over the weeks and months. That means staying sensitive to those changes. Also, for as long as we had the schedule, we stuck to it faithfully. With three babies, there isn't the luxury of flexibility. For us, spending individual time with the children was a top priority so we developed a schedule that would usually guarantee that one of us (my husband, helpers or me) would individually feed each baby rather than prop feed. It's a personal choice, but I was against prop feeding because I felt it took valuable bonding time away from each baby with us. This is especially important given the more complicated bonding process with triplets or more.

Household planning

Since time was at a premium, I sat down with our nanny to develop the best way of managing all of the daily routine activities and chores. To keep things running as smoothly as possible, we tried to plan tasks such as bottle sterilizing, solid food preparation and laundry in a way that made the most sense.

Fun times as a family

Our motto was this — let's try anything once, and if we don't succeed or go crazy trying, we'll either adjust the approach or shelve the idea for now. Even with three children all under age one, we were determined to continue doing many of the things parents do with one child. With that in mind, we rented a cottage for three weeks, and it was the best time we have spent together as a family. It was very relaxing for all, even the babies, and we really enjoyed ourselves.

Giving babies some space

Let the children have their own space, completely child-proofed, even if it means giving up a large portion of household living space. We cleared out our main floor living room and dining room for them, and the basement is also essentially their second playroom. It looks like a daycare centre with theme pictures on the walls, mobiles hanging from our dining room fixture, and laminated 8- by 10-inch colour copies of the whole family scattered across all the walls. I truly believe they enjoy and benefit from this creative environment.

Remembering our good fortune

Every night after kissing the babies goodnight, my husband and I were reminded how lucky we were to have three happy angels.

sleeping like a baby
Gillian Borowy

As a new mother, I was envious when I heard stories of babies who slept eight hours at two weeks of age. On the other hand, I also heard stories of children who were two years old and still not sleeping through the night, and I was afraid. My three boys, David, Michael and Kenny, are now six months old and finally sleeping well.

During the first two months I had enough day and nighttime help to feed the babies on demand. Then the help disappeared and I had to move towards scheduling because I couldn't keep going at the same pace. My husband and I started the process by feeding the boys at 11 p.m. regardless of when they last ate. After the last feeding, they would sleep for between four and five hours. That was the longest

home at last

period of time in which all three slept at the same time. During the day the babies were still fed on demand, except on those occasions when they demanded to be fed less than three hours from the last feeding. I wanted to try and break their snack-and-snooze cycle.

Things improved markedly when by two and a half months of age, at 12, 13 and 14 pounds, they would sleep seven hours or more. If one awoke before 6 a.m., I would give him just two or three ounces. I could get up, change the baby, feed him, and be back in bed within 20 minutes.

At three months, we were able to move the last feed back to 10 p.m. and the boys would still sleep until 6 am. During the day, I was still demand feeding because I was alone with them and I did not have the emotional strength to wake a sleeping baby. I was also intimidated by the thought of feeding all three at once. I was on call all day, not knowing when I would next be required to feed someone. I couldn't plan anything, not even a shower. I was definitely not in control. I thought it would be easier with the boys on a schedule, but I didn't know how to start.

Speaking with other mothers gave me the resolve to do it. They convinced me that it would only be difficult for a day, then my life would be much easier. To help me with the task of feeding three babies at once, I invited a neighbour for coffee. I felt good being able to say, "Come at 10 a.m. and you can help me feed the boys." I actually knew when I was going to feed them! After that first morning my confidence soared and I never looked back. The boys were on a schedule of 6 p.m., 10 p.m., 2 a.m., 6 a.m., 10 a.m. and 2 p.m.

By four months of age, the boys were sleeping for eight hours most nights. But then they caught two colds in a row, and their congestion caused them to wake up at night. After we were all healthy again, only David was sleeping through the night. The other two had forgotten how.

Instead of improving, things got worse. I was getting up three to five times a night as they took turns waking. I knew I had reached my limit the night I had to quickly put Kenny down on the hardwood floor because I thought I was about to faint.

Another mother recommended that I read some books on sleep. One of the books I read mentioned that sleep habits are being formed from three to five months of age. I realized we had created our own problems by always rocking Kenny to sleep, and by always

home at last

feeding Michael when he woke in the night. (He's the smallest and we were trying to help him catch up.) They learned to associate these actions with falling asleep and couldn't go to sleep without them.

Breaking these associations involved letting the boys cry for timed intervals and then going back in to reassure them. We followed the program exactly, even though the first night was hell. But on the third night, Kenny slept nine hours.

Michael took a lot longer to adjust. Unfortunately just as he was getting there, Christmas happened: 10 days of travel, visiting, and family get-togethers. Rather than let the boys wake the 15 other people sleeping in the same house, we started taking them into bed with us. They loved it, and it worked for those few days, but we had simply created another sleep association that needed to be broken. By New Year's Day, all five of us were glazed-eyed zombies.

These quick fixes to get the boys to sleep, such as feeding, rocking, or taking them to bed with us, all gave me and the baby instant gratification (sleep) but we weren't winning in the long run. We had to teach the boys to fall asleep on their own in the crib. No bottle, no Mummy, no Daddy. That way, if they woke up in the middle of the night, they would know how to go back to sleep on their own, instead of needing that bottle or pair of arms. We had to be consistent, every evening and every nap time. Now that they can fall asleep on their own, they wake up chatting instead of crying and are happier all day long.

Michael still doesn't sleep quite as well as his brothers, but we are on track. Now six months old and 18, 19, and 21 pounds, David and Kenny sleep 11 hours at night with two to three hours of nap time. Michael sleeps eight to nine hours at night, with similar naps.

Now if only I could get all those naps to happen at the same time…

the mystery and misery of colic
Anonymous

Crying triplets can put anyone's nerves on edge, but imagine adding colic into the scenario. We were fortunate that only one of our babies had it. Our son, who came home from the hospital first, was a perfect angel for two weeks. We could not have been happier … then it happened.

Two days before our two girls were to come home, he started screaming for what seemed to be no reason. We went through the usual checklist: bottle, diaper change, cuddle, tiredness? Nothing helped. Eventually he screamed himself to sleep. Then it happened again, and again and again. It tore my husband and me apart. Every day, we optimistically thought the next day would be better. In the morning he was fine, but by lunch, the screaming would begin, and continue unabated until he went to bed. More than crying, these were ear-piercing outbursts that would cause him to break into a sweat and turn his face blistering shades of red. At first, our doctor said that he was "just fussy" but soon changed his mind after hearing him go off in the waiting room! It wasn't long before he confirmed this was colic.

Coping through this period was the hardest thing we have ever gone through. My husband and I went from loving this baby to really starting to dislike him. His screams would shoot up my spine and by the time we finally got him settled down at night, I would be shaking. I lost 10 pounds and was taking a mild sedative. When my husband came home from work, he would take over to give me a break or send me out. He was the only person who saved me. I look back now and I can't believe we made it. I kept assuring myself that it would soon end.

There wasn't a helper who wanted to feed him; only my husband and I, it seemed, could take it. Finally, it reached the point where we used earplugs when holding him. For the first four months, I felt that I really missed some valuable time with my two girls. Frightened by the cries, they would become upset, so I always tried to have someone look after them in another room. But of course, they still needed and wanted to be with me. It would break my heart to see them in someone else's arms and not my own.

home at last

We tried every remedy that the pharmacy had to offer with little or no success. We tried car rides, hot water bottles, formula changes. Nothing worked, until one day, quite by accident, I was rinsing dishes and holding him with me at the kitchen sink, and he went quiet! I turned the water off and he started crying again, so I turned the water on full and he went quiet again. I was overjoyed. I just couldn't believe I had found something that would soothe him. As soon as my husband stepped through the door, I ran to tell him the great news. We were thrilled. Soon we found other kinds of white noise worked equally well as a calming device like the sound of static on the television or the radio. We had finally found something that could soothe him!

One day, at four months, I was preparing for the regular screaming routine and heard nothing. Could this be the day I had been waiting for? Please, please let this be the day he stops. It was! Life for us as a family changed that day in August. Thinking of those days now, I still don't know how we made it. I'm just glad we did. We now have the happiest little boy a year later, and after those four months I could finally look after all my children myself and not want to just survive another day.

it's never just a cold
Bev Unger

When babies get sick

"This room is really only meant to accommodate two people — it's awfully crowded in here." The nurse's words rang in my ears. She was clearly annoyed that I had two very sick nine-month-old babies in one hospital room. And things were about to get much more crowded. With my two daughters Brianna and Rebecca finally settled in their room, I rushed home to pick up baby Kaitlyn, who had grown seriously ill through the night while I had waited in emergency with the other babies. My husband, Jeff, had been home with Kaitlyn and our fourth baby Zachary, who was far from well himself. While Jeff stayed home with Zachary, I raced back to the hospital with Kaitlyn.

I returned to the patient room where Brianna and Rebecca

home at last

were still asleep and hooked up to oxygen and IVs for antibiotics and steroids. They also needed medication by mask every two hours. But I was thinking of my third baby Kaitlyn, in my arms, barely able to breathe, waiting for the doctor. Mercifully, the pediatrician agreed to examine Kaitlyn in the patient room, so we could bypass the whole emergency process. She was admitted immediately. By then, it was 4 a.m. In a couple of hours, my husband would need to bring Zachary to the hospital because there was no one else to care for him while my husband went to work.

I was tired. By the time Kaitlyn was admitted to the same room and my son had been dropped off for the day at 6 a.m., the nurse was far from happy. "This room is really only meant to accommodate two people." It was true. The two-bed room was crowded with three cribs, a cot for me, highchairs, playpen, IV units and a volunteer. But what was our alternative? I was stressed and not in the best frame of mind for offering sympathy to this woman. I snapped back, "And people are only supposed to have one child at a time — not four!" By the time the nurse left the room, I was raging mad and crying from exhaustion, concern for our daughters, guilt, frustration and uncertainty about how I was going to handle yet another hospital admission.

The culprit was almost always respiratory problems

Unfortunately, this was just one of our many hospital experiences over a period of eight months. Taken together, we visited the local emergency department 10 times and were admitted for a grand total of 43 days. Why? The culprit was almost always the same — respiratory problems. Often it was asthma, but in some cases, we were isolated with Respiratory Syncytial Virus. In any event, the treatment was oxygen and medications by mask and IV to relax their airways. These babies were sick! What always seemed to start with a cold very quickly escalated into full-blown respiratory distress. An innocuous little sniffle in other children and adults could spell disaster for us.

I always wondered why our babies got so sick, so often. We were always very careful not to allow anyone with a cold into our home. We also had very strict handwashing routines that everyone fol-

home at last

lowed as they entered our house. At first, visitors and volunteers
found it difficult to understand why I was so insistent. I went as far
as putting up a sign over the sink to demonstrate proper handwashing techniques. Soon the teasing for my strictness gave way to
an understanding when others saw firsthand just how sick the
babies became with even a common cold.

It was a difficult time for us when the babies were between
seven and 15 months old. We missed many family and social
gatherings and avoided going to parties and shopping with the
babies in an effort to protect them from viruses. Even with all
these precautions, the babies were still affected. I wish there had
been something available to protect against illnesses such as
RSV as there is today.

Back in the hospital, I was struggling through a particularly
stressful admission. The hospital staff was frustrated as well. Soon,
the head of pediatrics stepped in to remind the medical staff that
we were a family with four babies, three of whom required oxygen and inhalations by mask every two hours and another child
who could not go to a babysitter's house because he, too, required
medications and close monitoring. More importantly, he was sick
and he needed his mother.

> **quote**
>
> **A particularly
> stressful hospital
> admission**

Attitudes quickly changed and the staff soon began to work
with us to find ways of giving the children the care they needed. I
requested that we all be in the same room so I would not have to
divide my time between rooms. The five of us quickly learned to
adapt to being in the small room, along with the company of at least
one and often two volunteers I had arranged to give us a helping
hand, not to mention the nurses and doctors.

The next six days were long ones. My husband would drop
Zachary off at the hospital on his way to work and pick him up
on his way home. We coped. The nature of his work prevents Jeff
from taking unscheduled time off, particularly during exceptionally busy summer months, so we relied heavily on our volunteers.

It helped having a solid, strong base of people to call upon at the last minute

It also helped to forsake aspirations of being a supermom to each
child, especially during times when just one or two of the children were admitted and the others were at home with volunteers.

291

home at last

The challenge was to find coverage for those at home by some-one who knew the babies well enough and was responsible enough to takeover care all day at home. Each of our babies was on a dif-ferent formula — one regular, one high calorie, one soy and anoth-er, soy-free and lactose-free. Finding helpers who could manage the diets and cope with the demands of two and often three infants at a time was a constant challenge.

As the months passed, Jeff and I began to quickly identify the onset of symptoms and recognized when the babies needed medication to stave off full-blown respiratory distress. After many consultations with the pediatrician, we brought a com-pressor into the house, which allowed us to give the babies their inhaled medication before their symptoms became severe enough for hospitalization. This helped to keep hospital admis-sions down to a minimum.

But through those long eight months when the babies were between seven and 15 months old, I remember when a little cough would set off anxiety alarms. That was when we could look at our ill baby at 3 p.m. and know that by 7 p.m. that evening, the baby would be sick enough to warrant a trip to emergency. It was always top of mind at our house.

understanding respiratory syncytial virus (RSV)
Maureen Doolan Boyle,
MOST (Mothers of Supertwins) Inc.

RSV is a common and highly contagious respiratory virus that infects many children before the age of two. The virus typically causes significant cold symptoms and fever. In some cases, RSV can cause infants to become gravely ill. RSV is the leading cause of pneumonia and bronchiolitis in babies and is the most frequent cause of lower respiratory tract infections in young children.

Who's at risk?
Young children, especially those who were born prematurely or

those with medical problems, can be at risk for severe complications.
• Children age two and under, who were born prematurely
  (before 32 weeks gestation)
• Full-term infants under eight weeks of age
• Infants with congenital heart disease
• Infants with chronic lung complications (including asthma)
• Infants with compromised immune systems

When does RSV strike?
The season tends to run from fall to early spring.

Signs and symptoms
RSV initially resembles a cold with fever and runny nose. As the virus progresses, the child begins to cough and have difficulty breathing. Rapid breathing and/or wheezing are common signs. The condition can worsen very quickly.

How is RSV contracted?
It is very easy for a child to catch RSV through physical contact with an infected person (shaking hands) or breathing contaminated air droplets (through sneezing/ coughing). Often the virus spreads from an older sibling. RSV can survive for several hours on surfaces such as doorknobs, telephones, faucet handles, or used tissues. It's very common in areas where people are grouped together at home, in daycare centres or on public transportation.

Can RSV be prevented?
There is an injection of antibodies that can help prevent RSV in babies. It must be given once a month during the RSV season from October to April. If your babies are born prematurely, ask the hospital for information. It may be possible to start the first monthly injection before discharge. If the babies have been discharged from the hospital, follow up with your children's pediatrician.

People with a cold or fever should avoid being around babies and young children at risk. Parents and primary caregivers should wash their hands with soap and water diligently before touching the children.

With thanks to Dr. P. Neelands.

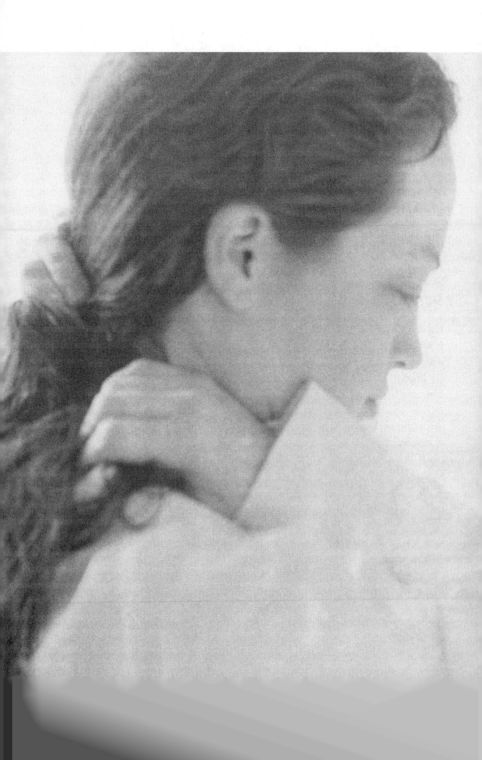

9

coping with stress & change

Courtesy of National Post

whose life is this?

Anonymous

Nothing was wrong, exactly. We had just changed our minds about children and wished there was a way out of our predicament

From the time we got the babies home at one-week-old until they were almost three months old, my life was filled with more intense feelings than I could ever remember. Lucky for me, I was emotionally anesthetized by hormones. Otherwise, how would I have endured?

At first, my life felt so foreign, so unbelievable and so unwanted at times that I couldn't believe that other women went through it. The strange thing was, we were doing really well. Everyone said we seemed calm and relaxed, the babies were thriving, sleeping well, and the doctors and nurses were full of praise. Our house was tidy, we were well fed by my mother, who helped out in every way.

It was not as if anything was wrong. We had just changed our minds about wanting children and wished there was a way out of our predicament. Of course, just having got off the phone with a friend who has a three-week-old baby, I realize this might actually be a normal response. But it caught me by surprise. There were a few other things.

- For the first month or so, when I was away from the babies, I forgot that I had them. I had to remind myself that I had babies. At first I thought it was in part because I didn't get too attached to them for fear of losing them during the pregnancy. I have since learned that newborn babies can still feel as much a part of you as an arm or a leg. If you are not looking at your arm, you don't really think about it, do you?
- It took months before I could think of myself as a mother. Maybe this holds for many women across the childbearing spectrum. Instead, I felt like a member of a caregiving team. The mother on the team was my mother, who was helping us out.
- I did not feel anything akin to love for the babies for many months. I'm still not sure what that bonding experience is supposed to be about. I love them with all my heart now, but it has been a gradual process.
- I couldn't get out of the house often enough, although I could never leave for long, because of breastfeeding. Perhaps this was in part a response to being in a hospital room for two months. I felt very tethered, and I wasn't used to it.
- I deeply regretted having wanted kids so badly. I did not want three babies. That was a distinct feeling that surprised me because during the pregnancy we had decided that in fact having three children was ideal. But it seemed clear that there were too many, and our home had become a house full of tension.

My husband was angry at me for my dogged determination to have children, which inadvertently resulted in triplets. It surprised me that he fell back on that position because he had been as disappointed as I was when our first attempts did not work, and he was as excited and joyful as I was when I did get pregnant. Also, he was the most nurturing and selfless caregiver during my three months on bedrest. We were both enormously excited about triplets. Later, he made it very clear he held nothing against the babies, and was extremely good and helpful with them, but his response to the stress was to blame me. The magnitude and suddenness of the lifestyle change had triggered clinical depression in him.

We were caught completely off-guard by this, but perhaps we should not have been. We knew about another couple in which the father left when the triplets were two weeks old. We had become friends with parents of two-year-old triplets who described how the father had thrown a bottle at the wall in a fit of rage and frustration. His wife said she was glad when her husband went back to work because there was less tension when he wasn't around! Another couple with triplets we know described the 14-hour days the husband would work, until he asked his mother-in-law to stop helping out. That was during a fight when the babies were about eight weeks old. Whatever the reaction, triplet fathers may have to be more involved than the father of a single baby, so their reactions may become uncharacteristic or amplified. But it does seem that the strange reactions disappear by the time the babies are about three months old — in other words, when normalcy sets in and the babies start to respond to the parents.

When the babies were three weeks old, I analyzed the situation. During my years at work, I had learned to look at problems as things to be solved. You just sat down, looked at all the factors, and figured out a plan. In applying this method to the family situation I found myself in, I decided that if worst came to worst, I would have to find other homes for the babies. I couldn't bear the thought of them going to strangers, so I mentally placed them with my sister, my mother, and my brother-in-law. I had to know there was an emergency exit, even though I knew that we would have to exile ourselves in Argentina for the rest of our painful lives if we ever did that.

I just wanted to go back to the way things were. "I'm sorry, I'm sorry, I'm sorry," I said. "I made a mistake, a big mistake. Is there no way out?" Somehow time passed and the fog lifted. My mother left when the babies were 10 weeks old. I was very sad to see her go, and felt vulnerable without her. My husband was deeply appreciative of all she had done, but he was ready for us to do it on our own. And so we began the phase of trying to have a settled life with triplets, and it truly gets better by the day.

Now it is one year later, and what a difference.

I remember a friend telling me that, despite the hardships of her life with toddler triplets, she wouldn't trade it for the world. I truly thought there must be something wrong with me, because there were periods that I would have traded it for anything in the world. But that thought started to disappear as the weeks accumulated.

I have often since asked myself why it must seem so unnatural at first. After all, people have been having babies a good long time now. Maybe it is the volume of babies. Maybe our less community-oriented way in Western cultures contributes to the challenge. I'm not sure if there is a reason that it has to be so hard. And in retrospect, it wasn't really that bad, to be honest. In fact, it's getting hard to remember.

keeping up appearances
Anonymous

Everyone thought I was doing so well... but inside I was alone and trapped

I don't know if what I had would be clinically diagnosed as postpartum depression, since I never consulted a doctor. But I do know that for a full year after my children were born, I felt very depressed. I know that feelings of inadequacy are normal in new mothers, but I was overwhelmed by them. I couldn't make simple decisions about the children's care or our own day-to-day living. (Frozen peas or frozen corn?)

There were the usual strains on what was previously a calm life: financial worries, no privacy with all the help and visitors every day, sleep deprivation and marital stresses, but my depression was coming from within myself.

I had difficulties with both breastfeeding and pumping, and felt that I had failed some important test of motherhood. I did not feel like a mother. I felt no maternal instincts. I was taking care of three crying babies because I had to, not because I wanted to. It felt like they were somebody else's children. I didn't love them and I wished that someone would just take them away. I didn't want this new life;

I didn't want to be a mother.

Feeling trapped, I used to daydream about running away, deserting my husband, my children, my family and friends. My marriage faltered. My husband was disappointed that our sex life did not resume after the bleeding stopped, and I got the distinct impression that he thought I should "pull myself together" although he never said it aloud. I had no energy for him, for us.

I was emotionally tuned-out. I would sit listlessly and hold a bottle or shake a rattle, but rarely sang silly songs or made faces. I attended to the physical needs of my babies, but I had a hard time meeting their emotional needs.

Always on the verge of tears and feeling sorry for myself, my sense of self-worth sank lower and lower. I was mad at myself for being such a failure, both as a mother and as a wife, but I couldn't find the strength to do anything about it.

If anyone called or visited (other than my husband), suddenly I would be fine. I could make cheery conversation, cope with the babies, offer cups of tea, do whatever seemed expected of me. Everybody thought I was doing so well and that I didn't need any help. The problem was that as soon as they left, I went back to sitting and staring blankly at the wall.

Why did I put on this act? Why, if I could do it for others, could I not do it for my husband or for myself? I don't know. Were my feelings normal? Do all triplet moms go through this? I don't know.

We made it through the first year, and things improved dramatically when I got a job. I probably should have done that much earlier. I am grateful to my husband for sticking by me through that difficult time, and now we are as solid as ever.

I wish that I had had the sense to talk to a professional and to fully explain to my husband the depths of my feelings. To this day he doesn't know what I went through.

in a cloud
of depression

Nola Beecroft

In the first few years after having triplets, people often remarked, "I don't know how you do it; I have trouble with just one baby!" I still remember responding, "I am just so thrilled to have babies, and still have to pinch myself every once in a while to be sure this isn't just a dream."

My husband and I had tried for three years to have children. After a miscarriage, an ectopic pregnancy and various operations, we finally came home with three babies. They were three little miracles as far as I was concerned, and the magic didn't wear off for the first year. I couldn't understand how people could possibly become depressed when they had such precious little gifts.

Then when my children turned 12 months, there were days when I didn't have much patience with them. I often lost my temper when accidents happened involving juice cups and clean floors, and I felt overwhelmed at the prospect of another day cooped up with three babies. We had recently relocated to a city where my husband had taken on a new job, and I didn't have the same help and support of friends and neighbours that I had in the first year. I still felt that the children were three very special gifts, and was angry with myself whenever I would lose my temper over insignificant things. There were times when I would go into another room and scream into a cushion to vent some of the anger. I knew I was upsetting the kids, but I didn't see any other alternative. I began to worry that my frustration might soon lead me to physically abusing the babies. I didn't realize that I was suffering from depression and needed help.

**Dealing with depression is not a matter
of just "getting out and doing things,"
it is a chemical imbalance in the brain**

Having triplets can be a very humbling and stressful experience. Many women dream of having a baby and being able to provide total care for that child. When the babies were newborns, I sat in the living room breastfeeding them one at a time during the night feeling guilty that I didn't have the energy to sing to them as they nursed. The guilt had started already! With the stress of providing constant care for three infants, sleeping between four and six hours a night, recovering from a cesarean, keeping a household intact, and the hundred or so other things I tried to accomplish in any given day — it's no wonder depression had a chance to take hold.

Dealing with depression is not a matter of just "getting out and doing things," it is a chemical imbalance in the brain. For the physical and mental health of both you and your babies, it is imperative that you seek professional help. There are varying degrees of depression, ranging from what I experienced in feeling guilty and overwhelmed some of the time to complete depression that requires hospitalization.

We all have days when we are tired and our fuse is maybe not as long as it should be. But if you lose your temper often or find a cloud of depression hanging over you for days or weeks on end, please seek help from your doctor. Those early years with the babies are so busy, and although it may not seem like it on some days, it really does go by very quickly. So many lives depend on you, and life will be so much easier and happier for everyone if you can start each day with a positive mental outlook. And the memories, which last a lifetime, will be wonderful.

Professional Notes from the Twin-Triplet Specialist

---

depression and anxiety
Linda G. Leonard, Twin-Triplet Specialist
Associate Professor, School of Nursing

"I can't manage and I feel so inadequate. I want to walk away. I don't have enough arms, legs, or brains to do this .... I haven't mastered going out on my own with the three children .... The anger just wells up inside me."
(A mother of infant multiples with postnatal depression)
Expectant and new parents of multiple babies normally experience a wide range of emotions. There are, however, about 25 to 30 per cent of families who may be affected by depression, severe anxiety, and even panic attacks. Depression and anxiety disorders, if not recog-

nized and treated, rob parents of the joy of having triplets, quadruplets, or quintuplets and can have a devastating impact on the woman, her children, and her family (Leonard, 1998*). Fortunately, the multiple birth experience does not have to be this way as the disorders in many instances can be prevented, and should they occur, respond well to support, counseling and other treatment approaches.

Research on depression and anxiety in parents of triplets and more

Although the cause of prenatal and postpartum depression and anxiety disorders remains a mystery, evidence suggests that biochemical, hormonal, psychological and social factors are involved. In the general population of childbearing women, estimates of depression in pregnancy range from four per cent to 28 per cent (Misri, 1995) while postpartum depression is thought to affect seven per cent to 10 per cent of women (Stowe & Nemeroff, 1995). A study of British women expecting twins revealed that at 32 weeks gestation, 31 per cent were depressed (Thorpe, Greenwood, & Goodenough, 1995). The average time of onset of postpartum depression is between three and four months after delivery, but a late onset at seven to eight months or even one to two years after birth is possible. The intensity of symptoms ranges from mild to severe.

There is limited but compelling evidence to suggest that the rates of postpartum depression, anxiety, and stress are much higher in mothers of multiples than in mothers of a single child. It is unknown if the rates are greater in parents with greater numbers of babies — quadruplets versus twins. Of the 1,200 Canadian mothers of twins and triplets who responded to a national survey, 42 per cent revealed they had experienced postpartum depression, while 35 per cent reported high levels of emotional stress (POMBA, 1993). An Australian study comparing mothers with infant twins to mothers with a single baby found the following: three times as many mothers of multiples reported high anxiety, five times as many, extreme depression, and nine times as many, exhaustion (Hay et al., 1990).

Two groups of French researchers have studied mothers of triplets since the births of their babies. One group found that after four months, 40 per cent of the 14 women reported that they were depressed, and at one year, 30 per cent of the women still exhibit-

*See appendix for references

ed depressive behaviour (Robin, Bydlowski, Cahen, & Josse, 1991). The second group of researchers, following a different group of mothers of triplets, found that one year after the births, the vast majority of the 12 women still experienced serious psychological disorders, with 25 per cent being treated for major depression. Fifty per cent of the women were affected by serious difficulties such as feelings of helplessness, anxiety, tension, irritability, and loss of body strength (Garel & Blondel, 1992). At two years, 33 per cent of these women suffered from anxiety and depressive symptoms and at four years, 100 per cent reported emotional problems such as stress and fatigue, with close to 40 per cent being treated for major depression (Garel, Salobir, & Blondel, 1997). I am unaware of recent studies of depression and anxiety in parents of quadruplets or more.

Are parents of multiples more likely to develop mood disorders?

I believe that expectant and new parents of multiples may be at greater risk for depression and anxiety disorders because of the enormous physical and biochemical upheaval during a higher order multiple pregnancy. They face the unrelenting demands of responding to and raising babies of identical age, maternal sleep disturbance and deprivation, social isolation and the pressure to measure up to personal and others' expectations. Many of today's parents of higher order multiples are older, well educated, have established careers, and are accustomed to feeling competent and in control. Multiple pregnancy and parenthood can be extremely challenging for those who have difficulty living with uncertainty or who have a strong need for control as there are so many factors over which parents have little or no influence.

The complexities of caring for more than one infant of identical age may play a role in depression. Despite a parent's belief that she or he should love and treat each baby equally, a parent of multiples may favour one baby over another or have difficulty caring for or relating to specific babies.

Adding to the parenting challenges are the special care issues associated with preterm, small, or sick babies. These may include extended stays in the hospital, frequent and slow feedings, infants' irritability, and equipment such as apnea monitors. Women may feel that they are shortchanging their infants and other children because they are unable to focus on one without thinking about or responding to the others. Guilt is a constant companion. Competition among the children for their parents' love and attention can easily lead to frustration and pronounced fatigue. Many parents of triplets or more are unable to find ways of adequately meeting their own personal needs, such as taking time to eat or having a break from parenting. Some lose touch with their partners because of the overriding demands of their children. Affordable and high quality childcare assistance is most often beyond the financial means of families with higher order multiples. Caregiver burnout is an obvious threat, particularly for those parents of multiples who constantly strive for excellence.

Recognizing depression

Prenatal or postpartum depression, collectively known as perinatal depression, is a name given to a constellation of symptoms, only one of which is feeling depressed. Women (or men) may experience a few or the majority of the following:

- Depressed mood most of the day or nearly every day
- Loss of pleasure in all or almost all activities: "going through the motions"
- Crying for no apparent reason
- Inability to sleep or wanting to sleep excessively
- Eating constantly or lacking appetite
- Lack of concentration, forgetfulness, confusion
- Obsessive or repetitive thoughts and compulsive or uncontrollable behaviour (see below)
- Irritability, intense anger, explosive rages
- Besieged with insecurities
- Feeling overwhelmed, inadequate, guilt, a failure, a burden
- Fear of being left alone
- Anxiety and panic attacks (see explanation below)
- Feelings of loss of control
- Losing a sense of self
- Unbearable loneliness
- Wanting to flee the situation
- Wanting to hurt the babies
- Contemplation of suicide

Uncontrollable anxiety and panic attacks may be one component of perinatal depression. Severe panic attacks in a multiple pregnancy can lead to preterm labour and premature rupture of the membranes. An attack comes without warning and may last a few minutes to over an hour. There is an intense desire to flee the situation triggering the attack and to avoid it in the future. Some signs are a pounding heart or thinking you are having a heart attack, sweating, trembling, shortness of breath or feeling that you are smothering or choking, chest tightness or pain, nausea or abdominal distress, numbness or tingling, especially around the mouth, feeling dizzy, unsteady, light-headed, and fear you are about to lose control and die.

Obsessive-compulsive disorder (OCD), as with panic attacks, may also occur as a component of perinatal depression. The obsessions are persistent ideas, thoughts, or images that intrude on your life and cause marked anxiety or distress. You might try hard to ignore or suppress, for example, the need for order. You might also have thoughts of contamination, repeated doubts, or horrific images. In order to reduce or prevent the anxiety or distress caused by the obsessions, the woman engages in repetitive behaviours such as uncontrollable hand washing, cleaning, or constantly checking door locks. OCD can take over a woman's life, denying her the opportunity to sleep, rest, and concentrate on her pregnancy or parenthood. The most frightening and terrifying obsessions for parents are thoughts of harming or even killing one or all of the babies. The obsessions may focus on drowning the babies for example, letting the babies fall, or suffocating them. Women are horrified that they could have these thoughts or images and are extremely reluctant to discuss them. What women with OCD may not realize is that they are not crazy and they do not carry out the actions that they continually imagine (Misri, 1995). Infanticide by a baby's mother is most often the result of a rare condition called postpartum psychosis, where the mother is no longer in touch with reality.

Mothers of multiples with depression and anxiety disorders have difficulty talking about the enormity of emotional pain they are suffering, even to those closest to them. Most women believe that they should be happy and grateful after giving birth to their babies, especially if the babies have been intensely desired. A woman may feel ashamed and fear that if she tells someone about her emotional nightmare, she will be judged incapable of caring for her children, will be hospitalized, or even that the authorities will take her children away. Women try hard to overcome feelings of lost control. In fact, some women appear to be coping well on the "outside" yet on the "inside" are falling apart. When they become scared about what they might do to the babies or to themselves, they often try to convey the depth of their feelings of inadequacy to their partners or close friends. Many partners are unable to understand the enormity of their pain. Even though there may be people around them, women with prenatal or postpartum depression feel swallowed up by their personal nightmares. In an effort to dull their distress, parents may turn to alcohol, smoking, or prescription drugs. A woman may decide that the only way out of the "living hell" of depression, excruciating anxiety, and constantly feeling overwhelmed is to take her life: "I didn't want to die, I just wanted this feeling to end." Sadly, some women with multiples and major depression do attempt suicide.

How does postpartum depression affect parenting multiples?

Parents with postpartum depression can feel totally overwhelmed by the number and constancy of infant interactions, especially if the babies require simultaneous attention. Physical care of the children is most often completed, but mothers often report that they don't play with the babies, and many in fact want to avoid the babies. Women who are run-down and depressed have a greater tendency to treat the babies as a unit, not recognize the uniqueness of each baby, and have less visual and bodily contact with their babies than nondepressed and nonfatigued women (Robin, Corroyer, & Casati, 1996). Depression and anxiety intensify when sleep deprivation occurs. Women experiencing depression are overly sensitive to certain behaviours of the babies, such as crying, screaming, whining, fast moving or clinging behaviours. These behaviours may trigger intense anger, anxiety, and panic attacks, and parents fear that they might lose control and harm their children. Unfortunately, some do. Mothers of triplets who are depressed have reported feeling punished (Robin et al., 1991): "I didn't realize it would be this way ... they are not a blessing."

Babies seem to sense and are affected when a parent has postpartum depression. Infants of depressed mothers have more disturbances in sleep, eating, and physical growth than infants of nondepressed mothers. They also tend to vocalize less, be less active, be more irritable, and elicit fewer happy faces and more sad faces (Field, 1995). It had been assumed that a mother's diminished mood and contact with the babies was the cause of the babies' behaviour. Now it is believed that certain infant characteristics at birth, such as irritability and difficulties being consoled, may contribute to post-natal depression in the parent (Murray, Stanley, Hooper, King, & Fiori-Cowley, 1996). The positive news is that infants of mothers who seek treatment for postnatal depression before their babies are six months old seem to show no long-lasting effects (Field, 1995). Other approaches that assist the babies' development are the pres-ence of another caregiver who can cuddle and talk to the babies, baby massage, mood music, and the mother getting professional assistance in how to respond to irritable, sad, or high need babies.

The effect of postpartum depression on a couple's relationship

Depression and anxiety disorders can seriously undermine a cou-ple's relationship. Friction can occur easily when partners feel over-whelmed, unappreciated, resentful, irritable, exhausted, and critical of one another. Communication can quickly disintegrate, leading to emotional and physical distance, frequent and colossal arguments, and physical violence. Physical and sexual intimacy deteriorates. Women report needing reassurance that their partners still love them, yet are often repelled by their partner's desire for sexual inti-macy. Unfortunately, her partner may interpret the woman's disin-terest as personal rejection. Men report intense anxiety, profound sadness, frustration, demoralization, and bitterness about the deteri-oration in their wives' mental health and their marriages. Many are burned out from trying to cope with work and life at home with multiple babies. They talk about not understanding what is hap-pening, wanting to have their wives back, and are unsure of how to help or what to do.

What can parents of triplets, quadruplets and more do?

Take preventive action: try to learn as much as possible about higher order pregnancy and parenthood from parents and other sources to become better prepared and to establish realistic expectations. Review your resources for reliable, long-term support. Realize that some women with multiples feel conflicted about securing childcare or homemaking assistance and are reluctant to accept offers of help. They often think there is something wrong with them if they need help. If you want help and can't get it or afford it, discuss strategies with a multiples club, your community health nurse, physician or social service worker.

Be aware that it doesn't mean that it will happen, but some mothers of multiples are at increased risk for developing depression and anxiety in pregnancy or after the births (see list below). Fathers are also at risk if they have a history of depression, are unemployed, or have a spouse who is not supportive or who was depressed either during the pregnancy or in the first few months after the births (Ballard, Davis, Cullen, Mohan, & Dean, 1994). Discuss these factors with your family and healthcare providers.

Risk factors for maternal depression and anxiety

- An unsupportive partner, marital breakdown, lack of supportive people and resources
- A partner with a history of depression
- Adverse or highly stressful life events such as a death, life-threatening conditions, history of sexual assault or abuse, complications during the pregnancy and after
- Maternal history of depression or anxiety disorders, previous postpartum depression, premenstrual syndrome
- Maternal family history of depression or anxiety disorder
- Maternal attitude such as not wanting to have a multiple pregnancy, serious doubts while pregnant about being able to cope with the babies
- Anxiety/depression during the multiple pregnancy and maternity blues after the delivery
- Infant and childcare stresses such as preterm, sick or high demand babies

• Unresolved breastfeeding difficulties, abrupt weaning, returning to work before eight weeks

Realize that if prenatal and postpartum depression and anxiety occur, it is not your fault, a sign of weakness or a reason to feel ashamed.

If you are emotionally distressed, talk as soon as possible to a supportive person about how you are feeling. That could be your partner, mother, another parent of multiples, your physician, public health nurse, lactation consultant, parent information/crisis line, or a postnatal depression support group.

Know that depression and anxiety disorders respond well to a variety of approaches tailored to the needs of each parent. These may include individual, couple, or group counseling sessions; self-help support groups and family education sessions; psychotherapy; and certain medications.

Many women fear taking medications because they are concerned about harming the babies, suffering side effects, being labeled "crazy," or becoming dependent on the drugs. Specific medications taken during pregnancy or when mothers are breastfeeding do not appear to affect the babies' development (Nulman et al., 1997; Wisner, Perel, & Findling, 1996), while others are or may be harmful. Discuss the risks, benefits, and safety issues with your family and health professionals before making a decision about medication. It may take about two weeks before an appreciable effect is gained from the medication and four to six months before you regain your mood. Finding the right dose and even the best medication(s) may take time. You will likely need to take the medication for about a year. Otherwise, relapse is probable. Some mothers of multiples with mild to moderate postnatal depression report success using herbal remedies under the care of a qualified health provider.

Self-help

The demands and realities of being the mother of higher order multiple birth children may make it extremely difficult to adopt some suggestions in the literature for overcoming postpartum depression and panic attacks. As a minimum, take steps to protect yourself and your babies. Become aware of what behaviours or situations trigger your anger and then develop a couple of ways that you can safely vent your anger or cool off before dealing with your

children's immediate needs. If you have suicidal plans or thoughts of
harming yourself or your babies, please reach out to a trusted person or to a crisis line.

Obtaining one night (or day) of uninterrupted sleep (minimum
four to five hours) has been shown to positively affect mood. Talk
with your family or friends about who could come in and take over
childcare responsibilities for part of a day or night while you sleep.
If at all possible, try to find a few moments of the day for yourself
— it is virtually impossible to constantly give out without replen-
ishing yourself.

How can partners and others help?

Practical help is a good place to start. Help the mother to develop
a simple routine that includes accomplishing one or two tasks
which are manageable in a day: to take breaks away from the babies
out of the house and to rest when possible rather than doing something like housework. Keep the kitchen stocked with nutritious,

quick and easy to eat snacks such as fruit, nuts, dairy products, and encourage her to eat. Support her in finding one (or more) babysitters or someone to do some of the household chores.

Become aware of the symptoms of depression and be prepared to take action and seek help for the mother. Emotional support is critical as her self-confidence and self-worth are at a low ebb. Encourage her to tell you how she is feeling and let her know that this is not her fault, that she is not going crazy, and that she is not a bad mother. Accept her feelings and help her find ways to protect herself and the babies. Support the decisions that she is able to make, and encourage her to take one day at a time and to focus on today. Help her to talk about what part of herself or her previous life has been lost and who she is now. Help her to examine what she expects of herself, to adjust those expectations and to take credit for the hard work she is doing as a mother. Discuss what physical expressions of affection she needs and realize (if you are her partner) that it is normal for a woman who is depressed to lose interest in sex and that it is not a rejection of her partner. Encourage her to make contact with others that can support her, such as friends and health professionals.

Care for yourself, as it is easy to get run-down, irritable, resentful, and even depressed.

A mother of triplets summarizes her experience with postnatal depression: "I take it day by day and see myself getting stronger .... I didn't realize what was happening to me .... I felt ashamed. I wish I had known what I do now and gotten help sooner. I missed so much with the babies." It is my hope that this information will help families accept that prenatal and postpartum depression and anxiety happens to multiple birth parents through no shortcomings on their part, and that if it does happen, excellent assistance is available.

More information on mental health support services in your local communities may be obtained from PASS-CAN (Postpartum Adjustment Support Services) in Oakville, Ont., the Pacific Postpartum Support Society in Vancouver, B.C., or your public health nurse.

a shoulder to lean on
John Lentz

With multiples, even the strongest relationships will be challenged

Many parents of multiple birth children realize the importance of devoting time and energy to their marriage. But it's easy for a relationship between a couple to be eclipsed by the seemingly endless hours of work and the constant fatigue that come with parenting three or more little ones. Even the strongest relationships will be challenged. Here are a few ideas that my wife and I have tried to keep in mind in our four years as parents of triplets.

Teamwork

Leave the egos behind. Both spouses have to be willing to help with all of the chores, such as diapers, laundry, baths, feeding, etc. Conversely, neither spouse should insist that he or she is the only one on Planet Earth who is able to fulfill a given duty properly (i.e., Bathing: "I am the only one who cleans behind the ears.") There will be duties that one parent is better at than the other. Work should be distributed accordingly. How the work is assigned will depend on the dynamics of the particular partnership and communication is the key, as always.

Do not be too proud to refuse offers of help

Family members and close friends who are reliable and experienced will often gladly volunteer their assistance. They will find your children a big attraction. If they are visiting and wish to assist with feeding, why not let them? You need the break. If they would like to babysit for the evening or weekend and are up to the task, consider it seriously. They may not offer a second time. One spouse may also act as babysitter, allowing the other to take some time away. This is especially the case if one parent is at home full time. Encourage that parent to take at least one evening per week off to help stave off the stir-crazy blues, particularly in the very early months and years. As the children get a little older, a mini getaway for the stay-at-home parent can help restore their energy and spirit. My wife went to New York City recently with girlfriends and left me (at my insistence) to care for our three-year-old triplets. She came home relaxed, and I bonded with the children and came out of the experience with a new understanding of what my spouse lives through on a daily basis. We also took a trip to Cape Cod over a long weekend, which did us a world of good.

Talk to each other

The few moments you have together and alone should be spent with each other. Talk about the babies, about your day at work, or gossip about the neighbours if that is what interests you. Try to share a common activity during those few moments. Try to resist sitting in two different rooms, reading two different newspapers, until it's time to fall asleep. You don't have much time together, so spend it wisely.

Be sensitive to each other's needs

Stay-at-home parents may feel that the adult world has passed them by, especially with younger children. They may long for adult conversation. Events that seem entirely mundane to the working-for-pay parent, such as workplace occurrences, might be welcome news to the partner at home. On the other hand, if one parent clearly wants to be left alone, the other should not impose himself or herself. As always, communication is crucial, even when it is nonverbal communication.

Finding time for intimacy

That may be a problem. After a full day of chasing several toddlers in several different directions simultaneously, getting into "the mood" may be a challenge. Many of us may find it very hard to recall what it was that led us to become parents in the first place. Mothers may find physical challenges in the first several months postpartum. First, try to find the time. This is easier said than done, but remember that babies do nap frequently. You may have to schedule things, as calculated as that sounds. Second, be patient with each other (perhaps this applies especially to us, dads). Your better half will be very tired, very often, and attempts at coercion will only backfire, one way or the other. Finally, remember the simple things such as holding hands.

Appreciate each other's strengths, weaknesses and differences

Your energy levels won't always be the same. Don't make your spouse feel guilty about being tired. One of you may be more positive and optimistic than the other — something that may be especially noticeable in families with children with disabilities. Some parents may have a great deal of difficulty coping, while their partner may wonder why they react in that way.

Have fun

Laugh with each other and with your children. Keep your sense of humour. Try to see the glass as half full, not half empty. It is a wonderful experience. Enjoy it.

how our marriage survived multiples
Mary Gallagher

How quickly we were thrown from being a happily married couple to a happily married couple of four children. There was no time to ease in and adapt to parenthood. Suddenly our lives were consumed with our babies. Every thought, every feeling, every moment was for our children. Preserving a sense of couplehood took more and more effort until we soon discovered we were calling each other Mommy and Daddy. I found that my whole day was spent hugging, loving, being close to a child and simply giving my whole self physically and emotionally. By the end of the day I was so exhausted from giving myself that I had no energy left, physically or emotionally, for my husband. Before we knew it, we spent very little time as a married couple.

The first year of our children's lives was so busy and hectic that I found I was grabbing at chances to be alone rather than with my husband. My husband is a very special person who has kept me sane and our marriage together. He gave me days out by myself, weekends away with friends and a trip to Scotland by myself to visit relatives, while he stayed home with the children. I'm not sure I would be sane today if I didn't have that break.

Unfortunately, my husband had very little time for himself after the children were born. Each day after work, he would come home and take over. And I was selfish enough to allow it, but it was all I could do to cope mentally the next day. When the children were babies and toddlers, my husband and I worked as a team doing shift work. Although it was hard work, we loved what we were doing. Our children gave us so much pleasure, and definitely four times the love. We stuck to a daily, organized routine and most importantly, we each held onto a wonderful sense of humour, which helped us get through most situations.

Time spent together is very important since physical closeness and intimacy reminds us of why we began our lives together. Although physical love sometimes got lost in all the chaos of the day, as a married couple, we have found it more important to remain emotionally close. Understanding the ups and downs, talking everything through and playing together has kept us strong. Hopefully our children see their parents as a strong, happy couple. We find that if we do get out for dinner together, we end up talking about our children and all the funny things they get up to, or how proud we are of them. We go to the movies and wish the children could have been with us. We go for a walk and see something that the children would have loved. We even had a fantastic opportunity recently to go on a Caribbean cruise, which was a wonderful trip away, our first in seven years. Yet even afloat, we talked about how the children would have had a great time there.

In many ways, our five children have become integrated into our marriage and we have to revolve around them. But taking time to notice each other, even if it is only for 10 seconds in a day, is very important. I feel that, although we were a happily married childless couple six years ago, our children have probably brought us closer

together. We have been through so many ups and downs, life and death situations (when the babies were born), seemingly endless stresses, and yet we remain together because we are a family, a happy family, and we look forward to the future.

Why we are still together today

- We kept a sense of humour
- We remembered why we got married
- We remembered why we both wished for children — even if it was only one or two wishes!
- We never tried to "win the war" on our own and cried for help from volunteers, friends and family, church groups and babysitters
- We found at least one hour a week to be together
- We tried to get out for the evening (or the day) at least once a month
- We understood each other's mood swings
- We talked through all our feelings or wrote each other letters about the day
- We wrote down thoughts about the children, which helped us realize just how wonderful and funny they are
- We never stopped thinking of ourselves as a couple
- We always remembered that our children could survive without us for a few hours. Children also need time away from their parents. We figured why not give them a break and another friendly face to drive crazy for a little while?

life as a single mom
Anonymous

Being a single parent places so many strains on an individual. But I found an inner strength I never knew I had

It's difficult and challenging enough to be a mother of triplets without managing on your own as a single parent. Being single again felt odd, particularly after the last of my friends got married. I think that when you separate from a spouse you go through different stages, just as you would if you had suffered the loss of a loved one. It's similar, but in this case, the person is still alive, although they are no longer an integral part of your life.

One of those stages is embarrassment — feeling that you have failed yourself and your family. All of a sudden, I felt like a statistic with a lost sense of belonging. It was very painful for me to remove my engagement and wedding rings. I felt as though I were amputating my finger at the same time. I was so self-conscious about not having a ring on that finger that I quickly replaced it with another: a gold band with three diamonds, one for each of my children. I was concerned about how society would judge me if they saw me without a wedding band and three children by my side. I worried that my kids and I would be viewed or judged negatively.

When I started my solo journey into parenthood, I was completely overwhelmed. Many questions plagued me for months. Should I try to reconcile for the children's sake? What if the kids don't understand how I arrived at the decisions I felt were best at the time? What if they resented me when they got older because of these decisions? How would my children react when their friends at school asked why their parents don't live together? Would any of the decisions that I have made affect their lives negatively in the future? And then, of course, there was the overriding question: how could I possibly raise three children on my own?

When I was experiencing my new way of life, I was very fortunate to have the support and love of my family and friends. My mom stayed with me for about eight months to help me get back on my feet, while my dad helped with minor repairs around the house and maintenance such as cutting the grass, shoveling the snow, landscaping and keeping my car clean inside and out. My friends and parents never judged me and supported my decision no matter what the outcome or consequences. There was the other side of the family, however, who felt uncomfortable with "the new situation" and, as a result, didn't feel the need to visit or telephone anymore. People sometimes drift away once they know you are back on your feet and coping.

Soon after I became separated from my husband, I found it very surprising that I was denied a volunteer. I assumed that if I explained my situation to the local public health department, I might qualify for a volunteer, even for just a few hours a week. But five years ago, government cutbacks were underway. I was told that resources were scarce. Believe or not, there were a lot of people worse off than I was. I was on my own.

I didn't feel much like socializing.
I disliked talking about my life because talking about it meant thinking about it

Many people suggested that I join a support group, but I never did, mostly because I had no one to look after the children while I was gone. I didn't want to burden my parents after they had already helped out so much. My mom was with the kids all the time on weekdays. She left for home on Friday every week and returned back on Sunday evening or Monday morning. My dad came to help out every second day. Also, I really didn't feel much like socializing. I disliked talking about my life because talking about it meant thinking about it, and thinking about it meant feeling upset. I tried very hard not to think about my life and how it had changed so drastically because I didn't want to drag myself down.

Being a single parent places so many strains on an individual. Emotionally you feel as though you have the world on your shoulders. You rarely get a break unless you depend on somebody to come over and give you one. The day-to-day struggles of dragging three reluctant kids to the grocery store, bank, post office, drugstore — on every errand imaginable — wore on me. It didn't seem to dawn on other people that this was a part of my day-to-day life.

Single parents miss out on social interaction with other adults, especially if they don't work outside the home and receive a pay cheque for all their hard work, stress and struggles. The chances of burning out faster are obviously higher, especially for the stay-at-home parent who juggles being a maid, a referee, a chef, an educator and a wicked witch who handles discipline. Once the kids are in bed, the day doesn't end. There is always something that needs to be done: the kitchen to be swept and dishes to be washed, clothes to be laundered and folded, floors to be disinfected, telephone calls to be returned. I find if I have been with the children for 12 or more hours that by 7:30 p.m., I'm running on empty and my patience is wearing thin.

What might be small, insignificant repairs to some — vertical blinds that come off their track, bicycle chains that need to be put back into place, toilet handles that break off, sliding door screens that get torn, oven coils and heating elements that need to be replaced – are monumental tasks to me and cause great frustration. I'm not at all handy with tools (not that I would have enough hours left in the day to do these repairs) so I always have to wait for somebody to come over and take care of it for me.

Financial strain is a reality after separation. There are more compromises and greater spending restrictions. Sticking to a strict budget worked best for me. It's amazing how I became so aware of where money is spent. I learned very quickly to record everything on a calendar: when the property taxes were due, how much I spent on clothing, groceries, gas, utilities, insurance for home and auto and all the miscellaneous expenses. I saw first-hand just how expensive it is to raise triplets. It's difficult enough adjusting to making ends meet on one person's salary after a husband or wife has given up his or her job to care for the children without having to stretch the money even further.

I feel as if I have been working on this story forever. Either the children have been ill with the flu, colds or ear infections, or I have come down with something. Sometimes I think I can keep going as though I were on a conveyor belt; but things eventually catch up and often manifest themselves through illness. By the end of the day, I am often physically and emotionally drained. I probably composed most of this story by jotting points down while I was doing housework or driving in my car to the supermarket. But writing this feels like another burden in an already hectic life.

I certainly can't take all the credit for how far I've come. I could not have done it without the love and assistance of my parents. I have met so many people who are quick to judge, but on the other hand, there are those very special few that offer encouraging words of praise like, "My hat goes off to you."

It's important not to worry about tomorrow, but take one day at a time. Equally important is to try and have a positive attitude and not allow unpleasant events in life to make you bitter.

Sometimes I think of my life as being like a boxing match where I get knocked down in one round only to quickly climb back up on my feet for the next round. I have discovered an inner strength that I never knew I possessed. I also learned one extremely valuable lesson through all of this — never judge others until you have walked a mile in their shoes.

remembering the older child
Sheena Judd

We wanted our eldest daughter to continue feeling unique and involved

Bringing a new baby home to a family with older children always has the potential to cause some friction. Knowing we would be bringing three babies home to an older daughter, my husband and I took very definite steps to make sure she didn't fade into the background of family life.

Our daughter was four when we found out I was pregnant with triplets. Although we had had many miscarriages in the past, we

decided to tell her the news immediately and made certain that she understood she was the very first person to know. Throughout the pregnancy, we included her in our conversations about the babies and always shared new information. We wanted our daughter to continue feeling unique and involved. After all, she had been an only child for a long time.

During the pregnancy we spent time doing special things with her. We asked for her input as we prepared a nursery for the babies. We attended a class specially designed for siblings at our local hospital, which talked about some of the feelings of jealousy and anger that older siblings might experience when the new additions arrive. While the class wasn't geared to children with multiple birth siblings, it did give our daughter some helpful guidance for preparing for the babies in a language and style that she could understand. She also accompanied us on a visit to the special care nursery at the hospital so she would not be frightened when she saw the babies with IVs or heart monitors in the incubators.

When the boys were born, she was their first visitor. Pictures she drew for each of her brothers were taped to their incubators. While I was pregnant, I purchased small gifts for her (crayons, colouring books, stickers, dollar-store toys and books) and wrapped them. When people visited with gifts for the boys, she was able to pick a surprise from the grab bag of these little items.

Things were difficult after we brought the babies home from the hospital because both my husband and I were exhausted. Looking after three newborns was more work than I had anticipated (and I anticipated a lot of work). I tried to breastfeed but stopped because it left me even less time with our daughter. At least with bottlefeeding, a helper could take a turn or even our daughter could give one of the babies a bottle as they sat in a car seat. She felt very important when she was able to feed her brothers and enjoys that even now.

One or two weeks after the boys came home, my husband took our daughter on a special outing to the circus. We tried to continue finding time like that just for her. Since the boys have just turned two and a half years old, they have yet to realize they are missing out on a little fun with these excursions. But as they get older, the outings will no doubt change. For now though, we feel it is very important for our daughter to be able to participate in special activities; her gymnastics program, for example.

Striking a balance between the age-appropriate needs of our daughter and our boys has been tricky. But my husband and I both believe that because we have made the effort to make her feel special and have maintained as many of her regular activities as possible, we have experienced very little sibling rivalry. Although her toddler brothers can annoy her in a very big way at times, for the most part, she enjoys being a big sister to triplets. After all, in Grade 2 there is a certain prestige that comes with having triplet brothers, and she is never at a loss for a story to show and share.

making room for three sisters
Melanie Smith

At school, people would hassle me about my mom expecting triplets

Hi, my name is Melanie. I am 18 years old and in my first year of college. When I found out my mom was pregnant with triplets, I was 15 and in Grade 11. I was also an only child.

I was excited, but also shocked and worried. During those long months when my mom was pregnant, things were difficult for me since I had to cope on my own. Medical complications during the pregnancy meant that she had to be admitted for bedrest in a Toronto hospital 45 minutes from home. Even though I knew it was the right thing for her to do, I was upset that my mom and I had to be apart for this period of time. I visited her often with my dad, but it was difficult to leave her all by herself at the hospital and go home with her not there. Later, when I found out that mom was having three girls, I found it hard to concentrate on school every day. People would hassle and bother me about my mom expecting triplets. I was beginning to feel like no one cared or loved me. I felt alone in the world. It's a feeling I had never felt before.

One day in November 1996, I got called down to the office late in the day. My aunt was waiting to take me to see my mom. The day had come for the arrival of my new sisters. When we got to the hospital, my entire family was there. We just sat around waiting patiently until finally my dad came out and told us I had three new sisters. Eventually, they were named Jacqueline, Leslie and Rebecca. While I was filled and overcome with joy and happiness, I have to admit it was a difficult time because people came to visit the kids and just ignored me as if I wasn't there.

We brought Rebecca home first and then the other two followed a week later. Even at home the attention was mostly on them. The hardest part was my 16th birthday that year, when my family came over to celebrate. Everyone's attention, laughter and joy were directed toward my one-month-old sisters. My dad noticed it and made me feel a little better about it.

As they grew older, it got better. I could play and have some fun with them. Today, things are both good and bad. Sometimes it is fun and sometimes, frankly, it is not. Everyone still ignores me, but it is better than before. After three years, I am still trying to get used to my sisters and the changes they have made in our home. The noise and the upheaval have had a big effect on me. I like to have my space and I don't always get it! I still sometimes wish everything would go back to the way it was. But then I wonder if I would miss what has happened and then regret what I wished for. I still wonder if anything else will change. Sometimes I get angry and sometimes I cry.

For those teenagers that will be experiencing this now or later, be ready for a rough ride, but try and enjoy it. I don't really have many suggestions for you because I am still going through it myself, but I would say, "Get used to it!" Maybe even more important is not letting people tell you how you feel or how you should feel.

All in all I have to say through these times, good and bad, I have learned that I should be happy for what God has given me: my three precious sisters, my mom and dad and a caring family that I love dearly.

being a big sister

Jerin Forgie (age 11)

How do I feel about it? Well, I'll tell you ...

I'm the sister of not one, not two, not three, not four, but five, five little kids running, crawling and crying around the house, past the terrible twos, past kindergarten, in Grade 4 — and boy, am I proud. How do I feel about being the sister of five, three sisters and two brothers, all born at the same time? I'll tell you.

When my mother and father were ready to tell me the great news, they sat me on the kitchen counter and my mother began to speak to me very slowly. She said that I was going to be the big sister to five little kids. I was two years old at the time and they probably expected me to go through some sort of phase, but I just sat there thinking it was perfectly normal to be a sister to five babies. But about seven months later ...

Hey, where are you going? You forgot me! My mother was being rushed to the hospital while I was left behind with a babysitter, and believe me, I was not pleased! My mother had never been away from me overnight and now she was gone for two weeks. Every so often my dad would come home to take me to the hospital to visit her. Sometimes that would only make matters worse because she wasn't exactly looking pretty. I would cling onto her and I wouldn't let her go. I couldn't bear another night without her home. After she had given birth to the quints, I couldn't visit her because she was unconscious for a few days.

When my mother was well enough to come home, she and I spent some quality time with each other, but she went right back to the hospital to stay with the quints. The quints were coming home at different times, some in one month, and others in two or three, depending on their health.

When they were all at home, the house was very hectic. It was filled with news reporters, TV stations, people coming over and letters from people we've never met or heard of. Then there were the nurses. They came over to see if the quints were developing correctly, which they were and still are. With all this commotion going on, it was impossible to get any sleep. So I made my final decision. I spoke loud and clear, "Okay! You can take them all back to the hospital now. I don't want them anymore!" My mother sat me down and looked me straight in the eye and said, "If we did that you wouldn't be a big sister anymore and Mommy and Daddy would cry." So I said, "Fine," thinking it wouldn't be very good if Mommy and Daddy cried.

The house finally started to calm down. But the thing was that since I was only two years old, I didn't understand why all these strange people came to our house or even the risk the quints were at for different health problems. The only thing I understood was that my life was somewhat different from other people's and my

mom wouldn't always be there.

The quints are nine years old now. With five nine-year-olds and one 11 year old, it would only make sense to set some ground rules to bring the fighting down. For example, each day of the week is a different day for people to do chores around the house, and we make our lunch every morning and walk to school.

Here comes the biggest event of the year — birthday parties. Some parents think it's bad having six kids over; well picture this: 35 six-year-olds all over the house. Just imagine the mess, the noise, the pain, but the presents. Whoa! Now here's where my little jealousy monster starts creeping around. Games here, hair ponies there, stuffed toys everywhere. Then one year it was just too much, so we had two parties, one for the girls and one for the boys, but no more parties after we're 10.

Unfortunately, that includes me.

I've come to realize that my brothers and sisters watch me all the time which means I'm an important role model. How I act will have an impact on how they act. Sometimes this is annoying, but I'm ready to face the responsibility. Without the quints, I would miss all the surprises that come with being a big sister. My life is different from most people my age but I've learned to accept and enjoy it, so I am and always will be the sister of the quints.

my life as a big brother
Josh Parker (age 4)

Hi, my name is Josh Parker. I have three little brothers; named Jacob, Oliver and Noah. I am four years old and I am a good big brother. I like having three brothers, but one of them bites. It is more fun at Christmas 'cause there are more presents and I get to play with them all. We also get to go to their birthday party. But it's not always fun. Sometimes I have to wait for my mom and dad 'cause the boys take too long. It is so nice to have a good, nice family and lots of people to love me. But maybe I will just take my own room!

being there
Laval Wong

Working from home, Dad becomes primary caregiver to four babies and a six-year-old daughter

I used to joke that I wouldn't mind having half a dozen children. So the arrival of Nadine, Sarah, Daniel and Cédric in our lives brought ecstatic joy, since we had been trying to give a brother or a sister to our six-year-old, Kareen, for quite some time. But they also brought some stress.

When our little ones came home from the hospital, I did my best to help my wife, Patricia, take care of them. After work, I would do my share of changing diapers, washing and sterilizing 24 bottles at the end of the day and preparing the formula for the next day. I made time for Kareen, and took charge of the last feedings of the day so that Mummy could get a few hours of sleep. And I accepted with a smile the mood swings of my better half, who was very tired, of course, especially in the first few weeks when she refused to get any help.

My training lasted six months, until it was time for my wife to go back to work. Fortunately, a special arrangement allowed me to work from home for the next few months.

The idea of staying home made me a little apprehensive at first. Frankly, I was scared knowing that I would have to spend a whole day at home with my little monsters. I doubted if I would be capable of keeping my sanity. Patience is not one of my strong qualities! But I was also looking forward to it because by then, our little angels had started responding to me when I talked and sang to them. In a way, I felt privileged to be given the opportunity to be with them.

There was no time to deal with fear. The babies were there and waiting to be loved and taken care of and that was just what I did. Very soon I was the one who knew everything there was to know about our children. Since our babies had come home from the hospital, we had been keeping a log of everything that happened during the day, and I found pleasure in writing down all the special happenings of the day that I knew Patricia could read about later.

working & parenthood

What I witnessed was priceless! I saw who needed special attention on one day, who went to the doctor, who smiled the most on a particular day. I saw how Sarah, tired of waiting to be served, got out of her highchair to steal her brother's food, or how Daniel slept soundly even as his brother and sisters screamed right next to him. I smiled, remembering how Nadine discovered a way to get out of her bouncer to go visit her sibling, and how Cédric took his first steps. One other thing that made these months special was the fact that I was there to welcome Kareen home from school every afternoon and listen as she related with so much enthusiasm what happened during her day at school.

These are precious little things that any parent who works may not have the chance to witness. They are unforgettable memories to be cherished. Such special moments are unfortunately accepted by most dads as being solely the privilege of moms! I cherished every moment spent with my children.

On the other hand, life was hectic. Once a week, when one of our devoted volunteers arrived, I usually went to the office for a couple of hours to report to my boss (and update my colleagues about the babies and the number of hours of sleep that I managed to get in the last week)! At home, my computer was always on so that whenever possible, I would try and work for a few minutes. There was no time to relax. I was always on the go, rushing here to take care of my little people, rushing there to grab something to eat, rushing again to be able to work. When Patricia came back home from work, she would take over with the children and I would settle down in front of my computer for the rest of the evening. There was not any time for us as a couple. All we would have time for was hello and goodbye. On one occasion, Patricia was running upstairs to get the laundry as I was on my way outside for some fresh air. After a near collision on the stairs, we started talking and after about 10 minutes, realized that this was the longest and first meaningful conversation we had had in months! In the early months, little misunderstandings between us could snowball into huge problems, since both of us were so tired and had so little time to talk through problems. Once the little ones started settling into a routine and I went back to work, our relationship returned to the way it was before.

Remembering our impromptu conversation, Patricia and I

started a little routine: when the children were finally asleep for the night, regardless of the hour, we would sit and have a cup of tea and talk. It wasn't elaborate, but it was special time spent together getting reacquainted. Even today, with life far less hectic, we still sit down for our nightly ritual.

The first two years seem a total blur. My wife and I took a day at a time and did what had to be done. We both knew that a more relaxing stage of life would eventually come when we would be able to appreciate all of our blessings. And we are certainly appreciating them at the moment!

back to work
Renate MacDuff

Every morning at 5 a.m., I would start the daily process of getting five women out the door for the day

With all of my children in school now, it's hard to imagine how chaotic our lives once were when I was working and the girls were just babies. We have four children — the eldest is nine and our three younger girls are seven. During my multiple pregnancy, I was working full-time and felt that with three new children depending on us, I would have to return after the birth for financial reasons. Following doctor's orders, I left work five months before the birth and returned to work two months and one week after the girls were born. My employer requested that I return, and I felt I had no choice. I needed that job.

After consulting with the babies' caregiver, I returned to work. I must emphasize that I have the world's best caregiver, which left me feeling reasonably comfortable with the idea of leaving them at such an early age. So every morning at 5 a.m., I would start the daily process of getting five women out the door for the day. The babies would naturally awaken around this time and I would feed and dress them. Then I would pack the diaper bags and make my lunch. Next our oldest daughter awoke, and we would rush to the bathroom quickly (potty training, you know) and then have some breakfast. The babies usually went back to sleep for a while during this time. After breakfast, I would take those sleeping babies out of their cribs, wrap them up and load them into the car. At age two, my big girl would get on her shoes and come out so I could get her into her car seat. Off we would go to the sitter's house, where I would unload three infants and a toddler, and leave instructions for the day for feedings, naps, sniffles etc. Then I would be off to work for the restful part of my day. One undeniable benefit of working was being able to eat my entire lunch without interruption while it was still warm. This was a rare treat, not experienced at home until many months later.

Not surprisingly, it was an arduous process day in and out. There were many days when I functioned with little sleep from the night before, which made the days even longer and more trying. I still can't believe that we kept the schedule and that we are still doing it to this day. Of course, circumstances have changed. I no longer have babies waking up at 5:30 a.m. wanting to be fed. Instead, there are four very sleepy girls that need to be dragged out of bed at 7:30 a.m. to be at school for 9 a.m. Morning cries have been replaced with conversation (too much on some days) and a chorus of questions: "What can I wear? Do I have to brush my teeth again? Will you do my hair? Did you pack my homework in my bag? Can you send some baking for this afternoon's special event?"

The days are still chaotic, but we have found a way to make the schedule run smoothly for the most part. As I look back now on the last seven years of being a mom who also works outside the home, I have only a few regrets. When one or more of the children were ill, I did not take time off work. The sitter was more than happy to look after sick children. My girls almost seemed to cope better with the illness at the sitter's home because there was always something to do and someone to fuss over them; if not the caregiver, then her family or other children.

Today, there are times when work prevents me from attending some of the girls' school functions and events, but my husband and I do manage to get to most of them. The girls seem to understand and recognize that there are other moms and dads that can't always make it to certain events as well. After-school activities like soccer, cooking and gymnastics keep everyone in the family busy all the time. But we believe these programs are valuable, and so we make the time.

Whenever I am feeling low or guilty about not always being at home with the children, I try to remember and hold onto one important thought: you have not failed and cannot fail if you love your children.

finding a balance
Jacquie Weber

I have been asked many times when I plan to return to full-time practice. I have found many creative ways to change the subject

When I sat down to write my story about working outside the home, I was amazed to realize how much effort it takes to make everything work.

I have been a lawyer for 10 years, practicing civil litigation. My husband and I have triplets, two boys and a girl, born in January 1998.

I was 24 weeks pregnant when I stopped working. I told my employers I would be back, but I was never really convinced I would return because my profession does not fit into a 9-to-5 schedule. When the children were eight months old, I had to make my decision. My husband agreed to support whatever choice I made. In a way, his support actually made the decision more difficult, because it would be my own (I wouldn't be able to blame him if it didn't work out).

The hardest part about making the decision was knowing the reason why I was so torn. Most people assumed I was struggling because I am a professional who spent many years in school and then several more trying to establish myself in a very competitive environment. How could I give all that up to be at home with my kids?

In truth, my dilemma lay in the realization that I needed to escape. In short, I found I was not the parent I had hoped to be. I didn't enjoy being at home every day. I did not become the patient and level-headed person I assumed childbirth would make me. I felt that everyone else I knew with higher order multiples was doing a better job than I was. No one raised their voices to their children and

working & parenthood

certainly no one ever called their husband at work begging him to come home early because they had had enough. I thought that since I was such a lousy parent, the kids would be better off if I was not their sole caregiver during the day. I know now that I had grossly underestimated myself. I may never win any parenting awards, but I am starting to believe people when they tell me I am doing a good job.

Along with having triplets came feelings of guilt that my children had to share everything from birth. They are rarely alone with either my husband or me. Of course, they don't know anything different, but I do, and as a mother, I have that uncanny ability to find things to feel guilty about. My initial thought was that if I only worked three days per week, I would have four days at home to spread over three children. They would have more of me than the children of a mom who worked five days a week. (I didn't say the practice of law always requires rational thought!)

I agreed to work three days per week at 60% of my former salary

I was very lucky. I managed to convince my employers that recent reorganizations at the firm meant they really only needed me on a part-time basis. I agreed to work three days per week at 60 percent of my former salary. My pitch that my former salary ought to be adjusted for inflation was met with a strong rebuke that my salary was high enough "for a part-time job." So began my marginalization.

Finding a caregiver was daunting. We ran an ad in the local paper six weeks before I was due to return to work and received only one phone call. I was beginning to panic. We ran the ad again and the response was greater, but I didn't feel comfortable leaving my kids with any of the applicants. I could not return to work unless I had absolute confidence in the person we hired as a caregiver.

Suddenly everything fell into place. Hayley came into our lives, with her two-year-old daughter and 10 years of experience as an early childhood educator. As I watched her sitting on the floor playing with our children, I knew she was the one we had been waiting for. The key to being a successful working mother of triplets is having a good caregiver. Hayley is undoubtedly one of the secrets to my success at work.

When I returned to work, I noticed immediately that my coping skills improved. I could enjoy three days with the kids and get excited about going to work on Monday. I'm generally the only happy person at the office on Monday mornings! I would never deny that it is a lot harder to be at home with my kids than at the office.

Like many working moms, I need to learn to quell my feelings that everything we do together must be FUN

The greatest challenges I face at home are probably no different from those of other parents of triplets or more. I think it's best described as an exercise in staying one step ahead of the next crisis. My organizational skills are now as finely honed as they could be when I'm dealing with three two-year-olds who have never moved in the direction I've wanted them to since they learned to walk. I probably spend too much time worrying about spending quality time with the kids. Like many working moms, I need to learn to

quell my feelings that everything we do together must be FUN!

When I first returned to work, I diligently checked my voice-mail and e-mail messages several times a day on my days at home. I began to dread this task because it always involved spending precious nap time on the telephone putting out fires. I eventually learned the best strategy is to try and ignore work during my days at home. I know other women in the legal profession who work four days per week, or "modified hours" (which usually means 40 hours per week in a large firm). Many have fallen into the trap of taking work home at night and on weekends so that it is now expected of them.

The greatest challenge I face at work is trying to keep people from noticing that I'm not always there. Despite my part-time arrangements, I am well aware that they could end at anytime, if anyone is inconvenienced by my absence. I therefore rarely leave my desk during the day, unless I am in court.

Part of my juggling act is a result of moving to the suburbs shortly after our children were born. In order to make the 90-minute commute and still leave the impression I am working 12 hours a day, I leave for the office shortly after 6 a.m. My husband greets Hayley as she arrives at 7 a.m. and then dashes off to catch his train. I leave work at 4:30 p.m. (a taboo in my profession) to get home by 6 p.m.

Despite what we read about employers trying harder to accommodate the needs of the family, this does not happen in the legal profession. What I do is not acceptable to many people. Consequently, the firm's clients are generally not told that I work part time (unless we want them to think we are progressive).

I have been told my career will be jeopardized because people will think I am not serious about my profession if I continue to work part time. Most of my colleagues do not believe I am committed to my job because in order to have a successful practice you must be driven to succeed. Many of my male colleagues and some women cannot understand why I would want to work less than the 60-hour week they feel compelled to work. The partners in my firm encourage me to think in the long term. I have been asked many times when I intend to return to full-time practice. I have found many creative ways to change the subject.

I have now been back to work for 18 months. We definitely have more wrinkles to iron out of our arrangements, but generally our family is very happy. I enjoy my job more than I ever have before and I appreciate the time I have at home with the kids. I have not ruled out the possibility that I may leave the profession at some point, but for now, we will keep juggling and with any luck, none of the balls will fall and hit me in the head!

music and motherhood
Karen Rotenberg

**My whole life had changed so dramatically —
I was different physically and emotionally.
Would I be able to perform as I had before?**

I am the mother of three-year-old triplets. I am also a professional musician (I play the oboe) and have been working on a part-time basis since my children were three months old. People always say to me, "I don't know how you do it!" Of course, they say the same thing about the experience of raising triplets anyway, even without the added pressure of a performing career. But to do both is another matter entirely! "You don't look exhausted," is another typical comment. Surprise! I'm not exhausted (a little tired, I admit). I'm happy, I'm calm most of the time, I love my family and I love my performing career.

I never expected to resume playing so soon after my children were born. But there were many reasons for my decision. We needed my income to help pay for the enormous expenses of caring for our children. Another major reason was to safeguard my future earning capacity. When the word was out in musical circles that I had given birth to triplets, my colleagues didn't expect me to resurface for five years at least. Unfortunately, in my line of work, if you are not available, someone else will be called in to do the job. There is always a risk that the call will go to that someone else the next time. So it seemed wise to maintain some sort of professional profile. Also, playing an instrument requires ongoing practice, regardless of performing commitments. The longer I didn't play, the harder it would be to get back into shape.

working & parenthood

I started playing again about three weeks after giving birth. I started slowly, only about 15 minutes a day. What a shock when I first put my oboe to my lips; I had lost all muscle strength in my abdomen from my pregnancy and the cesarean. But I persevered. Over the next two months, the 15 minutes increased to 45 minutes a day, which was the maximum preparation time I could manage for the first six months. Out of necessity, I had to become much more efficient in my practice than I had been before my children were born.

When I returned to work, I first performed with a very prestigious orchestra. To add to the pressure, the concert was taped for broadcast on television. I was sick with anxiety beforehand. I had not performed for six months. My whole life had changed so dramatically. I had changed both physically and emotionally. Could I perform as I had before?

The answer was yes, I could. It took me a year to get back to the level of playing I had achieved before my pregnancy, but even in that first difficult year, I was still able to perform well. Gradually, as my children grew older, I started to grow again musically and accepted more ambitious and challenging commitments when my responsibilities at home would permit. I discovered that being a musician has certain advantages for a woman with young children. Most of the work is at night and most of the preparation is done at home. It's rare that I am gone for a full day. I feel fortunate that I have been able to pursue my career and be at home most of the time with my children. I find the two roles of mother and musician actually complement each other. Playing and performing give me a break from the intensity of motherhood and raising three children the same age. Motherhood provides welcome relief from the intensity of performing. It's a busy life, but so rewarding in every way.

How do I do it?
Here's a short list of pointers for any mother of multiples who wants to combine career and family.

• Competent, reliable help is essential. We have had two nannies since the children were born. Both have been fabulous (the second is still with us). They have been willing to work long hours and/or weekends to accommodate the irregular schedules of two musicians (my husband is a musician as well). Our present nanny has been with us for over two years. The children are very bonded to her. She knows us very well and can carry much of the domestic load when I am busy and under pressure.

- A supportive spouse is very helpful. I could not have resumed playing without the encouragement and help of my husband. (He is pulling duty at our nursery co-op this morning so that I can write this story.) My mother has also been very helpful, coming over regularly to take the kids out with our nanny so that I can practice.

- Be organized and plan ahead. I could not survive without organizing ahead of time. Even when I am not working, the children's clothes are laid out and bottles prepared the night before. When I have to work in the morning, my oboe bag is packed the night before and my clothes are laid out. It is impossible to get my children or myself out of the house in the morning with some degree of calm and sanity without planning ahead.

- Realistic expectations. Do not take on more work than you can handle realistically, given your responsibilities as a mother. Regardless of how much help I have, the family still relies heavily on me. I run the household and make the daily decisions concerning the children. They always need to spend time with me, even if other adults are available. And I wouldn't want it any other way. Therefore I have to pace my musical commitments so that family life doesn't suffer unduly and that I am not run ragged. There is a limit to the amount of work I can accept and sometimes, if an opportunity requires a lot of preparation, I simply have to turn it down altogether.

- Invest in the future, both yours and your children's! This means enlisting enough help, either paid or from family, so that the children are well taken care of while you work. Sometimes this means spending more money in the short term, but the payoff in the long term is your health and sanity.

- Motivation for me is the key. I love my family and I love my work. You can accomplish great things when you are inspired. I had to struggle for my pregnancy and went through a dark period when I thought I might not be able to have children at all. Never in my wildest dreams did I expect to have three beautiful healthy children. They (and my husband) are the greatest blessings of my life. Before motherhood, my life centred on my music and self-fulfillment. Now my career is not just for me, but contributes to the support of my children and provides added financial security for the family at a time when working in the arts is tenuous. I am thankful that I have been able to maintain the continuity of my career now that I am a mother of three children. All are thriving! May it continue!

working & parenthood

i'm a working mom now
Donna Zidar

After many years of infertility, I was determined that when my children were born, I would not return to the workforce, but stay at home and do all the things I had longed to do. Little did I know that I would have quadruplets and that I would be doing all those things four times as much and as often as the average mother. I had been there day and night for them from the moment they were born. I had done the night feedings, the diaper changing, witnessed first steps, taught them to drink from a cup, helped them to learn to talk, toilet-trained them, kissed every boo boo, sang songs, watched thousands of preschool programs, taught them to ride bikes, and had been a part of all the wonderful things that little children experience. I had been their main source of security, learning and love.

The time passed so quickly. Before I knew it, they were ready to graduate from senior kindergarten and would soon be off to school full time. The prospect of having all that free time to myself was wonderful. Yet, I didn't have a clue about what I would do all day. I had worked so hard for the past five years that I could not imagine myself sitting around waiting for the kids to come home. I had always wanted free time to myself, but this was too much free time.

At the same time, the children were starting to become very expensive. There were no more donations and the costs of food and clothing were becoming outrageous. The kids were starting to want things that were very expensive: bikes, skates, baseball gloves, snowsuits, all times four. It seemed like the only option was to try and return to the workforce. But it was an intimidating prospect. I had been a legal secretary when I became pregnant, but after six years away from an office, technology had improved so much. I didn't feel I had the skills to compete anymore. After being at home for so long, my self-confidence had really slipped. I considered myself an expert at night feedings and toilet training, but the prospect of a job interview made my stomach turn.

My sister, also a stay-at-home mom, and I decided that our first step to getting back into the workforce was to upgrade our skills. Together

working & parenthood

we enrolled in a night school class at the local college on Friday nights. It was rather intimidating at first, but once we got going, we loved it. It had been a long time since either of us had channeled our energy into something other than childcare. We both graduated with A's and were on our way to becoming working parents.

Fortunately, when I approached the law firm where I had once worked, there was a six-month maternity leave position available, and they welcomed me back. Recognizing that my skills might be a little rusty, they were willing to train me. It was a very lucky break because I was able to return to an environment that was familiar and friendly. While I was excited and happy to be returning to work and to be doing something on an adult level, I felt extremely guilty and worried that the family wouldn't be able to cope without me at the helm.

The first few months were a major adjustment for all six of us. For the kids, who had just started full days at school in Grade 1 and an after-school program, the adjustment was difficult. There were too many changes, too fast, at the beginning of the school year. One of my daughters cried quite frequently at school that she missed me. I think that she not only missed me, she also missed her siblings, who were in separate classes for the first time. It broke my heart to see her go to school with a picture of me in her backpack that she could look at anytime she felt lonely. With some help from the teacher, it took her about three months to make new friends and to adjust to being on her own in the classroom. The other three kids adjusted fairly well with no real problems, (aside from complaints about being woken up for school). Now that they are in Grade 2, all of them are doing very well in separate classes and are coping quite well with mom working.

The biggest adjustment, though, was for my husband. Most of the responsibility for the kids now fell on his shoulders. Because my job is in downtown Toronto, I have to leave much earlier than him in the morning. He is doing a marvelous job as the parent who gets the kids ready for school (although I do as much preparation the night before as possible). He's also the one who picks them up after school, starts dinner, takes them to doctor's appointments, takes the calls from the school when someone gets hurt, etc.

The only way for me to continue working is for the entire family to pull together as a team. From the day our quadruplets were born, both parents cared for the kids and the house. Now we are encouraging the kids to contribute in their small way as well, whether it's helping with the lunches, making their beds (albeit rather lumpy) or setting the table for dinner. At the same time, hopefully they are learning a lesson that all members of the household need to contribute to make the house a "happy home" for everyone, including mom and dad. I also hope they will learn to appreciate how hard everyone has to work to earn the money that pays for the material things the kids long for.

Life as a working mother has been extremely challenging and often difficult, but it is also very rewarding. Whenever I miss a school trip or a sunny afternoon at the park with the kids, I wish I were home again with free time on my hands to just enjoy being with my family. But working has given me a chance to socialize, to build confidence in myself and most importantly, to contribute financially to improving the quality of life of our entire family.

After working for more than a year, I have come to realize there is a balance somewhere between home and work, but it's not always easy to find. It comes from all members of the family contributing to household chores (and allowing them to contribute and not feeling as though you're the only one who should do it). It comes from making the most of your free time with the family. Housework is no longer the most important thing. Spending quality time with my family is now my most important objective. It's what I'll remember. Life is too short to worry about the silly stuff and kids are only young once. So, although I'm a "working" mom now, I am still a mom who is trying hard to keep things in perspective and not miss out on what is truly important to me.

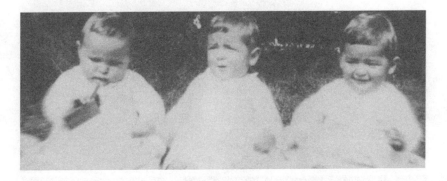

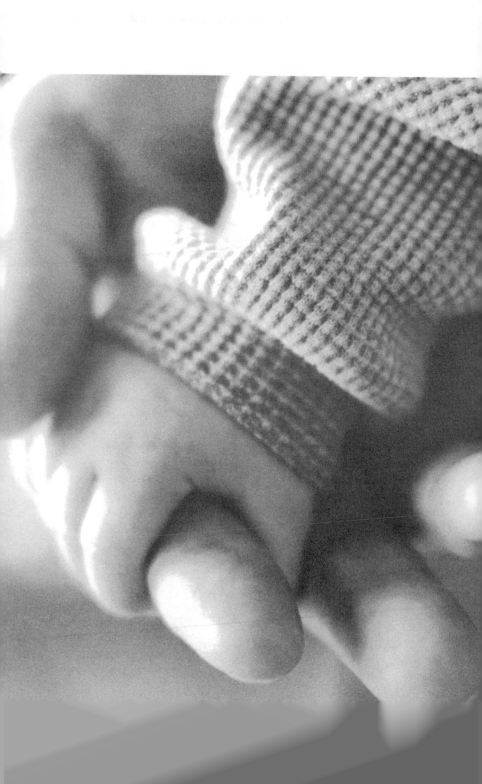

10

our supporters

telling it
like it is
George and Joan Eldridge

George

I remember as if it happened yesterday. Diane and John were expecting one child (so we all thought) and Diane was very ill. John had called to see if we would come down and take care of their first-born son, Craig, and Diane, who was not able to keep any food down and definitely not able to care for herself or her son. We were needed, so we came. At this point, we didn't know that we were going to become grandparents of quadruplets.

The day we found out that Diane and John were expecting four babies was a scary, bewildering and exciting day. Diane had an ultrasound scheduled early because she was getting so large so quickly. The doctor wanted to make sure that she had calculated the expected delivery date correctly. As John prepared for a month-long business trip to Hong Kong, we were planning to continue caring for Diane and Craig in his absence.

About two hours after Diane left the house, our son-in-law called from the doctor's office to tell my wife, Joan and I that Diane was having quadruplets. Joan exclaimed, "Oh shit!" and then in a panic, they both hung up the phone. Quadruplets! This was not something we expected to hear from anyone in our family. It was hard to grasp.

Joan

As her parents, our main concern at this time was for our daughter. She was so sick! George made Diane leek and potato soup. I think that's what kept her alive. She could only eat about half a cup at a time, but her father kept on cooking it because it was the only thing Diane would eat. I prayed that the babies and Diane would be fine. This was a wondrous experience. We had to tell everyone. I wished my mother was alive to see it. She just loved babies. When we started to ask about our family history, I found out that my grandmother's sister had twins, but one had died at one year old. There was no other known history of multiples on either side of the families.

George

Joan prayed, and I put my faith in the soup because I knew it could cure anything. We wanted to be there for our daughter. She needed us. Once Diane started to feel better, we headed back home, knowing that we would be needed again once the babies came home.

When the big day arrived, John called to tell us Diane was in labour and that the babies would be born that day. Then he called again to tell us that the babies — two boys and two girls — had arrived. Joan then called Diane's sister and two brothers. John suggested that we wait until the next day before visiting because Diane would be in recovery and the babies seemed to be doing fine, considering their prematurity. But we couldn't sit and wait for the next call. We jumped in the car, picked up Diane's sister, Lynne, on the way and headed to the hospital three hours away.

Joan

The children were in the hospital for two and a half months. It was scary. From day to day, we never knew who was going to be ill or well. I never told Diane, but I was very worried about Harrison. He was so sick. I gazed at all of the children in amazement. They were so tiny, so fragile. All we could do was place our hands on the children's backs and talk to them. It is really a miracle that our little grandchildren survived. Three of the babies arrived home and were joined a week later by Harrison. That's when the real work started.

As far as family is concerned, this experience seems to have bonded us together. Diane and her siblings began to appreciate that in times of need, family has to be there for each other. Diane knows, really knows, that she can count on her parents and siblings. Family participation from both sides was amazing.

George

In the beginning, Joan would head to Diane's place on Sunday evenings and stay until Friday. Joan jumped into everything. I mean everything! John would be sure to be home early on Fridays so that Joan could come home. I would cook dinner when she arrived home, but by the time it was ready, Joan was fast asleep in the chair.

Joan continued this for a few months. She was also joined or relieved by Diane's sister, Lynne, niece Amparo, or John's two older sisters, Joan and Sheelagh. The caregiver team rotated every few days or every week.

Joan

We were so amazed by the support of the community and all our friends. Diane and John's friends came to help and our friends were there for them as well. Every few months during the first year, we would call our friends Shirley and Ray to join us for a weekend at Diane's house since we felt that it was important for Diane and John to get away for a few days to rejuvenate themselves. Our friends were so pleased to be able to help. We have some great pictures of us feeding the babies. Each of us would be assigned a baby for the feeding. We would set up the highchairs in a circle in the living room, pull up our chairs and see who could get their child to eat the most or the fastest. Raymond always got Alison, who was the most difficult to feed. But he would sing to her through the meal to keep her eating. Once the babies ate, we had time to feed older brother Craig and make sure the dog was walked. Our friends quickly learned the routines and how to fill out all the charts. The men, who lived in a time when the tasks of babies and household were typically left to the mothers, learned through these children the work and joy of babies. George spent many of his hours at Diane's house washing dishes. We were all very tired, but exhilarated by the experience.

We also enjoyed taking one or two children to our home for a few days. It was a nice break for Diane and John and a great way for us to get to know the children better. It also gave the children a chance to be separated from each other and get some individual attention. The children were always eager when it was their turn to visit.

George

Diane used a cloth diaper service at home, but when they all came to our house north of Toronto, we had to wash the diapers. On one visit, people in the area noticed our long clothesline of drying diapers. They had never seen such a thing and had to come over to take a picture.

When Diane, John and the children arrive at our home, the house comes alive. We are lucky to have our children stay with us every year for Christmas. When they were very young, they worried that Santa might not know where he should leave their gifts, so we convinced our neighbour to be Santa. He arrived just before the children's bedtime to reassure them that he knew they were at Grandma and Grandpa's house.

We are so proud of all the children. Joan tells everyone about them. On more than one occasion, Joan would be out with Diane taking a walk with the children and people would ask the usual question, "Are they all yours?" to which Joan would quickly respond, "Yes, they are all hers. You know, you could come and help any time." And you know, they would!

Joan

I never sat on the floor so much in my life!

George

It's nice to be needed — and boy — are we needed!

Joan and George

Life is so precious. These children are not just Diane's and John's — they are our grandchildren! From one grandparent to another — be there!

doing the night shift
Kelly O'Sullivan

My summer job as a night nanny

On my fridge, there is a picture of four beautiful, smiling babies. On the back, it says, "Thanks for helping us through our sleepless nights and for playing with us every morning." I treasure this picture because it will always remind me of the five most memorable months of my life.

I had a very unique summer job. Four nights a week, I helped a family with infant quadruplets get a good night's sleep. I arrived at 1 a.m., after everyone was in bed, and the day was more than over. Officially, I was an overnight nanny. I stayed awake all night to feed and change four infants who were eight months old. I also did other things to help out, such as empty the dishwasher, fold laundry, dust and many other household chores. When the babies were younger, I also sterilized the bottles.

One night while I was cleaning highchairs at around 4 a.m., I began to wonder how many other 19-year-olds had the same privilege as me. Not many, I bet. I am pleased to say I became an expert at balancing a baby on my hip and doing virtually anything else. I could feed two and even bounce three babies at once. I also became rather talented at rocking, bouncing or soothing a baby to sleep. How on earth did I get this job? I asked myself that same question more than once.

How many other 19-year-olds have the same privilege as me? Not many, I bet

I had been volunteering with the family for about a month when I finished school. At that point, the family was looking for someone to work nights for them. When they asked me I was so honoured, and actually quite surprised. I couldn't believe they wanted ME to care for their precious babies. My only concern was that I would have to stay up all night. Could I do it? I had to try since the prospect of being such an important part of their lives was an honour. The fact that it would be a temporary position was perfect because I would be off to college in September.

Many nights, as I rocked a baby back to sleep, I found my eyes closing. I swear I will never again take for granted the privilege of sleeping at night. Even though I could sleep all day, nothing could replace that rest at night. Even still, I would not trade those peaceful moments with a baby for the comfort of my bed. There is nothing in the whole world as beautiful as a sleeping baby, and I saw four each night. However, just like their parents, I longed for the night when the babies would sleep through.

Generally, the babies would wake one at a time, giving me a chance to give them some one-on-one attention. When they were younger, they weren't as generous and I often had three or four hungry babies awake at the same time. During these times, one or both parents helped me out. There were also many very long nights because someone was teething or not feeling well. I had to rock them for hours at a time. Having the parents there or knowing they would help was a godsend. Usually though, it was just a matter of perseverance and finding that one perfect position or just rocking until they were asleep. But there were times, I must admit, when I didn't have the right stuff and only their mom would do.

Even though I was not their mom, they sure were happy to see me

The smiles that greeted me each morning and the sleepy cuddles as each baby awoke made every night worth it. For that few minutes before hunger set in, I had four of the happiest babies in the world to play with. And even though I was not their mom, they sure were happy to see me.

When the babies were awake by around 6 a.m., I got everyone changed and started as many bottles as I could while trying to keep everyone happy. Their mom usually came down to help with cereal around 7 a.m. Breakfast ran more smoothly if I had all of the bowls laid out with the cereal measured before everyone woke up. It was one less thing to do when everyone started to fuss. I left the house around 7:30 a.m. each morning, usually just as everyone wanted breakfast. Often though, I stayed until 8 a.m. because it was hard to leave when someone needed to be fed or changed or just cuddled. And someone always needed a cuddle.

I am so happy to have had the chance to watch these children grow and develop their own personalities, which are very different. I am absolutely in awe of how fast they are growing and changing.

Every now and then, the parents joke that some day I will also have quadruplets. Only time will tell, but I do know that I am almost a baby expert, and by the time I have just one of my own, it should be a snap.

Kaitlyn, Zachary, Rebecca and Brianna will always have a special place in my heart and I hope I have the opportunity to continue watching them grow up.

babies are
my favourite people
Cutie O'Reilly

When one of the quadruplets woke and began crying, I would pick him up and together we would dance to our special tune

I don't consider myself the perfect nanny. I don't know all there is to know about being a nanny, but there is one thing I do know for a fact: taking care of babies — whether singles, twins, triplets or quadruplets — is not just a job, it is a most enjoyable privilege.

Next to the parents, nannies have the awesome responsibility to help foster the emotional well-being of each child. Babies need their emotional tanks filled frequently. So when mom or dad is not there to fill the tank, a nanny is there.

I always think of the babies I care for as my babies. I often ask moms or dads, "How are our babies?" As long as they are in my care and even long after my service is no longer required, I consider them my babies.

To me, all little boys and girls are princes and princesses from a spiritual point of view. I recognize each child as an individual who is very special in his or her own unique way.

I once had the super privilege of caring for quadruplets. One of the boys, the one I nicknamed "Mr. Velvet Voice," had a problem understanding why the bottle was not put into his mouth the minute he woke up. The more I apologized and tried to explain, the more upset he became. So, I created a little tune and dance to pacify him until his bottle was ready. As soon as "Mr. Velvet Voice" woke and began crying, I would pick him up and together we would dance as I hummed the special tune.

It was a silly dance, really, and the tune was even sillier. I would feel a little odd if mom or dad were to happen down the stairs when we were engaged in our song and dance routine. But my little boss man totally enjoyed it. And it kept him calm and reasonable until his bottle was ready.

Have you ever been told off by a baby? I have. Her name is Jessica. I nicknamed her "Duchess." Her cry actually sounded as if she was quarrelling. If I didn't leave whatever I was doing to go to her as soon as she beckoned, she told me off in her baby language! I'm quite sure that along with telling me off, she threw in a threat or two about informing mom and dad about how really incompetent and slow I was in getting her changed.

If you don't have a good sense of humour, you can forget about taking care of babies.

Another of the quadruplets was my little blue-eyed blonde that I called "Mr. Handsome." The day I went for the job interview, I was so fascinated with the babies I decided to stay for a while longer after the interview had ended. It was definitely a love-at-first-sight experience. I took to mom and the babies instantly and I could tell they felt the same way about me. However, Mr. Handsome it seemed, wasn't quite convinced and decided to give me what I can only describe as the "acid test."

I had taken him upstairs to change him. Placing him on my lap, I took off the wet diaper and just as I was reaching over to get a clean diaper he squirted me in the face. "Let's see how she takes this, then we'll know for sure if she's the one for the job," I imagine he said to himself.

A couple of months later, when he didn't feel like sleeping and just wanted to hang out with me in the wee hours of the morning, he would lay back in his little car seat and just admire me with the kind of contented smile on his face that said, "Cutie, you're okay. I like you and I feel safe and loved when I'm with you, just as I do with mom and dad."

One night, Princess Monica woke up crying (she's one of the beautiful triplet girls I later began to care for). I went upstairs to the nursery, took her up and was walking back downstairs with her. She had stopped crying when I picked her up at first, but on the way down with me, she started to cry again. So I said to her, "Cut that out Monica! There's no need for you to cry now." She looked up at me, smiled the sort of smile that says, "Okay, Cutie, if you say so. But you can't knock a girl for trying to get some attention around here, can you?" She curled up in my arms with that knowing smile still on her face and she never uttered another sound. She was about four months old then.

Ah yes, and little Princess Annie from another set of beautiful triplet girls. She felt the best place to sleep was on someone's tummy. And when she decided she wanted an on-top-of-the-tummy sleep that night, you couldn't get her to change her mind if you tried.

She, too, had her special little silly tune and dance we created together, just for her, when she was feeling blue. No one else shared that tune and dance.

There's something special I could tell you about each of my babies. But they are all beautiful and fun to care for. Take it from a nanny who knows.

sweeping away the day's stress
Maureen Malloy

Getting my "baby-fix" as a triplet volunteer

The ad in our school newsletter read: "Volunteers Needed" for a mother expecting triplets. I raced to the nearest phone to call the expectant mother and offer my services. Volunteering would be the perfect opportunity for me, a person with more than my fair share of maternal instinct and no sign of grandchildren in sight.

I first met the family about two weeks after their three beautiful girls were born. It was a summer day and the babies were all sleeping soundly in their playpen in the backyard. The parents, though tired from the ordeal of the cesarean birth, non-stop care and adjustment to a new way of life, were radiant with pride and joy as they introduced me to Jacqueline, Monica and Lorraine. The parents and I sat, talked and became acquainted. I felt comfortable with them and sensed they felt the same way about me. I began my weekly visits as a volunteer, helping this young family with all the necessary routines of feeding, changing, bathing and making formula.

In the early months, I would arrive in the late afternoon to the heartwarming sight of mom watching her three babies nestled in their cradle seats. As they began to stir we readied the bottles and began the routine of changing, feeding, burping and changing again, with lots of time to rock and cuddle each little one. With every visit I could see the changes as the babies gained weight, began to smile and take part in our "conversations" with them. We were bonding.

Once a trusting and comfortable relationship was established between the parents and me, I began to help out by doing some dishes, sweeping the floor, picking up toys — things that gave an extra hand to the parents. There were many times when I felt tired at the end of the day but I didn't want to let the mother down so I would show up anyway. Very often, it was on those days I came away most rewarded by a small, happy event, with one of the girls taking a first step or speaking a word.

---

quote

"I remember holding and feeding baby Victoria one day. I realized at that moment how much I loved her. It reminded me of nurturing and caring for my own baby 25 years earlier. And I think I understood at that moment how adoptive parents can experience the same deep love for their children as natural parents."

Madeleine Rack
Triplet volunteer

Recruiting helpers from various walks of life

I told two friends, both confirmed baby addicts like me, about my experience volunteering. One friend had been a long-time volunteer with another family with triplets. When I asked her if she would be interested in starting over with newborns, she told me she would have to think it over. Within minutes, she called the mom and offered her time. My other friend, a kindergarten teacher with a 12-year-old daughter, also helped with the babies every Friday evening. In addition, there were many other volunteers, including co-op students from a high school graduating class, university students, a student nurse, neighbours, as well as family members. I commend the parents for having complete trust in the volunteers and for their initiative in recruiting people from various but related walks of life.

It has been more than two years now since I began to volunteer with the family. I have seen so many changes from week to week, month to month, from smiling, cooing and babbling to crawling, standing and taking their first steps, cutting their first tooth and talking. The miracle of growth has unfolded before my eyes. I particularly remember when Lorraine took her first steps. She wiggled up against the wall, outstretched her two arms in front and walked quickly but carefully with one step after the other across the room to me. She arrived with great jubilation over her accomplishment and, of course, to great cheers from her sisters and me.

The toddlers are very different from when I arrived on the scene two years ago. As I enter the house, the girls come running to the door into my baby-deprived arms, with hugs and kisses. My daily stresses are swept away! It's time to play and the child in me surfaces. Now it's time for mom and dad to take a well-deserved break.

Volunteering to help a family with multiple birth children has been a wonderful experience for me. It's a two-way encounter — the volunteer gives time and energy and the returns are innumerable. The girls have given me fun, joy, satisfaction, learning, fulfillment and love. We are going into year three, and I always look forward to my weekly "baby-fix" with Jacqueline, Monica and Lorraine.

11

overnight celebrities

thrown into the spotlight

Karen Neilson

Media and public attention can be overwhelming

When our quintuplets were born, the hospital held a news conference, which was our first experience speaking to an audience of reporters. The number of people inside that room, drumming their fingers on tabletops waiting for me to speak, was just staggering. As my husband, Tom, and I entered the huge conference room wired with microphones and video cameras, the reporters charged from their seats toward us to get their story.

Several weeks after the children were born, the media settled down and stopped staking out the hospital. Instead of just showing up for comments, they would make appointments for interviews. We granted some interviews, but we also turned many down because I was just too tired. Once we were at home, our local media were very understanding and didn't push to speak to us. When we did interviews, it actually became a very useful way of getting the word out that we were looking for volunteers. As well, I found I could use the media time to publicly thank everyone who helped us.

Of course, there are drawbacks. Television interviews involve setup time, which is never just the minute or two that is broadcast later. In all, it can take up to two hours, which is precious time I could have been using to get a lot of household things accomplished. Worse, if the kids were sleeping, an interview could throw a nap schedule completely out of sync.

Also, the notoriety, created not just by the media but through word of mouth, did have more sinister effects on us. There were people who wanted to see the kids playing and would walk right into our backyard just to watch them. One fellow came to the door and offered $200 to view the children for two minutes. I refused, and he upped the offer to $600. Again, I turned him down.

Another couple called and offered to take one baby off our hands because they couldn't have a baby of their own. One man called and fabricated a story about his wife expecting quintuplets and wanted to hear our story. We later learned that none of it was true. I had people come up to me that wanted to touch me or to get my autograph. Other people would approach the strollers and try to pick a baby up without so much as a word.

After all of this, I began to look at life more cautiously. I still have trouble letting my kids go out in the backyard to play by themselves because I think of the day when I ran inside my house for two seconds and then came back outside to find a strange man, who had walked into our fenced backyard to talk to the kids. That thought goes through my mind every time they go out the door. I still also find it difficult to be in large crowds for fear I will lose one of the kids.

Now that we have moved and the children are older, the public attention is beginning to fade. From time to time, especially on birthdays and anniversaries, we still get requests for interviews from the media in our hometown. I will sometimes grant them because our community really pulled together for us and it's one way of thanking everyone and keeping them in touch with our progress.

curiosity gets the best of them
Sheena Judd

We took a double and single stroller so we wouldn't be too conspicuous. It was no use

Parents and their multiple children face public curiosity almost daily. Our first experience was before we even left the hospital. At our local hospital, when you leave with your baby (babies), you stop by the gift shop and present the information card that had been on the baby's isolette and receive a package with samples and coupons. When I presented the information cards, the clerk did not believe me and demanded to see the babies for herself before we were entitled to our free gift.

Our first shopping trip as a family was unforgettable. When the babies were about eight weeks old and Christmas was approaching, my husband and I decided since we were going to be a family of six (two parents and four children), we had better get accustomed to striking out as a family. So we went on a simple shopping trip to our local mall, taking the double and single stroller so that we wouldn't be too conspicuous. The stroller strategy was no use. Clerks ran out of stores, people were staring and pointing; it gave us a small idea of what it must be like to be a celebrity. Needless to say, we didn't get much shopping done. But we did learn a few tricks along the way.

We find that if you are going out and you want to get anything accomplished you have to be almost dismissive. We tend to travel through the malls at a fast pace and try not to make eye contact with anyone. It is the only way to get the errands done. My personal rule is that I will stop and talk only to the elderly and other parents of multiple birth children.

My husband and I continue to split up: one parent with the double stroller and the other with the single, not walking together. Although people can be curious about twins, the degree of interest and questioning isn't as intense as it can be with triplets.

And, if all else fails, we simply smile politely and walk away. After all, time is precious and we can't afford to waste a single second.

responding to tactless questions

Oonagh Hastie

My children are very special. I feel I have been blessed three times over and I want people to walk away knowing that I am happy, not burdened

When people see triplets or quadruplets or more, I think they are so shocked they don't realize they are asking prying questions. They are just interested in finding out about such a unique and special situation. I actually don't mind the attention and most of the comments and questions. But certain comments such as, "There's a reason for birth control," or "Life must be hell," hurt me. But these comments especially hurt the children. People need to be reminded that their remarks, even those made in fun, can hurt the children. And they hear these kinds of jokes all the time.

Children are a blessing and, as a mother of triplets, I like to tell people how lucky I am. I found out very early, though, that I shouldn't expect to get anything done in a hurry at the mall. But there is always time to show off my beautiful family.

My children are very special. I feel I have been blessed three times over and I want people to walk away knowing that I am happy, not burdened.

Question after question after question ...

Wow are they all yours?
No, I collect kids.

I'm glad they are yours and not mine.
So are we!

Are you having any more?
No, it's my husband's turn next.

There's a reason for birth control!
Something your parents should have thought of.

If I touch one, will they all feel it?
No possible response to this.

Did your wife take drugs?
Just in the '70s when drugs were really good.

Did you take fertility pills?
Do you take birth control pills?

Do multiples run in your family?
Yes, from morning till night.

12

remember when

it seems like only yesterday

Ken Johnson

We're sitting in the family room at quarter to nine in the evening. The kids went to bed half an hour ago. They were really tired. We went out for pizza with all four kids. The house looks its usual "post-kid" day. Toys are everywhere — under the couch, under the kitchen table, in the foyer. Clothes and dirty diapers are waiting to be disposed of. We've been thinking about how quickly time seems to have gone by in the last two years. Shelley says, "It seems like only yesterday."

After five years of marriage, we had planned the perfect family: three children, boys and girls, born two years apart in the spring. You know, an idyllic situation.

Well, two years, one miscarriage, and many frustrated months later, no babies. Ten more months of pills, needles, doctors, sperm samples, inseminations and early morning trips to a clinic in downtown Toronto, and finally, "Bingo!" Pregnant. The nurse told us to prepare for the possibility of twins, which was an exciting thought. The next week after the first ultrasound, the doctor announced, "Congratulations, you're going to have triplets!" One week and another ultrasound later, the doctor said, "We have to talk; now there are four." Quadruplets! We had wanted twins, but not two pairs. After our feet hit the ground, we had lots of serious thinking about how we should proceed. Shelley was young and healthy, and probably could carry four at least 30 weeks, but it was still risky. After weighing all the alternatives, we decided to go ahead.

That was more than two years ago. It's unbelievable that those murky images (sacs of fluid) on the ultrasound screen are now four lively, noisy and lovable little toddlers. Our three girls, Brianna, Chelsea, and Brittany, and one boy, Devon, fill our days with activity. They are getting older by the minute, and our house, once always neat, is in disarray more than half the time. Shelley spent close to eight weeks of her pregnancy in the antenatal ward in a Toronto hospital. She says it seemed like forever! She did carry the babies for 31 weeks with only minor problems.

"Minor?" she interrupts. "You gain 76 pounds and stretch your girth by 54 inches, and call it minor."

So it wasn't minor.

But the babies had only minor complications. Chelsea and Devon needed ventilators for a couple of days. Then they were transferred to our local hospital after 10 days, and were home a little over three weeks later.

We will never forget the midnight feedings: two adults and four wailing babies. We would work for 45 minutes to get two ounces of formula into them, only to have them throw it up all over us. As the kids went through the rollover stage, the crawling stage, and the walking/running stage, it went so fast that we began to lose track. The bottles are gone and diapers will be gone before we know it (I hope)! Soon their vocabulary will grow into sentences and they'll be off to school.

"Off to school?" Shelley cries.

She knows that will be a teary day. Even now, she longs to turn the clock back to a day when they were just little babies, just for an hour, maybe even a minute. But you can't, of course. They're only babies once, and all you can hold onto is memories (and videotapes).

We don't know if time goes by as quickly for parents with single babies because quads are all we have ever known. We've learned to cherish the special moments in our lives: four little bare bums climbing into the bathtub and running around clean and happy after four hugs and kisses at bedtime or a chorus of "daddy" or "mommy" when one of us comes home.

"Well, it's time to clean up," Shelley says. It's hard to believe that in only 30 minutes the house will be transformed into orderly living space again. But there will be lots of reminders that four little toddlers call this place home.

Likely a few years from now, we'll be sitting in the family room again after a long day, and one of us will say, "You know, it seems like only yesterday."

a day in the life
Gillian Borowy

One fine sunny day when Michael, Kenny and David were almost one year old, we were finishing up that very messy adventure called dinnertime for the boys. I was cleaning the spaghetti sauce out of their ears and hair when I realized that Michael was being quiet, which is dangerous.

What I hadn't realized was that the boys had been in the wading pool with their dad just before supper, and Michael did not have a diaper on under his shorts. There he was, sitting on our kitchen floor, using a large poo as a crayon and colouring in the linoleum. He had covered a three-foot section and was travelling fast.

My first reaction was to grab Michael and head for the sink. No sooner had I turned on the tap than David made a beeline for the poo and started finger painting. What a fun game! As soon as I pulled one boy away from the mess, the other two dove in. They outnumbered me, and I could not keep all three of them out of it.

"Get out!" I cried. "Out of the kitchen!" Bad idea. The couch and carpet in the living room are beige. Luckily my husband walked through the door that second, his arms full of groceries.

He dropped the groceries and grabbed Michael. I cleaned David and managed to wipe the worst of it off the floor. "Uh oh," I thought. "Where's Kenny?" I ran out of the kitchen to see him sitting quite happily in the front foyer, quietly saying to no one in particular — "Na na ... na,na" while peeling the last of eight bananas.

morning has broken
Bev Unger

An hour with four 10-month-olds

One of my kids is crying pretty loudly. It's not usual to hear such a hard cry this early in the morning, especially from Brianna. A great day is one that starts with one of the kids rattling away at the activity centre in the crib. The rattle is the wake-up call that signals I have a few minutes to jump out of bed, do a quick stretch for my aching back, quickly throw on some clothes, move the baby monitors downstairs, say good morning to our dog, Tessie, brush my teeth, and if I am lucky, have the time to run a brush through my hair before the second, third and fourth are awake. By this time, they are no longer playing but are harmonizing in a way I know that says, "get me outta here, morning has broken!"

Today, morning breaks in a different way. I go to Brianna, who is wide awake, crying and breathing heavily, which is common for her since she often has episodes of wheezing and needs a puff of asthma medication. I roll her onto her side in hopes she will fall back to sleep since it is only 5 a.m. I am very tired, having been awake with Kaitlyn from 3:30 to 4:45 this morning for reasons I have yet to figure out. As I touch Brianna, I realize she is wet right through her diaper — again! I rush Brianna out of the room for fear of waking her sister. No luck. As we reach the doorway, Rebecca stirs and begins to whimper. As we head downstairs, Rebecca's whimpers turn into a full-blown cry from her crib. Brianna is quickly rocked back to sleep after a fast diaper and pyjama change and the puff of medication. We head upstairs to the nursery, tuck Brianna into bed and swiftly whisk Rebecca out in fear of waking Brianna again. Whew! It worked. We manage to get out of the room without a sound. Within seconds we hear Zachary and run to collect him out of the crib. At least Kaitlyn will surely sleep until at least 6:30 after her long night. No luck! I'm at the bottom of the stairs with Zachary and Rebecca, and away she roars! Doesn't it figure? It is going to be one of those days!

What can I do? I am exhausted from a rough day yesterday, a rotten sleep and an early rise today. I am starting out the day with three very tired, irritable little 10 month olds. My only saving grace is that Brianna remains asleep. Quick! To the basket of stuffed animals we go. The kids love them! I dump the animals out of the basket and hope for the best. As I start squeezing the animals, we hear the moos, neighs, meows, woof woofs, chirps and baas. Slowly, one by one, the cries fade away. Sad faces turn into little grins with looks that say, "I would still rather be crying and rocked by Mom." Three little, nearly happy faces look up at me and then back to the animals now scattered all around us. The big smiles and hearty laughs finally come. I grab the first pillow I see and toss my head down on it. The kids think I am still playing with them, as they frolic about with the toys. Little do they know I am really trying to grab an extra 30 winks. As usual, my head barely hits the pillow before Zachary and Kaitlyn begin crawling all over me and Rebecca shakes her arms and makes her noises which mean, "Mom, I need to learn how to crawl, I want to be on you too." I pull Rebecca over, and the four of us play and laugh for as long as I can to stretch out the inevitable wet bottom changes. If I wait much longer, I know their clothes will be soaking wet. So off to the change table ... one ... two ... three ... thank goodness Brianna was just changed at 5 a.m.. I am saved one more diaper change before the bottles start.

One of my big mistakes before getting down on the floor was only bringing one soother from the cribs. The soother stealing begins. We have a rule: if there is a soother in someone else's mouth or attached to someone else's body, it is personal property and no one else is allowed to touch it. If a soother is on the floor, it is free game! Try teaching that to four 10-month olds! Am I crazy?

The chorus of "ma ma ma mas" has started. Playtime on the floor is limited for me, because I need to get up and retrieve the bottles that were thrown into the pot of hot water. Back to the floor. As I pull Rebecca up onto my lap, I hear the now common "bang" as a soft head hits the hard ground. I am now accustomed to this sound as one of the four are always toppling over, ending up on their backs or their heads unexpectedly. The joy of 10-month olds — an age of exploring, investigating and challenge. It's an age where attempting something for the first time seems nearly impossible without a few whines, a lot of concentration, effort, struggle, cries of "ma ma" and "da da," and finally, accomplishment! It's an age where success always ends with big smiles and the clapping of hands, which makes the undertaking all worthwhile.

All of a sudden there are only two bodies against me. I look around to see Kaitlyn pull herself up to a standing position on a nearby chair. I take a deep breath and laugh at myself for not hovering over her every move, as I know I would do with a single baby. But I have four and I cannot be there for every fall. I accept that, but it is hard for me. I rationalize that I cannot be in all places at all times. You quickly learn to accept the fact the kids are going to explore and fall down with a little "whah," and often not much more. As my heart is in my throat they get back up again and go right back to where they just fell and start all over until they have mastered their quest. Then they move onto the next challenge. Realizing I am not always able to console the ouchies is one of the toughest lessons I have learned in the short time Kaitlyn and Zachary have been crawling. I am often rocking or feeding another baby, changing a diaper, answering a ringing phone, putting the dog out, consoling a sibling who has also just fallen, but a little harder, answering the door, making lunch and dinner, pulling a fax off the machine from work. (I have taken a one-year leave from work, but they still manage to find me!) The list is endless. I never seem to be where I am needed the most at any given time.

We have been very lucky to have a great pool of very dependable, hardworking and loyal volunteers. Today, as luck would have it, the first volunteer will arrive at 8 a.m. Soon I will be assured it's okay to safely get breakfast ready and put the first of many loads of laundry in for the day. Knowing there will be another set of eyes and hands to help watch over my wandering crew is very comforting. An extra pair of loving arms to help console, feed, give bottles, entertain, cuddle, change, fold laundry, clean, rock — you name it, our volunteers do it!

The moment has finally arrived. The "ma, ma, mas" are getting louder and louder. I have to find the strength within me to get up. As I try to make my way off the floor, I have six arms reaching for me and climbing on me. All I can think of is, thank goodness Brianna is still asleep, since there are usually eight arms and 40 fingers stretching toward me.

I spoke too soon! Brianna is awake! As I make my way to the stairs, Kaitlyn is on my heels. I rush to close the baby gate and keep going. Brianna is wide awake now and all she wants to do is cuddle. Cuddle time is hard when three hungry little mouths are crying at the bottom of the stairs, trying to get through the gate. We make our way to the change table and head into the kitchen to grab the already warmed bottles. As I reach the kitchen door I see Zachary reaching for the dog's water dish. Darn, I meant to put the water outside after I fed her this morning. Poor Tessie. She too has had to make big adjustments. I manage to get the dish just as the water spills all over the floor. Throwing a tea towel down, I think to myself, "I will clean that up before the kids get on the loose again." I pick up Zachary and place him and Brianna on the living room floor. I rush back to the kitchen and get the bottles. Rebecca sees them first, starts to cry and quickly, four sets of eyes are on me. The cries are so loud now I wonder if we will wake the neighbours! Each babe is looking at me. Tears pour down their sweet little faces, telling me how hungry they are now that they have spotted their breakfast bottles. Bibs are tied and their cries get louder and louder. As the bottles are put into their mouths one by one, the penetrating shrills are slowly replaced with a welcome calm. A hush comes over the room. Finally, peace and quiet. I close my eyes and take a deep breath. In the background, I begin to hear the music which was forgotten amid the noise in the house. I concentrate on the words. I laugh aloud hearing the words to one of my favourite songs through the sounds of sucking: "I am slowly going crazy, crazy going slowly am I."

I think I am already there and it's only 6:15 a.m.

toss and turn
Donna Patterson

Memories of a remarkable year

Toss and turn, toss and turn. What time is it? Only 4 a.m. I should try to get three more hours of sleep before Alanna wakes, I think to myself. Oh, the strange dreams that fill my head during this first trimester; they interrupt my sleep. Awakened by nightmares when all is quiet, I begin to wonder. What will triplets be like? Will they be healthy? Oh, that's the worst fear of all. How will we manage? Can we manage? What will my body look like? How big can I get — I'll be huge! How will I resume my career? How will we afford everything for triplets? Babies are a new life, a new beginning, but three new beginnings? Why is this happening to me? It's like a miracle — there aren't any triplets in our family. Well, there are now! Am I still dreaming? Are we really expecting triplets? *Toss and turn, toss and turn*

When I look in the mirror at 28 weeks, I don't know whether to laugh or cry. There is such wondrous life inside me — incredible, but the physical sight of me is also incredible. My belly seems to expand by the day. How large can I get?

No longer able to care for my three-year-old daughter Alanna or myself, I am admitted to the hospital at 30 weeks gestation. I knew it was time. Fatigue dominates this pregnancy. My physician has said she wanted to keep a close watch on the babies and me. I'm 30 weeks pregnant but look and feel 46 weeks. Crying quietly relieves some of the frustration and fear. *Toss and turn, toss and turn*

Being away from my three-year-old daughter Alanna is the worst of all because she is the most vulnerable. My mum and Alanna drive the hour to the hospital once or twice a week. Our visits together are always comforting but they are never long enough. As always, my little gal changes into her nightgown and hops into my hospital bed with me. My husband, Darryl, and I are so lucky that my mum is able to care for Alanna while I'm here in hospital. Thank you Mum for everything you do. You are so amazing to me in so many ways. Evening phone calls with Darryl are really good for us because we can be alone and not rushed. Darryl and Alanna come once each weekend and when they leave, I feel so empty. I miss you. I miss the three of us. *Toss and turn, toss and turn*

Baby A is becoming quiet in utero. Something is different with this baby. Ultrasounds show that she is smaller as well. Oh please, hang on baby, please grow. *Toss and turn, toss and turn*

Just before Thanksgiving weekend, our physician examined me and found that I was showing warning signs of toxemia. To avoid an emergency delivery over a skeleton-staffed holiday weekend, she scheduled a c-section for the following day. Yikes! Oh my God, we're going to have our babies! I hope 32 weeks gestation is long enough for these little babies and I hope that everything will be as it should be. But it will be a great relief to have this uncomfortable bundle removed from me! *Toss and turn, toss and turn*

On delivery day, surgery is scheduled for 4 p.m. No food or drink. A day seems longer when a pregnant mom of three can't eat or drink all day. I'm on edge, wondering how the babies are, what they will be like. The babies are very still today. *Toss and turn, toss and turn*

The delivery is an unforgettable experience, involving 14 medical professionals. The pain of three spinal epidurals slowly fades as, one by one, each beautiful tiny baby is born. Each arrives screaming — oh the wonder of life! Our babies, Victoria, Teresa and Jaclyn are considered "well babies" though they will be carefully watched. The first two days of the babies' lives are a happy blur of excitement and countless visitors. Then, on the third day, we begin to hear about the complications.

The babies are not digesting breastmilk or formula very well. The reality of neonatal prematurity has struck. My parents, Darryl and I learn quickly the feelings of stress and concern that families bear while their little babies must stay in intensive care. Our babies begin to suffer interrupted breathing spells. They endure feeding tubes and intravenous needles. They also lose the human contact and cuddling that babies need so much. Babies Teresa and Victoria soon overcome their digestive problems and then become jaundiced. They dislike lying under the lights and it pains me to see them so uncomfortable.

Since baby Jaclyn, our tiniest, has continued to reject breastmilk and formula, we are giving her TPN, a substitute nutritional product. She is alone now that her sisters have graduated to a hospital closer to home. Poor Jaclyn is so listless and despondent. *Toss and turn, toss and turn*

I spend a heart-wrenching afternoon with Jaclyn and my mum

in the Neonatal Intensive Care Unit. My mum weeps silently and whispers how amazed she is that this little creature holds my finger so tight that her knuckles are white. Jaclyn seems to be giving me a message that she is as scared as I am. Mum, I can't bring you in here if you continue to cry; it's too emotional for me. Just then, Jaclyn's neonatologist creeps by us, pats my shoulder and whispers, "She'll be the first to walk." *Toss and turn, toss and turn*

The day Jaclyn graduates from the NICU to Level 2 care, we hear that Victoria is ready to come home. What a remarkable day! But the next two weeks are chaotic. I spend every moment it seems feeding babies and driving to and from the hospital with a baby and older child. There is time for nothing else. Soon my erratic blood pressure and chest pains begin. I refuse to allow myself to dwell on my health concerns because there are more important things to do for my new, large family. *Toss and turn, toss and turn*

We want our babies home. Jaclyn arrives home six weeks after she was born, and on the same day that our beloved Aunt Louise

comes all the way from California to help care for these little babies of ours. I'll never forget the joy and relief at having Jaclyn finally with us. We are so anxious to get to know her and to have all our children together. My health problems begin to settle as the babies slowly progress. My husband Darryl has been so supportive and involved. We are a team together in the care of our big family. Not long ago, Darryl and I would look at each other with tears in our eyes. A quick hug or touch would restore some strength to the other.

My father has often said to us that life is a great equilibrium and that having triplets requires three times the effort of a single child, but the rewards and joy are three times greater.

I sleep more soundly now, as the uncertainty and risks of pregnancy, birth and prematurity become just memories of what life once was for us. Together we are a family, uniquely shaped by our multiple experience, but a family just the same.

Thank you for this gift.

lifetime experiences

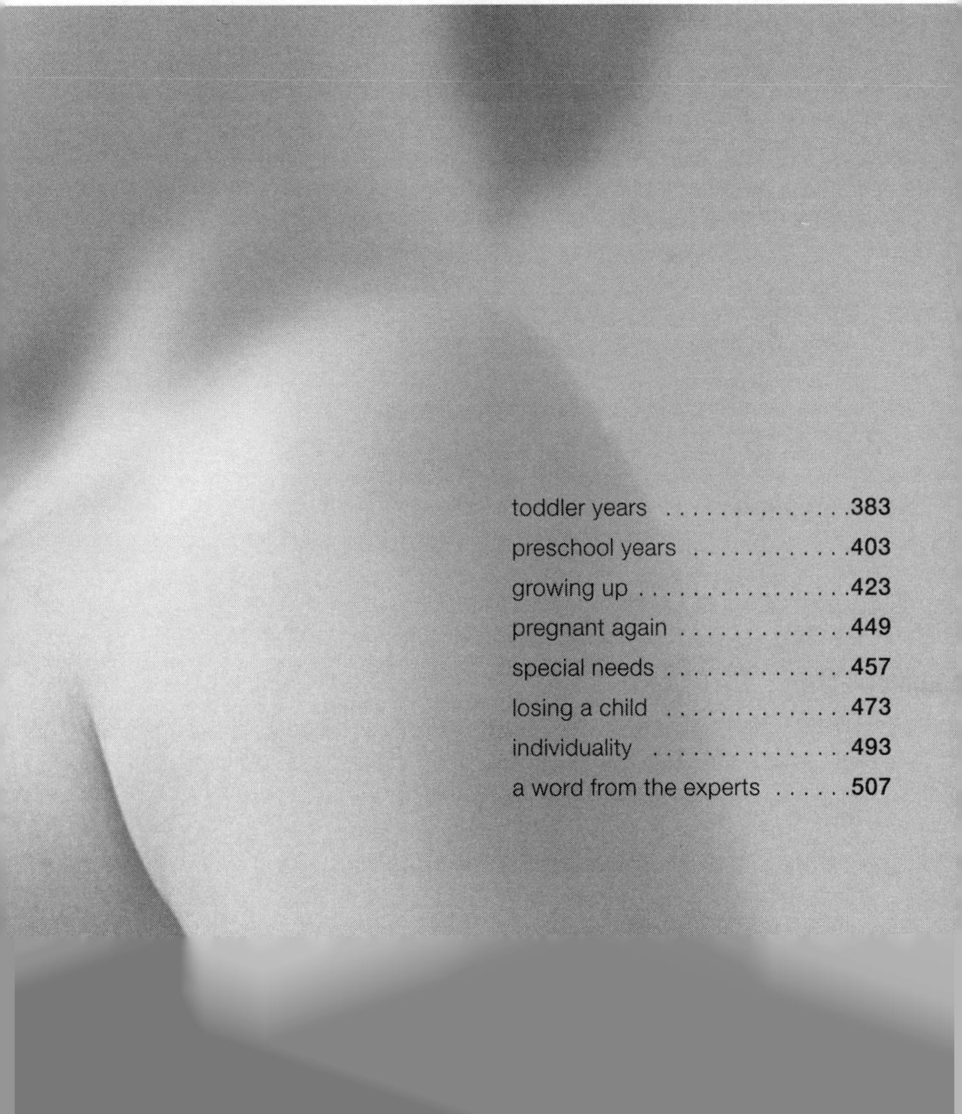

13

toddler years

discipline is a family affair
Sterling Gunn

As the adult, I know it's my job to model appropriate behaviour. That means discipline applies as much to me as it does to my children

It's a typical scene at our house. An unsuspecting toddler is busy building a house of blocks, taking great care to place every piece in exactly the right position. Her focus is extraordinary as she works on creating a whole new world where nothing is impossible. There is nothing else in her world. Suddenly, the world is shattered as another child arrives, pushing her over, then grabbing the house and running off. It's all over in a second — the toddler equivalent of a hit and run — and the perpetrator, mission completed, settles down with the blocks. The first child, crying, looks around and spies the local law enforcer. Calculating swiftly, she doubles the intensity of her crying. Simultaneously, she begins frantically pointing at her brother, clearly calling for justice to be done, and done swiftly.

We have a victim, a perpetrator and a witness. You are the law and it's clear what needs to be done: an arrest, a quick trial, a sentencing, and the perp does his time in the big house. It's an open and shut case, isn't it. Well, isn't it? The perp is getting what he deserves, right? Right? Well, maybe in the movies, but not in our house. In the movies, there is always a good guy, a bad guy, a victim, a judge and a jury. That's at least 16 people, not including any witnesses, and each has a role to play. The cop figures out the facts of the case, the judge ensures due process, the jury weighs the evidence and finds a verdict, the bad guy is punished and the victim gets to see the perpetrator punished. This is a very appealing system for administering criminal justice — 16 people involved in a very tidy, very rational and, all things said, very effective system. And in my opinion, with its emphasis on punishment, it's often very wrong for disciplining children.

Punishment is one aspect of disciplining a child, but I believe it's a rather blunt instrument that alone can lead to undesired behaviours in the future, such as aggression. If we don't talk to our kids about which behaviours are acceptable, they learn which behaviours to avoid while not learning which behaviours are acceptable.

Anyway, remember the 16 people needed for justice? That's a lot of people to have in one place. Our house is already pretty crowded with two-year-old triplets. So, to make ends meet, we the parents are often the cop, judge and jury. That's a lot of responsibility and, if you ask our kids, probably a conflict of interest. And, because playing so many roles can be so complicated, we know we're going to make mistakes. It becomes really important to have a clear objective for our disciplinary system and to keep the end in mind when we begin.

If we were to give one of our kids a 30-minute time-out, I don't believe they would learn very much; certainly not what they might do differently in the future. Discipline, on the other hand, involves sending the child to the time-out room until "you choose to behave." The child has an opportunity to choose how to behave in the future. I believe it's important for children to understand they make choices, and that their choices have repercussions. Of course, toddlers are a little young to be rational, but the idea still works.

We have a time-out spot near the front door, still in sight of the other kids and parents. Initially, we would put them there with a timer. Once the timer went off, they could return. Now, rather than a timer, we ask, "Are you ready to behave?" If so, off he or she goes. If not, we ask the child to please stay in the time-out spot. It doesn't always work, but we try.

Often in the usual chaos, someone is running around with something they shouldn't have — Daddy's glasses, for example. (You are no doubt wondering why Daddy's glasses were within reach of a toddler, but that's my discipline problem!) Usually, I'm just thankful they're not running around with a knife or scissors. Anyway, we try to get the contraband object by asking, "Do you know where Daddy's glasses go?" followed by, "Will you put the glasses on the table, or will Daddy?" Of course, our kids like to demonstrate their knowledge of the world, so they'll tell us, "The glasses go on the counter." Then it's just a matter of determining if they want to put the glasses away, or if they want Daddy to take the glasses from them. Most often, our children will quite happily put the glasses on the table. It's amazing how liberating choice can be.

Wow, that's pretty good advice for raising a well-adjusted child, isn't it? Unfortunately, the reality in our household can be, and is, different. Reading books is easy, raising kids isn't (at least, not for me). As they say, it's often hard to remember you set out to drain the swamp when you're up to your ass in alligators.

Even though I try, I don't always begin with the end in mind. There are times when I have just said, "Stop it." That's pronounced STOP IT!! The offending toddler is then herded off to the time-out spot and stranded with a parting "STAY HERE" while I hastily return to the scene of the crime. This happens when I'm too busy focusing on managing the event (whatever it was), rather than helping my child learn. Perhaps I feel I have a good reason — a bitten sibling needs consoling — but likely I've just forgotten about the big picture. I'm thinking about what I need right now (some quiet, no juice on the wall) and not about raising my children. If I were thinking clearly, perhaps I'd engage the biter in helping administer to the hurt of the bitten. After all, it never hurts to do a little empathy building.

There are a number of other things we try to do with our children. I think, for example, a lot of the screaming, hitting, pant pulling, throwing of toys and so on are just the child's means of getting our attention. A time-out may not be the best way to discipline a child. Consider the toddler hit and run. The perpetrator may be feeling ignored by the parent or sibling, and has engaged in this behaviour to gain attention.

If the victim has been truly hurt (a bite, for example), then we do try to focus on empathy building. The parent consoles the victim, and the biter, after the time-out, is invited to help make the oowie better. Biters won't always come and help, but at least they have a choice. In my mind, it all comes down to learning we make choices, and I want my kids to make good choices.

For a triplet, it's pretty easy to feel like a third wheel in a two-lap household

As the song says, I'm an adult now (well, I'm old enough to be an adult). If I don't behave the way I should, then how can I expect my children to behave the way I think they should? This leads me to the harsh realization that I too, need discipline. I need the discipline to do the right thing, not the easy thing, and to remember that I am responsible for the outcome of my choices. If I choose to punish my children rather than discipline them, then we will all bear the consequences.

Parenting is a life-long learning experience. As my parenting experience grows, I have come to know that discipline applies as much to me as it does to our children. I believe successful parents are disciplined parents — they are both teachers, and learners. Children are wonderful, and have a fabulous capacity to love, to learn and to enjoy life to the fullest. I also believe they're capable of making choices. I don't know if I am disciplined enough to raise perfect kids, but I'm going to try. After all, who else is going to help them get it right?

toddler teamwork
Lucy Carley

As I sit in the background and watch my three little ones play together, I resist the temptation to laugh with them and spoil their moment. They are playing their favourite game, a variation on "peek-a-boo," hiding around corners and jumping out, squealing and laughing as they crash into each other.

Our little ones are not that little any more — 18 months have gone by, and they are getting to know one another more and more each day. Their camaraderie was entrenched by the time they were crawling and then hanging onto one another for support as they learned to walk and other important life skills, such as wrestling.

Amy, our cautious little girl, Jeremy, an impulsive risk taker, and Storm, with an even balance of both qualities, are really starting to work as a team.

Jeremy, our little climber, was not content to climb out of his crib; he had to climb into others in the room as well. Soon mattresses on the floor replaced cribs. During the first night of sleeping (term used loosely) in their new beds, my husband and I tucked everyone in, gave kisses and hugs and bid goodnight. No more than 15 seconds passed before we heard the pitter-patter of feet running in all directions. Quietly, I crept up the stairs and opened the door just a crack and watched as they busily stacked their mattresses in a heap on the floor. Lifting in unison, these industrious toddlers positioned the mattresses as a ramp of sorts, which they then took turns running down. No one slept well in our house that night.

Still, I hope that they continue to learn from each other through their teamwork and interaction. During their first six months of life I often wondered — in fact, wished — that I had more time for them separately. I questioned whether there were enough hugs to go around and imagined how nice it would be to spend more time with each child separately.

Occasionally, one will climb onto my lap for a little one-on-one. It is our special moment together and there always seems to be just enough time before the other climbs up and then the other. There is a natural harmony about it.

I just can't imagine it any other way because any other way would mean they weren't together, and they are just absolutely adorable — together.

cookie? don't mind if i do
Shelley Johnson

I went upstairs for a few minutes to say goodnight to my husband, who had just come home from working the night shift. As we talked, we could hear the kids happily banging away downstairs on pots and pans. We actually thought we had five minutes to carry on a conversation without interruption. What fools we were! We should have known better.

The night before, I had made a batch of sugar cookies that didn't turn out very well. The whole batch went straight from the oven into the kitchen garbage. After talking to my husband for that few minutes, I came downstairs and found four toddlers messing around on the kitchen floor surrounded by pots and pans and eating sugar cookies right from the top of the garbage can. Everyone was munching and amusing themselves with the leftover crumbs. My mother-in-law laughs about it today and says, "I guess the cookies weren't as bad as you thought."

life's a circus with four mischievous toddlers

Mary Gallagher

For me, the most challenging stage of being a mother to quadruplets happened between the 20- and 24-month point. I had four little toddlers, each trying hard to assert his or her independence, but along with that came frustration and many, many tears and tantrums times four. They weren't able to talk but they knew exactly what they wanted.

By this time, I was on my own with the children during the day, except for two mornings a week when I had volunteers in to help. I felt very isolated in my own home since venturing outside with four little children alone was stressful and frankly, quite dangerous.

Thinking back to a few momentous events of toddlerhood, I can only laugh. But at the time ….

Testing mom to her limit was great fun. One Halloween, I went through stacks of their treats and divided them into four little boxes. I filled another bag with chocolate and tucked it away in the fridge.

The next morning while I slept, my four two-year-olds somehow managed to sneak unheard past our bedroom, downstairs and into the kitchen (which was gated and off limits as a rule) and help themselves to every treat they could find. By the time I walked into the kitchen, my chocolate covered children were occupied in a lively game of baseball using eggs as balls and a wrapper-strewn floor as the field. It should go without saying that a few of the baseballs got away from them. When they saw me, they took one look at my face and ran upstairs to their room. I charged behind, and after cleaning their hands and faces, screamed at them not to come downstairs until they were told. Then I tackled the mess in the kitchen. That done, I went back upstairs and witnessed the effects of chocolate on empty stomachs. The kids were running around destroying everything in sight! Mattresses were turned over onto the floor, sheets had been flung about. I walked in just as they were making a slide with the mattresses! They were just having the best time together, but I just stood there and cried.

Making a slide with the mattresses became a daily activity. It was just too much fun to resist. Standing on the dining room table and punching the chandelier was another fun pastime despite my many

> **quote**
>
> **Beautiful toys were cast aside — there were too many other interesting and adventurous things to tackle**

warnings, threats and physical removal of the offending child or children. Emptying the linen closet was another great game, the object of which was to dump as many sheets and towels as possible downstairs to the gleeful shouts of all four children. It didn't seem to matter how childproof we made our house, our children always seemed to find something to destroy. Beautiful toys were cast aside — there were too many other interesting and adventurous things to tackle.

I remember one lovely spring day when I ventured to the park with the four kids by myself. It was a five-minute walk for me but about a half-hour walk with the kids. Along the way, I reminded them about the importance of holding hands and staying beside me. Success! We accomplished that feat and actually had a very nice time at the park. Just as we neared home, the kids ran off in four different directions! I caught two of them and stood shouting for the others, knowing they couldn't have gone too far. The neighbours must have thought I was a raving lunatic shouting threats at my children. Then once I found the lost two, the other two ran away. When I eventually corralled everyone back into the house, my heart was pounding, and my exasperation came pouring out on the children in fevered shouts about safety rules and how naughty they had been. Back to their room they went, which, of course, wasn't terribly effective once the mattress game started ...

Meal times were a circus that seemed to only get messier as the kids got older. One day, I gave each child some yogurt in a bowl. I turned my back for two minutes and when I turned around, all four children had the bowl of yogurt on their heads with the yogurt running down their faces and necks! They were all giggling so hard that all I could do was join them, and promptly put them in a bath.

There were many days when I would call my husband at work pleading him to come home because I knew I had reached my limit and couldn't take any more. After rushing home, he would meet four beautifully well-behaved children sitting looking at books or watching a movie quietly.

When my children turned two years old, their behaviour improved, frustrations lessened, communication increased and life became more tolerable and actually enjoyable.

The children started nursery school when they were almost three. I was becoming quite concerned about their social skills outside the home because they were finding it very difficult to make friends with other children. Around others, they were extremely shy and quiet, but together they were happy to share, take turns, be polite (usually), and were generally very chatty, happy children who played well together. As soon as another child entered their "group" they would stand and stare, which only intimidated a potential new friend.

Attending nursery school did help to strengthen their social skills. But it's only now, at five years old, that they seem to be able to communicate individually with other children without as much fear or shyness. In our search for a nursery school, cost was obviously a large factor. I called many schools and most were willing to give some kind of discount for four children. The one I chose allowed one child free for the year, which really helped financially. All four were in the same class since I felt they were too young to be split. I had no idea how they would react to being in a different environment without me. I quickly discovered that as long as they had each other, it didn't matter if I was there or not! The first day at nursery school they waved goodbye to me and carried on playing. I walked out with a smile, gave a sigh of relief and wondered what I would do with my first free two and a half hours. Many possibilities occurred to me, but in the end, I chose to go home, sit down, put my feet up and have a cup of coffee … all by myself.

triplets travel well
Karen Rotenberg

Travelling with triplets may seem an overwhelming proposition to parents of young or even infant multiples, but yes, it can be done! Our little ones are almost four and we have taken a major vacation every summer since their birth. These trips have enriched our family life and widened our children's horizons far beyond their home environment. They have increased our confidence as parents and matured our children by exposing them to a variety of new situations. Our children follow a very stable daily routine in our household, which is vital to their well-being and our sanity. We experience less variation in this routine than the average family, so it's doubly (or triply!) important to make the effort to get away. It is also vital to us as parents to experience the excitement and freedom (a relative term, I know, when the kids are along) of travel and to have a break from the daily schedule.

Our first trip was a bold adventure. When the children were only eight months old, we drove to my relatives' home in New Jersey, a nine-hour drive. We left at 8 p.m., at bedtime, and drove almost without stopping through the night while the babies slept in the van. We only stopped for gas and once for a quick feeding. The advantage of driving at night? No hotels, no loading and unloading and minimum travel time. The disadvantage? Exhaustion for the adults because we missed a full night of sleep. As parents of eight-month-old triplets, we set out with a reasonable level of fatigue and the trip set us back even further.

We did take our nanny on this trip. Preparation was extensive, both in Toronto and in New Jersey. There were umpteen lists, a room-ful of clothing and supplies was laid out in advance — easily a week's work. My sister-in-law rounded up three portapens, a single stroller, infant seats for feeding and a change table. It was a major production!

The next summer, we rented a cottage for two weeks at Wasaga Beach, about two hours from Toronto. We found the perfect cottage for three young toddlers. It was sparsely furnished (less to worry about). It had a large kitchen with a long harvest table. Upstairs was a large bedroom with two double beds. When these were pushed to one side, there was enough room for our three portapens. The best feature of the cottage was a huge screened-in porch overlooking the Nottawasaga River. It was perfect. We could be outdoors and the children could be completely safe. We divided our time between the beach and that porch. This trip was a lot of fun. We took my nanny and my mother along to help because my husband had to commute to work part of the time. Again, preparation was mammoth; in fact, we had so much stuff — three portapens, three booster seats, a double stroller, single stroller, clothes and food for seven people for 14 days, etc., etc., etc. — that we had to enlist a friend with a pickup truck to drive up all the supplies! One word of advice: if you are thinking of renting a cottage, especially if your children are very young, go and see it first. We drove up in May to view this cottage to be sure it would suit our needs.

Our third family voyage was our most ambitious. The next summer, we flew to Los Angeles for two weeks when our children were two and a half years old. Poor health prevented my mother-in-law from travelling to see her beloved grandchildren. Only such a powerful reason could motivate us to make the long and expensive trip to California. This trip required momentous planning. Tickets were purchased months in advance. About six weeks prior to departure, a six-page fax was dispatched, detailing the minimum childproofing for my mother-in-law's house, the van to be rented (with two integrated car seats plus an additional car seat for the third child), and again, three portapens that had to be rented because the children were still in cribs. About three weeks before, I began rounding up a bag of tricks to keep my little ones occupied on the plane during the five-hour non-stop flight: books, crayons, stickers, little cars and trucks. Lists abounded: carry-on lists, luggage lists, lists of food for the plane.

Finally, D-day arrived. A friend drove our van to the airport. I'll never forget the feeling I had when we went through security and waved goodbye to our driver and our nanny. Excitement yes, but also fear and strain. The burden of responsibility for our threesome was upon us. This was their first flight. How would we manage if all three became needy under the stress of travel? Five hours is a long time when you're not having fun! We got off to a rocky start. My son refused to be buckled in for takeoff, and inspired one of his sisters to follow suit. He screamed like a banshee for the first 15 minutes and was a man on the move for the remainder of the flight. Normally a quiet child with excellent concentration, he could not sit still. Favourite books held his attention for only a minute or two. Cars and trucks did not interest him. Walking up and down the aisles did! The girls, on the other hand, were angels. Every activity and toy I brought for them, they played with dutifully. Luckily, the flight was not crowded and we got some help from the flight attendants and from other families with older children on the plane.

Once we had arrived, the trip was very successful. We were treated royally. The kids were showered with beautiful gifts, each in triplicate. The visit was an enormous amount of work, with almost no respite. What did we do in Los Angeles, the city of glitter and stardom? Oh, we hung out at Ralph's, the local supermarket. The trip was an exhilarating, but exhausting experience.

This past summer, we returned to New Jersey. This time we made the nine-hour trip in two days with an overnight stopover halfway at a hotel. I figured four to five hours of driving with a rest stop would be quite manageable for our three-year-old brood. And it was. The trip went very smoothly. I brought many car activities along: reusable sticker books, little blackboards with chalk (a big hit), small colouring pads with crayons, finger puppets etc. I had a cooler in the van with enough food for the kids for two days, so that we were not dependent on restaurants or a grocery store en route. When we settled in a hotel room, I would feed the kids from the cooler while my husband would order in food for us. Then the kids would nibble off our dinners as well. We ate breakfast in the hotel restaurant or somewhere close by. Sleeping arrangements were relatively simple. One adult, one child in each double bed, and the third child slept on either a roll out couch or on a single bed brought into the room. What a change from the portapen days! The kids loved the trip, loved the hotels and loved staying with their aunt, uncle and cousins. Mom and dad had a great time, too.

After this last trip, a friend expressed surprise to me that we had gone away. "It never occurred to me that anyone with triplets would travel!" Well, parents of triplets do travel and travel well. It is easier as the children get older, but all our trips have been worthwhile. My advice to fellow parents of multiples is — go for it! Plan ahead because thorough preparation means a more successful trip. When preparing for our trip to California, I even faxed pictures clipped from a catalogue of the portapens and car seats to be rented, so that no mistakes would be made. Keep sleeping arrangements as consistent as possible when you travel, especially when your children are very young. If they are used to cribs, do not have mattresses on the floor waiting for them in a strange environment. Take familiar bedding, pillows, and stuffed animals with you to ease their adjustment. It's worth it. Finally, be realistic in your planning. If we had attempted our nine-hour drive to New Jersey in one day, we might have met with more grief.

You might wonder what we plan on doing next summer. The kids will be four and a half years old. Do you think we're ready for camping?

Tina's morning
Tina Spigarelli

The coffee is hot, the crying is loud,
the bottles are warming, and breakfast is out
The lunches are waiting to be packed in their bags,
The spills on the counter, where are my rags?
Diapers need changing, and beds should be made,
The toys! I'm tripping, oh, what a save.
The lunches are packed, the kids all dressed,
Now if only a maid to clean up this mess.
Mornings are short, holy cow, it's 8 o'clock,
Kisses and hugs, and two are off.
Wipe the highchairs and faces because it's playtime
for the four little tykes left behind.
My hair is a mess from their eight little paws
Naptime is near, here come the yawns.
The laundry is sorted and ready to wash
The chicken is soaking while I cut up the squash.
Muffins are baking, and the dishes are clean.
Yes this is my life, it's not a dream
Now tucked in their cribs and stories are told
Hard to believe this day is just three hours old.
A sip of my coffee, oh no, it's cold.

this age of 18 months is a delight
Ross Thomas

Life seems so much more organized than a year ago. An illusion?
Perhaps. But my wife and I find the increased independence of our
foursome — the walking, self-feeding and new words — make
childcare much easier. The other day Sara put a slipper on (the
wrong foot, but by herself) and the room was shaken by gleeful
shrieks at the accomplishment (her mother's).

safety

safety

what will they think of next?

Barbara Morrison

Staying one step ahead of toddlers

Childproofing for triplets is a test of ingenuity. We started in the family room and removed every piece of furniture except the couch. We cordoned off areas using gates, tied fireplace doors closed and plugged up electrical outlets with safety plugs. We thought we had it covered. Wrong!

First, the boys played on the hearth, so we covered it with sleeping bags, foam and blankets. They also played with the fireplace doors, so we put up a barrier, which they managed to get around. We added a second barrier. It will be nice to see our fireplace again.

Before the boys were walking, they learned how to climb the gates with holes just large enough for little toes. Taping cardboard over the gates stopped the climbing — now they just pull off the tape and chew the cardboard. Toys curiously make their way to the base of the gate but have yet to give them that extra boost in height needed to scale the barrier.

The boys are allowed in the kitchen now that we have cleared out all the bottom cupboards, leaving empty containers and lids. A bungy cord holds the oven door closed and the blinds have also been tied up. To prevent them from cutting their heads, we had to put foam under the table to cover the metal tracks. The kick plate on the bottom of the fridge had to be tied down since it has springs and makes a great toy. And to stop them from pulling at the wires at the back of the fridge, we had to block it off with a piece of wood.

Unfortunately, childproof locks are not designed for our style of cupboards. After the boys started locking each other in the cupboard, we found masking tape was an effective temporary solution to stop them from opening the door in the first place. From the cupboards it's on to windowsills or to licking dirt out of the sliding glass door track or to a tasty sample from the floor. They pull out the vents and put their bottles and food down the shafts. We glued the vents to the floor, but unfortunately the boys are persistent and still pull them out. They also like to store food on the windowsills and paint the windows with their bottles. Will the house ever be clean again? They like to move the chairs, knock them over on each other and have learned to climb them and dance on the table. We no longer have chairs in our kitchen.

When the boys were 18 months old, we decided to let them watch some children's programs on television. We used an old broken freezer as a base because it was just the right height to stop the boys from reaching the television. There were no sharp corners to worry about once we removed the handle, and it was securely locked to prevent anyone from opening it and climbing inside. And it was too heavy to be pulled over. We taped the cords to the wall behind the freezer, taped the TV to the freezer, and taped the VCR on top of the TV. This arrangement seems to work and gives people a good laugh when they come to visit.

There is no possible way to prevent all dangers and to protect our children from everything, but as concerned parents we try to do our best. Many people have the view that childproofing is a sign of bad or lax parents who haven't taught the children to listen when a parent or caregiver says, "No!" But parents of multiple children know that life is different. We believe if you want to keep it, remove it.

safe and sound at home
Lucy Carley

People often ask how we manage with three busy toddlers at home whose little hands and feet take them in all of kinds of directions to exciting new adventures. Unfortunately, those adventures can also be risky. For safety as well as peace of mind, my husband and I have taken every conceivable step toward baby-proofing our home. Since our eyes cannot be everywhere at once, it's impossible to stop every potential accident or injury just before it's about to happen. Instead, we think it's best to prepare by creating a safe environment.

Many of our baby-proofing ideas are the products of both common sense and innovation, since we have found that many store-bought safety items aren't strong enough to withstand the combined

safety

strength and collaborative teamwork of three toddlers. For example, we discovered that a standard staircase gate, when used as instructed, would not withstand the combined weight of our children. So we had to take some additional steps to secure the gate to the wall.

Our three children are three times more likely to hurt themselves by breaking apart, moving or pulling over large pieces of furniture. In fact, we just had to remove a large heavy easy chair from our living room because the children could move it when they teamed up.

Electrical outlets are a particularly common threat for curious, wandering toddlers, who see them at eye level. A simple plug-in gadget will keep fingers and objects away. You may also want to keep metal objects away from your children that could possibly be inserted in an outlet. Electrical cords should always be out of reach. Little hands love to pull on things, which could result in serious injury.

tip

Be ready for emergencies by taking a CPR course and updating your skills every year

For our little explorers, we had to install window locks and a barrier to stop roaming hands from getting caught in the tracks of our sliding-door closets. When our son was only one, he was able to climb out of his crib and into the other cribs. Now what? Since the children were too young for beds, we placed their mattresses on the floor, each in a corner of the bedroom, and framed them with pine planks attached to the floor and walls. They are about the same height as futons.

If your children are very frisky, you may want to invest in stove and refrigerator locks. Stove rails can also provide safety against pots slipping off the stove.

Child-proof doorknob covers can be used to keep children from rooms that are off limits. Some parents use latch locks at the top of a door or cover the doorknob either with a store-bought plastic device or a piece of cloth. If you're making your own doorknob cover, use a six-inch circle of slippery scrap cloth (polyester or satin works best) and loosely sew a thread around the circumference, leaving long ends to tie around the stem of the door handle. Pull and tie the ends tightly around the door handle so the material covers the knob and gathers into the stem. Young hands cannot grip the handle well enough to open the door, but adults can manage easily. A doorknob cover may also provide a viable alternative to a bathroom lock, which can be problematic if the children wander in and lock themselves in and parents out! You may feel reassured dismantling the lock altogether for a while.

Our dining room is now a child-free zone. We have separated the living and dining room to give us two areas, one designated for the children and a clutter-free escape room for adults. Many of our friends and relatives laugh at how extreme our baby-proofing renovation seemed. But drastic times call for drastic measures.

It is very difficult to teach three, four or five children the true meaning of word "no" all at once! It quickly escalates into a game. So it may be easier in the beginning to just remove all fragile items. You can always bring the pieces back a few at a time as your children become aware of special and breakable articles.

Remember that things change quickly as children grow. The one cupboard that's out of reach will very soon be accessible. Medicine and poisonous household cleansers/chemicals should be locked away or stored in a cupboard that's very high and impossible for the children to reach. Even with all the precautions, it's a good idea to keep your hospital's poison information telephone number posted on the fridge.

Protecting our children is often an exercise in ingenuity. But for their safety and our peace of mind, we always try to err on the side of caution.

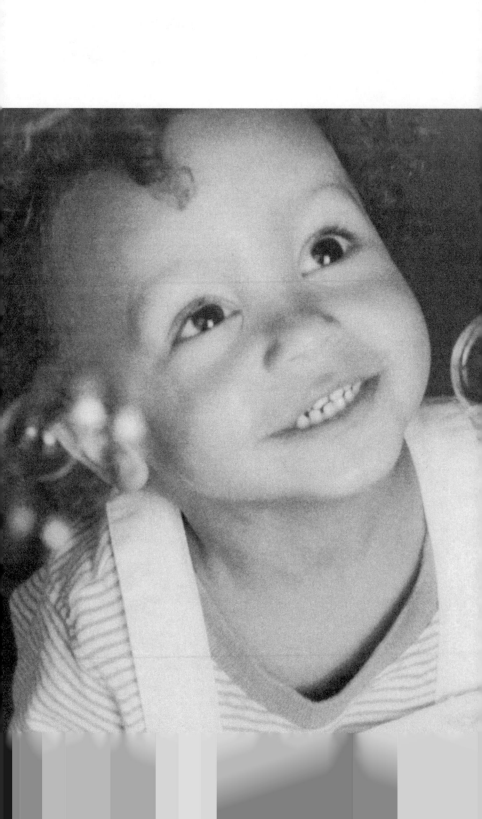

14

preschool years

stepping out in the world with preschoolers

Suzanne Lyons

How does a simple craft become a mind-splitting, heart-pounding, hair-raising experience? Give three or more two-year-olds a little paint, paper and glue, and watch them *express* themselves.

Because my three young boys were not in daycare where crafts and other creative activities are often part of the routine, I tried to make a point of exposing them to these kinds of learning experiences at home. I realized that it would be more difficult with three two-year olds. And yes, it would involve more planning, more organization and steely composure. No matter. I was determined to stimulate and enlighten my children!

Looking back, I think my "enlightenment phase" lasted about a month. And then, I surrendered. Why? Crayons became the afternoon snack of choice for my three boys. So did modelling clay. For them, the simple exercise of cutting and pasting shapes onto paper wasn't nearly as fun as squeezing glue across every horizontal surface in sight. Focusing 10 seconds on one of the boys as he tried to master a new skill was at my peril. Distracted and impatient, the others would slip away to a more pressing agenda, kindly remembering to leave tracks of glitter and glue with every step. It became obvious that I couldn't cope with these kinds of activities at home.

But I remained convinced that our boys needed to be involved in some kind of structured activity soon after their second birthday. Left to play on their own, they would be content only for minutes. Then the fighting — and biting — would begin. Unable to communicate well with each other and still rooted in their *me* stage, Andrew, Joel and Quentin's playtime stopped just short of becoming full-out war. In playgroups or at birthday parties with other children, the conflicts never amounted to more than a typical preschool squabble that was easily settled. Back at home, however, blood could be shed with alarming precision and speed.

We needed a diversion. Here are a few programs we joined.

Library groups

Our community library offered a free reading, song and craft session that helped introduce Andrew, Joel and Quentin to structured activities in a group environment. Outside their familiarity of home, the children were attentive for small blocks of time and began to interact with others their own age. It wasn't all smooth sailing, of course. The boys had only just celebrated their second birthday and were not accustomed to sitting still for periods of time. And to join the group, I had to assure the library staff that another adult could accompany us. Admittedly, it would have been a challenge on my own. I would have spent the hour corralling the three boys and disrupting the group (which the library made a point of mentioning as we signed up).

Libraries can be an invaluable resource of information about available programs for children ages two and older, especially during March and summer breaks. Often, they'll present puppet shows and small plays that can be a delight for all age groups. Remember to check the community bulletin board for notices of other shows and events for young children — particularly around special holidays.

Parks and recreation/community programs

We are fortunate to have an abundant choice of programs for toddlers and preschoolers where we live. Before my boys were two and a half years old, they attended a few preschool sessions where parents stayed and participated. After that, they joined a playgroup without parents twice weekly, which worked very well. While they can be a costly investment, city-run programs offer a valuable change of pace and scenery to young children, who otherwise stay at home with a caregiver. Remember to ask for a multiple discount (usually 10 per cent to 15 per cent off second, third and fourth enrollments). In one program, I volunteered to help in two sessions over the 12-week program and received a significant discount from enrollment fees as a result.

The benefits of joining these groups for stay-at-home parents go without saying. Aside from giving mom or dad a couple of hours of time to re-energize two days a week, the kids were often happier after being exposed to new experiences and were very proud and eager to show the work (paintings and crafts) that they completed in "school."

Preschool/nursery programs

Stepping up from a two-hour session twice weekly to part-time preschool or daycare was a goal that proved elusive for us. Because I work from home, I constantly sought out opportunities to enroll the boys in a half day program, but found them either prohibitively expensive or filled to capacity. I checked in community centres, local schools and daycare facilities to no avail. Finally, just as the boys were to begin junior kindergarten and we no longer needed a program, I happened to notice a cooperative preschool program, which was not run by the city, but advertised in the classified section of the community recreation guide.

Parent magazines and local community newspapers often advertise these kinds of enrichment programs. The choices vary from one area to the next. Good, inexpensive programs are rare gems, but they may be available if you dig for the information.

Family field trips

By the time our boys were three years old, we had visited every park, zoo, museum and fair in our vicinity and beyond. Daytime excursions were a great way to spend a day or just a couple of hours. The boys always enjoyed new adventures and it was a way for me to feel as though I was still connected with the outside world.

One of the best advantages of taking very young children to the zoo, museum and other attractions is that there is rarely an admission charge to pay for them. An adult and three or more children can spend a relatively inexpensive afternoon wandering through the halls of a science or discovery centre pushing buttons that light up, pounding on drums and exploring space ships — all for a single adult admission.

Needless to say, outings like these with young children and one adult can get a little hairy. I was fortunate that my children were not wandering explorers and always stayed in sight. Obviously, certain expeditions will not be suited to fearless adventurers who will bolt from the moment you step through the door. Without the weekend crowds though, I found my crew had more space to branch out and were very easy to keep in sight.

Home-made fun

I remember one mom with young quadruplets telling me that she could keep everyone happy by coming up with a "special" event or activity for each day. She tried to keep the outings simple but spontaneous and fun. A walk around the neighbourhood became a parade of musicians banging pots and pans and any other instrument of choice. Another day, the big event was potato races across the floor. The activity wasn't as important as the idea that something special was happening.

Sometimes event planning for two- and three-year-olds feels as though it will deplete your already shallow reservoir of time and energy. And because things won't always run as planned, there were times when frustration and exasperation tested my patience.

More often though, creating or finding diversions for the children was worth the effort. They restored my energy. It was fascinating and funny to rediscover the world through the eyes of preschoolers. As their mom, I initially thought of myself as a teacher who would bring the world to them. What I didn't realize is how much their experiences and observations would bring to me.

sheltered lives
Donna Patterson

Community programs often inaccessible to multiple birth children

In front of me is a stack of community newsletters describing children's programs that I've been meaning to browse through to see if my triplet gals and I can enrol in an activity of some kind. All of us need to get out of the house!

Our local parent-child centre will be my best bet for finding programs organized by child-loving educators. Either I'll pay for a networking program this semester (a weekly seminar for adults with childcare) or I'll use the drop-in centre on any given morning where the girls can play while I watch. Alternatively, we could enrol in a short preschool program that involves parents and caregivers. My girls love the 30 minutes of playtime with mom and another 30 minutes in a separate room with a teacher who tells stories and leads singsongs. I just hope that the program has three openings because I am finding that all too often, enrollments are restricted to one or two at a time.

Next, I'll check the local library listings. From experience, I know we cannot join the preschool reading groups unless we have one parent or caregiver attending for each child. This participatory program would provide some useful enrichment for my kids. I'll call my mother to see if she can join with us. Then I'll phone the library and beg them to bend the rules.

When I read the swimming rules for toddler lessons or leisure programs, I see that it's impossible for us to join. The ratio for lessons is one adult per child. That means swimming lessons will need to be delayed for a few years.

My community service guide outlines some "tot camps" for ages two to three, but the children must be toilet-trained. My girls aren't trained yet and probably won't be until age three, so we'll need to postpone this as well. It's difficult to find the patience to wait. I am anxious to move forward with my gals.

Another possibility is a toy lending library. It wasn't my favourite outing last year (the toys didn't seem clean enough) but, as a last resort for a diversion or change of pace, I think we'll go anyway. At least the girls will benefit from learning that they need to return a toy that isn't theirs to keep, in exchange for a new toy on loan.

I feel a bias toward our family of six. We certainly don't fit into society's ideal profile of a 1.5-child family, and it shows! As Canadian families are shrinking, large families face many obstacles when they try to join programs that have not been designed to accommodate more than two children of the same age from the same family. Sadly, while all children benefit from these programs, I believe multiple children can especially benefit. Why?

• With three or more preschoolers, parents can sometimes find that even the most mundane outings require mammoth planning and energy. Simple things like walks, eating in restaurants, or just running a few errands are all possible, of course, but they take far more time. As a result, multiple toddlers and preschoolers are at a higher risk of being secluded socially and losing valuable opportunities to learn. One mom with two-year-old quadruplets told me that she found a simple walk to a park nearly impossible to coordinate. All the experiences from which children learn, however simple or elaborate, are more difficult to manage and thus tend to be undertaken less frequently.

• Very often, multiple children are cared for in their homes by stay-at-home parents or by a hired nanny. In some provinces, regulations restrict the number of infants cared for in a private home to two infants. (Isn't it interesting that parents of multiples are expected to care for their children without help, a situation that would be considered illegal for hired caregivers in many provinces?) For childcare options, we must look at either large daycare centres or nanny care. Given the convenience of keeping the children at home, many parents opt for bringing a nanny into the home. Childcare expenses are tax deductible only if both parents work outside the home.

• Playtime among three or more toddlers or preschoolers often requires considerable diversion tactics, since congenial play can easily turn ugly as toys are snatched and teeth bared. Playgroups and external programs can break the tedium and encourage the children to recognize that others exist outside their group. I think it's an important step of socialization.

So, as I continue to scan these pages hoping to discover a suitable tots group or lessons, I remain hopeful that program planners will begin to recognize our unique circumstances as families with multiple children and open their doors to us as participants.

getting a good night's sleep
Daphne Gray-Grant

With preschoolers who have PhDs in delaying bedtime

At four years old, my children have reached the age I once longed for during those hours of pacing the floor with crying babies, wrestling with the breastpump in the wee hours of the night, or standing at the stove cooking meals I was too exhausted to prepare, never mind eat. I used to fantasize about how blissful it would be when they were four.

Now Claire, Duncan and Alison have almost hit the magic number, but somehow life doesn't seem any easier. True, they are toilet-trained (translation: I know every bathroom within a four-mile radius of my house). And yes, they sleep through the night (the bedtime ritual takes three hours). They can tell me exactly what they want and need (ohhhh boy, can they tell me — it's just that they won't stop telling me). So I've come to terms with the fact that raising triplets is not a 100-yard dash, it's a marathon. Along the way there are the milestones and the rewards. Here is one we accomplished last year.

Goodbye cribs — hello beds

Getting rid of major gear is always an achievement and none more so than saying goodbye to the cribs. I have to admit our kids were practically old fogies before we pried them out of theirs at the age of three. Our kids, who could climb bookcases and hang from stair banisters like monkeys, never made the mental leap and figured out it was possible to climb out of their cribs. I used to joke that I practiced a little-known technique of mass hypnosis to prevent this knowledge from infiltrating their tiny minds. But finally, a crisis loomed — my husband was facing hernia surgery and I didn't want to do any more lifting than absolutely necessary. Cribs? Gone.

Anyone contemplating this bold move should be advised that an orderly bedtime will collapse into pure chaos, literally overnight. My mother, who still comes to help one evening a week, claims that my children have PhDs in delaying bedtime. Still, I'm prepared to offer this advice:

- Have a predictable bedtime ritual established long before the children make the transition to beds. Do things in the same order each night (we always brush teeth before stories, for example). If your kids are very young, be prepared for some weird rituals. At age two, our kids used to kiss a fabric wallhanging of llamas each night — go figure. Whatever you do, make it as soothing, calming and ritualistic as possible. And get that routine carved in stone before you bring in the beds.
- Put a baby gate on the bedroom door, or two (one on top of each other) if necessary. Or invest in a so-called Dutch door (bottom can be closed while top stays open). You may need to contain wandering children during the first few weeks.
- Remove anything dangerous from the room. If they want to empty drawers, consider moving the chest of drawers (or bookshelves) temporarily.
- There's no need to invest in an expensive toddler bed, which will only last for a short time anyway. We went directly to adult twin beds and have never regretted it. Consider putting the mattresses directly on the floor for the first few months. When you move them up to the box spring you may also want to invest in bed rails, which are relatively inexpensive.
- To safeguard the mattress, look for a mattress protector made of waterproof quilted cotton — it's far preferable to heavy plastic. Buy at least four of them, so you have a spare to cover for "accidents."
- Let your children help choose their sleeping arrangements. We have our three in a small room. At first we put their beds around the perimeter. After finding them in each other's beds a number of times, we finally pushed all three beds together — and they love it.

calm sets in
with four-year-olds
Lucy Carley

As a mom of triplets who are almost four, I can't help but look back to a time when things were different and life seemed unreal. We've certainly come a long way. When our babies were born prematurely at 27 weeks, our lives were about hospital trips, sleepless nights spent worrying, the exhilaration of finally bringing them home, and then more sleepless nights. Then came crawling and climbing and baby-proofing, walking, running and more baby-proofing, talking, talking and more talking, toilet training, night training and on and on ... what an adventure it has been!

Through the years, I've learned one very important lesson: to go with the flow since things just never seem to go exactly as planned, and our lives always seem to be changing.

So has our home. When I look around, I am amazed by how much stuff we collected and how cluttered our lives became with car seats and high chairs, bottles, day cradles, bathtub rings, and diapers. I am often asked by other moms, "Does it get easier?" Absolutely!

They still keep me busy but a sense of normality and calm are also setting in. Our furniture is back and our home resembles more of a home and less of a romper room. Although I'm sure we have many challenges yet to face, I'm looking forward to life with our four-year-olds.

fun times

Elizabeth Massarelli

Here's a typical conversation at our house these days. It starts with the big question, "Is it Christmas now?" followed by that vague adult response "soon" which translates into "tomorrow" which means "not now" which really means "no."

The kids are mostly delightful and only sometimes demanding and very rarely, horrible. They are all out of diapers now, day and night (with fingers crossed), and can to varying degrees do some of the dressing and undressing, making that aspect of caring for them much, much easier. They play marvelously together in all sorts of imaginative games. Most recently, we overheard them putting on special "mittens" in preparation for a doll delivery by cesarean section.

toilet-training
our toilet-training marathon
Barbara Morrison

Starting too early may have prolonged the learning process

With triplet boys, the very thought of toilet training scared me. I consulted many mothers, read numerous books and articles, and watched and waited for the signs that they were ready. For their second birthday each of the boys was given a potty. At first, they thought the potties were toys, then a box for their toys, and then they tried them on as hats. After they started hitting each other with them, we put them away.

We tried to get everyone used to the idea of using the potty at bath-time — they were happy to sit it on it and do nothing. As soon as they got into the bath, they would tinkle on their brothers and burst into fits of laughter.

During the winter, they were not ready and neither was I. Then came spring, a move to a new house, and weeks of adjusting to a new

toilet-training

home and neighbourhood. But by late spring, we thought we were ready to try again. The boys were about two and a half. We put training pants on all three, explained they were special underwear, showed them the potty and encouraged each to use it. Finally, Patrick decided he had to go and did. He then wanted to dump the potty into the big toilet. Of course, both his brothers had to come and watch. Then, Bradley and Mitchell decided they had to go as well. Bradley did not want to sit on the potty. I said, "Try sitting on the potty, Bradley." He refused. Then it was my husband's turn. "Try sitting on the potty, Bradley." No, go. Then his brother Patrick said, "Sit down!" and Bradley sat down, much to Patrick's delight.

After Mitchell and Bradley had gone, they also wanted to dump it into the big toilet. Before I managed to put the potty back together, Patrick had to go again, so I just held the cup in front of him so he could go. After he dumped it into the big toilet, suddenly Bradley had to go. Patrick very nicely held the cup in front of Bradley as Mommy had done and Mitchell patted Bradley on the back as he went, offering a congratulatory "good job!"

For every success though, there were many setbacks, and soon toilet training gave way to diapers again. But with the start of a diaper-free nursery school looming in the fall, I began to worry and started

the effort again later that summer. I was amazed to see how often their reactions to the potty changed. Patrick seemed to grasp the concept the first day we resumed, Mitchell was at a complete loss, and Bradley was undecided. The second day Bradley looked at the potty as if he had never seen it before, Mitchell did well and Patrick was undecided. Responses seemed to change either daily or twice daily.

At the suggestion of a friend, who is both a mother and grandmother of twins, I tried having them tinkle in a bucket, something unusual to interest them. Everyone enjoyed that little activity immensely so the bucket went with us wherever we went. But soon the boys expressed their distinct preferences. One preferred the toilet, another liked the potty and the third used the bucket. I thought I was running before. On some occasions, all three wanted to go in the bucket at the same time. One day, one wanted to go in the little bucket and Mommy had to hold it. At the same time, his brother wanted to go in another small bucket, which Mommy had to hold as well. It was a good thing the third did not have to go, as I was only blessed with two hands.

We developed a reward system using stickers rather than candy, since the boys were active enough. In addition to receiving a small reward for every success, they also collected stars or stickers to post on a special chart on the fridge. Once the chart was filled, we promised to buy a special toy. But that became difficult. When Bradley finished his page and was able to purchase a toy, Mitchell and Patrick were devastated. The next day, Mitchell completed his chart, but Patrick was slow getting off the mark. In the end, we purchased a toy for everyone because Patrick was heartbroken. Admittedly, it was the wrong thing to do from a purely rational perspective. And I knew it. But sometimes as a parent, I have done things that I know are wrong — and gone ahead anyway — because my heart tells me to do it. I don't know. The reward system can be very tricky to manage with three or more competitive children.

Toilet-training kept me running in three different directions for nearly a year. I realize now that we started too early at age two and half and allowed the demands of nursery school to dictate how and when we approached the process. In the end, we found it wasn't the right nursery school for us anyway, and I enrolled the boys in another school that was more accommodating with children learning to use the toilet. Once the pressure was off and the boys reached their readiness point over age three, we enjoyed complete success with no accidents day or night. I see now that the process of reaching our goals could have been a little easier, faster, and um, far less messy, had we waited just a little longer.

if at first
you don't succeed
Karen Neilson

Toilet-training. With five children, I was ready to hire someone to do this for me — seriously. At two years old, the kids experimented with the potty and definitely weren't ready. So we let it drop. By the time they were three years old, I started working on it more seriously.

As recommended by a friend of mine with quadruplets, I purchased five potties, some Smarties™ and essential reading material. I placed all the seats in a row in the kitchen (I know, I know) because the bathroom wasn't large enough. Everyone's diapers came off. First I sat Spencer down on the seat to demonstrate to the others. I then escorted Mitchell to the potty, then Regan, and so on. By the time I got to Nicole and Lucas, Spencer was dragging his potty off somewhere out of the room. Mitchell was wearing his as a hat, Regan was trying to put her diaper back on, and Nicole was screaming because she didn't want to sit down. Lucas wanted to stand in his. It was a complete disaster. So I waved the white flag and surrendered on our first attempt. Then everyone sat down and ate all the Smarties.™

oh, pooh!™
Howard Parker

We decided that it was time to introduce the boys to the concept of "big boy poo" and how they would, when they were ready, of course, enjoy being "liberated" from the diaper world. Just like all two-year-olds, the boys viewed a toilet bowl as a toy that made noises, gushed water, got them wet, and best of all, sent Mum and Dad into a frenzy of activity cleaning both them and the bathroom floor.

So, our initial approach was to point to the toilet and say, "Big boys like you go poo in here." Each of them looked at my wife, Mary, then at me, then pointed to the bowl and chorused, "poo."

Several days later, the toilet became blocked. Mary made heroic efforts with a plunger to no avail. Out came the rubber gloves and down went the hands to grasp … something. But it wasn't coming out in a hurry.

We had a choice: get a plumber and not feed the kids for a month, or learn how to dismantle a toilet in one easy lesson. Grandad Frank arrived and we went to work. Oh what fun on a summer afternoon! After much grunting, sweating and more than a little cursing, we were close to the offending article. Grandad Frank finally grasped it in his hand and triumphantly pulled it out — a cute model of Winnie the Pooh!™

The boys, who had been watching intently, beamed and pointed to the bowl. "Pooh!" they said.

toilet-training quadruplets
Valerie Koning Keelan

The year our sons Geoffrey, Alan, Richard and Paul turned two, we tried giving each boy a turn at using the toilet, if he seemed interested. Nobody was, as I remember, and we just kept them in diapers because we weren't about to clean up after four tykes who didn't mind wearing wet diapers. Since their nursery school allowed children to attend in diapers, it wasn't a pressing concern for us.

Several months later, my husband, Bryan, had taken two weeks off at Christmas. We decided to use that time to teach the boys what life would be like without diapers. We took them out of their diapers and gave them training pants to wear. We showed them where the toilets were and how to use them.

toilet-training

The boys seemed to gain control of their bowels more readily than their bladders. After a day or two of accidents, they began to realize that training pants weren't the same as diapers. But with two adults always there, one to clean up and one to keep an eye on things, it was manageable. By the end of the holidays, three of the boys were fairly reliable. The fourth took another few months. We soon realized that he was so engrossed in play that he would ignore the signals until it was too late.

We opted for a total, rather than gradual approach to toilet training the boys because we felt it took less time and energy in the long run. I think the fact that the children were older made this approach more feasible as well.

My experience with my sons has taught me that it's not a matter of "training" a child to use the toilet. We can teach the child how to use a toilet, but in the end it's up to the child to decide when to use one. And I do believe that old adage that no child will ever go to school in diapers.

15

growing up

our first year at school
Donna Zidar

I stood waving goodbye with big tears rolling down my cheeks

For parents of very young children, September is probably no different from the other months of the year. But for those with children in school, September is always an exciting, busy month of preparation, adjustment and new experiences.

Sadness and worry

Looking back to the first year of school for my four children, I remember feeling so many emotions at once — including exhilaration that the kids were finally going to school and I would have every afternoon to myself. I imagined endless shopping trips, long lunches, hot baths, peace and quiet. The list went on and on. Yet there was also a great sense of sadness and worry. Sadness that the kids were growing up so fast, and worry that I hadn't done a good job as a parent.

The preschool years seemed to fly by, and I could barely remember their first year at all.

Could these four little kids really be ready for school? During the first four years, they were never very far away from me. How would they cope? Would they get along with the other kids? Would they behave and listen to their teacher? Would they be treated differently because they were quadruplets?

First day

On the first day of school, the kids were dressed in their best clothes and very excited to be on their way. My husband and I made sure that everyone arrived at the school 15 minutes early so we would have a lot of time to take photos and make some home videos. It was a big day for us, and we didn't want to forget any of it. When the bell rang, the teacher asked the children to line up and make a chain holding each other's backpacks. Off they marched with big smiles on their faces, waving wildly and looking suddenly like they were grown up. I stood waving too, but with big tears running down my cheeks.

The school staggered the start for the junior kindergarten students. The first week, they went one day, the second week for three days, and then finally, they went every day. The first two weeks went very well. But in the third week, Catharine was sick and had to stay home with Mom all by herself. She rather enjoyed herself at home and refused to go back to school. Meanwhile, the three at school cried the entire afternoon because they thought they were missing something at home. The teacher, who had 25 kids in the class, had a hard time getting control of the situation because she had at least eight kids crying at the same time.

No choice

One particular day of crying at school snowballed to the point where on the following Monday, all four kids screamed and cried that they didn't want to go to school any more. For about a week it was extremely difficult to get them into the classroom. Just as I would get the first two settled down, the second two would start crying and refuse to go into the class. Eventually, I just had to tell them that there was no choice. They had to go to school, so they might as well have fun. Then I would turn and walk away and leave all four crying for me. This was extremely difficult, but they did come around and the crying stopped. After a couple of weeks, a new attitude developed and they really enjoyed and looked forward to school.

Together or apart?

As with all parents of multiples, my husband and I had to decide if we wanted all the kids to be in the same class or separated. I felt that they had not spent enough time apart and were not quite ready to be separated. I never dreamed that they would miss me as much as they did and I realize now that I made the right choice keeping them together. It gave them the chance to get used to being away from me before they had to cope with being apart from each other. Now that they are in senior kindergarten, the teacher and I agree they are ready for separate classes. Only time will tell if this is the right choice, but I feel much more confident that they will be able to cope better now.

Life after school

Once we settled into our new school routine, life did improve greatly. I was able to grocery shop, clean the house, pay bills, paint or wallpaper, all while the kids were at school. These chores no longer occupied 95 per cent of our weekends. My husband, who works quite close to home, was able to occasionally take lunch during the day, and we were finally able to spend some quality time together again. As for my concerns about the kids being treated differently because they were quadruplets, I am pleased that it hasn't become a big issue so far. To the other children in the class, my four are just like any other kids in the class. Kindergarten kids don't seem to understand the concept of "quadruplets."

"We're not the quads, we're the Zidars"

However, Jonathan did come home one afternoon in October asking why he was a "quadruplet." Apparently, a few of the children had picked up the term (probably from their parents). The teacher assured me that she never referred to the kids as "the quads," but rather as "the Zidars," and she encouraged the other kids to do the same. Now my children tell people — "We're not the quads, we're the Zidars!" I guess they really are learning something at school.

The first year of school was very rewarding for all of us. The school trips, Halloween party, Christmas concert, and Mother's and Father's Day gifts have been real treats. And seeing all our kids up on stage dancing in a school concert or dressed as clouds in a play has made us so proud. Not only of our kids, but also of all the hard work, love and devotion that my husband and I have put into each of our four kids. If you have small children right now and are finding it hard to cope from one day to the next, try to imagine your kids up on that school stage. It's worth all the hard work, and the rewards are indescribable.

school debate
Melody Parent

Are kids better together or apart in class?
As the mother of preschool triplet boys, I have wrestled with the issue of school for some time. One of the hardest decisions that parents of multiples have to make is whether or not their children are going to start school in the same class. But I do have one advantage on my side for making this decision; I am a teacher and I have had the opportunity to teach two sets of quadruplets.

I was a Grade 2 French teacher to the first quadruplets I taught. It was the first year they were separated into two different classes. Since I was not their regular classroom teacher, I was not involved in the decision-making process about whether they were kept together or separated. The second set of quadruplets was in my regular Grade 2 class. Since it was a very small school with just one Grade 2 class, the children had to stay together. I have learned much from these children and their parents and want to share some of the knowledge I have gathered about parents' roles in their children's education.

Have a plan
Many teachers and principals have their own views on whether multiples should be separate or together. It's unlikely that you will be questioned if you request separate classes, but you should be prepared to defend your decision if you would like them to remain

together. Make sure you have reasons for keeping them in the same class and an idea of how long you intend to keep them together.

You might say something like this: "Here is my plan. I would like my children together for junior kindergarten because they have never been in childcare and I want them to help each other adjust to being in school. Socially, they are quite dependent on each other, and I think it would benefit them to be in the same class. I would also like to keep them together for senior kindergarten and Grade 1 and then separate them beginning in Grade 2. By that time, they will have been in school long enough so that I will be able to tell who will manage best on his own. Each year, I intend on switching who is on his own, so that each child has that experience. I am basing this plan on discussions I've had about the separation issue with other multiple parents, and I have come to the conclusion that it is a good plan that has security built in, yet allows for independence and equal pairings."

Triplets are the hardest splits to make because one will almost always have to be alone, since there are very few schools that are large enough to have three classes of one grade.

Talk to the teacher

You need to discuss your expectations regarding how you want your children treated within the class. Are they allowed to play together within the class or would you prefer them to be separated as much as possible? You may feel the need to make it very clear to the teacher that, during an interview, your children are not to be compared with each other and should be discussed on an individual basis. Interview time for the quadruplets was a very long process, with each student allotted 15 minutes. Only that student was discussed and he/she was not compared with siblings in any way.

The parents were able to share information with me about how they interacted at home and I was able to tell them about how they got along at school. In most cases, it wasn't very different. The more information you provide about how you want your children treated, the less guesswork involved for everyone. There are many teachers who have never had experience with multiples or perhaps, their experience has been quite different from the one you envision for your children. Ask questions to find out the teacher's views.

If you have decided that you want your children separated after they have been together, discuss your decision with the teacher. He/she may have some valuable insights on who can work independently and who would make the best combination. If you don't make your preferences known, the teacher will make the decision for you. In one case, the parents only requested that their children be separated, but did not offer any suggestions as to who they wanted paired together. As a result, I chose who went into which class. I based my decision on the fact that there were two boys and two girls and one of the girls was very dependent on her sister socially. It was to the point that she didn't want to join any clubs or do any activities outside the classroom that didn't involve her sister. It was my hope that this separation from her sister would give her more confidence and foster a stronger sense of independence.

The best time to make requests for the next year's class is at the beginning of May because class lists are usually completed by the end of that month.

Know your kids

Base your decisions on what your children say and how they interact with each other. You can tell a lot about your children and their relationships at school by listening to them at the dinner table. Be prepared to hear an entire replay of the events that happened and many versions of the same story. Ask your children who they play with at school and learn how much time they spend with their siblings and other children at school. Who do they spend the most time with at home?

Are they at ease with the idea of being separated? Do they enjoy quiet, independent activities? Is one of your children too dependent on another for things such as comfort, acceptance, or in social situations? These kinds of things will continue at school, so it is your decision as to whether your children will function better together or apart.

You may feel that your children are mature enough to make their own decision about whether they should be together or not. But they need to know that in most cases, the decision they make is final. They should be aware that teachers are different and offer a variety of learning experiences. The children may have to accept the fact that they may not go on as many field trips as their siblings do, or that their art activities aren't as good as in the other class.

These issues are common to all children, but they seem more dramatic for children from the same family in the same grade.

Reasons for keeping your children together

Here are a few reasons why you may decide to keep your children together:

- The children find comfort and strength in each other's presence and would find separation traumatic. For many multiples, the beginning of school is extremely stressful because they may be faced with a double separation. The first separation is from their parents and the second from their siblings.
- They may be independent enough to grow socially and academically while remaining in the same classroom. Their ability to socialize together and with other children may be an asset to the rest of the class. I found the quadruplets' interactions quite fascinating. When they referred to each other, they never said "my sister or brother," they always used their first names. They rarely chose each other as partners and only the girls interacted together in the schoolyard. When they received invitations to separate birthday parties, no one was upset with being excluded because they each had different friends. The main reason they were separated was because the parents requested it. If they had suggested that they be kept together for the next year, I probably would have agreed to it.
- Because a teacher's particular style is better suited to your children, you may wish to keep them together in that classroom.
- Many parents find it easier to deal with the homework if their children are in the same class working on the same thing. Helping with homework can be overwhelming for some parents when they have to deal with different assignments and expectations from different teachers.

As a teacher, I found it easy to have quadruplets in my class because they each worked independently. Part of this ability came from their separation the year before. It is important that if your children are going to be kept together, they know that they will be expected to work with other students for most activities. You might ask the teacher not to refer to your children as the quads even when discussing them outside the classroom. This helps the teacher to think of them as individuals rather than as a group. I never referred to them as the quads in my room and I always used their names instead of saying "your sister/brother." The only special attention focused on them came as a result of their comments about being quadruplets. I never refer to my children as the triplets so I was probably much more conscious of the label than another teacher would be.

Reasons for separating your children

• Their personalities are either so similar or so different that they would benefit from being in different classrooms. Many times, one sibling is more social than the others and would cope very well with a separation and a chance to be independent.

• You want them to have the benefit of spending time with each sibling. Changing which child is paired with whom each year seems to be a popular approach for ensuring that they benefit from different pairings.

• The competition or comparisons have become so great that they cannot function efficiently in the same room. The differences in abilities of children are never more apparent than when they are in the same classroom. All good intentions aside, it is very difficult to keep children from comparing themselves, or to keep other children and teachers from comparing them. Separating them may give them the opportunity to explore their individual talents.

The decision to keep your children together or to separate them can be an agonizing one. Ask for advice from other parents who have already been through it. There are positive and negative points to both sides and you will have to evaluate what is best for you and what will prove to be most beneficial to your children.

in a class of their own
Suzanne Lyons

A short time ago, as my three five-year-olds and 20 other kids charged out of their morning kindergarten class, the continuing debate about whether to separate our boys or place them together for Grade 1 the next year was inadvertently settled by a classmate.

In his parting comment to Andrew, Joel and Quentin, the young friend called out, "Goodbye triplets!" Of course, it wasn't the first time they had been called the triplets. But at school, it was becoming increasingly apparent that the boys were becoming recognized and known as triplets first, and then as individuals. I realized that the only way to be certain they were seen as complete individuals in the eyes of their classmates would be separate classes the following year.

From our perspective, the decision to separate the boys marked a definite change of course in parenting. Until that point, we were concerned primarily with their comfort level at school and their ability to settle in after four preschool years spent together at home during the day with either my husband, me or their granny. But as they grew, our priority was shifting from ensuring their comfort to helping them take what could be an uneasy but necessary step toward independence.

Andrew, Joel and Quentin are identical (monozygotic) triplets, making the issue of identity especially complex and challenging for them as well as for those around them. While they have distinct personalities in many ways and dress differently, determining "who's who" is a challenge that takes more than a quick glance from people who don't know the boys well, or in situations where the group is large and there is a great deal of activity.

Through the last two years of junior and senior kindergarten, casual observation tells me that many of the kids have difficulty identifying the boys individually from appearance alone. As their mom, I've naturally come to see their distinguishing characteristics without effort and so it sometimes surprises me at first to see others struggle to identify them. I almost forget just how alike they are, not just in terms of appearance, but also in temperament, language and articulation skills, and in reaching other developmental milestones.

The boys' teacher has been especially kind, accommodating and eager to distinguish Andrew, Joel and Quentin from each other. She often makes a point of noting their individual progress to my husband or me. Still, because the boys are very alike, reading report cards over the past two years has become an exercise in spotting a phrase or two that might differentiate one report from the others. Restricted to using point-form notes prescribed by the province to describe school progress, their teacher is resigned to sending home three virtually identical report cards each term.

And despite our best efforts to discuss each boy individually, parent/ teacher meetings invariably become a discussion of the boys as a group. We begin by discussing Andrew, for example, and reviewing his workbook, but the conversation will almost always drift to the others. Comparisons are inevitable, even helpful at times, for assessing development and progress. But in separate classes, the boys will be measured against other classmates first, rather than each other.

Despite the many compelling reasons to separate the boys, the final decision was not an easy one. Whether by nature or nurture, Andrew, Joel and Quentin are very close. They play together, sleep in the same room, and attend an afterschool program together. In fact, the boys spend virtually all of their waking hours together, not because they insist on it necessarily, but because our lives are organized that way. Consciously or not, my husband and I tend to plan activities for the boys as a group. We assume, often rightly, that what one will want to do, the others will want to do as well.

Is it because they are multiples and want to spend time together that everyone wants to go tobogganing, to play hockey, or to see the same movie? No — it's because they are all five years old and share similar interests. Maybe we are helping to entrench a dependence on each other by allowing them to do so many things together. But to do otherwise at this stage would feel as though we are forcing separation unnaturally.

At school, there is a unique opportunity for multiple children to begin sampling life as individuals, while still sharing the experience of school. As Andrew, Joel and Quentin get older, their interests may or may not take them on different paths. As their parents, we want to ensure that they at least consider separate paths as an option.

Part of that self–discovery will occur at school next year, where we are fortunate to have three Grade 1 classes. So far, the boys are open to the idea. Maybe my husband and I have instilled the importance of asserting themselves as individuals better than I imagined. Or maybe come September, as the kids form lines outside different doors that lead to different classes, one of the trio will swing around to joke with his brothers and realize for the first time that neither one is there.

I can only hope that with that realization, he will find the confidence to turn back around and take a big step forward.

Together or Apart? Points to Keep in Mind
In a class of their own

Many schools are taking the cue from parents today about keeping their children together or separating them at school. Once the initial plan is set, though, it's helpful to stay in touch with the teacher from time to time to see how the children are behaving in the class, and, equally important, how other children are relating to your crew. Be prepared to change your way of thinking.

Enough classes to go around?

In schools with just one or even two classes at the same grade level, the questions and options are quite different. Dividing quads into two classes is an option — triplets present a dilemma. Two in one class, the third in another? It might work for some families, depending on the dynamics of the relationships among the children. For our three boys though, I suspect that kind of uneven split, particularly since they are separating for the first time, would alienate the one boy on his own and reinforce a stronger bond between the two in the same class. I wonder if that alienation would extend to home as well.

The size of the kindergarten enrollment (morning and afternoon) is a useful indicator of how many classes to expect of that grade as the children progress through the years. Remember to account for split grades in which two grade levels occupy the same class. The incidence of split grades depends largely on the policies of your local school board as well as on the enrollment of the school. And it can vary from one year to the next.

Hitting the books

Because homework assignments vary from class to class even in the same grade, each child could very well require a different type of assistance from his or her parents. If your children are in the same class, group homework sessions are more feasible. On the other hand, separate classes will mean more one-on-one time with each child.

school days
Karen Neilson

With quintuplets in Grade 3, the problem isn't separation issues, it's the homework

I think adjusting to school was harder on me than it was for my quintuplets. For the first time, someone else would be responsible for them. It's not as though I didn't enjoy having half a day to myself. But the anxiety of wondering whether the teacher would be waiting there for them so they wouldn't get lost in the school, or whether they would get on the right bus to come home, kept me from relaxing. Yep, I'll admit it: I followed the bus to school the first day and watched as they got off, and I was there again after school to make sure they got back on the right bus!

In our northern community, there was just one class of every grade from kindergarten through to Grade 2. Splitting the kids into different classes wasn't an option for us. After we moved to another community, we did take advantage of the school having two classes of every grade, and split the children up in Grade 2. I asked that my two girls be separated because Regan was outgoing and a social butterfly, whereas Nicole was initially quite shy and preferred to hang around with her sister and the friends that Regan made.

I wanted Nicole to learn not to depend on her sister quite as much. The adjustment was difficult for Nicole, but in the end, she did learn to be more outgoing. When Grade 3 came along, we continued with the same pattern to continue encouraging Nicole to make special friends of her own, and it has worked out well.

The only problem I am having now is homework. My children were in French immersion in senior kindergarten and Grade 1. Since schools in our new community didn't offer French immersion programs until Grade 5, we had to switch everyone back into the English program. When they entered the new school, none of the five children could read a word of English. They have done well catching up, but it has been a difficult challenge for two of the kids. We now spend three hours a night on homework, Monday to Friday, with weekends off.

Given the growing diversity of homework assignments, I plan on requesting that all of my children be placed in the same class for

Grade 4 so that we can work on the same subjects and have the same homework together at night. Even though they are in the same grade, each teacher has his or her own way of teaching and expectations. I am hopeful that once the children can work more independently on their homework, we can split them up again.

It doesn't concern me that they are always together. When they were in the same classroom before, the average person would have been hard-pressed to point out the quintuplets in the room. Since they each have their own distinct personalities, they also have unique interests, likes and dislikes. Whenever they walk into a room, they spread out and go their separate ways, which is the way it has been since they were toddlers.

you are the expert
Bracha Mirsky

I am not arguing against separating multiple birth children in school. Apparently, many can find success if separated. But it seems there is no voice for those who need more time

I don't know if I am ready to write this one; it still cuts too deep. But I will do it for you, my friends, linked through our shared experience as mothers of multiples, because I must caution you.

The only advocate your children truly have is you. Professionals, teachers, psychologists and others may pressure you into doing something you don't feel is right for your children. Don't be pressured. Don't let their scare tactics beat you down! Speak up and be heard.

I should have voiced my opinion, but didn't. And I regret it so much. Multiples are different from other children in many ways. There can be learning or developmental problems to watch for. Don't rely on the school to catch it. Take the lead with your children. Review their homework with them and find out for yourself where their weaknesses lie.

Here's an example to illustrate my point. Aharon, one of my triplets, couldn't read until he was 11 years old. The school had no idea there was a problem. Teachers said nothing. His report card was average. He was bright and pleasant in class, but he couldn't read! Aharon is gifted with a brilliant memory. He memorized anything he needed, even pages read aloud in class, by listening to others. I only found out by asking him to read for me in Grade 3, and not letting him wiggle out of it. Through investigation we found out Aharon had an eye coordination problem which made tracking in a straight line difficult. We worked together to help him with this problem. Aharon is now an honour student in high school.

Example two: Rochel, sweet and creative, and happy to go to school in kindergarten. In junior kindergarten, the triplets were together. But for senior kindergarten, the school recommended that Aharon go to another class, as he and Rochel were too "into each other" and not paying attention. "We know what we're doing, we're professionals. We've read a lot of books on multiples." I go for every parent-teacher day and ask, "How is Rochel doing?" "What a wonderful child you have. She's so artistic, look at all the drawings. She is such a pleasure." Two years later, Rochel is in trouble. Another year, and in Grade 3 they ask us to remove her from school. "She just sits outside the class and cries. She won't go in." We transferred her to a special school where she would get more attention.

I met the senior kindergarten teacher during that year, and she asked me how Rochel was doing. I told her we had to switch schools, and she said, "I thought it wouldn't work out. She used to hide under the desk in class all the time. But of course you knew that. I'm sure she did that at home as well." I was speechless! "No, I didn't know that! Why didn't you tell me? She never did that at home — or anywhere else, except at school!" My heart broke. I spoke to a specialist in light of the new information, and it became apparent that it wasn't attention deficit disorder or any one of numerous other possible conditions. It was separation anxiety created as a result of being separated at five years old from her brother. Too soon, too young. We worked hard, Rochel worked hard — she's now in high school and doing well. She loves her school and her friends. Her art has always been with her, and she has won a second year of scholarships to take special art courses.

Oh, this one really hurts. Same school (don't ask why). Our younger twins are age seven. We walk in on the first day of class and they have been assigned to different classrooms! I protest — "But I want them together ..." and hear, "It's our policy to separate twins.

We've consulted many experts and this is best. We've had a lot of experience with twins and this has always worked very well. If you don't separate them, the weaker one will become dominated by the other." The suggestion I would be ruining my sons' lives if I didn't agree was clear. But worse was the knowledge that I tried to negotiate, but I didn't fight. Once the school planted that seed of doubt, I was done, but I should have listened to my heart. One year later, one son is at the bottom of the class. "It's just a period of adjustment. He'll be all over that next year." By the end of Grade 3, he was withdrawn, and they recommended removing him from the school. "Put them back together!" I wanted to scream. This time they agreed. Every year since, his marks have gone up. He is already equal to the class in most things and beginning to pull ahead in others. He is in Grade 6.

Why did he have to suffer so much? How could I let myself be coerced? I should have known; I should have known!

It seems a lot of experts and many books recommend multiples should be separated and even go to different schools. But this view does not necessarily meet the unique needs of our children. I am not arguing against separating multiple birth children. Apparently, many can find success if separated. But it also seems there is no voice for those who need more time.

You are the only expert of your children. If it doesn't feel right, it isn't. Don't let anyone coerce you by suggesting there will be dire consequences if your approach is taken. Keep seeking specialists and others for information and objective methods to ascertain if any of your children are heading into trouble at school. By the time a child can no longer cope, you may have waited too long and there will be a long road to travel back — sometimes needlessly.

finding themselves
Barbara Morrison

The next step — separate schools — may seem drastic, but it's necessary

One day last winter, I received a call from the school principal about one of my nine-year-old boys. Apparently, Mitchell had been caught throwing a snowball in the playground and had been hauled into the office to face the music. After speaking to the principal and later to all three of my boys, I discovered, in fact, that the offender wasn't Mitchell at all, but one of his brothers. The wrong boy had been singled out of the crowd.

I wish this was an isolated incident, but unfortunately, with monozygotic (identical) triplets, identity confusion has become a real problem. Few people, including teachers, principals and Cub™ leaders, can tell the boys apart. Having two of the boys in one class and one in the other class of the same grade hasn't appeared to help. The teachers have tried diligently to involve them in different activities, but once on the playground, they are known as the Morrison brothers — red-haired, rambunctious and very high profile in their elementary school. And together, they are rascals, pestering and wrestling not with others, but with each other. For us, the next step — separate schools — may seem drastic, but we have reached the point where we know this is a necessary step if the boys are to look out, see and experience a world that exists outside themselves.

Guess what? The boys are thrilled with the idea. Bradley and Mitchell welcome the change of schools, and while Patrick is adamant about staying in his school, he cares little about being separated. I suspect that's because they are simply fed up with being viewed as a set. We appreciate the difficulty people have in distinguishing our children from each other, so we have tried to maintain a colour-coding system in which each boy wears clothes in his favourite colour. But of course, that doesn't always work. I recall one day as early as age four when Patrick and Mitchell refused to wear their baseball uniforms since they would all look exactly alike. Patrick insisted on combing his own hair to look different from his brothers "so people will know me!" Later that year, it became an issue again with school uniforms. "We do not want to look the same; no one will know us."

But on the other hand, Bradley, Patrick and Mitchell crave each other's company. At home, they gravitate toward each other. To foster one-on-one friendships with neighbours and classmates, I always encourage each of the boys to invite a friend to play at our home. If someone does play host to a classmate, I have made a rule that the two are given time to play together without interference from the others. Otherwise, the unsuspecting friend gets swept up in the frenzied activity of my three and leaves (or rather escapes) us with little hope of return.

From a social standpoint, I am convinced that our children need an opportunity and an environment to discover themselves as individuals. For us, that means separate schools, separate programs and separate camps. Patrick will soon set off without his brothers on a camping trip with a new Cub™ group. In spite of remarks from leaders, including the question, "Are you sure you want to?" he will not be dissuaded. He is determined to go and I am proud of his decision.

Finding a balance between encouraging independence and supporting the bond among my children has been an unbelievable challenge for us because the circumstances always seem to change. For my children at this moment, they need to be separated. Others need to be together. That's why it is so essential that schools not develop strict policies for multiples, but rather, take the cue from parents. Every situation is unique. Every child is unique. I just need to give each of our boys the opportunity to discover what makes him unique.

the screaming meanies
Bracha Mirsky

Have you ever become the worst possible character you could imagine of yourself? Well, I did. In retrospect, it was a great turning point in my growth as a parent. I can't even contemplate what would have happened if I hadn't changed course. My mind just won't go there.

What did I want most at that point in my life? I wanted to be a great mom and wonderful wife. A mother who would be patient with her children, always kind and encouraging. Able to guide them, building a relationship based on friendship and trust. Insightful. Yes sir, that was going to be me!

Any parent can experience pressures, but for parents of multiple birth children, the demands and pressures are intensified. I really don't know when the screaming began. I had actually been handling things quite well. Before I knew it though, calm communication with my children was replaced overnight by this absolute screaming witch. I wasn't even conscious of what I was doing!

I believe I was saved from the horrors of a destroyed family by one brief moment, by one gift. It was a morning that started like any other. I was up at 7 a.m., dragged myself out of bed, put on my housecoat and went to wake up the triplets, who were six years old. I snapped on their light. "Hurry up! Get out of bed or you'll be late for the car pool!" My usual morning greeting. Next I went to the twins' room. They were one year old. My husband warmed their bottles, while I changed diapers and brought them downstairs. In the meantime, I was shouting at my three oldest, "Breakfast! Hurry up or you'll go to school hungry!" Breakfast proceeded under a dark cloud. The children didn't laugh or talk, as I kept my eye on the clock and admonished them to quicken their pace.

Then it was upstairs to brush teeth and change into school clothes. While I was downstairs with the twins, I let my voice do the work. Yelling and yelling … "Carpool will be here soon! You're not dressed yet! You're not trying. How can you be so lazy? If you don't get down here right now, all dressed for school, you are going to get it!"

To tell you the truth, I no longer remember what I said. I was in a frenzy far beyond myself. But I remember being in the living room, looking upstairs through the stair railing. By then my blood was boiling. I yelled again. Then I looked up. There between the spindles was the sweetest face of my son Yossi. He was sitting on the floor, face looking down at me. His eyes were wide, his mouth gaping in amazement. This sweet little six-year-old had obviously never seen an adult "lose it" before. Our eyes locked for one brief second, and that look went straight through my heart. For one brief moment in time, I saw how I must look to my children. It was an ugly picture. I had to look away. It struck me so hard. Yet, I could still not stop screaming and yelling.

Finally, the carpool arrived and I sent the children out the door with the usual terse, "I love you," and closed the door behind them. I collapsed on the couch and lay there thinking as my heated emotions bled out of me. I kept thinking over and over again. I tried to stop. Why couldn't I stop? Why did those hateful words keep coming out of my mouth when I didn't want them to?

It took me months of work, but I was determined to be true to that moment — that warning. Through trial and error I realized certain truths:

- Time pressures put a phenomenal amount of pressure on adults, while children are innocent. Keeping things in perspective is important. The world will not end if we are late. For routines that are too pressured, it is up to the parents to analyze them, and change what is necessary. If you have to wake up 15 minutes earlier to make things work, that is your obligation.
- Setting the tone of the home is strictly in the hands of parents. Every word we say and how we say it is of primary importance.
- Everything becomes habit. Habits can save you or sink you. Consciously make good habits and routines for yourself and your children. Anything you say with a sharp tone or terse admonishment can also be said with a kind word, gentle voice and soft smile. And it will work much better too! Save your children and save yourself from the cuts of unkind words. The screaming meanies can be beat. Within six months I was in control. We were back to a more relaxed family full of smiles and laughter. The screaming meanies were beaten! (It did not hit me until two years later how profound the change was.) I woke up at 6:45 a.m., put on my housecoat and went to wake up the children, now eight years old, with, "Good morning, time to get up. Did you sleep well?" I turned on their light. Soon they came downstairs for breakfast all dressed and sat at their places around the kitchen table ... and started to sing!

the summer of hormones
Nancy Parish

It seems like only yesterday they were running around in sagging diapers. Suddenly they are running around in tight jeans

It doesn't seem that long ago we were up to our knees in diapers around here. My triplet daughters arrived just as my first son passed the one-year mark. Diapers were stockpiled around our house. Now that 11 years have passed and diapers are a distant memory, we're facing another stage of growing up that rivals those days — adolescence!

My children seemed to have matured early, at least physically. Four of my five kids are competing to see who drives the others the most crazy. There are days when things as simple as a backpack sitting on a chair can cause streaming tears and foot stomping. Backpack location has a lot of power in our house. It is far too precious an item to sit on the floor.

Nitpicking has become sibling-bashing. What was once simply annoying is now punishable by slow death at the hands of the offended sister or brother. No one can do anything right according to the others, which in turn, causes snide remarks and looks of utter disgust.

We all know "the stage." That time of life when a kid without label designer jeans runs the risk of forever being cast out into the wastelands of the uncool. We have all been through it to some extent, and I am no exception. I was prepared for my kids to go through it as well. But for some unknown naive reason, it never occurred to me that I would have four kids going through it together.

Getting them into the bathtub was once a battle; now getting them out is a war. "Please change your clothes," has become "Why do you have so much laundry?" Once-dirty hands are now adorned with blue nail polish. Cheeks are speckled with the latest glitter. Those cute little baby outfits are long gone, replaced by designer labels. Cute outfits are now rejected. "Oh Mom, that is sooo tacky!"

The highest point on Earth has recently changed from Mt. Everest to my laundry pile, and shows no sign of being challenged. For some reason, girls at 11 have an irrational urge to change their clothes four times a day, leaving the three previous outfits strewn across the floor waiting for the day Mom cries, "Clean up your room!"

There aren't really any differences between triplets going through puberty and single children. It's just that there is a lot MORE of it! Anyone who has multiples knows that the workload doesn't increase in linear degrees. It goes up exponentially. Two is not twice the work of one, it is four times the work. Three is 12 times the work, and four boggles the mind!

A sense of humour, flexibility and patience must be firmly intact if one expects to emerge at least sane from the other side of the puberty years. Of course, I am assuming it will end ….

Girls have different needs at this age than boys. Mom gets to sit down and explain menstruation to bug-eyed faces uttering remarks like, "No way!" or "Eeewwww, gross!" and the like. Moms get to introduce bras, sanitary pads and acne facewash to young girls who insist that, "Well, none of that is going to happen to me!"

My daughters all reacted differently to this information. One's reaction was, "Okay, cool. Can I go now?" Another hid her face and blushed for three days after. The third had great concerns that she wasn't growing breasts yet and would need implants. Of the latter two, one can't wait to go through all of this puberty stuff, while the other would sell it all in an instant.

Tempers flare but we are learning to be very forgiving. Life is never simple and straightforward. I suppose it would be boring if it was, but I would still like to try "boring" for a day, just to see for myself.

I no longer buy diapers in bulk. I buy sanitary pads in bulk, facewash by the gallon, and am currently looking for a discount on bras. I have become an expert at finding second-hand designer clothing and running shoes in good shape.

It seems like only yesterday they were running around in sagging diapers. Suddenly they are running around in tight jeans.

being a multiple is the greatest gift

Bracha Mirsky

My triplets, five years old at the time, came home from kindergarten very excited one day. They had made a new friend! As they tried to describe their new friend to me, there was deep concentration on their happy faces as they searched for the words. "He's a single," Rochel said. Yossi and Aharon quickly agreed.

But I didn't understand. "You mean he doesn't have any brothers or sisters?" I asked. A look of confusion crossed their faces. "No, a single, an only one!" They popped up and down excitedly, sure I would understand now. No, I was still confused. Exasperated at my inability to understand their concept, they pressed on. "Mom, you know, when he was born, there was only him!" They all nodded, solemnly. That such a thing could happen to their friend. To be born alone! This drew an instinctive response of sorrow from these three children, who kept each other company in the womb and beyond.

To be born a multiple connects our children in a way we can only wonder about. It attunes them to another human being on a deep emotional level. There is an emotional understanding or sensitivity that their peers may not share. When they were six, my children asked, "Mom, why do some kids at school call other children names? Don't they know they're hurting them? With very little encouragement, multiple children seem able to grasp the feelings of others as a real and tangible part of a human being, which needs consideration and protection. It's a totally normal way to look at others. But it bothers them when other people don't seem to care. Why can't they understand? And if they could, wouldn't the world a better place?

Many people will learn over time, even in adulthood, the concept of the emotional "core" of people. But very few will live and breath it all their lives, as multiple birth children do.

As teens, my children are still asked the question, "Isn't it weird being a triplet?" It seems ridiculous to them. "How can they keep asking that? No, of course not! It's perfectly normal. I've been a triplet all my life. To me the thought of being a single would be weird!"

You are what you live. The closeness of multiple birth children is a special gift. Encourage it and they will have a bond that others can only dream of having. A sense of humanity and an understanding of family, friendship and loyalty that will strengthen them all their lives.

16

pregnant again

another baby?!

Mary Gallagher

I am very aware of a bond between baby Claire and me that is different from what I share with the quads

After trying for five long years to conceive and eventually using fertility drugs, our quadruplets were born. So you can imagine the surprise when we found out that I was pregnant for a second time when the quads were three years old. This unplanned pregnancy was initially shocking and horrifying for both my husband and me. Then fear set in as we wondered if we were going to have twins or triplets. I knew we wouldn't be able to cope. We were even discussing fetal reduction if it was a multiple pregnancy, a discussion that overwhelmed me with anxiety. The first few weeks of the pregnancy were a very difficult period. It was probably more stressful than what we had already endured in the last three years with our other children.

This pregnancy came just two weeks after the quads had started nursery school. Finally I was getting two mornings all to myself to do whatever I wanted, and now I had to deal with being pregnant and having four preschoolers.

An ultrasound showing just one fetus came as a great relief. But then I had to deal with horrible morning sickness. I had endured 20 weeks of morning sickness with my multiple pregnancy and here I was with the same sickness with just one baby! So instead of enjoying my free two mornings a week, I was home, nauseous and exhausted for the first 18 weeks of pregnancy, thinking, "What have I done?"

Once the nausea subsided and the baby started to kick, I really began to enjoy the pregnancy and looked forward to having one baby to love and share with the other children. The quads were amazingly attached to this little one while it was still inside me. After explaining to them why I was so tired and how they would have to help me, their behaviour changed (most of the time) and they really didn't mind me frequently napping on the couch.

This second pregnancy progressed very quickly and without any complications. I was truly amazed at how different I felt compared with the multiple pregnancy. It seemed to take forever for my belly to expand, and I was able to bond to this one little baby and know its every movement and kick. I was thoroughly convinced that this baby was a boy, so we called him Stephen through the whole pregnancy. You can imagine our surprise when the baby born at 41 weeks was actually a 9 lb. 11 oz. girl. I had hoped to deliver her vaginally and have everything as "normal" as possible, feeling that everything had been abnormal with the quadruplets. But due to some minor complications, she was delivered by cesarean section.

Claire was the most beautiful little baby I had ever seen (after my other four, of course), and she was a mixture of all the other four put together.

Instead of being bedridden for two days after the c-section, as I had been with the quads, I was up and about that same night. I couldn't believe how different I felt.

Not being able to breastfeed the quads, I was desperate to breastfeed this little one. I persevered and it became one of the most enjoyable experiences of my life. She was breastfed for 10 months.

When I came home from the hospital, I felt really good. But about one hour later, after many, many questions from the quads, and them wanting to touch the baby and follow me everywhere, exhaustion took over and I just stood and cried and cried, wondering how on earth I was going to cope!

Our 17-year-old niece came to live with us for 10 weeks in the summer, and I thanked God every day for her. Claire was a high demand baby who loved the breast and never slept and who also developed that wonderful condition called colic. The other four would have been truly neglected if our niece had not been there.

But even through all of that, I have always been very happy that Claire joined our family. She took our focus off the quads and gave them the responsibility of being a big sister or big brother. They learned very quickly how to be gentle and quiet while around her and all the time they showed great love and respect for her. While she sat happily in her bouncing chair, they would show her books or their drawings. Claire's daily entertainment was to watch her sisters and brother playing. They always marvelled as she reached another step in her development. I am sure she has developed so quickly through their examples. She rolled over at eight weeks, sat up at five months, crawled at six months, walked at eight months and ran at 10 months. Today, now that she has just turned two years old, she dashes to play with all their toys with barely a glance toward her own.

Claire and her siblings exchange hugs and kisses all the time. I can't imagine having the quads without her. She has shown me what motherhood is really about: sharing precious moments through breastfeeding and special time together. Claire always knew who her mother was. I never had to wonder if my baby was mistaking a helper for her mother. Having the time to treasure each and every moment of her development and love and having time to laugh with her and cry with her meant so much to both my husband and me.

Although I am so proud of Katie, Emma, Louise and Michael, and I know that they have turned out to be very special, wonderful little children, I still have tremendous guilt for not being able to give each one of them as much time as they really needed with me. I am very aware that the bond that I have with Claire is very different to the bond I have with them. I hope one day when they are older they will tell me that they understand and that they still love me.

Claire has been given to our family as a gift.

and baby makes six
Amy Mammarella

Now our family is complete

My husband and I still yearned for another baby when our triplets (one boy and two girls) were nearing 18 months old. We hoped to have another boy to give our son a brother. He was already being excluded from some of the "girl play" at home. When I became pregnant, we were both ecstatic and terrified. What were we thinking bringing another baby into our very young family?

We realized our threesome would have to grow up quickly. Baby bottles, cribs and diapers disappeared by the time they turned two years old. These transitions were successful, but implementing them exhausted me. A minor heart condition resurfaced and I began to feel early contractions. I was warned not to lift my children after 20 weeks of pregnancy. Try telling that to three young toddlers! Of course, I pushed my limits and was sent for hospital rest twice before the due date. In the last seven weeks of pregnancy, we had household help. Unfortunately, our children never adapted to having strangers in our home and it was a difficult time for everyone. We all waited impatiently for the birth.

Quite a different experience

Fortunately, all went well and I delivered another healthy son. To our delight, our eldest son was and still is, awestruck by his baby brother. A mutual love has developed.

Now, instead of triplets plus one, we are more often described as a family of two boys and two girls. We feel that this baby has normalized our family. The spotlight on our multiples has dimmed and, like most of their friends, they have the experience of helping and playing with a younger sibling.

Also, my experience with this baby was quite different than with my older three. Breastfeeding, particularly at night, took on a whole new feeling as I relaxed and focused on just one baby. I have spent time marvelling at his fingers and toes instead of watching how he interacts with his siblings. I have more time to cherish his every action, sound and facial expression, as my eyes aren't constantly darting from one baby to another.

We have been blessed with four incredible children and now feel that our family is complete. I can't imagine life without any of them, or without the experiences of both the multiple and single pregnancies.

When parents of multiples ask my opinion about having more children, my answer is always positive. Know your personal limits and be ready for more fatigue, but otherwise enjoy the big joys that come with an extra-large family!

17

special needs

when the world changed

Allison Bourne

I have read often how mothers like me with special needs children are chosen or special, and I can tell you that I feel neither

I remember touching my stomach in anticipation as I sat in the back of an airport limousine bound for a business flight to Texas. The night before the stick had read blue and confirmed what I had been feeling — pregnant. My husband, James and I had been married eight years, and although I was in no hurry to have children, this seemed like the right time. We had lived in England for a couple of years, renovated and sold our house and built a good foundation. I think back on that time as the last moments of my "other" life, the life that was untouched by substantial pain and disappointment. The life that is only a faint memory now.

Triplets — the words filled me with terror. Although this was my first pregnancy, I appreciated the huge responsibility of having one baby, let alone three. I was not happy, to say the least. And when I spoke to other moms of triplets who referred to my situation as a "blessing" and a "gift" I knew I was in trouble. I think the realization that I was in for a big change helped me in many ways. I did not go into motherhood thinking it would be at all easy, but I had no idea at that time how much things would really change for James and me.

In October 1995, Libby, Madeline and Annie were born, relatively healthy for 31 weeks. They went through a "normal" preemie course and began to arrive home in December. The first night I had one baby at home I sat on the floor and cried. How the hell was I going to be able to take care of another two? I was terrified. It would be the first of many moments where I was overcome with fear. Somehow it is that fear that serves me well now.

Looking back into my heart, I think I knew that there was something wrong with Annie from early on. I asked the doctors at one point if she was okay and was assured she was fine. I knew they were wrong. The following summer Annie was admitted to the hospital with infantile spasms. She was a very sick baby and suddenly the world of hospitals and doctors was my world. Knowledge about Annie's condition was the first step toward getting her better. I read and e-mailed and faxed everyone who knew something about seizures. I was a doctor's pain in the ass. If they did anything, performed any procedure, I wanted to know what it was and why they were doing it. Don't misunderstand me — I respect and admire members of the healthcare profession now more than ever, but I also realize that part of the process lies in knowing what is going on. I expect Annie's doctors and therapists to be honest and straightforward. In return, I promise not to yell too much. While Annie was in the hospital over the summer, my other girls were at home. I am thankful that I found in our little community a wonderful nanny and friend to look after Libby and Madeline. Knowing that they were happy and well taken care of helped me to direct my energies toward Annie.

My biggest fear for Annie came in July 1996, two months after she began her treatment. She lay on her bed bloated from the drugs, breathing with difficulty and unable to move, feel or recognize my touch. I felt I could handle any problem Annie had as long as she knew who I was. I could not live knowing she didn't know me. I faced many things that summer — the things every parent fears the most. But one thing I know for sure is that the fear is bigger than the reality. Fear drives you. Annie eventually came home. That first month home, she smiled for the first time in 120 days. It was September and her first birthday was October 28th.

It was the beginning of my life as a mother of a child with special needs. It was a world that I have gone into screaming and kicking, not wanting to be part of it, but knowing that I have no choice. All the misconceptions I had about developmentally delayed children came to the surface. There were painful memories of childhood where the "funny" kids would be in one class and us in the other. It is about seeing things for the first time and having empathy in my heart for every parent of a sick and disabled child.

The things that have helped me get through this won't be for everyone, but I think part of the process is for each individual to find out what works and what doesn't for them. I have read often how mothers like me are chosen or special, and I can tell you that I feel neither. I am not a "better" person because of Annie but I see the seeds of great women being sown in my other daughters. They will live with more compassion, caring and acceptance than I ever have or will.

I found that joining support groups was a hard match. While I had much in common with these women, I also realized that we weren't going to be automatic friends because of our children's disability. I go to support groups now and then when I want to feel like I am not going crazy, that the things I am feeling are normal or within the limits. The hardest thing about Annie without question is other parents. The stares we have endured in doctors' waiting rooms, the ignorant questions and the plain stupidity never cease to amaze me. I refuse to let anyone disrespect Annie and if you ask me an inappropriate question, be careful of the answer. I am not a very religious person — don't expect me to accept your blessings on my child or your story about how your "friend" had a child like Annie and how she is now in university. I know Annie's limitations and expectations. I also expect that she will fit into my world, despite the hardships of doing so.

I also don't chase every new therapy or drug that I read about, and I have no time for guilt. I expect her to be the brightest and the best within her limitations.

Annie came into my world and taught me many lessons at a very high price. I wish it never happened. I wish she didn't have special needs, but she is also exactly the daughter I wanted. She makes me feel grounded to life and holding her and having her touch my face is the closest thing to God I can imagine.

If you have recently had a child diagnosed with a disability, I can assure you that the things you feel today will not be there in a year. The things I feel today, approaching birthday number two, will be eased by next year. This is what I cling to — that life goes on. There will be days when you will not think about your child's condition and there will be days when you will sink into despair. But those moments become fewer and you will manage ways to keep that door shut. I also realize that I am lucky to have a partner such as James. He is, without a doubt, a better "mother" than I am, and when I feel desperate, he is a rock. He reminds me that everything is okay.

Today I picked up Annie and her sisters from daycare. I was handed her artwork and told about her day. She had rice for lunch and enjoyed circle time. As I scooped her up in my arms, Annie smiled and reached up to stroke my face. Annie makes me wonder, at times like that, just what everyone is so afraid of.

living with special needs
Jeanette Niebler

A long, difficult journey from diagnosis to acceptance

When you are faced with a higher order multiple pregnancy, one of your main concerns may be the effect of that pregnancy on the future health and development of your children. It's unfortunate but true that there are many risks, including disorders resulting in special needs, associated with higher order multiples. Since many special needs are a result of prematurity, it is not uncommon for families with multiples to be faced with multiple challenges. Although it is always devastating to be faced with one or more challenges, it is often possible to live with them and even to thrive as a family.

Whether you find out during your pregnancy or afterward that one or more of your children faces additional problems, the news can be devastating. Often you are forced to realize that the hopes and dreams that you had for your child will not come to pass, and you will likely go through a period of mourning for your "normal" child. This is nothing to be ashamed of — it is a common process of coping and proceeding through life to do what is necessary for your child or children. The initial diagnosis or hints that something might be wrong can seem unreal. When doctors told her about her son's cleft lip and palate, Barbara Skinner remembers, "I really didn't hear all that they were saying. It was if mouths were moving and no words were being said."

Depending on when you are given the news, there can be many other factors that will also affect your feelings. They include hormonal overload if you are pregnant or have just delivered the babies, exhaustion and sleep deprivation in the first few months, and the overwhelming logistics of dealing with multiple toddlers, preschoolers or school-aged children. Professionals involved with your children can be very helpful to you, especially if they are aware of other stressful factors in your life. As parents, we may assume that other people realize the stresses of having multiples. But it's better not to make assumptions. Instead, communicate openly with professionals so that you can access all the support services you and your children need. Don't be afraid to ask for help or to explain what you need.

Getting a diagnosis

Often it is the parents who bring a child's challenges to the notice of professionals. It's easy to dismiss our fears for our children, since society tends to tell us that our kids will "catch up" or that they are "slow learners" or that "multiples develop more slowly than singletons." While all of these theories have some merit, it is also true that parents' intuition can be the most valuable tool for identifying and describing challenges that young children face.

If you suspect that there is a problem, there is a good chance that you are right. As a mother of autistic triplets, I noticed at 14 months that their babbling didn't seem to be progressing into speech in the same way as my friends' kids. We had been followed closely by a developmental program at our hospital since they were born. The kids were now down to yearly visits since the consensus was that everyone was doing well. Because I knew that preemies were often speech delayed, as were multiples, I wasn't too concerned about their lack of language. But at about 16 months, I asked our pediatrician about it. He wasn't concerned either and said that we should wait until they were two years old before we started worrying. Thanks to some friends on the Internet, I pushed and pushed to get them evaluated before then. We moved up a two-year appointment at the hospital to 18 months. That was the first time that I heard the wonderful phrase "autistic tendencies."

If you suspect your children are having difficulties, have them evaluated. You can often access evaluation services through the hospital where they were born, through your pediatrician, or by calling your public health unit and asking for a contact number. Many doctors and pediatricians want to wait until children are two years of age to start the evaluation process, but most therapists would prefer to start working with children as early as possible, so don't take no for an answer.

The diagnostic process itself can be filled with frustration and anguish, especially if it carries over many long, drawn-out months of tests and appointments. Unfortunately, not all of our children can be easily diagnosed. You and the doctors may know that something is wrong, but identifying and putting a label on it can often be exceptionally difficult.

Diane Myers describes her experience with one of her quadruplets: "At six months, we began to notice some differences in Harrison. He could sleep through anything. After a conversation with the children's doctor a hearing test was scheduled. This test led to many, many months of frustration. First came ear infection after ear infection, then a suggestion to insert ear tubes, a complication, a new ear, nose and throat specialist, faster service, tubes in, hearing test complete, a diagnosis of severe hearing loss in both ears, fitting for hearing aids, and finally, relief. Harrison didn't get his hearing aids until he was 18 months old. How frustrating! By this time, Harrison was getting out of hand. He was very frustrated. The other children were beginning to talk and communicate their needs. Temper tantrums were his most effective form of communication. And boy, was he getting good at them!"

> **quote**
>
> **The diagnostic process itself can be filled with frustration and anguish**

Finding support

Getting a diagnosis is only the first step. After dealing with the initial shock and grief, it is vitally important that you educate yourself to provide the best possible services for your child. It is unfortunate that parents are forced to work as our children's advocates instead of just being able to rely on professionals, but that is often the way things turn out. There are many, many excellent sources of information available on any type of challenge. Try contacting your provincial or national multiple birth group to find other parents facing similar challenges. National and international organizations for almost every type of special need can be your best sources of information. Use the Internet extensively if you can, but be aware that many sources of information can be inaccurate or misleading. The more you read and learn, the better you will be able to distinguish good advice and information from bad.

Local support groups may also be helpful, but it is often difficult for parents of higher order multiples to get out to meetings, and when you do, you may find that they were not as helpful as you wished. As we all know, there is a huge difference between having one child with a special need, and having higher order multiples, where one or more of the children are affected. But support groups are worth a try. These parents from your community may have already dealt with local services and can help you navigate the maze of services and doctors.

Depending on exactly what form your child's challenge takes, it can be very difficult dealing with the general public. If your child looks or acts differently in public, it can be a heartbreaking experience. One thing that support groups can offer is the chance to compare stories and receive support from other people who understand what you are going through. The value of relating to similar experiences cannot be underestimated.

Keeping a balance in the family

In any family where there is a child with special challenges, there can be a tendency to place that child at the centre of importance in the group. Everything revolves around that child's needs. Not only is this often unnecessary, it is extremely destructive to the family as a whole. It is very important to keep time and energy for your other children, for your spouse, and perhaps most importantly, for yourself. Having a child with special needs can be even more of a life-long commitment than having a typical child, since you don't necessarily know that at the end of 18 or 20 years, the child will move out and go on to live an independent life. This is a long haul, and you must nurture yourself because the demands on you may not go away. Do whatever it takes to make sure that you are as fulfilled a person as you can be. It will pay off for you as well as for your family. Above all, nurture your relationship with your partner. There is reportedly a higher than average rate of divorce among higher order multiple families, and there is definitely a higher divorce rate in families with special needs children. It is vitally important that if you want to remain a two-parent family, you keep the lines of communication open. It is not unusual for one partner to have more trouble than the other in adjusting to a diagnosis or in coping with the extra demands of special needs children. To make the relationship work, both parents will need to show a lot of patience with each other, as well as commitment.

For a child struggling with a challenge, small milestones may represent a huge effort that a typical child would never have to make

There is no question that having one or more children with special needs brings extra challenges. Watching one or two of your children lag behind the rest, or suffer more than the others, is so difficult. Although we as parents of multiples are indoctrinated early with the idea of not comparing the children with each other, it becomes increasingly difficult to do when the differences are obvious. It is very important to try to see the children as individuals, and not compare the achievements of one with another. Seeing the development of some children can be heartbreaking if you see delays in your other children. There is no easy way to deal with this except to try and see the achievements of each child for what they are and to try your best not to make comparisons. For a child struggling with a challenge, small milestones may represent a huge effort that a typical child would never have to make. They deserve as much pride as any child.

So how do you handle the practical demands of having a child with special needs among a set of multiples? Sometimes you may have to change the way your family does things in order to accommodate that child. In our family, Dylan's sensory issues didn't allow us to go many places as a family, especially areas with loud noise or busy crowds. So if there is somewhere I think the girls would like to go that Dylan couldn't tolerate, someone else either has to take them or I have to arrange care for Dylan so that I can go with them. Family activities are limited to familiar places or to areas with less intense sensory activities. Each family will have to work out caregiver arrangements in their own way.

One of the main problems for families of multiples with special needs is coordinating the many visits to therapy, doctors' appointments, schools and hospitals. One child with special needs may need to spend his or her days in a different setting than his or her siblings, which can lead to horrendous logistical problems for parents. A doctor's visit can be a nightmare if you are trying to talk to a doctor about one child while the others run rampant in a waiting room or office. One solution is to develop an effective support system, which can come into place as needed. Many parents received help when the babies first came home from the hospital. Try to tap into the goodwill of these people. Contact your local multiple birth organization to see if there is any way that they can help. Utilize any services provided by your community that you can, and don't be afraid to ask for help. With certain types of challenges, such as developmental delays, ask about including the siblings in therapy as peer models. Ask your caseworker about respite care or babysitting services as well as sibling support groups. As a parent of higher-order multiples, you are already in a high-need situation. When you add one or more high-need children to the equation, there is no reason that you should not utilize any services that you can.

Have a large calendar or white board by your phone to help keep appointments straight. With more than one child, you will be surprised at how quickly your calendar fills up. These are just some suggestions but, above all, be creative and consider your own family's needs and desires to find what works best for you.

Sibling relationships

Another big issue that frightens parents of multiples when one or more of their children develops a challenge is how that condition will affect the sibling relationship. There is no question that siblings of special needs children can have a difficult time understanding why their parents have to sometimes give extra care to a brother or sister with special needs. They must also deal with society's reaction to their sibling's condition, as well as to fears that they too may develop the same condition, or guilt that they "caused" it in some way. Almost every national support group should have information on sibling relationships. Most local support groups or agencies will also offer workshops or reading materials. Although many of us tend to see sibling issues in a negative light when we think about special needs, there is no question that siblings can also be the greatest asset to the affected child and vice versa.

Sibling relationships, along with every other issue that you face with a child with special needs, seem to magnify once it's time for school. It can be hard for siblings to deal with their classmates when it's obvious that their brother or sister has a special need. When parents consider the possibility of their child being teased or ostracized, it can be heartbreaking, and siblings seem to bear the main brunt. There are no easy solutions. Some families split the children into different schools or grades, while others make the effort to keep them together. Utilize whatever resources are available for making the decision that's right for your entire family.

Despite the huge list of problems that families of multiples with special needs face, it is not all pain and hardship. There is no feeling like watching your child struggle and achieve something that you weren't expecting, or develop a new skill that you didn't think was possible. Our children are the light of our lives, and we have a difficult time understanding why society doesn't accept them as we do. As Diane Myers says about having one child with cerebral palsy and another who is hearing impaired, "Having children with labels can lead us on a very different path in life. A lot depends on availability of resources, the severity of the child's disability, and our approach to our different circumstances. After being involved with people with labels both professionally and personally, I have learned that we truly must look at the child first. All my children are very special in their own way. I have learned much from them and their reactions to the world. Not one of them will react the same way to the same situation. As a parent, it may be hard for me to deal with, but it definitely makes life more interesting and, yes, very challenging."

**Professional Notes from the Speech Language
Pathologist and Mother of Twins**

---

the more the merrier
Paula Moss

Speech and language delays are common problems among twins and higher order multiple children. In fact, approximately 30 per cent of twins and higher order multiples have communication problems, with boys being at greater risk.

Why are speech and language problems so common? There are no known certainties but many theories abound:

- Reduced opportunities for interaction between caregiver and child. This also holds true for a second or third child in a family. The more children in a family, the less time parents have to spend talking with them individually.
- Caregivers in families of multiples tend to use more directive language in an effort to get through essential, everyday routines. There is typically less time to engage in normal verbal exchanges, which is the means by which children learn the art of conversation.
- There is more competition to be heard. Children speak more quickly to get all the information out at once before someone else jumps in to tell the rest or to steal mom's attention. Naturally, faster speech is often not articulated as clearly and often leads to less use of the key muscles typically used when speaking.
- There may be significant prenatal or birth histories that affect the child's speech and language development. Premature and low birthweight babies are at increased risk. Children born under 2,500 grams should be monitored and those born 1,500 grams need to be watched very closely for communication problems. Children who suffer from recurrent ear infections are also at greater risk since fluid can remain in the ear and possibly interfere with the child's ability to hear. Hearing loss is directly related to speech and language acquisition. The greatest learning period of language occurs during the first 24 months of life, which is also the critical time period for monitoring potential hearing deficiencies.

Research findings on language development in multiple birth children

Multiple birth children are more likely to:

- Be later to develop first words.
- Have reduced vocabulary at school entry. Children with a limited or lower vocabulary also tend to have reading problems.
- Be later to develop walking and play skills. The research shows that late walkers are more likely to be late talkers.
- Have fewer verbal exchanges at home where life is hectic and the opportunities to spend time one on one are limited.
- Experience social delays.
- Have problems articulating sounds.
- Experience difficulties with spelling and reading.
- Engage in autonomous language or "twintalk." In spite of its name, the language is really not autonomous but rather a variation of the language of the child's environment and a delay in the development of sound patterns, which is reinforced by same-age siblings. The cycle continues unless parents constantly reinforce correct language and articulation.

Possible interventions

Children need to learn how to listen and follow directions. They also need to learn how to express themselves. Try to use the following suggestions during everyday activities:

- When you talk to your child, make sure you have his or her attention. Call the child's name before you say anything or touch him or her gently on the arm.
- To ensure you have full attention, get down to the child's level and make eye contact.
- Try to eliminate as many distractions as possible. Turn off the television and clean up toys before engaging in a conversation.
- Use gestures and facial expressions along with directions to convey your message.
- Speak clearly and not too quickly so that the child has time to take in what you are saying. Children are more likely to listen to directions broken into single steps or short phrases.
- Encourage your child's attempts to communicate. If your child

uses a word incorrectly, repeat the word back correctly and emphasize the word or sound he or she is having difficulty with. Do not insist that the child repeat the word back to you because he or she may repeat it incorrectly again, which may discourage further attempts. It's better to simply provide ample opportunities to hear the words and sounds used correctly.

- Give your child enough time to respond. It can take a long time for a child to organize his or her thoughts and feelings before putting them into words. Avoid the temptation to interrupt and finish the sentence. All too often we, as busy parents, fail to give our children time to communicate with us.
- Be aware of the words, sounds, sentence patterns or grammar that your child should know and model them clearly.
- Talk out loud about what you and your child are doing using simple sentences.
- Expand on what your child says by adding new words and ideas to their remarks.
- Sing and read to your child to develop his or her listening and speaking skills. These are great ways for developing language and sharing a conversation.
- Finally, try to relax and have fun together. Remember, when it comes to talking, the more the merrier!

18

losing a child

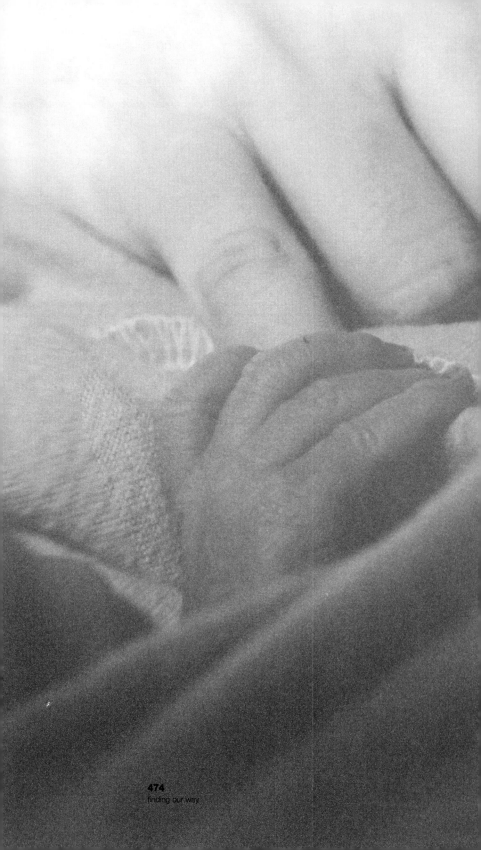

our short time together
Craig Mahood

A precious life measured in moments

"I have some good news and some bad news," our obstetrician said. "The good news is that your fetus is fine. The bad news is, there's more than one." Jan and I were talking to our family doctor about an ultrasound report she had just received. We looked at each other. Twins? "No, there are two more than one." Jan and I began to laugh, then Jan began to cry, then laugh again. We were stunned. Triplets! "Three viable fetuses," is the way the doctor put it, sitting nicely in Jan's uterus, growing comfortably. Three lives to think about when just 12 weeks ago, after seven years of marriage with no plans for children, Jan discovered she was pregnant. We decided that we should keep and love this child. But now triplets! One to three! How big a difference can that be? As our obstetrician put it on our first visit, "You know you're in trouble when there's more of them than you."

Jan was high risk, so we went under the care of an obstetrician in a downtown Toronto hospital. His office was on the main floor. The Neonatal Intensive Care Unit (NICU) was on the third. Through the pregnancy, we didn't think one way or the other about the likelihood of our babies ending up there. The excitement and anticipation was inspiring as we stepped onto the path to becoming an instant family of five. It was fun telling our family and friends. They were so disbelieving when we first told them the news and so shocked when we convinced them we weren't kidding. We laughed a lot. It somehow seemed funny. We were the focus of many conversations. Spontaneous triplets had made us fertility stars in a group of friends and relatives that had more than one couple in invitro programs trying to conceive. The trouble is that on the path, our family of five became a family of four. Only Alix and Maxine survived. Sarah died.

It's a long way from 12-week-old embryos and the excitement of incredible news to 40 weeks and the birth of 6-lb. babies that are pink and fat and can breathe on their own. Twenty-nine weeks is a tough burden for a little baby to carry, and 29 weeks is when our three had to make it on their own. Two days after my girls were delivered, Sarah had a large brain bleed, went downhill fast, made a slight recovery, lost it again, and died. I remember where I was when Jan called me and told me to come to the hospital. Sarah was in trouble. I was at work renovating a house, not worrying about anything, feeling confident that everything was under control. What could go wrong, now that the babies had been delivered? As I left the job site and made the short drive to the hospital, something was changing. Dread rose from the pit of my stomach. I came to the sinks at the door of the NICU and quickly washed my hands. I walked though the door backwards and looked toward the desk with panic and worry. I saw the look of sadness and sympathy from the nurse. Sarah's isolette, visible from the entrance, was surrounded by doctors and nurses. I don't know how many, I just know I couldn't see my baby, or even the isolette. I had to walk away from Sarah to a small private room in the corner of the NICU where Jan already was. Our tears began to flow. Our short vigil began.

I was unsuspecting when I went to work that morning. I didn't understand the struggle these small babies make to keep going.

They lie in their isolettes, a subconscious will to live pushing them forward. They take breaths on their own when they can. They digest the milk we give them through tubes, when an umbilical cord would be better. They control all systems with an imperfect determination. With the help of a caring group of medical professionals that know so much about helping these kids survive, they begin to make their way in the world. But for me, things had changed. I lost my confidence. My daughters were sick.

Three hours after I arrived at the hospital, Jan and I were holding each other waiting to see Sarah's body. There was nothing anyone could have done to help her.

Sarah's brain had been profoundly damaged. She was unable to survive. The nurse that had been with Sarah that morning when her problems began brought her to us. She was dressed in a small white christening gown that spoke of a more complex life than she had had. As soon as we were alone with her, without speaking, Jan and I began to take her clothes off. We felt compelled to look at Sarah, as she was when she was born, untouched by machines, untouched by clothes, simply naked and innocent. She was beautiful, her features not masked by full-term fat, or a trip down the birth canal. Slender, graceful arms and hands, perfect legs and feet. Her face looked a little like Jan's side of the family. The Liberto nose. We held Sarah gently and cried. She was just a little baby. We carefully put Sarah's clothes back on, making her look like part of a world she had never belonged to. Such a short life. Gone before it started. Our sadness was coming from thoughts of what might have been, not from things that had been. You can't give such a little person a life they didn't have, can't grieve for the things they haven't done when they haven't done anything. I grieve because Sarah was on the path with us and is now gone. I had a picture in my head of what these three girls would look like standing in our backyard, and now one spot is empty.

Jan and I were living two lives. A life of hope and love and positive energy when we were in the NICU with Alix and Maxine, and a life of sadness when we were in Jan's hospital room alone. It just wasn't supposed to be like this; we were supposed to have three babies. I guess this is what the doctors meant by high risk. You arrive in the situation naïve, and if things go well, you leave naïve because the people helping you through keep a positive power about them. It's only when things go wrong that you can see how fragile the strings are that hold these babies to us. We were overloaded with emotions, but the important thing was to keep connected to Maxine and Alix. We spent as much time in the NICU as we could, just being with them, hoping the power of life would carry them forward. I'm sure we felt a lot closer to the edge than lots of parents that had children in the NICU. We started with three isolettes to visit, and then we had two. When we left the NICU with Maxine and Alix, our thoughts turned to Sarah and that sadness hung on us. We would rest in our hospital room, emotions numb from the emotional roller-coaster we were on. Jan also had the extra load of pumping breastmilk for Alix and Maxine, and recovering from the cesarean. The first bit of relief from the numbing first week of parenthood came when Jan was able to leave the hospital and we were home again. Just being away from the room where Jan and I shed so many tears was good. The world was bigger now, not institutional 24 hours a day. Maxine and Alix began to make small gains, which gave us back a little confidence.

Something else that helped was my brothers visiting from Vancouver. First, Warren and his wife, Diane came for a week, then Brent and his wife, Denise. It was so nice not to be alone, to share the fears that Jan and I had, and also to share the progress as Maxine and Alix's age climbed into their 30s — measured in weeks. It also gave them a better understanding of the babies' situation, to stand at an isolette and watch them breathe. There's a calm but vigilant air about the NICU: closely watched young babies breathing in stops and starts, the more relaxed attitude about the babies who are about to graduate to Level 2 care. It was Denise who looked at me one day when we were beside Alix and said, "These kids are really sick, aren't they?" We stay positive and celebrate each gram they add to their body weight.

As the days passed, I talk to Jan, my brothers and my friends about what happened to Sarah and how Alix and Maxine were doing. I realize that part of me has to cling to the time when the three girls were with Jan, before their birth. And as one-sided as that relationship might be, it's the only time there were five of us and everyone was healthy and happy. I love telling the story about us finding out we were having triplets, or how the ultrasound technician, not letting on that there were three babies, rushed us out of the office and dashed for the phone to tell our doctor the news. Or the time spent planning and laughing, and wondering what life would be like with them. "Wouldn't it be wild if they're identical and we can't tell them apart," we would say. We used to lay on the bed and contemplate where the babies were placed on the globe that was Jan's tummy, and try and think of names. It's a good thing they were girls since we had so many names picked out.

This was my relationship with Sarah. I couldn't hold her or touch her during the time I spent with her, but I loved her. She is a part of our family. If Sarah's early death did anything, it made me focus on the moments she was alive. These are moments I'm not sure I would remember very well if the outcome had been happier. I reach within myself to feel the few hours I spent with her after she was born, and the 29 weeks when she was within Jan. This is my time with her, and this short piece of time means so much to me.

finding strength in the memory of my son
Janet Hardy

I can't say his death is getting any easier — just that we are getting stronger

I can tell you for certain that May 27, 1995, was a warm, sunny day. My boys went for a bike ride that afternoon and asked to go again after supper. My husband, Blair was on his way to go fishing in New Brunswick. I let the boys go again, and watched as they came home later that evening, one by one. I saw Craig cross the dirt road in front of our house. I turned to speak to a repair man, who was just leaving, and then, suddenly, our world came crashing down. Craig was struck by a truck and killed. This was a nightmare. How could this happen? I fought so hard to carry them as long as I could through my pregnancy and now at age seven, one of my beautiful children was lost. Craig had the most beautiful smile. People said God loved his smile and knew how special he was, and that's why he was chosen.

losing a child

We had to plan a funeral for our little boy. It was the hardest thing we have ever faced. Blair said, "I never thought I would be burying one of my boys." We now have an emptiness in our hearts when we see all the boys together. Craig still and always will hold a special part of us together. We are learning to cope with the loss of a son. I can't say it is getting easier, just that we are getting stronger. His last school picture was beautiful, probably the best. We had it put on his tombstone for all to see.

Craig's death was very hard on our other boys, but especially Alex. He had shared a room with Craig for years. Brad and Darren moved in with Alex for a while. We took them (and us) to a therapist for help. But they weren't ready to talk. Now they talk about Craig, but not about the accident. They talk about his funny stories, since he always had one to tell. He was always there to lend a hand to anyone. Craig was special to me — he was my helper. He was my strength, and still is through his memory.

Every Christmas season, we buy a wreath for our front door. Then on Christmas Day, we all go together to place the wreath on his grave. Our family will never forget the son we lost. We miss him and love him very much. For those who have a child, cherish them with care. Love them every moment and show them how much you care.

supporting
a grieving mom
Valerie Powers

Guilt-ridden and retreating to cliches, I struggled to find a way to help a mother whose babies had died

During my pregnancy with triplets, my husband and I felt alone in this new world of multiples, of which we knew very little. Our family physician referred me to an obstetrician as though I had contracted some rare disease. There was just one other family that we knew of who had triplets, but they were just coming home from hospital and needed more support than I did. That's when I vowed I would always make time for new families so they wouldn't feel the same as we did.

In May 1994, my chance to make someone feel secure and accepted (my goal as a support person) finally came. Loretta was about 15 weeks pregnant with three girls who were due in November. We talked every week and became close friends. If there was a question I couldn't answer, I referred to our association and networks to find the answer so that Loretta could feel reassured knowing that answers and help were available.

Most of the questions I had anticipated because I wanted the same answers myself while I was in her position. Truth be told, I think I provided great support. At 25 weeks, Loretta was hemorrhaging and admitted to our local hospital. The labour stopped only to start again within 24 hours. She delivered three girls Dana, Isabell and Leah. Dana and Isabell died within 24 hours and Leah was on shaky ground.

What do I say? What must she feel? How do I feel? Questions to which I had no answers. Her early delivery brought back my personal memories of my children's premature birth. But losing not one, but two babies — the thought was inconceivable. I told her it was meant to be (how lame); just what she wanted to hear. I told her that the two died to save the third. All my advice was very logical but did it help her? No. I wasn't doing what my gut instincts told me to do. So I gave up trying to explain why but started to focus on her. I put myself in Loretta's position (the best way I could)

481

and felt what I thought she must be feeling and I cried many times. Then guilt began to gnaw at me. My children were alive, well and thriving. My next instinct was to stay away and break off all contact out of fear she would resent me.

I was afraid to call but more afraid of not calling

Did she feel that way? The next few months were filled with good and bad weeks. I so wanted baby Leah to survive! I was afraid to call but more afraid of not calling. What would become of Loretta if I abandoned her at that point? How will I handle it? I witnessed her pain, joys and little hurdles first hand but was not quite able to feel the anguish. Was I really helpful or was I a constant reminder of how life might have been? In preparing to write this story, I called Loretta and asked her permission. More than two years have passed since our first contact. We usually speak to each other three or four times a year, on birthdays, Christmas, in summer and fall, but our last conversation was very different. We talked about how things would have been. She wondered what her life would have been like with triplets. Revisiting our experience together has eased some of the mutual pain. Time allowed us to ask and answer questions that neither dared to ask before. Our phone calls have become more frequent and our positions are now laid out. I no longer feel guilt. I won't ever hesitate to call for fear she may not want to talk to me. A new door has been opened.

Since then I've been a support to two other families. Once again, there was another very sad loss and one very happy outcome. But the second journey down fate's lane was easier for me to find appropriate ways of lending support. But no loss is any less painful.

grief and loss
Eunice Gorman, Diane Savage, Diane Schaller

Loss of a baby (or babies) in pregnancy, during labour and delivery, or in the newborn period, can happen whether they were conceived spontaneously or through assisted reproductive technology. It also occurs as a result of fetal reduction. Your own need for information and support will be different depending on your history, cultural/religious background and personality. As with any grieving process, individual reactions vary greatly. There is never a right time or right way to grieve. The following information represents some common feelings women and their families may experience, but it may not reflect how you feel.

Prenatal
Loss of a multiple during the antenatal period can be frightening. Having mixed feelings is not at all unusual. Many women will have experienced a previous pregnancy loss and the reminders during this stressful time may be powerful.

Common reactions following the loss of a multiple in pregnancy include:
- Fears about the well-being of the remaining babies
- Fears about your own health and the impact of carrying a dead baby/babies
- Guilt
- Numbness, anger and denial
- Fear of becoming attached to the remaining babies
- Too worried to be hopeful
- A deferral of grief and sadness
- Negation of loss from family and friends
- Secrecy about the number of babies

Fears about causing harm to mother or baby/babies
Some women are acutely sensitive to the physical sensation and/or psychological images of their dead baby/babies inside them. They worry about this being unhealthy, and have thoughts and even dreams about what the baby may look like at the time of delivery.

You may find yourself wondering whether you will want to see your baby that has died. You may even be informed that burial or cremation arrangements will be necessary, depending on the gestational age of the baby at the time of death, and the legal requirements where you live.

What may help

Physicians can reassure you of the risks you have and can address your questions about the impact of loss for your remaining babies. Sometimes taking the opportunity to see your baby that has died provides a sense of comfort.

Guilt and sadness

Feelings of guilt may be related to your hope that the remaining babies survive. You may also feel guilty for protecting yourself from further grief and not allowing yourself to get too close to the babies. Efforts to postpone attachment until after amniocentesis or other test results are common. If you have experienced a previous pregnancy loss, you may try to hold back until you have passed the gestation of your other loss (losses). Sometimes, people can feel totally unprepared when their babies actually do arrive, having been able to focus only on staying pregnant.

What may help

It can be helpful to realize that your feelings are quite normal. You may be experiencing two things at once: grief for your baby/babies that died, and a need to focus on the rest of your pregnancy. Talking and planning for some of the bereavement issues you will be faced with may make it easier to then put some of those feelings aside for the time being.

This is often when people begin to deal with the question of how many babies there are going to be in the family story. If there were triplets and one baby died, many parents find it comforting to acknowledge that there were three babies and to continue talking about the pregnancy in those terms.

Friends and family

Well-meaning family and friends do not want to see their loved ones sad and upset about any loss. They may handle this by not asking questions, by offering platitudes such as, "It's all for the best. At least you have one, two, three." They may also worry that openly grieving may cause harm to you or the babies. Grandparents may be experiencing their own feelings of loss as well as worry for their own children.

What may help

Talk with family and friends about what you are experiencing and try to be honest with them about what they can do to be helpful during this time. If you are on bedrest, be willing to accept offers to help with meals and housekeeping. If you are finding it helpful to talk about the baby(s) that has died, seek out family, friends, or professional supports that will listen.

Pregnancy reduction

In some settings, pregnancy reduction is available to those who would like to try and lower the risks to remaining babies. If you have made this decision, you are likely to experience any and all of the following feelings. You may have experienced a previous pregnancy loss and have found the decision to go through a reduction very complex. You may find your feelings about the baby(s) that has died to be very confusing, and may be less inclined to acknowledge the full number of babies for fear of being judged or misunderstood. As well, perinatal centres do not always offer the same supports to families in this situation.

What may help

Recognize that the loss of a baby, no matter the circumstance, has an impact on you and your family. If you have feelings of grief and sadness, find a way to address them, even in your own private way as individuals or partners.

If you would like to be able to talk openly with family and friends but are uncertain how they might respond, it is sufficient to explain that one or more baby/babies has died in utero.

In hospital

Knowing that one or more of your babies has died prior to the actual delivery can make the birthing experience one of conflicted emotions. Some parents report feeling only sorrow for the baby/babies that died and find their thoughts preoccupied with their loss. Other parents may find they focus on their living babies until they are assured that they are well and out of danger. Still others find their grief delayed by a few years as they adjust to life at home caring for those babies that did live. Parents may also be grieving the loss of the prestige of having multiple babies.

Similar emotions can be expected if the death of a multiple occurs at birth or in the newborn period. Some parents report a tugging back and forth between loving and celebrating the life that lives and grieving the life that is lost. Consequently, parents may feel they are only doing "half" a job dealing with either emotion. If the baby/babies that lives remains critically ill in intensive care, some parents may find it difficult to bond for fear that the baby will die too. Emotionally, parents may feel numb and overwhelmed, alternating between celebrating and grieving. They may also feel guilty and responsible for their babies' death in some way. They may also feel ambivalent. Through all these feelings, mothers are also experiencing the physical and hormonal changes that come with giving birth.

Parents who have one child in the hospital and another at home may find it a challenge to balance their time between both places. If the hospitalized child dies, some parents may feel an increased intensity in their feelings of guilt of not being there for their baby. For some parents, the loss of a baby from a multiple pregnancy may come after years of infertility. For parents where all the babies from a multiple gestation pregnancy die, the grieving for so many lives at the same time may be overwhelming. Given the intense mix of emotions and varied scenarios, a family may find this initial period not to be the ideal time to make a permanent decision about the future. As survivors reach landmarks in their development such as being discharged home or baptized, parents may feel sorrow again for the baby/babies that died and joy for the life they do have. Finally, almost all parents feel discomfort in labelling their family in terms of the number of survivors since it would not acknowledge the baby/babies that died, or that they are in fact twins, triplets, etc.

Affirming your babies

Whether your babies die prior to or at delivery or in the newborn period, you may find it helpful to plan ways to acknowledge each of their lives and the unique experience of a multiple gestation pregnancy. Spend time, see, hold and name your baby/babies that died. Take photographs of your babies both together and separately and photograph or videotape yourself holding the deceased baby/babies. Hand and footprint impressions using an inkpad and recipe card or plaster molds can be taken of all the babies. Some parents keep a clip of hair as a keepsake. Ultrasound reports and any other tangible evidence of the babies together are another option. Having tangible momentos of all your babies together as well as individually can help to separate the confusing and conflicting experience of their birth and death. Sometimes, a photograph, or a composition of all the babies may be a possibility using newer computer technology or by having an artist sketch a portrait.

Many parents choose to bury their multiple birth children together. If the living babies are critically ill, some parents delay the funeral of the deceased baby/babies until they are certain the others survive. Waiting leaves open the option of burying the babies together should one or the others die also.

Determining your own way to acknowledge the babies that died and weave them into your family story both in the immediate period and over your lifetime is part of grieving your loss. If some of the multiples remain in the hospital, the name of their deceased sibling could be written on the crib cards. Photographs could be taken and placed in their incubators. This also alerts healthcare workers that these babies are triplets, quadruplets etc. Some parents may choose to send out joint birth and death notices. Keeping a journal of memories about the pregnancy, labour and delivery and how you felt holding each of your babies can create a remembrance both for you to acknowledge each baby as well as for those babies that live to remember their siblings.

Holidays and anniversary dates can also be periods of intensified grief. Your expected date of delivery, the day your babies were born on and died on, or shopping for birthday gifts and new clothes can be a reminder that there should have been more babies to shop for and celebrate with. Some parents continue with their traditional celebrations while other make changes such as separating anniversaries by a day or two to allow them to mourn their loss and celebrate without conflicting feelings. Still others opt for a vacation away from the immediate reminders of their loss.

Family and friends

Some parents may feel the need to go through the experience of labour and delivery and/or the death of their baby/babies in the hospital without the presence of their family and friends. Other parents may find it helpful to include family and friends into parts of the experience so they may also get to know the babies that died and feel a connection and understanding of the emotional trauma often experienced by the parents. The reaction of family and friends can vary from recognizing and acknowledging your loss to ignoring the babies that died and sending you messages that you need to focus on the living baby/babies. They may not be comfortable talking about the babies that died. When all of your babies die at birth, family and friends may feel as if they too are overwhelmed with the thought of losing so many lives at one time. Sometimes the people close to you are so relieved that the mother is okay physically that they may not be able to focus on anything else.

Family and friends may have expectations about how long you should grieve and when you should take care of any loose ends such as extra baby equipment. People around you may be pregnant themselves with either single babies or multiples. Perhaps you connected with another family expecting multiples earlier on in your pregnancy and their children survived. Coping with pregnant women, baby showers, and Mother's and Father's Day may intensify your feelings of grief. Distance may be a factor in how much an extended family can be supportive with their presence or their understanding of your loss. Overall, family and friends are often the main source of support for many families and as such can offer a much-needed listening ear or babysitting service that will allow you time to yourself away from your living babies. Family and friends can be invaluable in supporting you to find your own path or to find time for you and your partner to acknowledge each life. Remember that grieving the loss of your babies is important.

At home in the postnatal period

Once you are home, the reality of your loss may be brought painfully to the forefront. Friends and family may already be struggling with whether to talk about what you have experienced. There is pressure to focus on the baby/babies that you have, especially if they are premature or at risk for health problems. There may be concerns about work, finances, your relationship with your partner or the unique stresses of single parenting. Your other children may be grieving and/or reacting in ways that you might not have predicted. Friends may seem unsupportive with a subtle reminder that infertility treatments present higher risk for multiple births and therefore prematurity and miscarriage. Others may, in an attempt to be helpful, quickly dismantle the "extra" crib or put away all the clothing that won't be needed now. Still others will try to encourage you by saying that you still have the other baby/babies.

And in all of this, there is you and your partner. Both of you can cope in very different ways. Your partner may feel betrayed and that his or her chance for a "miracle" is gone. He or she may feel chosen and then "unchosen."

Partners may throw themselves into work or activity and want to become intimate again when all you feel is exhausted, ill and sleep deprived. They may speak of "trying again" while you may be feeling fearful and uncertain about the future and how you could cope with nine months of pregnancy again.

If you have other losses — previous infertility, other pregnancy losses, a less than ideal birthing experience or concurrent crises and losses within your family — your grief may be magnified. To delay, suppress, or deny your grief can ultimately cause further problems. The challenge, of course, is how to grieve when you are called upon to care for your surviving babies, when you are juggling feeding, diapering, transporting, bathing, carrying and loving. How do you take care of yourself and relationship when you have children who may be premature, have low birthweight or are at risk for physical disabilities? How do you cope with the chronic sorrow that may accompany the "last chance" pregnancy? How do you mourn when you have a surviving child/children who is being welcomed by relieved family because he or she is still with them? It is indeed a bittersweet time, but somehow you must find ways to:

- cry
- rest
- stay connected with friends or family
- eat
- go outside and walk
- pray, mediate — have faith

quote

You are struggling with two of life's greatest transitions at the same time — birth and death, attachment and grieving, love and sadness, hello and goodbye, celebrating life and mourning death

- read: self help books, shared experiences
- connect with a professional: clergy, public health nurse, social worker, doctor
- find someone who will listen and talk
- hope
- accept all forms of help: childcare, meals prepared by others
- lower the expectations on yourself
- take comfort in music or relaxation therapy
- enjoy comfort food
- write in a journal, write a letter to the lost baby/babies
- find a "drop in" for new mothers
- uses the baby's/babies' name when you talk about your family
- decrease or cut out use of alcohol
- feel: confused, hurt, bitter, disappointment, sad, lonely, disoriented, disorganization, grief, cheated, angry, blame, yearning, despair, exhaustion, denial, fear, uncertainty
- talk about the delivery, plans for your lost child/children
- get information on what happened
- ask for what you need
- get help if you feel resentful or upset with your surviving children and fear that you might harm them
- make it simple: cook in bulk, use disposables, don't bathe all the babies every day, "top and tail" instead
- find a support group, Internet sites, chat lines, telephone tree, newsletter or some other connection with others who have lost a child/children
- talk to your other children and make sure they don't secretly bear some guilt for the death of their sibling(s)
- do not idealize the dead baby so that the surviving children fear that the wrong child died
- consider combining a memorial for your lost baby/babies with the christening for those who lived
- create an immortality project in honour of your baby, plant a tree, create a scrapbook or memory book, have an "angel cake" at birthdays
- tell someone if you fear investing in your surviving babies in case they too die
- speak to someone if the loss of your child/children brings up issues from the past with your partner. (If your spouse was initial-

ly reluctant to have children, you may blame him, thinking he was somehow responsible for the death.)
- ask for help, if you are ill, exhausted, housebound, feel inadequate, isolated or overwhelmed
- recognize that many women report intense sadness, even depression at three months, six months and even three years after the loss
- understand that apprehension about future pregnancies is normal
- recognize that birthdays, anniversaries, holidays, hearing your lost child's name, or explaining your living children's status (i.e., surviving triplets) may always cause sad feelings to rise to the surface
- talk about the loss of your dreams for the lost baby

Death ends a life not a relationship.

19

individuality

what makes you so special?

Suzanne Lyons

The quest for individuality

In the two years since Andrew, Joel and Quentin were born, my husband and I have been asked literally hundreds of questions about what life is like with monozygotic (identical) triplets. "What did they weigh at birth? Are they healthy? Do they get along?" Of all the questions, I prefer the kind that I can answer fast — "Yes, they're a handful," or "Sure, they play well together," or "Yes, we have just the three children."

When the subject shifts to personality traits, as it invariably does with identical triplets, I'm less certain with a response. People say, "Well, they look alike, but they must have very different personalities. Who's the bold one? Who's the loudest and most demanding? Who's the most easygoing?" I have been asked these questions countless times and I still struggle with a response. "We'll see," is the standard response that gets me off the hook and through the grocery checkout counter. But, truthfully, I'm still not sure.

Have we found enough time to spend one-on-one?

These kinds of comments often leave me thinking about personality development and whether my husband and I have been able to dedicate enough one-on-one time and attention to each our sons. I wonder if one of the boys is more outgoing in certain situations and, in the chaos of day-to-day living, we just haven't noticed. I worry sometimes that we've missed some of the important subtleties in each of their characters that distinguish them. And by missing those differences, is it possible that we've failed to reinforce them?

From the start, it's been extremely important to my husband and me that our boys learn and grow as individuals first, while respecting the powerful and mystifying bond they share. But promoting individuality in a household of multiples can be more difficult than it sounds. The realities of scheduling in the early days often demand group feedings, assembly line bathing and group visits with grandparents. In later months, activities and outings are the same for the group whether or not one sibling would prefer to do something else. I realize this is also necessary for children of different ages in families, but conforming to the will of the group comes at a very early age for multiples.

Monozygotic siblings face greater challenges in asserting individuality

As near-mirror-images of one another, our children face an even greater challenge in establishing a distinct identity from the others and finding ways to be visually recognizable by family and friends. Dressing in identical outfits can make that challenge all the more difficult. The decision to dress your children in identical clothing is a personal one; however, conventional wisdom discourages it. Dressing in different clothing assumes, of course, that you do not have three stubborn 18-month-olds demanding to be dressed exactly the same way.

In this regard, we have been fortunate. Whenever, Andrew, Joel and Quentin received the same clothing as gifts, one of the boys invariably adopted all three identical outfits as his own. "No, all of

Batman™ tracksuits are mine!" This makes for less variety in his wardrobe but has helped reassure us that each of the boys is demonstrating individual preferences and, more importantly, a desire to distinguish himself from his brothers. I'm not sure if we have taught them to value their individuality or if they are naturally inclined to express themselves that way.

Being a parent is a process of discovery and surprises. My husband and I are not experts. And while I once believed that being a good parent meant that I should know everything there is to know about my children, I am now beginning to realize that there will be aspects about the boys that I'm not sure I will ever fully understand. For parents like me who grew up as single babies, the relationship among multiple children can be an enigma that's beyond comprehension, but is deserving of respect.

With parenting multiples comes a need to accept certain things. One of those is that one-to-one time between parent and child does not happen as often as we would like. But, when the opportunity does come up, it's an experience that is rarely taken for granted and always appreciated. I, for example, look forward to taking one of my sons to a regular doctor's appointment. As others in the specialist's office grumble about waiting one, two or sometimes three hours, we chat happily without interruption about the many thoughts and surprising observations only a two-year-old can make. It's precious time that allows me to get to know him and how he views the world with greater understanding.

I'm always trying to find ways to spend similar time with my other sons, but admittedly, it doesn't happen often. I'm not as concerned as I once was about making the time because I know I am conscious of the issue of individuality. I hope that even a few minutes of individual attention spent day-to-day, or making an effort to listen and respond appropriately to each of the boys' comments in a chorus of conversation can send an important message that each child is important. It's my hope that by recognizing and treating the boys as individuals in small ways, we'll help foster their development into well-rounded and independent adults.

identical? no, but we can't tell them apart

Mary Anne Moser

It was easy to get our boys mixed up as newborns, especially when they were snuggled in their bunting bags and only their tiny faces peeped out. Before they were born, we knew they each had their own placenta and their own sac. So how could the two boys in our set of triplets possibly be monozygotic (identical)? We were in denial for many months. Hey, we insisted, many singletons would probably look this alike if they were seen together at the same age. Besides, we knew three embryos had been implanted.

Through the Multiple Births Association, we learned about a doctor doing a study of twinning who offered DNA testing for multiples for only $100 (normally this test would cost well over $500). Knowing it could take months to get the results, we settled into our comfortable state of denial once again. How could it be that we needed a laboratory test to tell us if our boys were monozygotic? It was because we did not want them to be, but I think we knew all along that they were. When the letter arrived in the mail, I anxiously waited for my husband to come home before opening it. Together, we looked at the first sheet, "dizygotic." I threw my hands in the air with a yelp of joy. "No, wait," my husband said. "That was the test result for Grace." Not a surprising result, since she was our one girl. So we turned the page to find the results for the two boys. Monozygotic. I could actually feel my spirits sink.

Why did it matter? The black cloud that hung over me that day was annoying because it was fruitless. I delved into my books, especially the ones on twins, which suddenly seemed more relevant than they did when I thought of our kids as simply non-identical triplets. By the end of my reading session, I felt a lot better again. Basically, I concluded, that it doesn't make any difference if they are mono- or dizygotic. They are individuals, and we would have treated them the same way in either case. The only difference may be that we will be treated to little surprises, when genetically influenced traits or behaviours are expressed. And that was that.

I am glad we did not know right from the start. The volume of babies overwhelmed us, and I am afraid that the thought of having "identicals" in the group would have further confused my already mixed emotions. We were not happy to get the news that we were having triplets, but during the course of the pregnancy, we came to see it as a wonderful and exciting proposition. Once they were born, in response to the stress, we fell back to our first position that we did not want three babies. In fact, my husband had gone back to his position that he did not want any babies. So it would not have been a good time to know that we had two versions of the same child.

Of course, it is ludicrous now to even think of our two one-year-old boys as being duplicate copies. While they look alike, they are certainly individuals. At that newborn stage, however, we had yet to see them that way. Our transition from seeing them as copies to seeing them as individuals has made me laugh in the face of the cloning debate. Our children are as unpredictably different as they are unpredictably similar.

Having monozygotic twins in a set of triplets added another layer of interest to our already delightful family life. While I did not see it as a positive aspect at first, I have come to see it as wonderfully intriguing. From a "selfish gene" point of view, it is quite clever to have "identical" twins. (Of course, we orchestrated it.) And it adds another topic to my expanding list of interests, which I appreciate. Lately I have been reading about birth order and its possible influence on personality and preferences. While I do not think there is any clear-cut relationship between all these things, it is clear that with multiples, the age factor is eliminated as one obvious means by which children find their niche within the family. With monozygotic multiples, some other inborn differences may also be eliminated. But as they all grow and develop, differences will emerge. Given the room and support to discover their identities, we believe they will do so quite ably.

Some children may find they can attract more attention as half of a pair rather than as distinct individuals. It is easy to see how this could happen. There is something awfully cute about the doubling effect. However, since it is unlikely that they will be content as adults to be seen only part of an identical pair, we have decided to set them on paths as their own people and to let their similarities and differences play themselves out against this foundation.

four very special individuals

Mary Gallagher

It is so easy to get caught up in the fact that our children are quadruplets. But somewhere in that foursome are four very special individuals, each with different needs and talents.

Now that our children are four-year-olds, their differences are becoming increasingly apparent. I think my biggest fault is comparing them to each other. It just amazes me how four very different babies could be born at the same time from my body.

They each have different learning abilities, talents, tastes in clothes (already), personalities, looks and very unique needs and wants out of life. Katie has shown us her wonderful talent for art and writing, but still has difficulty getting dressed by herself. Emma just adores ballet and loves feminine and pretty things, but she still has difficulty reading and writing. Louise is very good at reading and doing puzzles and has an extraordinary memory, yet the slightest thing can set her off in a temper. Michael has shown us that being a boy is inborn and not learned. He loves sports and riding his bike and identifies so much with his Daddy.

My husband and I have tried our very best to encourage our children to be the best they can be and to always try without fear of making mistakes. But they compete with each other and sometimes that competition leads to lack of confidence and frustration.

Not unlike other multiple siblings, our foursome has a leader, Katie. With a strong, outgoing personality, she often assumes authority over the other three, becoming the boss, the decision-maker and the bully. Emma, the shy, quiet one, has allowed Katie to dominate her from a very early age. As parents who have believed in promoting individuality from the beginning, our biggest hurdle was to prevent Katie from answering every question for Emma. Emma now gets very angry and frustrated with Katie whenever she tries to take over, which has led to a very tense relationship between them.

When the children started junior kindergarten, we placed them all in the same class since I felt that they were not ready to be separated. I think it was more of a maternal response rather than reality. The children have really enjoyed school and are developing well but

quote

Last Christmas, we started a tradition. Each child goes on a special outing with a parent of their choice to a place of their choice. That's our gift to each other

they have found it difficult to separate into their own group of friends. In class, they mainly played together and would basically stand and stare at other children, their own age, playing together. Michael and Emma became very good buddies in kindergarten, creating major disruptions in the classroom and neglecting their projects. At home, we saw reflections of their classroom relationship. Whenever they played together, the duo would unwittingly cause destruction and chaos. By the end of that year, their teacher and I came to a decision that Michael and Emma should be split up for the following year. We also decided to keep Emma and Katie apart to give Emma a boost of confidence in the classroom outside the shadow of Katie. Over the year in senior kindergarten, I have seen each

of them begin to interact individually with the other children at their own paces.

Spending time with the children individually is very important but very difficult to accomplish through all the chaos of the day. Our children take turns going to the grocery store with me or to the mall. I try to make our outings a little special. They know there's a small treat in store.

When the girls were younger, I never dressed them in identical clothing except for very special occasions. Even then, the clothes were similar and not identical. Many items of clothing were shared among the three girls since they are the same size, but as they have got older, they each began to suit different styles. Now I buy clothes with a certain daughter in mind. They just love having their own clothes.

Last Christmas we decided to give each of our children a special day out with the parent of their choice to a place of their choice. We usually buy a special gift for each of them at Christmas to add to Santa's gifts, but they never seemed to appreciate it. So this year, we decided to give them something they would always remember. Each day was so special!

Katie chose to go out to dinner to a "big restaurant" with Mommy and then to the movies afterward. We went for a lovely meal, which I enjoyed, but she didn't touch. But we had lovely conversations and a wonderful time together. After our movie, I bought her a special piggy bank as a souvenir, which she is so proud of!

Emma chose to go to "see the ballerinas" with Mommy, so I took her to the ballet. She was so excited the whole time she was there and we both loved the show. As a special gift, she got a beautiful silver necklace with ballet slippers on it, which she still treasures.

Michael, of course, wanted to go "somewhere with Daddy." So Daddy took him to see a professional basketball game. They both had dinner before the game and came home with a snazzy baseball cap to remember the evening. What a great time they both had!

Louise wanted to see a special ice show with Daddy and took home a cartoon mug as her special gift. They both had a very special time together.

Those gifts were just as special for us as they were for them. They still talk about their "special day out." We hope we can continue to have Christmases like this for many years to come.

And I hope that through their childhood years, I can focus on their personal needs and help them recognize their own individuality. I will try to guide them toward self-confidence and allow separation from their siblings to be a gradual process, but only when they are each ready to do so.

odd-man out
Bracha Mirsky

Two of them acted as though they were on the same frequency, while the other was exasperated by the nonsense

Since every person and family situation is unique, not everyone will experience what I call the odd-man-out syndrome. But you should be watching for it.

What is the odd-one-out? In higher order multiples birth children, it means that one of the group is alienated. Note that perception is everything with this. It is my belief that as a parent of triplets you must watch and intervene if you notice a trend. We all know we cannot make everything "perfect" for our children, nor should we, but if one child feels snubbed by his/her multiple birth siblings, it can be very traumatic and difficult to understand. Parental support and encouragement will go a long way.

When our triplets were about eight years old, they were able to play board games without adult help. This was a great love of theirs. As the novelty wore off, these games quickly became a source of frustration and tears for Yossi. Through deeply felt tears, he repeatedly accused his brother and sister of ruining the games. After carefully keeping my eye on their exchanges, this is what I learned. Yossi took the game very seriously. He had the ability to understand the importance of a strategy and was more mature in many ways than his brother and sister. He could maintain his concentration on the game longer, while they became bored and began acting silly together. Rochel and Aharon were not malicious in their behaviour, but the two of them acted like they were on the same frequency, finding the same things funny and so on. Yossi acted like a little scientist looking deeper into the world around him.

They weren't ganging up against him. Yossi had pulled away and matured beyond them. A gap now existed, and it would leave a mark on their relationship. I could not make Rochel and Aharon mature quicker, nor could I teach Yossi to be any less mature.

It was very hard on him, but by explaining the situation as I saw it and trying to meet Yossi's needs, I hoped to ease his pain and keep the love and closeness among the siblings strong. As children grow older, the competition increases. Sometimes hurtful words and actions can be tossed back and forth. I make it clear what is allowed and what is not. You may not have to share, but you cannot insult! You must allow another to join a game or the game will be removed. Physical violence is not tolerated at any level. (Boys do tussle, which is different.)

As the triplets hit their "tween" years, they became divided along gender lines. It was the boys against the girl. That was hard for Rochel, but again, she was not left alone. She had parental support and understanding. The boys were curtailed in what could become relentless teasing. And Rochel was encouraged so that she could bear some teasing in good grace and not be pulled into battles she could not win. All of my children were taught that the only person he or she can control is himself or herself. If they allow another person to control them (by teasing, making them sad or angry), then they control nothing in their lives.

Eventually this phase passed as well. The "teens" united on common ground — they shared a sense of independence, taste in music and the ability to see each other as potential allies against a common foe — their parents. Good luck!

20

a word from
the experts

my life as a quadruplet
Alison Myers, age 7

My name is Alison Myers and I am a quadruplet. We were born at 27 weeks gestation. I have one big brother, Craig, who is eight years old, and one little brother, Mac, who is five years old. I am seven years old and I am one of the quads. Harrison, Jessica and Kenny are the other quads. Harrison has a hearing problem and I have cerebral palsy. When I was born, I was two pounds and six ounces.

I share my room with Jessica. Kenny shares his room with Harrison and Craig shares his room with Mac.

On weekends, Mommy is a lazy head. Mommy washes almost 100 clothes a day.

We all go to school. I am in Grade 2. Craig is in Grade 4 and Mac is in kindergarten.

I have one sister and four brothers and they all are big pests. Harrison, Kenny and Mac are very funny. My favourite colour is yellow. Jessica's favourite colour is purple. Kenny's favourite colour is green. Harrison's favourite colour is red, and so is Craig's. Mac's favourite colour is blue. We have some video games. Craig rocks at them and I suck at them. My favourite things to do are art. Sometimes reading and writing.

growing up as a triplet
Sandra Tibbo

quote

I don't remember feeling we were different from other families

What is it like to grow up as one of triplet siblings? At one time, my first response to this question was to think that my life was just like millions of other people's lives. Why would it be any different? I still believe this is true, but I also recognize there were differences and challenges that our family faced that I can appreciate now as an adult. As a child, I either didn't notice or accepted them as part of life. Recently I've spoken to "the other two" and my father about their memories of our early years. Unfortunately, our mother, to whom I give most credit for our feelings of normalcy, died many years ago.

The big event took place on July 8, 1960, in St. John's, Nfld. My mother, who was 39 years old, delivered three near-term babies through natural childbirth. Together, two girls and a boy weighed just over 16 pounds. My brother weighed 5 lb. 6 oz., my sister 5 lb. 6 oz. and I was the bully at 6 lb. 7 oz.

From what I've been told about the early years, there was a lot of work without government subsidies, extra help, free diapers or anything else. My mother said that she never slept in the first year. We were bottlefed, with bottles propped. Her biggest fear was that we would come down with an illness and that she wouldn't be able to cope with three sick babies. She also voiced her frustration about people wanting to touch us, especially our hands, as this was another way that we could come into contact with germs. Thankfully, we did pass through these years without any major illnesses.

Our school years were typical. Our elementary and junior high schools had three classes of each grade so that from Grade 3 onward, we were separated, until certain classes in junior high where there was some overlapping, which we were not particularly fond of. It was only the occasional person who couldn't (or wouldn't) remember "which one" we were, even though my sister and I are not identical. Personally, the part of life that annoyed me the most was being stared at. Whenever we were out together, people stared and sighed, "How cute."

Life at home for us was quite typical. There was a lot of "sibling rivalry," and I mean a lot! It seemed there was always a squabble of some sort. Any game that started in fun ended in a fight. Our mother handled this by yelling and grinding her teeth. Her response intimidated us as children, but as we got a little older, it actually became quite funny. When I asked her why we were never spanked (I'd heard in the neighbourhood that other children were) she said that it was because she was afraid if she ever started she might never stop. As a mother myself now, I can appreciate her self-control.

We were to be treated equally. Even the cherry in a can of fruit cocktail was divided into three

One strict rule in our home was that we were to be treated equally. There was absolutely no preferential treatment — even the cherry in a can of fruit cocktail was divided into three! When a visitor bearing gifts decided to give my brother a little something extra, he was informed that we were to be treated alike. I can't explain why, but I remember feeling very comforted by this idea. Because friends sometimes found it difficult to deal with gift giving on such special occasions as birthdays, these events usually were family affairs. Our only really big blast was our eighth birthday, when we turned eight on the eighth of the month. A big celebration was in order that year.

When it was time for high school, I made my big break, announcing that I didn't want to be one of the triplets any longer, so I set off to a different high school. By this time, we each had different friends, although my sister and I spent a lot of time together with common friends. From this point, we seemed to drift into three separate lives, which is fine because we were, and continue to be, three very different people. Today, we are separated geographically, but we keep in touch.

As an adult, it is obvious to me that people do not plan or expect to become the parents of triplets. To my parents' credit, I cannot remember ever feeling that we were different from any other family, with the exception of our birthdays. We were treated as three individuals with no expectations that we would be alike because we were born together. As a parent I now have some insight into the challenges they faced. And I can now appreciate the time, effort, work and patience that must have been involved.

breaking away
Maria Noussis

Finding our identity was a struggle for us

I am the second of three lucky deals born in Toronto in 1975. Until now, I never imagined I would have an opportunity to write about my experience as a multiple. As the story begins, my parents, Helen and Jim, aimed for a third child to add to their family. As it turned out, there are five of us now in total.

The three of us were born full term at approximately 40 weeks. Elizabeth, the first born, weighed 5 lb. 5 oz., I was 4 lb. 5 oz. and Nicolas weighed 3 lb. 5 oz. He remained in an incubator for two or three months. When we came home, the government provided a nurse for about a month, an arbitrary time period obviously decided upon by someone who had no experience with multiples.

When we were born, my eldest sibling, Steven, was only three years old, and my sister Mia was just a year and a half. Five little "monsters" running around with the help of a nurse for only a month seems a little ridiculous. If it wasn't for my grandmother helping full time back then, I'm not sure how my mother would have handled the situation. Soon, having my grandmother's help wasn't enough. Once the nurse left, my father arranged for our grandmother's sister to fly in from Greece. She stayed for about a year. When she went back home, my favourite aunt came out to lend a pair of hands to our family for yet another year.

When I was asked to write about my experience as a multiple, the first thing that came to mind was the nuisance of not being regarded as an individual, even though Nicholas, obviously a boy, has no resemblance to Lisa and me. He closely resembles my father. We identical girls resemble our mother. Lisa and I dressed alike, and continued to do so out of our own free will well into our teenage years.

Looking back, I see that was a big mistake. When it came time to graduate from high school, we struggled to find our own identities.

Lisa and I are extremely close. I believe that only multiples can understand the close-knit bond we share. But closeness can lead to confrontation. For some, it can even lead to resentment and envy. Based on my experience, I firmly believe that identical multiples should not be dressed alike at an early age. Individuality should be instilled right from the moment of birth.

Others may disagree with me, and each is entitled to his or her own opinion. In fact, I have spoken to other multiples who would agree or disagree with me. There is no correct answer, only choices.

together and apart
Suzanne Lyons (for Jeff Jarvis)

"I never really thought of myself as being one of three. But we were very often together"

There is an amusing little story that Jeff Jarvis likes to tell when he's asked to describe the relationship he shares with identical triplet brother Greg. It happened many years ago, some time after the Second World War, when different jobs and family responsibilities had taken the three boys — Jeff, Greg and fraternal (dizygotic) brother Blair — in separate directions to separate lives.

"We stayed in touch, of course," Jeff, now 75, recalls, "but Greg was living in Vancouver and I was in Montreal, so we didn't meet face to face very often. One New Year's, when we were in our late 20s, we arranged to meet in Toronto to celebrate. I bought a new suit for the party and so did Greg. Wouldn't you know — we both arrived wearing exactly the same suit! So, I guess you could say we did share a connection that's quite uncanny. But I'm quite certain that if Greg fell down the stairs, I wouldn't feel the bumps on the way down."

Greg and Jeff did share a connection — both excelled academically, even had their appendixes removed on the same day when they were nine years old. What about brother Blair? "Oh, he was a little different," Jeff laughs. "He was a true athlete. I think there were many places he would have rather been than in high school. You know, as we were growing up, it never seemed to me that Blair felt left out in any way. But later as adults, I heard him mention that he did feel that way at times. I guess as a child, I never appreciated how he must have felt."

Born in Toronto in 1925, the Jarvis boys were the youngest in a family of six children that included two other boys, one of whom died very young in a flu epidemic, and one girl. "Our brother and sister were very good and kind to us," Jeff says. "Once when our older brother, John was taking a girl up to the lake for the day, he piled us into the back of the car. He would have been about 16, and we were 11. Well, the look on that girl's face as we pulled up to the driveway to pick her up for the date. Unforgettable!"

When they were very young, Jeff, Greg and Blair dressed alike, slept in the same room, played together and had relationships with many of the same friends. But soon, different interests took them in new directions.

"In those days, being a triplet was even more of a novelty, but I don't remember it as being top of our minds much. And it certainly wasn't onerous in any way," Jeff says. "Our parents treated us as independent children who simply happened to have been born together."

When Mrs. Jarvis went into labour, the doctor had been expecting to deliver twins, given her size. "My father said he would help lift her legs onto the bed while she was pregnant because she was so large. As the story goes, the doctor delivered two babies and left the delivery room, thinking the main event was over. Apparently, the nurses ran and called him back — when it became very obvious that things were definitely not over."

Both parents were happy, if not shaken, by the sudden addition of three babies. "When my father finally left the hospital, he walked outside into a very cold night. The car had been sitting for some time in the parking lot and wouldn't start, so my father dug into his pockets to fish out some money to take a cab home — he didn't have a cent with him. Back into the hospital he went, hoping to borrow a few dollars from the doctor. But the doctor had long since gone back to sleep, knowing he would have to be awake again soon to deliver another baby. So my father walked home — a good half hour in the blistering cold. As he arrived home from downtown Toronto to our home in north Rosedale, he was greeted by the housekeeper, and told her the news about the babies. He must have looked and sounded miserable after that walk because when she heard about the babies, the housekeeper tried to reassure our father by saying, 'Don't worry, Mr. Jarvis. They can't possibly survive.'"

But survive they did, born nearly full term and weighing more than five pounds each. Fortunately, none of the boys suffered exceptional health complications as babies or throughout their lives. After a period of time as young adults when distance separated them, eventually the Jarvises returned to the Toronto area, where they remained for 30 years. "We didn't live on each other's doorsteps, but we did stay in touch," Jeff says. "I think we managed to find a balance between the bond and our independence. I remember when I was teaching one year, there were two 19-year-old twin girls in my class. Both dressed exactly alike, looked alike and sat together all the time. I remembering feeling worried for them a bit."

Jeff is the last surviving triplet and delivered eulogies at both of his brother's funerals. "I felt good about doing that," he says quietly. "Through my life, I never really thought of myself as being one of three. But we were often together, until circumstances moved us apart."

the times of our lives
Barbara Jane Baker-Jardine

Valentine's Day of 1951 was rapidly approaching as the scene unfolded at Mount Hamilton Hospital. Mum was expecting again, and there was something unusual about this pregnancy, but nothing had been confirmed. There were complications with her first pregnancy, but it ended happily with Glenn, a healthy baby.

During a recent check-up, Mum's general practitioner, Dr. Fred Overend, thought that he could detect two fetal hearts, but it was possible that one was an echo in the amniotic fluid. Just to be certain, he booked an x-ray. That may seem unusual but of course, during those years, there were no fetal monitors or ultrasounds. All the doctor had was a stethoscope attached to a headband and his hands with which to palpate size, position, engagement and so on.

February 10, 1951

Mum never made the appointment because her membranes ruptured one night later at 11 p.m. — a full six weeks before "the baby" was due. Dad recalls dropping Mum off at the hospital and then going back home, since he had to work the next day at his pharmacy. The next morning at 6 a.m. labour began, catching the doctor, delivery nurses, dad Roy, extended family and the entire Niagara Peninsula off guard. No one could guess what was about to happen — nearly two months ahead of schedule God's plan was unveiled with the arrival of triplets; two sisters and a brother for Glenn. The support team was in place, and what a team it was! No sacrifice was too great, no obstacle insurmountable for the Baker team. We couldn't help but live, and thrive.

Mum had been given an anesthetic known as "laughing gas" that put her "out" for the delivery so she was blissfully unaware of the situation at hand. For in rapid succession a few minutes past 7 a.m., there was not one, not two, but three identical-looking black-haired, fragile babies, each estimated to weigh less than three pounds. Mum was sure that a teacup would fit over each of our heads. The first was named Bonnie Elizabeth, then me, Barbara Jane, and the third was a boy, the largest, but in the most critical condition. His name was Allan Edward.

Surely Dr. Overend was cursing the choice of anesthetic as he struggled to make Mum realize the reality of the situation at hand. The whole thing struck Mum as being very funny and she was unable to take the doctor seriously until the effects of the "laughing gas" wore off. He kept saying, while Mum laughed, "Mrs. Baker, this is serious. You have three very small babies who may not live." And she thought it hilarious that she only had a few diapers on hand. Poor Mum. Who could blame her? It wasn't her fault. I'm sure that she was shocked and maybe feeling sad that she had laughed at the wrong time. Mum has always had the greatest respect for and faith in Dr. Overend, and she knew that we were in the best of hands.

The hospital called Dad with the news and he was quoted as saying later, "You could blow me over with a feather." He was allowed to see us through the window, but not touch us. Dad went to several neighbours with the news and walked to work. Mum didn't see us for two days. We were not weighed at delivery by order of Dr. Overend until our conditions were assessed and stabilized. On day 10, we were weighed: Bonnie was 2 lb. 8 oz., I was 2 lb. 9 oz. while Allan was the heaviest at 2 lb. 11 oz.

The incubator was not like the incubators, or isolettes, of today. Back then, it was a rectangular metal-framed box with glass sides and top. To care for the baby inside, you had to lift the whole side of the incubator or the top lid. A rubber mattress lay on top of a metal frame that could be raised or lowered. The box stood on legs. There was a temperature dial plus a thermometer inside the incubator. Hospital nurses in the '70s referred to the incubators of the '50s as leftover "heaters." Each regular nursery usually had one heater plugged in at all times. Typically a baby was placed inside after delivery until he or she was warm enough to bathe. Then it was back inside the incubator, until the baby's temperature reached 36.5 C.

Since there were no portholes to minimize heat loss as a baby was being handled, the sick babies were handled infrequently. For some time, our bodies were covered with cotton balls to keep us warmer. For those who needed it, oxygen was pumped into the incubator through a tube connected to a large, white funnel positioned near the baby's mouth and nose.

Mum and Dad were not allowed to hold us until discharge. Bonnie asked Mum about how she found it possible to bond and develop a relationship with us. Mum assured Bonnie that she could and did.

February 12, 1951

Mum reported in a letter home to her mother and sister Lilian that "the babies haven't been washed yet, or dressed. Feedings for Bonnie and Barbara started yesterday, and Allan was to start feeding today. Allan is the weakest and holding his own, but the doctor doesn't seem too hopeful for them coming home soon. We have a very good doctor and I'm sure he is doing everything he can for them."

Our earliest feedings consisted of a sugar solution, administered by a small needle through the skin in the chest area. Tiny scars remain today as a reminder of this life-saving technique, which was a forerunner of intravenous lines later used to deliver nourishment.

The doctor was so unsure of our prognosis that on February 14, he came to the nursery with his camera. He snapped a black and white photograph of each of us lying in the incubator with oxygen funnels at our faces. A special Valentine's gift for Mum and Dad, I guess, just in case we didn't survive. We were very small, and breathing was difficult. All of us had respiratory distress syndrome but it was obvious that Allan was facing bigger problems after four days. Allan was born with a large depression in his chest area, caused by overcrowding and pressure from the other babies (possibly due to head positioning). He required forceps during delivery and signs of retardation were evident as he reached his second birthday. Since I can only speculate now, it also seems likely that his lungs were smaller and less developed. But Allan fought this courageous battle and won.

There was a second photo taken by Dr. Overend on March 10, 1951, and our conditions appeared to have improved. We no longer had oxygen funnels at our faces, but there appeared to be oxygen being pumped into the incubators. Yet we were filling out and looking good.

Mum told us that the doctors didn't know much about oxygen regulation and the risks to the eyes with prolonged use of concentrations above 40 per cent. We were fortunate not to have suffered any visual damage at the time, although we did eventually require glasses. Due to numerous ear infections and perforated eardrums, Bonnie and I developed severe hearing losses due to an overgrowth of scar tissue in the eustachian tubes. We received a series of cobalt treatments to eradicate that tissue, but we still suffer from minimal hearing loss.

Back at home, a small nursery was being prepared in blues and pinks and cheerful patterns of wallpaper borders. A friend of Dad's

a word from the experts

made a bassinet frame out of wood surrounded by a rail, so the three baskets couldn't be pulled onto the floor. In fact, these were wooden meat baskets lined and made cozy by Mum. A chest of drawers, a chair, and a laundry box completed the room. Eventually, our bassinet converted into a large wooden playpen for us.

Plans were made for Mum's mother Rose and youngest sister Laverne to come to Hamilton in the summer. A neighbour living behind the house who happened to be a registered nurse also offered to help out, especially during feedings and bath times.

March 31, 1951

According to a report in the local newspaper, we were discharged home from the hospital on March 31, 1951. Bonnie was weighed after being fed to ensure she had reached 5 pounds. Barbara was 5 lb. 3 oz., while Allan tipped the scales at a whopping 5 lb. 6 oz.

Behind these happy scenes apparently were some intense negotia-tions. The hospital refused to release us until the premature baby-care bills were paid. Dr. Overend worked out a deal that was satisfactory to both the hospital and our parents. The hospital kindly reduced the bill and for many years Mum and Dad signed over the baby bonus cheques monthly to the hospital, until the account was paid in full.

So home we went in the arms of some of Dad's family in a bor-rowed car, since we had no vehicle of our own. At home, we met one excited brother, Glenn. Visitors to the house were banned by order of Dr. Overend. Mum and Dad worked around the clock nursing us until we thrived. They spent most of the nights feeding us. Since we didn't know how to suck from a nipple when we came home, one feeding would often run into the next because we fed so slowly. Mum and Dad were exhausted. Dad was away from approximately 8:30 a.m. until 10 p.m. during the week, and got very little sleep at night before he would have to be back at work.

A few weeks later, our parents hired a woman to come in for night feedings, but I don't think that she lasted more than a shift or two. One night, it seems she somehow broke almost all of the bot-tles. Our neighbour, Arliss Hall (RN), came as often as she could, and Mum and Dad have always felt indebted to her. Since our family had no car, Mum felt especially housebound. The grocery store would deliver groceries and Woolcott's shoe store down on Concession Street brought our baby boots to the house to be fitted.

Dr. Overend came over to the house for check-ups carrying his black bag, but it would be very late at night when he was finally fin-ished for the day. He would tell Mum and Dad to leave the front door unlocked so that he could let himself in after they had gone to bed. He would get us up, undress us, check us over, redress us and tuck us all back into bed, and leave a note on the kitchen table. On the way out, he locked the front door behind him.

Our brother Glenn was just a very small toddler himself at two and a half years. He would drink the milk left in the bottles after our feedings, and he would carry a used diaper by the very tips of the corners to the diaper pail. He was a very good boy, but one day he threw sand in our faces as we lay in the carriages. Mum thought it a wonder that we weren't smothered.

We had two carriages. One was a borrowed double that held two babies side by side and the other was a single. Then the

Sunshine Company contacted Mum and Dad, expressing an interest in making a triple stroller for us. In return, they took photos of us sitting in the stroller on a cold day wearing the snowsuits that Mum had made. The picture, which appeared on the cover of their magazine, showed off a wide grey-chrome stroller with a large handle at the front. The unpadded seat was made of leather.

We also had a large wooden playpen that was large enough for the three of us. Mum remembered one year when the Christmas tree actually stood in the playpen to protect it. Our cribs had metal strips with our names on them, and for a period of time Bonnie and I wore small engraved wrist bracelets because we were so alike in appearance. One Sunday morning, Mum and a neighbour built a wooden bed for each of us while Dad was at church. One of the beds has stood the test of time and we still have it.

We all grew and thrived, and we were active playmates. We developed our own special language, which we all understood. We broke eggs one day when we got into the icebox. Once we could get out of our cribs, we sometimes got downstairs faster than Mum. Occasionally she would catch us playing in the toilet and eating the toilet tissue. When Mum had to go downstairs to the basement (perhaps to the washing machine) she would sit us in our highchairs and put corn syrup on our hands then put puffed wheat on our trays to amuse us.

To dry our clothes, there were either long lines outside or rows of lines strung up and down the front hallway. There were dozens of diapers hung out, and one washing machine wore out in a year under heavy daily use.

Our parents were struggling financially for many years, and Mum used her sewing talents to provide the family with home-made clothes. She sewed almost everything we ever wore until we got well into the high school years, when finances improved. The assembly line method worked as she tried to fit in sewing among so many other demands of everyday living. Often she bought material by the pound, some of it at the mills, because it was cheaper that way. Allan, Bonnie and I wore handmade identical nighties, diapers, and flannelette jackets, sweater sets, overalls, undershirts, panties, slips, T-shirts, dresses, snowsuits, coats, hats, winter leggings, sleepers, housecoats and pyjamas. One of the only purchased items was four dozen pairs of training pants. Mum also made much of the bedding;

sewed for Dad, Glenn and herself; and even mended rubber boots on the sewing machine. She often said that it was difficult sewing three of everything. By the time she had made one or two, she grew tired of that project. It was a pity that necessity took the enjoyment out of sewing for Mum in the end, but it was a labour of love and it helped us survive some lean times.

Glenn quickly grew into Mum's best helper and he often undressed us while Mum bathed us as we got closer to walking. He was as fast and proficient as Mum was, except when Allan would pull his shoelaces into knots. Glenn had no patience when Allan refused to sit still so the knots could be untied.

One day around our first birthday, the milkman opened the door to deliver four quarts of milk, and Bonnie and I crawled out. The poor fellow didn't know whether to drop the milk, and grab the kids or what. So he just yelled, "Hey lady, call off your kids."

December 1952

For some reason that was unclear to Mum, she decided to take all four of us to see Santa Claus that year for the first time. Mum bundled us all up, got us settled in the triple stroller and headed off with four-year-old Glenn in tow towards the bus stop. This may sound easy enough, but it was no small feat. She had to push through the cold and the snow, then wait for the bus. The kind bus driver got up to help (what choice did he have?!) as Mum unloaded the babies and handed each one over to the driver, who in turn found passengers to hold us. Then the stroller was loaded aboard and away we went, down the only major road to the lower level of the city where the large department stores were located. Once there, the transfer procedure was repeated. From then on, Mum was on her own.

When she arrived at the particular store, she soon discovered that the cart was too wide to fit through the door. Someone alerted the store manager, who took all of us on a freight elevator. Finally, we reached Toyland and Santa's castle. Mum stood in line and took off our snowsuits for the photograph with Santa. This photo is the last one taken where we three are together, and facing the camera. Very soon after, Allan began to deteriorate and he was gone before the next Christmas. Allan looks very well, although his eyes were closed, and his smile is so precious. I believe maternal instinct led Mum on this mission. She was exhausted but so thankful later that she had made the effort. The photo has always been one of our family's favourites.

Allan's health had begun to fail at age two soon after having surgery for strabismus. While in hospital, he caught measles, which seemed to weaken him further. Mum and Dad had no car at that time, so it's unlikely that Mum got over to see him while he was in the hospital in Toronto. Dad hitched a ride over with a friend to visit once and borrowed a car to bring Allan home when he was discharged from the hospital. Mum and Dad were shocked at his appearance and scarcely recognized him because he had lost so much weight. Our parents nursed Allan around the clock but he continued to weaken and he died unexpectedly, but peacefully, at the age of two years eight months at home on Glenn's fifth birthday.

October 11: Thanksgiving Day 1953

Glenn remembers that day. Suddenly there was much crying and commotion around him that he couldn't understand. The first break in the circle of three. Life would never be the same. The inner strength and faith of our parents in the face of adversity has never failed to amaze us. Mum was a great believer in the philosophy that everyone is put on this earth for a purpose or to complete a mission, however short.

Two days later, Allan's funeral was private, yet complete strangers turned up at the funeral home. They were turned away. Mum needed her privacy at a time of intense grief. Mum's mother and siblings lived 1,500 miles away and didn't attend the funeral since it would have been a huge financial burden for them. Our kind neighbour, Arliss Hall, helped Mum and Dad out in their hour of need. Mum didn't have a good outfit in which to bury Allan — just a partially completed two-piece white knitted sweater and leggings with yellow ducks. Mrs. Hall, who had just completed the same outfit, traded hers for Mum's. It was a touching gesture.

Just two weeks before Mum's death in 1997, she recalled Allan's last day at home. Allan had the strength to sit up and eat a good breakfast, but later that day, he faded and lost consciousness, dying peacefully in her arms. Mum was totally unprepared for Allan's death and it affected her deeply.

We surviving children have worked hard to keep Allan's memory alive because he's an important part of our family. Two nephews bear his name and his christening romper has been used by all of Allan's nephews for their own christenings and baptisms. Allan's framed picture, his white christening rompers and bible, the terrycloth bib trimmed with blue and embroidered with his name, booties with the blue bunny faces, his baby book, cradle roll picture and the small bonnet that he wore home from the hospital — all have lovingly been passed on to Glenn. His baby boots, later bronzed, remain on display in the family home. We did not forget Baby Allan at the time of Mum's sudden death on Sunday morning in May 1997 at her home. Although she slipped away quietly by herself — we are certain that Baby Allan and others were there with her.

We placed a photograph of Allan in Mum's hands along with a card that pictured a young angel painting stars. I wrote a note on

Allan's behalf welcoming his Mummy at long last. How appropriate for Mum to enter eternal rest just one week before Mother's Day. I was glad to think that she would be "home" to spend Mother's Day with the baby son that she loved and missed so much.

My brother Glenn, an ordained United Church Minister, used Allan's small white bible for the committal service at the cemetery. Then we took a flower from the casket spray over to the small baby grave where Allan lay. Every member of our three generations of family for the first time joined hands thanking God not only for the gift of Mum, but for the gift of Allan.

Glenn remembers Allan but Bonnie and I don't. We have often wondered why Allan was taken before we had a chance to know and remember him. No matter what his challenges, our family would have been there for him. It would have been an honour and privilege for us all to have loved and provided for him.

Growing up

Bonnie and I always liked the same clothing styles, and that continues today. Whenever a particularly nice item catches our eye, we will often buy two of the same outfit and send the second outfit to the other. Once she sent me a beautiful embroidered blouse that I already had hanging in my closet. One other time, Bonnie and I both purchased cards for Mum, and they were identical even though they were bought 1,500 miles apart.

Growing up, Bonnie and I always shared a room at home, which was a little unfortunate from Bonnie's perspective, since I was a bit more laid back in the tidiness department. Many nights came and went with Bonnie flipping on the light after we were supposed to be settled because she thought something was "messy." Her house is as neat as a pin even with six children at home and she's remarkably organized. I always admire her tactful restraint at my house, which has a somewhat more lived-in look. I know it drives her crazy.

Our most special toys stayed in our small bedroom. Even when we were very small, Bonnie and I were baby crazy. We had identical wooden doll cribs, white-lined bassinets on stands, turquoise and beige doll carriages that converted to strollers, and our very special love was our one-year-old dolls.

Our childhood years were quite typical of those of an average family in the '50s, '60s and early '70s. But twins and multiples have always caused a stir, and we were no exception. We were always being asked which one we were. I would usually answer, as an attention getting device, "I'm the one with the hole in my head," referring to a small indent on the left side of my head, presumably caused by someone's crowding around my head in the womb. Our kindergarten teacher couldn't tell us apart, so she asked Mum to put different socks on each of us. Apparently, Bonnie and I used to sit down on the curb and trade one sock so that we both arrived wearing one pink and one blue sock.

Our fondness for babies carried through adulthood and we both became nurses, hired to work in maternity. We loved the work and caring for all the children. But we dreamed of marrying and having our own children. Bonnie married and is the mother of six children (all single births), three girls and three boys. I'm not biased when I say that Bonnie is the most devoted, loving and maternal mother that I know.

After Bonnie married, I was having quite a difficult time adjusting to our new separate living arrangements. But soon, I too met someone and fell in love and was married in 1979. My husband and I went on to have a family of three girls and one boy, all of them single births. Glenn has two children, both single births.

Glenn has made many subtle remarks over the years that suggest he felt overshadowed by us three, and then by us two. Even today he refers often to "the triplets" when talking about years gone by. I feel so bad because Mum and Dad would never do anything to hurt Glenn deliberately, but our bond has taken its toll. Is it possible that Bonnie and I have always been a unit that didn't necessarily need Glenn or anyone else as long as we had each other? I realize this exclusion may have been a big mistake on our part. Our family has always recognized the need for Bonnie and me to remain in close contact, and they have all sacrificed much while my sister and I perhaps have selfishly not shared ourselves enough with the rest of the family.

Bonnie and I are very similar in many ways of course (one being that our children cannot tell Bonnie and I apart on the phone at times). But as we have grown and matured, we have also discovered differences that have surprised us and prove that we are definite individuals. I can honestly say that wearing the same clothes, having the same interests, mutual friends, and pursuing the same activities have not had any harmful effects on us — at least that we are aware of. As people get to know us, they discover that we don't have the same personalities and that we each have different talents.

No one has ever understood our special bond as Mum did because she was with us at home most of the time. Mum fought the school system for years on our behalf so that we could remain in the same classroom, but the school never respected her wishes. At summer camp, Bonnie and I were separated by a partition running down the centre of one cabin. The camp authorities did not wish to have us together but we were most upset, depressed and crying until they finally gave in and moved us together. We always knew that Mum understood us and our needs most, and she was most respectful towards the bond we shared.

Bonnie, Glenn, Dad and I last saw Dr. Overend at the funeral home when Mum died. He had seen the obituary and said that he just had to come. What a powerful tribute. This doctor was one of a dying breed who continued making house calls to our home whenever he was needed. During the baby boom, he delivered 300 babies a year. He always respected and trusted Mum's instincts and concerns. And to this day, the Bakers hold a special place in their heart for Dr. Overend.

Our Special Bond
Barbara Jane Baker-Jardine

Children may need the comfort of side-by-side proximity to their siblings. It may not last forever, but I believe it should be respected for as long as it remains important

Unless a person is born a multiple, or has lived within this realm as a parent or sibling, one can never know the magnitude of this most powerful bond. Until professional educators and child psychologists stop debating among themselves long enough to listen and to respect the emotional, physical and psychological needs and well being of the world's multiples, there will continue to be much grief, and for some, permanent scars from premature childhood separation crisis. Too often, self-proclaimed experts have maintained an almost militant stand on the so-called best approach to raising multiple birth children, and have paid little or no attention to the children themselves, who have in many cases remained voiceless and lost in the shuffle. Parents even today are encouraged to do all in their power to encourage the growth of individual identities. I see no problem with that, as long as the children's own needs and feelings remain the utmost priority.

It is the children themselves who know best about what their personal needs are at any given moment. To cope, they may need the comfort and side-by-side proximity of their siblings. This need may not last forever, but I believe that it should be respected and met for as long as it remains important to them. Even after 18 years of separation, Bonnie and I are as close as ever. We write, speak into tape recorders, telephone often, and even if we are not together physically, we are there spiritually with the other — rejoicing, advising or helping to carry a heavy load. During periods of stress or anxiety Bonnie and I have discovered that an identical dream haunts us both regularly until the real life issues are worked out. The only difference is that in my dream, I'm failing school because I've played hookie all year. I'm seeking Bonnie everywhere to rescue me from failing the high school final exams. In Bonnie's dreams, she's the unprepared person who seeks me out for help. How can one explain such coincidences?

We'll always be womb-to-tomb mates, best friends and supporters. There is no way to adequately describe a bond so deep yet elusive that defies and surpasses total human understanding.

a view from the outside

Nancy Griffin-Mazeika

This is of necessity, a view from the outside. I am the fraternal (dizy-gotic) one of the three, the others being identical (monozygotic). These are most of all musings on individuality. I can tell a story from the outside. I can't tell my sisters' stories. They belong to them. And in an ever-unfolding circle of three, we grow in the pleasures of individual lives. Sometimes together, sometimes apart. I know I am glad for the way it was and now, the way it is.

My sisters and I were born nearly 55 years ago. The birth was a rarity at the time and came not many years following the birth of the Dionnes. That birth brought with it what we now know were the makings of tragedy. The wonder of it was turned into a specta-cle. The Dionnes may have been the inspiration for my parents' commitment to raising distinct individuals. All these years later, the distinction is very clear and though my sisters and I share some fam-ily characteristics, we are very much our own individual persons.

I recall being amazed by a story I read a few years ago. This story about family generations so clearly revealed how individuals can be in the same place, experiencing the same event, and yet have quite

a different perspective of what happened in the end. So it is with my sisters and me. Despite the uniqueness of our birth, our responses to life are not dissimilar from members of any family.

From the beginning, the quest for individuality began as our names were chosen: Joann, Nancy and Cynthia. Each is distinct. Our clothing was chosen with care and an eye to difference. At most, the outfit may have been the same but the colour was always different. So too, these years later, is the colour of our lives. Each of us stands in our own place. We are mindful of the others but quite separate.

My favourite picture of my sisters and me as young girls is one that shows me standing on the outside. Usually we were placed in birth order with me in the centre. In the one I love so much, I see a photographic image of the way I remember feeling — somewhat on the outside. I remember snippets of being singled out. I looked different, I was different and most people addressed me by my name, knowing that Nancy was the "odd one." The link of sameness was probably more difficult for my sisters. As we have grown older, we share a family resemblance, but my sisters could still pose a challenge to identify if they were seen together.

As the years have passed, we have entered into that space of life where sibling rivalry has all but vanished. We are content in the presence of one another. It can be said however, that should my sisters compete in a game of Scrabble, they would demonstrate a competitiveness that is breathtaking to watch!

A tale is told from the day we first went to school. At the end of that day we arrived home in tears. Everyone had been gesturing and exclaiming, "Look, the triplets are here." We, not knowing that we were "the triplets," came home devastated that we had not seen them. School had definite challenges, especially for me. At that time, there was no choice as to classroom placement. We were in the same class each year for nine years. Not until high school was there any option or choice. It was always a challenge to professionals to celebrate our differences rather than our sameness. Sometimes this was brilliantly accomplished, other times not. I struggled with the inevitable comparisons inflicted by what I judged to be unenlightened ones. I now see that difficulties provided me with great opportunities. I learned to have a certain tenacity when confronted with obstacles. Those lessons stay with me today. The lessons also teach me to delight in my individuality and allow me to honour the sameness that is simply a part of the human condition.

Experience has taught me that there are many people who are utterly fascinated by those born in multiples. I suspect that we are seen to have a special affinity. This beckons to those who live in an often alienating and lonely world. It is with this knowledge that I have grown patient with unknowing comments and questions from those who might seem to be insensitive.

There are stories of multiples rejoicing in their sameness. For them it seems to be the only fulfilling way to live. Though this has not been my experience, I have no judgment except to express that each family, each group of multiples, must find their own way. Long ago, I disavowed any notion that there is only one way to manage. In the long run, each life is its own journey.

Caregivers in the lives of the fraternal ones surrounded by identical siblings need a special vigilance. It can be lonely on the outside. The outsider will need encouragement to stay on the journey toward the awareness of a special kind of belonging. You see, the outsider has a tremendous advantage. From there, everything can be seen. From there, the choices unfold. From there, you may enter in after the time of observation has ended. It is a wondrous place to be. Should you find it to be your place, honour it and rejoice.

appendix 1

References

Depression & Anxiety
Before and After the Birth of Triplets, Quadruplets or More

Ballard, C., Davis, R., Cullen, P., Mohan, R., & Dean, C. (1994). Prevalence of postnatal psychiatric morbidity in mothers and fathers. British Journal of Psychiatry, 164, 782-788.

Field, T. (1995). Infants of depressed mothers. Infant Behavior and Development, 18, 1-13.

Garel, M. & Blondel, B. (1992). Assessment at one year of the psychological consequences of having triplets. Human Reproduction, 7 (5) 729-32.

Garel, M., Salobir, C., & Blondel, B. (1997). Psychological consequences of having triplets: A four-year follow-up study. Fertility and Sterility, 67 (6), 1162-1165.

Hay, D., Gleeson, C., Davies, C., Lorden, B., Mitchell, D., & Patten, L. (1990). What information should the multiple birth family receive before, during and after the birth? Acta Geneticae Medicae et Gemellolgiae, 39, 259-269.

Leonard, L. G. (1998) Depression and anxiety disorders during multiple pregnancy and parenthood. Journal of Obstetrical, Gynecologic and Neonatal Nursing, 27 (3) 329-337.

Misri, S. (1995). Shouldn't I be happy?: Emotional problems of pregnant and postpartum women. New York: Free Press.

Murray, L., Stanley, C., Hooper, R., King, F., & Fiori-Cowley, A. (1996). The role of infant factors in postnatal depression and mother-infant interactions. Developmental Medicine and Child Neurology, 38, 109-119.

Nulman, I., Rovet, J., Stewart, D., Wolpin, J., Gardner, H., Theis, J., Kulin, N., & Koren, G. (1997). Neurodevelopment of children exposed in utero to antidepressant drugs. New England Journal of Medicine, 336 (4), 258-262.

Pacific Post Partum Support Society (1998). Postpartum depression and anxiety: A self help guide for mothers, 3rd ed. rev., Vancouver, BC: Author.

Parents of Multiple Births Association of Canada (POMBA), Research Committee. (1993, March). Results of the national survey. Stratford, ON: Author.

Robin, M., Bydlowski, M., Cahen, F., & Josse, D. (1991). Maternal reactions to the birth of triplets. Acta Geneticae Medicae et Gemellologiae, 40 (1), 41-52.

Robin, M., Corroyer, D. & Casati, I. (1996). Childcare patterns of mothers of twins during the first year. Journal of Child Psychology and Psychiatry, 37 (4) 453-460.

Stowe, Z. & Nemeroff, C. (1995). Women at risk for postpartum-onset major depression. American Journal of Obstetrics and Gynecology, 173 (2) S., 639-45.

Thorpe, K., Greenwood, R., & Goodenough, T. (1995). Does a twin pregnancy have a greater impact on physical and emotional well-being than a singleton pregnancy? Birth, 22 (3), 148-152.

Wisner, K., Perel, J., & Findling, R. (1996). Antidepressant treatment during breast-feeding. American Journal of Psychiatry, 153 (9), 1132-1137.

with great
gratitude

A very special thank you to each of the contributing authors for inspiring us with their honesty and wisdom.

There are a lot of people, ideas and work that go into seven years and more than 500 pages. Without them, *Finding Our Way* could not have been possible. A big thank you to the many contributors who donated time, money, professional services, fundraising and photographs to our book.

Your generosity helped us turn words into pages.

Generous Financial Supporters

Health Canada
D.S. Smith & Family
Durham Region Parents of Multiple Births Association
Multiple Birth Families Association of Ottawa
Serono Canada Inc.
Toronto Parents of Multiple Births Association
Diane and John Myers & Family
Maureen Tierney and Peter Pearson & Family
Bev and Jeff Unger & Family
Barrie Parents of Twins and More
Donna and Darryl Patterson & Family
Maternal, Infant and Child Ltd.
Candi Cuppage and Paul Forget & Family
Patricia and John Harber & Family
Alice Bluemke
Guelph Parents of Twins and Triplets Club
Newmarket Parents of Multiple Births Association
Brant Parents of Multiple Births Association

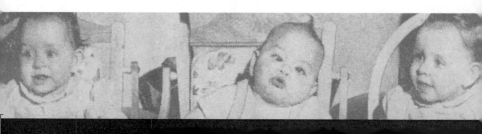

London Multiple Birth Association
Mississauga Parents of Multiple Births Association
Alanna Patterson and Friends' Lemonade Stand

The views expressed herein do not necessarily represent the official policy of Health Canada.

Generous Professional Supporters

Suzanne Lyons, Precise Communications	*Editor*
Dyan Parro, Aline Proulx, Thumbnail Art Direction+Design	*Art Direction and Design*
Peter Czegledy of Aird & Berlis	*Legal Advisor*
Valerie Edward of Aird & Berlis	*Legal Advisor*
Kirsteen MacLeod	*Proofreader*
Webcom Limited	*Printer*
Mel D'Souza	*Illustrator*

Publication Team

Patricia Harber	*Financial and Legal Manager*
Suzanne Lyons	*Editor*
Diane Myers	*Project Manager*
Donna Patterson	*Creative Consultation & Promotion Manager*
Maureen Tierney	*Research Manager*

Through the evolution of this book many other individuals have participated on the publication team– Gillian Borowy, Patty deLaat, Suzanne Lavallee, Judith McGill, Kimberely Rullar, and Eileen Taylor. We thank you all for your special contributions.

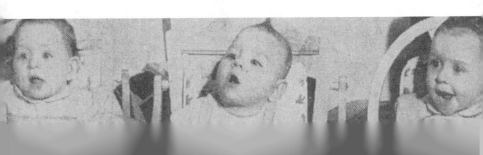

Special Thanks to
Elaine Stirk, Mary MacCafferty and Paul Jones for starting TQQ in 1987.

Finding Our Way is the result of Suzanne Lavallee and Debra Muenz's dream of sharing our experiences and truths with others.

Editorial Review Team
DR. JON BARRETT MBBch, MD, MRCOG FRCSC.
Specialist in Maternal Fetal Medicine and Director Multiple Births, Sunnybrook and Women's College Health Science Centre, Associate Professor University of Toronto. Chair SOGC Multiple Pregnancy Group. Ontario

GILLIAN BOROWY
Mother of fraternal triplet boys born in 1996. Living in British Columbia, Alberta or Ontario, depending on when you catch her.

MAUREEN A. DOOLAN BOYLE
Mother of 5 (3 of which are triplets) and Executive Director of MOST (Mothers of Supertwins), Inc.
An international support network of families who are expecting or are already the parents of triplets or more.
www.MOSTonline.org. USA

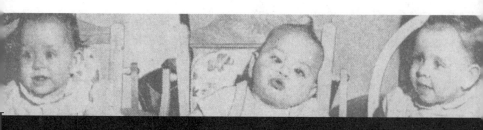

ELIZABETH MARY BRYAN MD, FRCP, FRCPCH, DCH
President of the International Society for Twin Studies, the
Founder and Medical Consultant to the Multiple Births
Foundation, Honorary Consultant Pediatrician at Queen
Charlotte's and Chelsea Hospital. London, England

PATTY DELAAT
Mom of triplets born in 1992, two girls and a boy. The diapers are
long gone, now we've got attitude! Ontario

LINDA G. LEONARD RN, BSN, MSN
Associate Professor, Multiple Births Specialist, School of Nursing,
University of British Columbia. British Columbia

DR. ELIZABETH MASSARELLI AND DR. ROSS THOMAS
Parents of quadruplets, two boys and two girls, born in 1990, who
are the focal point of our lives. We also share a practice in family
medicine. New Brunswick

JUDITH MCGILL
Of Lifepath Consulting is a writer and adult educator in the field
of disability. She is currently the Project Animator of the Support to
Aging Families Project and spends a lot of time with families who
have children with disabilities to help them reimagine their
sons/daughters futures. Ontario

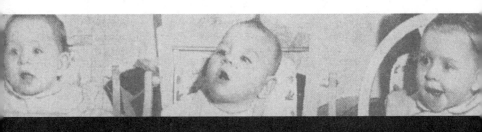

DAWN MONTAGNE-MALEY
New Zealand Triplets Plus Club President & mother of 4 including triplets born 1996, Dunedin New Zealand

MARY ANNE MOSER
Currently in charge of communications for several advanced technology organizations, and is in the midst of a Ph.D. on technology and social change. She is the editor of Immersed in Technology, published by MIT Press, and was founding editor of the Banff Centre Press. She tampered with technology in 1995 and is now the happy mother of two boys and a girl, all born in June 1996. Alberta

JEANETTE NIEBLER
Parent of triplets, two girls and a boy born in 1995. All autistic and all wonderful. Ontario

ANNA WAUGH
Certified Childbirth Educator, President of NovaMed Diagnostics Inc., and most valued accomplishment: mother of 5 children including triplets. Ontario

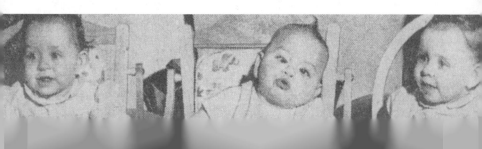

JACQUIE WEBER AND STERLING GUNN
Parents of Alexander, James and MacKenzie, born 1998 (BBG).
Active members of TQQ. When we first shared our news, a friend
quipped "But of course, lawyers and bankers always do things in
triplicate". With that warning always in mind, we continually strive
to support the individuality of our children. Given their expressive
and very different personalities, that's not difficult. We are currently practicing the discipline of keeping our sanity. Ontario

DONNA WILSON, RN, BSL, BScN, MN,
Clinical Nurse Specialist, Perinatal Program & Multiples Clinic,
Sunnybrook & Women's College Health Science Centre. Ontario

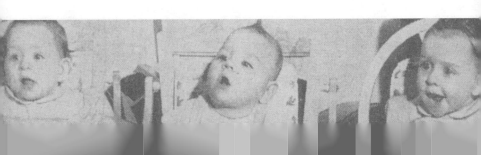

Publication Team

PATRICIA HARBER

I am the mother of four-year-old triplet girls and a 19-year-old daughter. My husband John is the outnumbered, but wonderful father to our precious daughters. My involvement with the Triplets, Quads and Quints Association (TQQ) started when I was about 26 weeks pregnant. Since then, my involvement with this organization has given me many opportunities for interaction and tremendous support. Working on this book has been an inspiration for me and I hope that it benefits all who read it.

SUZANNE LYONS

My three delightful boys were the motivation that drew me to this book. Andrew, Joel and Quentin were just two years old when we started compiling stories. Now, at age six, they are as familiar with many of the stories as I am. Many thanks to them and to my husband Rick for happily sacrificing many hours of time and attention at home so that this very worthwhile volume could be completed.

DIANE MYERS

The main event came for John and me in 1990 when Craig, our first born (1988), became the big brother to Alison, Harrison, Jessica and Kenny. Our family was finally complete after the birth of our youngest son, Mac, in 1992. TQQ has given me a unique opportunity to share fears, joys and tears with so many families, and for this, I feel privileged.

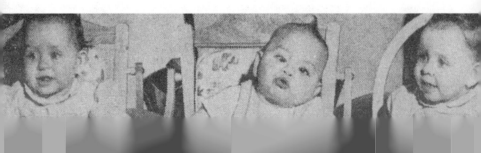

DONNA PATTERSON

My husband Darryl and I are the proud parents of 10-year-old Alanna, and her sisters Jaclyn, Teresa and Victoria who were born 1993. Motherhood is a wonderful and rewarding role for me. I have also enjoyed many years volunteering with TQQ as Treasurer, a new parent contact and, of course, as a contributor to this exciting endeavour, Finding Our Way.

MAUREEN TIERNEY

I am the proud mother of triplets Jacqueline, Monica and Lorraine born in 1995. After three years at home, I returned to work as a social worker. Volunteering for this book was very exciting for me. I enjoyed talking to and persuading families to share their experiences as honestly as possible. I believe honesty is the greatest benefit to our readers. I would like to thank my husband Peter Pearson for his patience and my parents Martin and Bridget Tierney for babysitting. Without them, it would have been impossible for me to work on this project

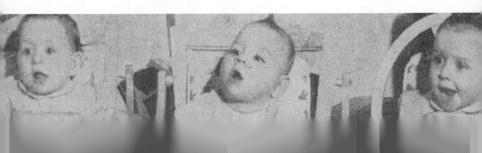